"OUR HEMISPHERE"?

ALSO BY BRITTA H. CRANDALL
Hemispheric Giants: The Misunderstood History of U.S.–Brazilian History

ALSO BY RUSSELL C. CRANDALL
Drugs and Thugs: The History and Future of America's War on Drugs

The Salvador Option: The United States in El Salvador, 1977–1992

America's Dirty Wars: Irregular Warfare from 1776 to the War on Terror

The United States and Latin America after the Cold War

Gunboat Democracy: U.S. Interventions in the Dominican Republic, Grenada, and Panama

Driven by Drugs: U.S. Policy toward Colombia

The Andes in Focus (coedited with Guadalupe Paz and Riordan Roett)

Mexico's Democracy at Work (coedited with Guadalupe Paz and Riordan Roett)

"Our Hemisphere"?

The United States in Latin America, from 1776 to the Twenty-First Century

Britta H. Crandall and
Russell C. Crandall

Yale UNIVERSITY PRESS   *New Haven and London*

Published with assistance from the foundation established in memory of Philip
Hamilton McMillan of the Class of 1894, Yale College.

Yale University Press books may be purchased in quantity for educational, business, or
promotional use. For information, please e-mail sales.press@yale.edu (U.S. office) or
sales@yaleup.co.uk (U.K. office).

Printed in the United States of America.

Library of Congress Control Number: 2021931532
ISBN 978-0-300-24810-4 (paper : alk. paper)

A catalogue record for this book is available from the
British Library.

This paper meets the requirements of ANSI/NISO Z39.48-1992 (Permanence of Paper).

10 9 8 7 6 5 4 3 2 1

We dedicate this book to Professor Riordan Roett, the indefatigable director, over four decades, of the innovative and spirited Latin America Studies program at Johns Hopkins University's School of Advanced International Studies (SAIS). Each of us owes a great debt to Professor Roett in ways big and small, including his time as doctoral advisor to both of us.

Contents

Time Line of Our Stories

1791–1804	Haitian Revolution
1810s–1820s	Widespread Latin American independence movements
1819	Adams–Onís Treaty between the United States and Spain
1823	Monroe Doctrine promulgated
1845	Texas enters the US as a slave state
1846	US invades Mexico; Bear Flag Revolt in California
1848	Treaty of Guadalupe Hidalgo is signed, ending the Mexican–American War (known in Mexico as the US Intervention in Mexico)
1855	Filibuster William Walker invades Nicaragua
1889	Secretary of State James Blaine convenes first Pan-American conference in Washington, DC
1895	Venezuela Crisis of 1895
1898	USS *Maine* sinks in Cuba's Havana Harbor
1901	Platt Amendment is passed
1903	President Theodore Roosevelt recognizes the new Republic of Panama
1904	Roosevelt Corollary builds on the Monroe Doctrine
1909–13	Dollar diplomacy, the concept of elevating corporate and economic interests over solely military ones, was most associated with President William Howard Taft and Secretary of State Philander C. Knox

Midterm (handwritten annotation spanning 1898–1909–13)

1910–20	*Midterm period*	Mexican Revolution
1914		Panama Canal opens; Tampico Affair in Mexico
1916		US Punitive Expedition into Mexico
1910s–1930s		So-called Banana Wars involving US hemispheric interventions, most notably the Dominican Republic, Haiti, and Nicaragua
1933		Good Neighbor Policy begins; the diplomat Sumner Welles begins his tenure in Cuba
1934		Nicaraguan nationalist rebel Augusto Sandino is executed
1938		Mexican populist president Lázaro Cárdenas expropriates foreign oil assets
1944		Argentina becomes the last Latin American country to declare war on Axis powers
1945		United Nations comes into existence
1948		Organization of America States (OAS) founded
1950		US diplomat George Kennan tours Latin America
1954		Guatemala's leftist president leader Jacobo Árbenz is ousted by a Central Intelligence Agency (CIA)– hatched covert operation
1959		Fidel Castro comes to power in Cuba, ousting strongman Fulgencio Batista
1960		US near-total trade embargo on Cuba commences
1961		US-backed failed Bay of Pigs invasion in Cuba; the tyrant Rafael Trujillo assassinated in the Dominican Republic
1964		Brazilian leftist João Goulart overthrown by the country's military
1965		US military intervention in the Dominican Republic
1967		Argentine-born revolutionary Che Guevara is killed in Bolivia
1971		Marxist guerrilla group's kidnapping of Salvadoran businessman Ernesto Regalado Dueñas helps ignite the country's civil war
1973		Chilean socialist president Salvador Allende overthrown; the US Drug Enforcement Agency (DEA) is founded

1976		Orlando Letelier, an outspoken critic of Chilean dictator Augusto Pinochet, is killed in a car bombing at Dupont Circle in Washington, DC
1978		US Senate ratifies Panama Canal Treaties
1979		Nicaraguan Revolution culminates with the overthrow of the Somoza dictatorship
1979–92		Sustained US nation-building and counterinsurgency in El Salvador
1980		Salvadoran archbishop Óscar Romero assassinated
1980s		Latin America's debt crisis
1982		General Efraín Ríos Montt comes to power in Guatemala
1983		US invades Grenada
1985–87		Iran–Contra scandal
1988		Chilean dictator Augusto Pinochet defeated in a national referendum
1989		US invades Panama; President George H. W. Bush launches the counternarcotics Andean Initiative
1990		Sandinista president Daniel Ortega loses power in Nicaragua
1991	*Midterm period 2*	Democratically elected Haitian president Jean-Bertrand Aristide toppled
1994		Trilateral North American Free Trade Agreement (NAFTA) comes into force; Colombian drug kingpin Pablo Escobar is killed by state security agents; Mexico devalues its currency, the peso; US military intervention in Haiti
1996		170 kilograms of cocaine are found on a plane commissioned by Peruvian president Alberto Fujimori
1999		Panama Canal handed over to Panama
2000		Washington unveils Plan Colombia; seventy-one-year tenure of Mexico's ruling PRI party comes to an end
2001		Inter-American Democratic Charter adopted; civilian aircraft mistaken as a drug courier is shot down by Peruvian authorities, killing, among others, a US missionary and her infant child

1998–2002	Argentine Great Depression
2002	US tacitly endorses a short-lived coup against Venezuela's populist president Hugo Chávez; Colombian rightist president Álvaro Uribe elected, unveiling his Democratic Security policy the following year
2005	Bolivian coca union leader Evo Morales is elected president
2007	Washington unveils Mérida Initiative for Mexico and Central America
2014	Seventy thousand children from the Northern Triangle cross the US–Mexico border; US and Cuba restore full relations
2016	Colombia's peace accord ends its five-decade internal war
2017	President Donald Trump backtracks on Obama's Cuban policy and reimposes restrictions
2018	Trump enacts "zero-tolerance" anti-immigration policy
2019	Mexican drug boss Joaquín "El Chapo" Guzmán sentenced by a US federal judge to life imprisonment; Evo Morales flees Bolivia after seeking a controversial fourth reelection bid

"Our Hemisphere"?

Introduction

Since its emergence as a major global power in the late nineteenth century the United States has played an outsized role in world affairs. It often seems to be everywhere at once, waging wars in the Middle East, part of NATO in Western Europe, going head to head with rival superpowers—the Soviet Union during the Cold War and China in more recent times—in economic, cyber, and interstellar domains. But there is one locale that is often overlooked in the national dialogue: Latin America. At times top US officials have explicitly diminished the importance of the region. In June 1969 National Security Advisor Henry Kissinger told the Chilean foreign minister, "You come here speaking of Latin America, but this is not important. Nothing important can come from the South." When the insulted minister claimed that Kissinger knew nothing about the region, Kissinger replied, "No, and I don't care."

But Kissinger's opinion leaves out a big story. Most US administrations actually considered what went on in Latin America as central to US national security and kept a close eye on events in the region. Indeed, Kissinger himself later became intimately involved in regional affairs. For Latin America wasn't just another foreign policy portfolio for the United States; it was the landmass on the doorstep as likely to inspire opportunity as augur competition, in terms of economics, ideology, and security. In the early years of US history where Latin America ended and the nascent United States began was a matter of hot debate and sometimes even bloody conflict. For all these reasons US policy makers often referred to Latin America as their backyard. And ever since the founding of the United States in 1776 the relationship between it and its southern neighbors has been of the utmost strategic importance to both sides, encompassing confrontation and cooperation, solidarity and suspicion—often at the same time.

This book focuses on uncovering the range, depth, and veracity of the relationship of the United States with the Americas through the lens of forty-two vignettes, each focusing on a particular historical episode. The approach is not to describe what the relationship should be or had been, but rather the reality of what occurred based on the best available historical records. This is a much-ploughed field, with a vast and dizzying array of scholarly studies that have often had very different interpretations of the same events. We do not seek to present the last word in the interpretation of US–Latin American relations; rather, we hope to showcase the wide range of critical accounts alongside our own interpretations.

We don't claim absolute neutrality, however, amid the mayhem of accusations, explanations, and op-eds that mark the analysis of US–Latin American relations. Our motivation for writing this book stems from our desire to tackle what we have often found to be a common view: that the US has relentlessly pursued a monolithic, hegemonic agenda, using its political, economic, and military muscle to force Latin American countries to do its bidding. This approach, propagated by President Theodore Roosevelt at the beginning of the twentieth century, was the so-called Big Stick. In this interpretation the United States involves itself in regional affairs only to achieve strictly limited national interests. There is much in the conventional, usually critical, assessment of US motivations and actions in its backyard; the ownership implied by the term itself, "backyard," hints at Uncle Sam's proclivity to mold the region. A historical legacy of United States Navy gunboats, plots by racist filibusters to legalize slavery in Central America, and CIA machinations to oust democratic presidents, supports the often-applied description of the US as empire or malignant hegemon. Ultimately, much of the current understanding of US policy toward Latin America is contoured by the extremities of one particularly painful episode in interhemispheric relations: the Cold War. Seeking to advance its political and economic interests, the US dispatched soldiers and diplomats to figuratively and literally comb the jungles and scale the mountains of Latin America carrying the tools of persuasion, coercion, and military force to combat the perceived threat of Soviet and Cuban communism.

But undermining the idea of a monolithic US agenda toward Latin America is the two-centuries-plus tenure of unexpected, sometimes staggering, regional interactions. An unprejudiced reading of the salient evidence reveals a relationship in which at times the Latin Americans exercised power vis-à-vis their northern, very potent neighbor in Washington. Latin America's periodic independence from the United States was not, as is often assumed, present solely in the decades following the end of the Cold War in 1991. In fact, Latin American autonomy existed from the beginning of the interhemispheric relationship two centuries prior. Washington's relationship with the region, then and now, has thus relied on cooperation and mutual respect and interest, means that rivaled Roosevelt's Big Stick.

Each historical era, the postcolonial, post-1898, Cold War, and post–Cold War periods, had its own zeitgeist and imperatives, even if one can discern common underlying trends like paternalism, realpolitik, and the spillover of domestic politics into foreign policy. Our dive into the historical records illuminates these themes, among others, not via prescriptive commentary but vicariously through the soldiers, intellectuals, private citizens, and politicians that have shaped US policy for centuries. We consider the outsized impact that individual politicians oftentimes have on policy. For example, Congressman Henry Clay of Kentucky in the mid-nineteenth century and the ultra–right wing senator Jesse Helms of North Carolina in the late twentieth century exerted a tremendous influence that forces one to think beyond the monolithic, although frequently indispensable, concepts like Washington or US policy.

The Monroe Doctrine and "Our Hemisphere"

A statement made by President Donald Trump's national security advisor, John Bolton, in January 2019 illuminates the complexities and contradictions of US policy toward Latin America. In the wake of disputed elections the strongman Nicolás Maduro was reelected as president of the crisis-stricken country. But, having largely scaled back US involvement in regional affairs since assuming office in January 2017, Trump unexpectedly recognized the opposition leader Juan Guaidó as Venezuela's legitimate ruler. Asked by a *New Yorker* journalist why the Trump administration had involved itself in Venezuela, Bolton replied, "The Monroe Doctrine is alive and well. It's our hemisphere."

"Our hemisphere." The phrase smacks of paternalism, a heavy-handed, overbearing approach to regional affairs that seems to fit squarely with the preconceptions of American involvement in coups, CIA intrigue, and botched military interventions. But Bolton's mention of the Monroe Doctrine, an early-nineteenth-century US policy that stated clear opposition to any European political interference in the Americas, is salient: the United States had expanded its involvement in Venezuela after reports that Russian aid was propping up Maduro's regime. Despite Trump's inclination to focus on "America First," the facts of the matter triggered a response that recalled principles enshrined in US policy a century earlier. Russian support clearly comprised outside interference in hemispheric affairs, a situation the United States had historically refused to tolerate. It resembles an episode from more than a century prior in which the United States Navy faced off against German and British ships in Venezuelan waters, as President Theodore Roosevelt threatened Kaiser Wilhelm of Germany with war if he did not commit to international arbitration.

Yet tracing the wake of President James Monroe's declaration reveals a deeper, more collaborative and unifying aspect to the phrase "our hemisphere." When ratified by Congress in 1823, the Monroe Doctrine implied little other than a self-issued permit for US influence to proliferate unchecked throughout the region: a unilateral warning to European powers not to try to reconquer the New World. But as the century wore on, the doctrine evolved into a multilateral framework consecrating the principles of noninterference that helped foster a sense of regional identity and ultimately led to the formation of the Organization of the American States in 1948. (The idea of a regional union had originally been proposed by the Latin American independence leader Simón Bolívar in the early nineteenth century.)

Just as the United States has often thought of Latin America as "our hemisphere" in the narrow sense—a place where it can exercise control and shape outcomes amenable to its national interest—it can also be said that the idiom captures something of the inextricable connection between the United States and Latin America. After all, the two "neighbors" rallied around cooperative landmarks such as US-backed Pan-Americanism in the nineteenth century and, in the 1920s and 1930s, the Good Neighbor Policy of hemispheric solidarity and multilateral cooperation.

Our Approach

In *"Our Hemisphere"?* we give readers a comprehensive sense of the multifaceted, often contradictory or hypocritical elements in inter-American affairs, one gleaned not only by taking a scholarly lens to Washington's machinations and effectiveness but also by scrutinizing those of its Latin American counterparts, both allies and foes. We do not provide a blow-by-blow or exhaustive account of either American foreign policy or world history; rather, we exfoliate insightful stories and syntheses of history that serve to introduce readers to the topic of US–Latin American relations. For the distant historical periods of the book (e.g., 1776 to 1898) we rely almost exclusively on key secondary sources, reevaluating established research in an attempt to offer new perspectives and original interpretations. In the final chapters, which trace events since the end of the Cold War, we depend instead on our own research (almost all previously published and cited accordingly) or field notes from the time we spent in US government service. Throughout the book a large proportion of our mostly secondary sources is from the United States, not Latin America, as the latter is simply beyond the scope of an already sweeping topic. The origin of our sources, which emanate predominantly from Washington, isn't as limiting as might be expected considering that this book is intentionally focused on US policies—hence the critical subtitle, "The United States *in* Latin America"—and how they contributed to the broader bilateral and multilateral relationships.

Our mantra for the historical storytelling is "explain, don't justify" so that readers are better able to make conclusions for themselves. We trust that readers will prefer getting our truest sense of the facts and stories told rather than the most morally or ideologically reassuring depiction. While we can never fully jettison our own ideological habits—between the two of us we have roughly four decades of teaching and executive branch policy stints—we intend to give the US record in the Western Hemisphere a rigorous, thorough scrubbing and present it in a new light.

Our conclusions about US policy over time are inherently circumspect and incremental but will hopefully stimulate additional reflection and dialogue in the reader. Furthermore, we believe that such an approach has tangible benefit in the real world today. From our vantage point, the only way current and future challenges, threats, and opportunities in the region can be identified and solved is to have both a nuanced and thorough understanding of its history.

PART I

CONTINENTAL CONSOLIDATION
AND CONQUEST, 1776–1898

It is tempting to begin a history of interhemispheric relations with the fateful events of 1898: the sinking of the USS *Maine,* the ensuing Spanish–American War, and the rise of the United States to a regional hegemon. But to do so would neglect the era from the American Revolution in 1776 through the latter decades of the nineteenth century, a period which represents a deeply significant and controversial component of our story, including consequential episodes of cooperation and respect. Indeed, before Theodore Roosevelt commanded his vaunted Rough Riders volunteer force against the Spanish in Cuba circa 1898, there was US recognition of and euphoria over events in the region. The string of countries in Latin America that gained independence, roughly half a century after that of its North American brother, won great admiration as the nascent states separated themselves from the Iberian powers Spain and Portugal. A further cause for US celebration, however, originated in their neighbors' incipient liberty. Nevertheless, the era witnessed its share of deeply salient expansionism: US continental growth in the era of Manifest Destiny, including the annexation of the Republic of Texas and a full-scale invasion of Mexico; a Tennessee filibuster who took over Nicaragua; and a Civil War army hero and then president who almost annexed Santo Domingo (today's Dominican Republic), the latter a scheme that had considerable support within the fledgling Caribbean island nation.

At the time the size and breadth of American national power was a fraction of its twentieth-century counterpart. In 1898 the departments of War (later Defense) and State and the US Navy fit into a single building adjacent to the White House, an unimaginably economic organization given today's vast bureaucratic machine. Yet Washington's underdevelopment did not stop US policy makers and politicians from critically assessing the hemispheric agenda—for ill or good: the still-salient and controversial Monroe Doctrine address from 1823 shows how enduring the ramifications from those early years are. Thus they are paramount to our broader understanding.

It is crucial to recognize the disproportionate role played by US actors throughout this period, no matter the degree to which it was official. This was an era in which the actions of a few could have consequences for millions. As the 1846 American invasion of Mexico alone demonstrates, even if the nineteenth-century State Department could fit into a single wing of the post–World War II Pentagon, that does not mean that US actions did not have catastrophic consequences for its neighbors. The map of the Americas changed dramatically in this period, both through liberation from European powers and through bloody conquest. This time of principle and political expediency, the former often serving as a cover for the latter, was a trend that would form a theme to US–Latin American relations throughout the next two centuries. And despite the regional clout that emanated from Washington, it remains history perhaps better remembered in Latin America than in the United States. For many Mexicans the US attack on Mexico City in 1847 sparked a strong and lasting national antipathy toward their northern neighbor. It's best we scrutinize the time that would leave a potent legacy on interhemispheric relations.

1 • The Black Spartacus Who Balanced Washington

The Haitian Revolution, said to be the biggest slave rebellion since Spartacus's uprising against the Roman Empire almost two millennia earlier, resulted in many firsts. Haiti was the first nation in Latin America to gain independence and remains the only country to have gained independence through a slave revolt. It was also the first country to outlaw slavery and to be ruled by former slaves and people of mixed race. The revolution was of great interest to many, including US abolitionists—those who, before the Civil War, supported the total and immediate abolition of slavery—who sought a case study of a stable and prosperous freed-slave republic to challenge both entrenched beliefs about black inferiority and slaveholders in the American South. It is also a case study in the power of the individual; how, in this case, an astute soldier and diplomat paved the way for the improbable outcome of nationhood and slave emancipation, all the while avoiding becoming embroiled in the machinations of rivaling France and the United States and fending off British and Spanish attempts to gain control of the island.

The Haitian Revolution

Established in 1697 and encompassing the western third of Hispaniola Island, Saint-Domingue was France's most lucrative New World colony; colloquially, it was known as the most "profitable stretch of real estate on the planet." According to the historian Edward Baptist, the colony's world-leading exports of sugar and coffee—shipping more than Jamaica, Cuba, and Brazil together and representing 40 percent of sugar and 50 percent of the coffee

9

ingested globally—as well as chocolate, indigo, and cotton served as the fuel for France's "imperial engine." Ships from the Americas and Europe sailed to and from its lively ports, nearing five hundred voyages to the United States alone. The colony's flourishing trade, belying its physical stature close to the state of Maryland, created more wealth for France than the combined thirteen North American colonies produced for Great Britain.

Extracting this "fuel," however, would have been impossible without the colony's massive, enslaved labor force. Comprising 480,000 enslaved Africans, which, by 1789, represented some 50 percent of the enslaved Caribbean population, Saint-Domingue's enslaved workforce far eclipsed the colony's population of whites (30,000) and freed persons of color (28,000). The colony's slavery model was considered "perhaps the most horrific . . . ever seen in human history." Amid wretched conditions and slave owners wresting the maximum labor out of their bodies, one in 20 slaves died each year, constantly replaced by the robust slave trade. Given the high ratio of slaves to whites, as well as the abhorrent treatment by the European minority, an uprising was only a matter of time, and in late August 1791 that time had come. The self-liberated slaves of Saint-Domingue revolted, torching fields of cane and massacring their masters. Free people of color in Saint-Domingue, enraged by French landowners' refusal to extend them citizenship, joined in taking up arms. By the time the independent Republic of Haiti was established in January 1804, the revolution had taken its toll: upward of 350,000 Haitians and 50,000 French troops had been killed (the troops mostly from yellow fever), and the island nation's economy laid in tatters.

To place the Haitian Revolution in historical context, it is important to remember that this was not a run-of-the-mill bilateral war pitting Saint-Domingue the colony versus France the colonizer. Rather, with the 1789 onset of the French Revolution, the colonial administration in Saint-Domingue collapsed, facilitating both the uprisings which marked the beginning of the revolution as well as the opportunity for both Spain and Great Britain to get involved militarily. By spring of 1794 Great Britain and Spain controlled much of the colony. Throughout the thirteen years of fighting, allegiances shifted between and among slaves, freed blacks, Creoles, European planters, the Spanish, French, and British. Further, the issues of independence and emancipation often became muddled in this multifaceted conflict. The new French revolutionary government, for example, abolished slavery in all its territories in 1794, luring many black fighters to its cause, among them, ultimately, Toussaint Louverture.

Louverture's Regional Realpolitik

While a West Africa–born rebel leader called Dutty Boukman guided the initial mass uprising, history has tended to laurel François-Dominique Toussaint Louverture—rebel leader, former domestic slave, and autodidact—as Haiti's Founding Father, an "idealistic herald of slave emancipation" and a black nationalist. Between the onset of revolution in 1791 and Haiti's independence in 1804 Louverture worked feverishly to abolish slavery on the island and carve out a new independent state without provoking the great world powers. His deft handling of political rivals in conjunction with his prowess on the battlefield catalyzed Louverture's meteoric ascent in Saint-Domingue politics, and by 1798 he was in de facto control of the island's political and military affairs.

Louverture's mastery of domestic affairs was echoed in his shrewdly calculated diplomacy: although his nation was far weaker than the looming imperial empires of Spain, France, Great Britain, and the United States, he skillfully maneuvered Saint-Domingue through their regional strife. Louverture's diplomatic calculations were especially complex when it came to navigating the competing interests of France and the United States. France had come to the aid of the nascent United States in the latter's rebellion against Great Britain; but after the US won independence, Washington promptly expanded trade with its prior colonizer and declared neutrality in France's conflict with monarchal Great Britain. In a further indication of cooling ties, the John Adams administration (1797–1801) stopped paying its debts to Paris. In retaliation for these snubs, France seized a fleet of US merchant ships off the East Coast of the US, sparking what would be a two-year-long period of undeclared hostilities—known as the Quasi-War—from 1798 to 1800.

As the two navies battled in the West Indies—the conflict had the unusual character of being conducted almost exclusively on the open seas—Saint-Domingue assumed a perhaps unenviable but strategic importance in the contest between the two powers. Given its colony's loyalty, France toyed with the idea of freeing Saint-Domingue slaves with the purpose of invading the United States. This might seem a gross mismatch today, but the vaunted Continental Army had disbanded after the American Revolution, leaving Saint-Domingue the more formidable military force, at least on land. With rumors of a black army marauding through the American South, in July 1798 Congress placed an embargo on all trade with France and its colonies, including Saint-Domingue.

In an attempt to repair relations with the Americans and lift the trade embargo, Louverture dispatched a discreet, capable representative, Joseph Bunel, in late December 1798 to Philadelphia for consultations with Secretary of State Timothy Pickering. Bunel, who as a white man hoped to be accepted more openly, was successful in achieving his ultimate goal: by February 1799 the US Congress had given President Adams the authority to exempt from the embargo any French colonies not menacing American merchantmen. The law's patent intention to apply to Saint-Domingue earned it the moniker the Toussaint Clause.

Louverture's and Bunel's success may have been helped by good timing. The New England–bred Adams, not a slave owner, was more disposed to entertain Louverture's solicitation than his predecessor George Washington or successor, Thomas Jefferson. Secretary Pickering, for his part, was an early supporter of independence, fearing that status quo as a French colony could facilitate either Saint-Domingue's use as a base for French military action against the United States or French anti-US pressure. Although formal recognition of the Caribbean nation did not happen until 1862, when Abraham Lincoln was in office, the Adams administration was much inclined to reestablish trade ties.

In negotiating a cessation of the US embargo, Louverture had to arrive at an agreement with the British, as Great Britain's naval superiority meant that all goods flowing to Saint-Domingue passed through what were, in effect, British waters. Fortunately, the British diplomat Thomas Maitland arrived in northern Saint-Domingue on May 4, 1799, with a joint agreement between the British and the United States in hand. Britain and the US were willing to resume trade with Louverture in one or two ports if Louverture promised to not incite a rebellion in the British colony of Jamaica. Louverture readily agreed to these terms, as the resumption of trade with the US was fundamental to his own domestic agenda.

Notably, Pickering chose the physician Edward Stevens, one of President Adams's close friends and himself born in the West Indies, as America's first consul general to Saint-Domingue. (An interesting aside: in the fiscally challenged early years of the new American republic, Stevens brought along all sorts of wares to sell in the Caribbean locale to underwrite the diplomatic endeavor.) French colonies were expected not to engage in diplomacy outside of France's colonial purview, but Louverture boldly met with Stevens when he arrived in April 1799. To many this would have been an irreparable blunder, but this was the same highly calculated leader as before: when speaking to the American emissary Stevens, the evasive Louverture focused on Haitian independence; with Paris, he continued to profess that he was "proud to be [France's] adoptive son."

Managing French expectations for Louverture's support of its broader geo-political goals, however, proved to be an ongoing, delicate matter. Using the rationale of the revolt for imperial ends, French officials pushed Louverture to promote the Declaration of the Rights of Man and of the Citizen through an attack on either the British island colony of Jamaica or the American South. (It appeared that Pickering's concerns were well justified.) French authorities, after all, had already used former black slaves for just such a campaign in the neighboring island of Guadalupe. But Louverture would have none of it. According to his biographer Philippe Girard, "He did not want to risk his life in some harebrained adventure overseas, even one that offered the promise of altering the course of world history. His long-term goal was not universal emancipation but abolition in Saint-Domingue, his political rise, and the colony's economic recovery, none of which could take place if he needlessly provoked the two main naval powers of the Caribbean. He chose to pursue cooperation instead."

To make things all the more complex, in addition to the liberation struggle Louverture was at the same time dealing with internal battles. While he was fighting with free black men in the north of the colony, on the horizon to the south was the army of his rival André Rigaud, a mixed-race general who controlled the south of the colony. Without food and guns from America, Louverture recognized that his chances of defeating Rigaud were slim. But with the reopening of Cap-Français and Port Repúblicain on June 13, 1799, to US trade, Louverture again proved that his military prowess was rivaled by his skill as a diplomat. Louverture's pragmatism not only elevated his troops over Rigaud's, in a savage civil war that was soon dubbed the War of the Knives, but also miraculously managed to keep him out of conflicts with France, Great Britain, and the United States—for the time being.

A New Empire of Slavery

From the French perspective, Napoleon was eager to restore dominion over Saint-Domingue and decisively end the revolt. In 1801 he dispatched one of the largest invasion forces ever to sail from Europe to the New World, comprising upward of fifty thousand troops and led by his gallant brother-in-law Charles Victoire Leclerc. The French dictator's orders to his subordinate were clear: "No more gilded Africans." Napoleon deliberately enlisted mixed-race and black officers into his force in order to add credence to his public promise not to restore slavery.

The following year, a second force some twenty-thousand-strong, initially sent to reestablish French control over Louisiana, was redirected to Saint-Domingue to reinforce what was by then a faltering mission. By this point the players had changed. Louverture had been captured and shipped off to prison in France; General Leclerc had died of yellow fever, a fate that awaited the majority of his expedition; and several of the force's black generals had mutinied. In November 1803 Haitian guerrillas fought the remnants of Leclerc's besieged force at Vertières, situated close to Louverture's birthplace. With the rebel troops prevailing, the French forces fled the island. Ultimately, Leclerc's failed counterinsurgency was critical to Napoleon's subsequent decision to sell New Orleans and all of French Louisiana (530 million acres at three cents per acre) to the United States, thus doubling the size of the fledgling nation. The irony is that the liberation of Haitian slaves had now, as Baptist put it, "delivered the Mississippi Valley to a new empire of slavery."

"Death or Liberty"

Contrary to what one might expect, abolitionist movements in France, Great Britain, and the United States viewed the Haitian Revolution with a combination of hope and trepidation as they waited to see if freed slaves could run the sugar plantations of the former colony without coerced labor. Slavery apologists had long contended that only slaves would submit to the harsh conditions of plantation work in the sweltering Caribbean climate; if they were freed they would simply resort to sloth, destroying the crop-based economy.

Abolitionists, by contrast, contended that the plantations would continue to prosper with wage labor. Abraham Bishop, from Connecticut and a political follower of Jefferson, was in the firm minority as a citizen who welcomed Haiti's independence. "If Freedom depends upon colour, and if the Blacks were born for slaves, those in the West-India islands may be called Insurgents and Murderers," he declared in his essays "The Rights of Black Men," published in Boston. "But the enlightened mind of Americans will not receive such ideas," he goes on. "We believe that Freedom is the natural right of all rational beings, and we know that the Blacks have never voluntarily resigned that freedom. Then is not their cause as just as ours?"

Louverture was celebrated by abolitionists around the world as someone who had dealt a blow to the evil scourge of slavery. The French abolitionist Victor Schoelcher, in his nineteenth-century biography of Louverture, describes him as a "man of genius." The radical American abolitionist John Brown read up on Louverture's military forays when devising his own raid on Harpers Ferry in 1859. Even proslavery voices in America praised the Haitian leader for his willingness to forgive his former masters and to force the free slaves back to the plantations. According to one, Louverture was "the only true great man yet known of the negro race." People who would have never endorsed the intellectual merits of slaves or their ability to achieve self-government could not help but admire Louverture's ability to keep his nerve when challenged by foreign powers. Africans living in America were also emboldened by Haiti's singular example. In 1800, for example, a tradesman named Gabriel, the "American Toussaint," commanded a failed slave insurrection in Virginia under the slogan Death or Liberty. Along with over two dozen of his fellow conspirators, he was convicted and executed, but his attempt (and inspiration) did not go unnoticed.

Despite receiving global praise, Louverture did not live to see his dream of independence realized. In early 1802 Louverture surrendered to General Leclerc's expedition force in exchange for what he thought was a French commitment not to reestablish slavery on the island. Months later Louverture was sent to the dingy Fort-de-Joux, a castle turned prison, in the Jura Mountains in France. He never set foot in Haiti again. Within a year, after suffering from intense interrogations and tuberculosis, Louverture died on April 7, 1803.

On January 1, 1804, Louverture's successor, Jean-Jacques Dessalines, put forth the Haitian Declaration of Independence, ending the thirteen-year revolution. France would not recognize independent Haiti until 1825—charging Haiti 150 million francs for the slaves and property lost during the revolution—but Louverture and his achievements would continue to inspire social revolution across the Americas into the twentieth century. Overcoming enormous odds to set his country on the path to independence, Louverture exemplified shrewd diplomacy and prowess on the battlefield.

Under Dessalines, Haiti became the first country in the world to permanently bar slavery. This incredible feat, however, would be somewhat tainted by Dessalines's order to wipe out the entire residual white population in the country, a genocide known as the "horrors of Santo Domingo" (and now, as the 1804 Haitian massacre). Leaving three thousand to five thousand people dead in its tracks, the massacre's victims included women and children and whites sympathetic to the new black order. Eager to court favor with the US, Dessalines wrote to Jefferson, but the Virginian never replied. To the contrary, the American commander in chief suspended relations between the two countries

Toussaint L'Ouverture, published by the prominent African American Underground Railroad conductor George DeBaptiste, circa 1870. (Library of Congress Prints and Photographs Division, Washington, DC)

from 1806 to 1808. Washington did not recognize Haiti's independence until long after France: in 1862 President Abraham Lincoln dispatched the New Hampshire judge, teacher, and diplomat Benjamin F. Whidden to Haiti to present his credentials.

2 • When Americans Loved Simón Bolívar

There will come a time when she is a giant, a colossus even, much to be feared in those vast regions. Then she will forget the benefits she received from others and think only of aggrandizing herself.
—Count Aranda, Prime Minister of Spain to King Charles III, 1783, in reference to the United States

The George Washington of South America

Although chroniclers of nineteenth-century US policies toward Latin America frequently (and rightly) bemoan the Colossus of the North's unyielding ambitions and expansion, Latin America's biggest impediment to cherished independence was in fact Spanish power, not the nascent United States. And revolt against European control was something Americans could certainly empathize with in the first decades of the eighteenth century. The United States came to share a deep solidarity with its South American brethren, hoping for, and at times directly assisting, a similar outcome to that of 1776 in order to further the project of New World liberty. Revolutionary rhetoric in the United States had embraced *universalist,* as opposed to national, themes like democracy and individual liberty even before American colonies were freed from British control. Writing in 1776, for instance, Thomas Paine declared that "freedom hath been hunted round the globe" and that his fellow citizens needed to "prepare in time an asylum for mankind." Once it had attained its own revolutionary republic, the United States turned its revolutionary passions and hopes to Latin America—and generally liked what it saw.

Simón Bolívar often headlines the discussion of Latin American independence, and although colloquially he is known as El Libertador, the first attempt
at liberating Latin America was coordinated by another learned Venezuelan
leader, Francisco de Miranda. Miranda arrived in the United States in 1783
after fleeing Spanish-held Cuba and promptly tapped into the prorevolutionary sentiment to further his cause. Over the next few years this revolutionary
forerunner would meet with the towering founders of the American democratic experiment: George Washington, Alexander Hamilton, Thomas Paine,
Samuel Adams, and Thomas Jefferson. Miranda's plan was to liberate Spanish America and form a confederation of hemispheric governments.

Not all US revolutionaries, however, were convinced by Miranda's vision.
John Adams was dubious about the South American's wide-eyed visions of
independence, while Thomas Jefferson, although happy to dine with Miranda,
conversed tongue-in-cheek. He did not see the US revolution as being export-
able to Latin America and even flirted with the idea of actually taking over the
Spanish American colonies. Writing to an acquaintance in 1786, Jefferson
held that taking Madrid's colonies for the United States was not out of the
question, but he feared that Spain was "too feeble to hold them till our population can be sufficiently advanced to gain it from them piece by piece."

While not receiving a unanimous seal of US approval, Miranda's venture
north was a success. He had piqued the interest of an illustrious audience
among the US political class, testament to how Spanish-American independence resonated in a very young United States. In 1811 President Madison,
while shying away from recognition of Latin independence, nonetheless described to Congress "an enlightened forecast" in the "great communities" in
South America. His nation, he argued, had "an obligation to take a deep interest in their destinies." The question now was whether this would entail the
United States taking an ideological, revolutionary interest and supporting
independence, or working to ensure that US interests would be served by the
new order that emerged.

Bolívar on a Roll

Born to a patrician family and steeped in literature, Bolívar towers as the
most formidable intellectual, political, and military leader of Latin America's
protracted wars of independence. His fortitude and streak of victories were
recognized around the globe (even if the latter came after multiple defeats),
and the accounts of his continental crisscrossing reads like a history textbook.

Before the Republic of Bolivia, formerly known as Upper Peru, was declared in 1825, Bolívar had liberated New Granada (today's Colombia) in 1819, his native Venezuela in 1821, Quito (today's Ecuador) in 1822, and Peru in 1824. As if this wasn't enough to secure his legacy, Bolívar continued to emboss history with his thumbprint when the independence struggle wound down. Swapping his sabre for a feathered quill, Bolívar served as president before installing himself as dictator in the newly formed Gran Colombia, comprising Colombia, Ecuador, and Venezuela, in 1819–30 and in Peru in 1823–26.

While the Venezuelan's achievements were and still are momentous, they didn't occur in a vacuum. Bolívar's liberation efforts conveniently aligned with the Napoleonic Wars in Europe. Distracting imperial attention from Latin America, Napoleon's invasion of the Iberian Peninsula in 1807–8 created a crisis of legitimacy in the Spanish Empire, with Napoleon engineering the abdication of both King Carlos IV and his son Ferdinand VII in May 1808 and appointing his brother Joseph as the new king of Spain. Legions of Spanish citizens were unwilling to accept Bonapartist rule and soon organized under a central junta to repel the invaders and their Spanish lackeys. Throughout the Spanish Empire, local elites, mostly of the *creole* class (people of European descent born in the New World), had to choose allegiances: either to the deposed Carlos IV and Ferdinand VII or to the new Bonapartist leadership. Many creoles called for outright independence, even if a remarkably liberal constitution had been promulgated from junta-controlled Spain in 1812.

Spain had expelled Napoleon by the end of 1813, and Ferdinand VII once again held the crown. Ruling as an absolutist monarch and turning his back on the junta's liberal constitution, he committed to restoring Spanish dominion over the recalcitrant colonies. The question, though, was whether there could ever be a return to the status quo ante in a rapidly changing New World where creole leaders like Bolívar had read Locke, Voltaire, and Montesquieu, witnessed the incredible events in North America in 1776 and 1789, and even tasted liberty in the case of Venezuela. Bolívar took full advantage of the moment, fundamentally changing the shape of the power dynamics in the hemisphere.

Bolívar Mania

Riding high on a surge of republican patriotism after the War of 1812 with Britain, the United States celebrated Latin American independence successes as if they were its own. Throngs of US citizens, not just white males but also blacks and women, northerners and southerners, applauded the advance of Latin American independence, calling the rebels "brothers and countrymen and Americans." "Appalachian farmers," wrote the Northwestern University historian Caitlin Fitz in her exquisite tome *Our Sister Republics,* "read poetry about Andean independence; sailors wore cockades for revolutionary Montevideo; boozy partygoers sang in honor of Colombian freedom." In taverns, inns, and public squares toasts that were novel before 1812 became commonplace. In Philadelphia, for example, US soldiers toasted the "Patriots of South America" and revelers in Virginia cheered roundly after crying out, "May our example excite them to imitation." By the early 1830s more than two hundred American children had been named after Bolívar. Meanwhile, rebel leaders worked hard to influence public opinion in the United States, "persuading their hosts," as Fitz writes, "that the latest [Latin] American revolutions were a glorious tropical reprise of 1776."

While ordinary US citizens appeared united by their joy at the outbreak of revolution in Latin America, US leaders were more ambivalent toward backing the rebels, at least at first. From his retirement lair atop the butte at Monticello, Thomas Jefferson rooted for the Latins but was wary of their ability to self-govern, writing in December 1813 that "history . . . furnishes no example of a priest-ridden people maintaining a free civil government." The good news, he hoped, was hemispheric sovereignty: "[I]n whatever governments they end, they will be *American* government, no longer involved in the never-ceasing broils of Europe. . . . America has a hemisphere to itself." John Adams, now seventy-nine years old, rehearsed his earlier skepticism of Miranda's dream of independence in a letter of March 1815 to the former Massachusetts senator James Lloyd: "What could I think of revolutions and constitutions in South America? A people more ignorant, more bigoted, more superstitious, more implicitly credulous in the sanctity of royalty, more blindly devoted to their priests, in more awful terror of the Inquisition, than any people in Europe, even in Spain, Portugal, or the Austrian Netherlands, and infinitely more than Rome itself." To Adams any dream of a Miranda-style "confederation of governments" was as "absurd as similar plans would be to establish democracies among the birds, beasts and fishes." Monroe's secretary of state, John Quincy Adams, shared his father's apprehension regarding instability in Latin America: "Venezuela, though it has emancipated all its slaves, has been constantly alternating between an absolute military government, a capitulation to Spanish authority, and guerrillas black and white, of which every petty chief has acted for purposes of war and rapine as an independent sovereign.

There is finally in South America neither unity of cause nor unity of effort, as there was in our Revolution."

And what certainly came as a deep disappointment to those who wanted to see the United States backing South American liberty, just nine months after the Battle of New Orleans, the final major battle of the War of 1812 that vaulted Major General Andrew Jackson to national fame, President Madison barred US citizens from locking elbows with southern rebels in their campaign against Spanish dominion. Although Americans still found ways to lend a hand, any romantic sense of hemispheric camaraderie wasn't the sole motivation. In a letter first published in Charleston's *City Gazette* and then picked up by numerous other papers, an American living in Venezuela urged his fellow citizens to become arms dealers for the cause of both liberty as well as profit. US merchants ended up selling upward of 150,000 guns, 1 million flints, and hundreds of tons of gunpowder and ammunition for the South American independence cause.

Fitz writes that on top of the sale of arms, many out-of-work American mariners made redundant by the post-1812 peace dividend decided to seek pay and adventure by joining rebel navies. More than three thousand seafaring men eventually departed the United States, leaving the Spanish and Portuguese to wonder how Washington could maintain its supposed neutrality while "letting its citizens prey on royalist forces." Hoping to fend off a war with Madrid, Adams eventually moved to stamp out the privateering with the Neutrality Act of 1817. Supporters called the act a "bill for making peace between His Catholic Majesty and the town of Baltimore," the city from which many privateers launched their excursions to Latin America. But the legislation failed to stop the enlistments. The notion of mariners actively working against the aims of policy makers raises a larger point for this book about what scholars call the multivocality (read, varying interests *within* and *outside* the foreign policy establishment that impinge on policy) of US policy toward Latin America: a persistent theme in the two-century US involvement in the region.

Elusive Recognition

For President Monroe and Secretary of State Adams restraint was in order, no matter how euphoric the pro-Latin mood at home. Explaining their more cautious approach in regard to recognizing new republics was the fear of raising the ire of Spain. This would have not only complicated commerce with Cuba but also jeopardized American plans for Spanish-held Florida and the

Columbia River Basin. As the historian Louis A. Pérez has mentioned, early US presidential administrations had designs on Cuba; but if the United States could not have the island, then it was incumbent on Washington to make sure that other European powers did not take it away from Spain. So, needless to say, the relationship was complex. Not to mention the unignorable ideological conflict between the US South (predominantly) and an independent Latin America where slavery was outlawed and racial mixing was permitted.

Not all voices were unified in their position toward these nascent republics. The Kentucky congressman Henry Clay, incensed after Monroe chose Adams over him for the administration's top diplomatic spot, believed that the United States needed to serve as a "rallying point" by offering prompt economic and diplomatic aid to republican dreamers around the world, Latin America above all. Pro-independence Latin Americans in Washington also were indefatigable in their diplomatic efforts to persuade the Monroe administration to officially recognize the new republics. A breakthrough occurred in mid-June 1822, when the Colombian envoy Manuel Torres entered the White House. John Quincy Adams describes the scene:

> At one o'clock, I presented Mr. Manuel Torres as Chargé d'Affaires from the Republic of Colombia to the President. . . . The incident was chiefly interesting as being the first formal act of recognition of an independent South American Government. Torres, who has scarcely life in him to walk alone, was deeply affected by it . . . moved even to tears. The President assured him of the great interest taken by the United States in the welfare and success of his country, and of the particular satisfaction with which he received him as its first representative. The audience was, as usual, only a few minutes.

Torres had dedicated years to achieving this recognition, working the diplomatic circles, yet ultimately it was Bolívar's stunning successes on the battlefield that convinced Adams and Monroe to finally give him credence. Exhausted but relieved, Torres returned to his residence in Philadelphia, eager to dispatch the stunning news to Bolívar. Within just a few weeks, though, the Colombian patriot had died. Torres's funeral was attended by US military personnel who gave him full military honors; all of the vessels in Philadelphia harbor "drew their colors at half-staff." Amazingly, Bolívar was "at such a remove in the depths of the equatorial cordillera" (the Andes) that he would not learn about North American recognition of the fledgling Colombian state for another six months.

Henry Clay, engraved by John Sartain from the original picture, 1843. The
subject stands before a large column and gestures toward an American flag
and a globe turned to show South America. The globe alludes to Clay's support,
during his early career in the House of Representatives, of Latin American
insurgents and new republics. (Library of Congress Prints and Photographs
Division, Washington, DC)

By the end of 1822 Secretary of State Adams opted to back the recognition
of other newly declared republics of Latin America. In the case of El Salvador,
soon after its independence in 1821, liberal (meaning free trade and national
development in the spirit of the American, French, and Haitian revolutions)

elites from the country petitioned the US for statehood, which was denied; the reasons for Washington's unwillingness seem to have been mostly lost to history. Congress also endorsed Adams's move, with only one nay in the House of Representatives and three in the Senate. A new defiance had possessed Washington, reflective of the growing confidence that the European monarchies would not punish Washington for taking this step. Moreover, as Florida was now in America's hands following the Adams–Onís Treaty of 1821, Monroe and Adams could use recognition as a way to send a sharp message to Spain. In addition American solidarity was, quite simply, good politics for Adams's insatiable presidential ambitions.

The significance of the US's formal recognition of its new Latin American neighbors was immense. In the past Americans had often looked askance at the radicalism in Haiti and France in the late 1790s, yet now, with Roman Catholic nations emancipating their slaves, the US populace appeared to welcome the racial universalism of the Latin American rebellions. To an extent, many US citizens lauded revolutionary movements with goals that they would never tolerate at home, especially in the slaveholding South. Only US blacks and white abolitionists were consistent in arguing that the Latin rebels were achieving the "egalitarian promise" that was as yet unrealized in the United States.

On New Year's Day, 1825, many of the nation's distinguished political leaders—Monroe, Adams, Clay, and Senator Andrew Jackson of Tennessee—gathered to offer a toast "to General Simón Bolívar, the George Washington of South America!" This was exactly the sort of reception Bolívar had hoped for from the United States, and by his battlefield gallantry he had earned it. One scholar wrote, "Not Alexander, not Hannibal, not even Julius Caesar had fought across such a vast, inhospitable terrain. Charlemagne's victories would have had to double to match Bolívar's. Napoleon, striving to build an empire, had covered less ground than Bolívar, struggling to win freedom."

The problem for Bolívar, though, was that recognition of Gran Colombia from Great Britain (1825) and the United States did not free the Great Liberator from myriad separate obstacles. Pro-Madrid royalist sentiment remained a blockade to be reckoned with as he moved from a successful campaign in Quito to Peru. And as Bolívar's political struggles became more and more evident, US politicians and envoys began to worry whether "South Americans were no better off for their revolution." However, in this initial, searing phase of Latin America's revolution, the United States commented from the sideline; it played primarily a peripheral, only occasionally supportive role, despite its well-earned subsequent reputation for hemispheric heavy-handedness.

After President Monroe's 1823 pronouncement of what came to be known as the Monroe Doctrine, which opposed European colonialism in Latin America (and by extension allowing the US to exert its influence without imperial competition), US policy toward Latin America was more equivocal and unplanned than the common interpretations of history suggest. Equally important is that while inspired by the North American model and Enlightenment ideas, Latin America's liberty was achieved by Latin American military and political relentlessness. Latin Americans owned their independence, a fact that helps make sense of events when this embryonic experiment in Latin American unity and strength ran off the rails.

3 • La Doctrina Monroe

Hemispheric Hardball

The new Latin American republics were soon under threat. Despite winning diplomatic recognition from the United States, they were not yet safe from the possibility of reconquest by their former European masters. US diplomatic recognition of the newly sovereign Latin American republics, while popular domestically in the US, did little to address the threat of European reconquest of the continent's erstwhile New World possessions. Buoyed by the Holy Alliance of Russia, Prussia, and Austria, a French army quelled a constitutionalist rebellion in Spain in 1823, paving the way for the Spanish monarchy to punish its recalcitrant colonies. Meanwhile, Tsar Alexander I of Russia was laying claim to Oregon, thereby challenging US continental ambitions. From the US perspective, the fear was that if Tsar Alexander and the Holy Alliance were able to continue to make gains in the New World, the United States could say goodbye to its territorial ambitions on the Pacific Coast, and Latin America could once again fall under the control of imperial Spain—or even predatory France.

Itself a constitutional monarchy, Great Britain had little patience for the absolutism of the Holy Alliance and wished to expand its commercial ties with the Latin republics. Despite the fact that the British had torched the White House only a decade earlier during the War of 1812, George Canning—described as the "balding and brilliant" British foreign secretary by Caitlin Fitz—approached the Monroe administration with a proposal to devise a dual declaration against the anticipated interference by the Holy Alliance in the Western Hemisphere. Canning was offering the Americans a "marriage of convenience" wrapped up in a "flattering and tempting proposal" entailing a joint renunciation of territorial additions.

At the time, Great Britain was the global power, while the United States was little more than, as Fitz depicts, a "second ring show in the high-strung Atlantic circus." President James Monroe (1817–25) supported increased cooperation with Great Britain, as did his secretary of war, John Calhoun. And in a letter written on October 24, 1823, Thomas Jefferson, responding to a solicitation of advice from his friend, the former president and fellow Virginian James Madison, urged Monroe to add Britain's geopolitical heft to the US cause. John Quincy Adams, however, was skeptical of the Europeans' ability to reassert themselves in the New World, making the benefit of any alliance with Britain moot. Much more prudent, Adams sensed, was to make a *unilateral* declaration against European forays into the hemisphere. In so doing the United States could build up its own credibility as a regional power while not appearing to be merely a lackey of Great Britain. Even if Adams's hunch was wrong and the Holy Alliance did intervene, he believed the British would still ultimately join with the Americans to check this continental power grab and provide the necessary military muscle.

US policy ended up reflecting Adams's position of unilateral independence; having rejected the British offer, the US would apply the same cunning diplomatic logic that ultimately led to the formulation of the Monroe Doctrine. This sweeping declaration called for a hemisphere free of European interference, pledged US nonintervention in the Old World, and affirmed that the United States would view European attacks on its hemispheric neighbors as aggression against itself. Adams contributed to the outline of Monroe's address, which the president delivered to Congress in December 1823:

> The citizens of the United States cherish sentiments the most friendly in favor of the liberty and happiness of their fellow-men on that side of the Atlantic. In the wars of the European powers in matters relating to themselves we have never taken any part, nor does it comport with our policy so to do. It is only when our rights are invaded or seriously menaced that we resent injuries or make preparations for our defense. With the movements in this hemisphere we are of necessity more immediately connected, and by causes which must be obvious to all enlightened and impartial observers. The political system of the allied powers is essentially different in this respect from that of America. . . . We owe it, therefore, to candor and to the amicable relations existing between the United States and those powers to declare that we should consider any attempt on their part to extend their system to any portion of this hemisphere as dangerous to our peace and safety.

Foreign powers were inclined to agree with the estimation of a British newspaper that at the time concluded that Monroe's address was at least in part about future US machinations in the region. "The plain *Yankee* of the matter is that the United States wish to monopolize to themselves the privilege of colonizing . . . every . . . part of the North American continent." However, the reality of the matter was that the United States had little ability to back with force such audacious aims. Luckily for the Monroe administration, keeping out the rest of Europe helped Great Britain as much as the United States. Thus it could be a free rider of sorts, benefiting from the support of the Royal Navy.

"Unity! Unity! Unity!"

Officials in the newly independent Latin republics were for the most part delighted. Reporting of Monroe's statement did not hit Bogotá until early 1824, by which time an editorial in the *Gaceta de Colombia* (possibly written by Vice President Francisco de Paula Santander) rejoiced that the United States had now commenced playing "among the civilized nations of the world that powerful and majestic role which befits the oldest and most powerful nation of our hemisphere." In a letter of February 7, 1824, the US envoy in Bogotá described how the Andean capital city's "unaffected joy was expressed on the arrival of the President's message . . . regarding the feelings and policy of the United States in the event of European interference in the political affairs of this continent." This same year Washington and Bogotá signed the Anderson–Gual Treaty, named for the Gran Colombian minister Pedro Gual Escandón, the first bilateral pact that the United States negotiated with another American nation.

Panama Passions

Simón Bolívar shared the US desire not to see European monarchies in the New World. In his words, "European ambition forced the yoke of slavery on the rest of the world, and the rest of the world was obliged to answer with an equivalent force. . . . This is what I call the equilibrium of the Universe."

Yet, critically, Bolívar had no patience for the United States acting as Latin America's protector. This explains why his diplomats could at once be both genuinely grateful to Monroe for this emphatic anti-imperial directive, yet remain wary of North American culture and motives. Bolívar wanted Latin

American nations to stand together on their own terms. He envisioned the freshly minted republics themselves setting the diplomatic wheels in motion to establish a new league of Spanish American nations that would resist common (imperial) foes and promote solidarity. In late 1824 Bolívar issued invitations for "an assembly of plenipotentiaries" to meet in Panama in June 1826. He did not invite the United States, Haiti, or Brazil to this inter-American conference, as they were not former Spanish colonies, even if Great Britain got the nod due to its undeniable global potency. In the end, though, other leaders, like Santander, issued invitations to the United States and Brazil, likely behind Bolívar's back.

John Quincy Adams, now as president, dispatched envoys to the inter-American conference with strict instructions not to sign any regional pacts. Once again many southerners were vehemently opposed to having Washington join a federation opposed to slavery. The newly appointed secretary of state, Henry Clay, however, saw beyond the immediate ideological conflict; he believed that participation would help give the United States a toehold in the burgeoning and lucrative inter-American system. It was indeed the *Yankees,* not the Latins, who were trying desperately to join the hemispheric solidarity fiesta. Famously, after Congress dibbled and dabbled for four months before approving the mission, neither of the two delegates were able to attend the conference, as one died on the way to the isthmus and the other arrived after it had concluded.

The delayed US arrival was just one of the conference's hiccups. Bolívar opted not to attend so as to reduce the chance that the outcomes could be written off as his own preferences. Yet only Peru, Gran Colombia, Mexico, and the Federal Republic of Central America attended the conference. Chile, "wrenched by internal conflagrations," was missing, and the United Province of Rio de la Plata (parts of today's Argentina, Bolivia, Uruguay, Paraguay, and Brazil) skipped too, citing its "horror of too early a union," especially if said union was a decidedly pro-Colombia, that is, pro-Bolívar, affair. While newfound liberty bonded the Western Hemisphere, rivalries, some bitter and some trivial, were still afoot, and they were often as much Latin-on-Latin as opposed to gringo-on-Latin.

In the end the conference was a profound failure. As the Peruvian author Marie Arana described it, "Delegates gathering in the stuffy Franciscan monastery in Panama's sweltering capital had been all too eager to be done with the debate. Some were ailing, others fearful of the pestilential climate; all were anxious, about the motives." Only New Granada ratified the vacuous resolutions. Here is Bolívar writing to a trusted colleague: "The institution was admirable like that mythic madman, perched on a rock in the open sea, thinking he could direct the ships' traffic." One British envoy attending the proceedings in the inhospitable climate found the conference participants "far less republican than I expected."

The divisions between the new Latin American states—illuminated by the conference—were in part a consequence of the intense struggles for independence that had won them their very own freedom. Liberty in Latin America had cost an enormous sum in blood and treasure, infinitely more than in North America. Arana writes, "A revolution begun by [creole] polite society on the assumption that its wins would be painless had become mired in two decades of catastrophic losses, rivaling in carnage the twentieth century's more heavily armed conflicts. Populations had been cut in half." The forecast was dire. In Arana's words, "The Americas that were emerging under Bolívar's horrified eyes were feudalistic, divisive, militaristic, racist, ruled by warlords who strove to keep the ignorant masses blinkered and under bigoted control." Indeed, Latin America's much larger battle was domestic, as new leaders attempted to forge nations out of exploited colonies with profound racial and economic schisms.

Monroe Doctrine's Bark over Bite

As the historian of diplomacy Walter McDougall has written, the "Monrovian principles" were hatched for essential American security imperatives but also for a widespread defense of Latin America's autonomy vis-à-vis Europe. However, despite the fierce reputation the Monroe Doctrine would gain in future decades and centuries, the pronouncement did not check moves that violated Monroe's admonitions, such as the British annexation of the Falkland Islands in 1833 or Madrid's renewal of colonial dominion in Santo Domingo in 1861 or, most infamously, Napoleon III's bold gambit to establish a French puppet regime in Mexico during the US Civil War. John Quincy Adams pithily explained this less active interpretation of the doctrine's exhortations: "America does not go abroad in search of monsters to destroy." One must also keep in mind that until very late in the nineteenth century the United States grappled with becoming the master of its own continental territory, focusing on its westward expansion to the Pacific Coast as well as forging its own national identity before meddling in affairs down south.

Nonetheless, in what was a policy—not a treaty as is sometimes assumed—the Monroe Doctrine turned Latin America into an effective sphere of influence for the United States. And its goal of preventing any European meddling in the Americas quickly became sacrosanct for many. In 1923, on the one hundredth anniversary of the Monroe Doctrine, Mary Baker Eddy, the guiding force of the Christian Science Church, proclaimed, "I believe strictly in the Monroe Doctrine, in our Constitution, and in the laws of God." It didn't matter that it wasn't until very late in the nineteenth century that the US Navy could challenge, say, its Chilean counterpart, "much less an imperial power that chose to meddle there."

Stricken with tuberculosis and ostracized politically in what was still Gran Colombia—although it would implode the following year and split into New Granada, Ecuador, and Venezuela—Bolívar died on December 17, 1830, at the age of forty-seven. But while the Great Liberator's Pan-American conference had failed to create a legal federation of states, it set the stage for the modern Organization of American States, through which the idea of "pan-Americanism" would endure. For the first half century or so after Bolívar's death, the Pan-American push was largely a result of Latin American governments and diplomats, at times intentionally without US or Brazilian participation, until the United States picked up the mantle in the last decade of the century.

The Monroe Doctrine has assumed a singular importance in the history of American political thought. It symbolizes the beginnings of the United States' often proprietary relationship with its so-called backyard. But one should not forget that the doctrine represented symbolic more than military might in that the United States lacked the ability to enforce Monroe's stated goals. Moreover, while this period is best known for US unilateralism, the complex multilateral and bilateral relations that also marked hemispheric dynamics during this time should not be overlooked. Latin American countries welcomed the Monroe Doctrine when it was first announced. As the governor of Buenos Aires wrote in a December 1824 message to the congress of La Plata Provinces that clearly reveals this broader mindset, "We are under a large obligation towards the United States of North America. That Republic has solemnly recognized our independence."

4 • Destiny Manifested

They consider themselves superior to the rest of mankind and look upon
their Republic as the only establishment upon the earth, founded upon a
grand and solid basis, embellished by wisdom, and destined one day to
become the most sublime colossus of human power, and the wonder of
the universe.
—Luis de Onís, Spanish envoy to the United States, 1808–19

Go West, young man, and grow up with the country.
—1851 editorial, Terre Haute *Express*

Each year millions of American high school students learn about Manifest
Destiny—the "quasi-theological" rationale for the nation's continental designs
in the 1840s and 1850s—as a distinct *era*. And the ostensible voice of this era
was the young John O'Sullivan. As the editor of the *Democratic Review*, a na-
tionally well-regarded political and literary magazine, O'Sullivan navigated
the magazine toward the principles of Jacksonian democracy and supported
Martin Van Buren's and James K. Polk's presidential candidacies in 1840 and
1844, respectively. Often less glorified during the high school history lesson,
however, is how O'Sullivan's prose was decidedly a manifestation of the
already surging nationalistic, racialized zeitgeist. "The far-reaching, the
boundless future will be the era of American greatness," the influential writer
contended. O'Sullivan's justifications for such action reflected America's mid-
century spirit of God-given exceptionalism, national progress, and—most important for understanding hemispheric relations—outward expansion and
destiny. In his 1839 essay titled "The Great Nation of Futurity," O'Sullivan told
his readers of the miracle of the United States of America born in 1776:

America is destined for better deeds. It is our unparalleled glory that we have no reminiscences of battle fields, but in defence of humanity, of the oppressed of all nations, of the rights of conscience, the rights of personal enfranchisement.

We have had patriots to defend our homes, our liberties, but no aspirants to crowns or thrones; nor have the American people ever suffered themselves to be led on by wicked ambition to depopulate the land, to spread desolation far and wide, that a human being might be placed on a seat of supremacy.

O'Sullivan's religious vision was a Union consisting of "hundreds of happy millions, calling, owning no man master, but governed by God's natural and moral law of equality, the law of brotherhood—of 'peace and good will amongst men.' " For O'Sullivan, America's "birth was the beginning of a new history." Six years later O'Sullivan's widely read 1845 essay "Annexation" actually coined the phrase "manifest destiny." The author applied the term to the immediate goal of bolstering the case for incorporating Texas into the Union— an issue that had festered in Congress and the nation ever since the Republic of Texas was born in 1836. "It is now time for the opposition to the Annexation of Texas to cease," he wrote. But there were bigger issues at stake, namely the "fulfillment of our manifest destiny to overspread the continent allotted by Providence for the free development of our yearly multiplying millions."

What is often overlooked is that Americans had been preaching and practicing Manifest Destiny–style expansionism since the nation's founding. As the scholar Walter MacDougall points out, despite Manifest Destiny being first consciously applied toward Texas and Oregon in the 1840s, "expansion was implicit in U.S. doctrine and explicit in its behavior from the moment in 1781 when Benjamin Franklin demanded of Britain all of the lands east of the Mississippi." Take this editorial by the *New York Evening Post* preceding the Louisiana Purchase from Napoleon in 1803: "It belongs *of right* to the United States to regulate the future destiny of *North America*. The country is *ours*; ours is the right to its rivers and to all the sources of future opulence, power and happiness, which lay scattered at our feet."

Foreign Policy and Filibusters

After the Louisiana Purchase in 1803 came American settlers' takeover of "West Florida" between 1810 and 1813; afterward, the seminal Adams– Onís Treaty, ratified in 1819 with Spain, annexed Florida into the United

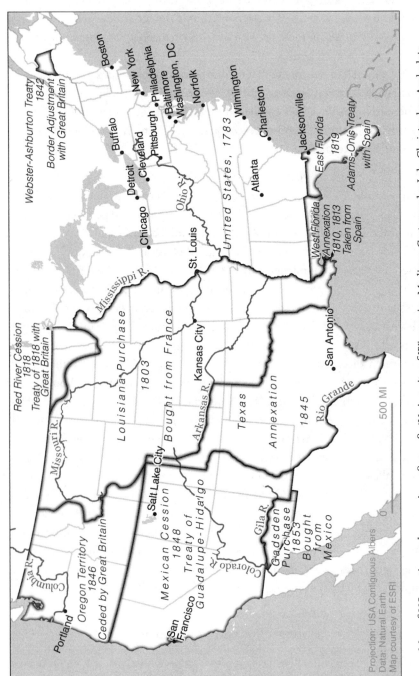

Map of US continental expansion, 1803–48. (University of Wisconsin–Madison Cartography Lab. Christopher Archuleta, cartographer)

States and determined the border between New Spain and the US; and then the Indian Removal Act signed into law by President Andrew Jackson on May 28, 1830. All of this is to show not only how closely linked the Monroe Doctrine of 1823 was with the era's unrepentant expansion, but also that it wasn't just O'Sullivan's commentary that sent pioneers westward. In fact, John Quincy Adams might have first made the explicit inference of the term when he coined Monroe's address, using "destiny" and "manifestation" in the same phrase.

Manifest Destiny was not a monolithic concept of state policy: it evolved over time and was subject to very different interpretations. Political expediency and profit played their part too, as did private citizens. Starting in the 1850s Manifest Destiny turned into what scholars have called Sectional Destiny. After the continental annexations, slaveholding southerners paid for or personally led motley (and illegal) but consequential imperial campaigns to Mexico, Central America, and the Caribbean, almost all of which invariably ended in failure. This phenomenon, the *filibuster* (Dutch for freebooter or pirate), emerged as a categorical label for slavery-driven, private US foreign campaigns in the antebellum era. The most infamous filibuster, William Walker of Tennessee, was well educated and a disciple of Manifest Destiny. "The grey-eyed man of destiny" thought the United States had committed an inexcusable sin when it failed to snatch more land from Mexico after bringing the country to its knees in the Mexican–American War. In 1853 Walker led a campaign in Baja California with forty-five fighters, a scheme that started with his invasion of the city of La Paz and was followed by Walker's installation as president of a nearby Mexican region and the instatement of slavery in the so-called Republic of Lower California from 1853 to 1854.

The redoubtable Walker, the "prince of American filibusters," then ventured to Nicaragua, Central America's largest country. He ruled there from 1855 to 1857, first as commander in chief and then as president through a rigged vote plagued by "the California style of ballot stuffing." Albeit late in his time in power, he again enacted slavery in a gambit to entice slaveholders from the American South. But as the scholar Michel Gobat writes in his essential book *Empire by Invitation,* more of Walker's roughly twelve thousand US supporters who joined him in Nicaragua were from the North and "not only opposed the expansion of slavery but also sought to uplift the native masses and free them from allegedly despotic elites." A notable case is that of the "suffragist, temperance lecturer, and abolitionist" Sarah Pellet, who gained notoriety by being the first woman to apply for admission to Harvard University. Finishing up her first stint in Walker's Nicaragua, Pellet spoke repeatedly to audiences in the United States, championing Walker's campaign to promote liberty. In addition to idealistic Americans such as Pellet, legions of Nicaraguans embraced Walker's ascension "in the hope that it would end the civil wars plaguing the country since it gained independence from Spain in 1821." Nicaraguans affiliated with the Liberal Party coveted being annexed by the United States as a free state.

During his tenure holding the reins of Nicaraguan power, Walker had both domestic and foreign ambitions. In Nicaragua he mandated that English should be the nation's official language, while abroad he set his eyes on conquering the entire isthmus. Yet Walker's white supremacist dreams would never come to fruition. Other Central American governments aligned against the American interloper, and, having also gotten crosswise with the business titan Cornelius Vanderbilt's Accessory Transit Company, a major political player in the country, Walker was all but finished by May 1857.

As the scholar Victor Bulmer-Thomas has argued, this tale would have been "dismissed as '*opera buffa*' " had the Tennessean not had what might be considered a puzzling link to President Franklin Pierce (1853–57). In 1856 Pierce extended diplomatic ties to Walker's regime, and in 1859 Pierce's successor, James Buchanan (1857–61), pardoned Walker after he'd been arrested by US forces. Walker's luck, however, would be short-lived. Arriving at the Honduran coastal city of Trujillo on his way back to Nicaragua, Walker was handed over to British Royal Navy officers, who then handed him back to the Honduran government, which executed the indefatigable filibuster on September 12, 1860. Walker was thirty-six years old. Lasting but two years, Walker's Central America odyssey nonetheless represented the first time that American citizens had taken over a country outside the continental United States. His escapades riveted the US public, which was still "enthralled with the expansionist spirit of Manifest Destiny."

McDougall offers an astute explanation for *when* and *why* this "civil religion," hatched in 1776, grew so much in the mid-nineteenth century: "Geography invited it; demography compelled it." Senator Stephen A. Douglas described the phenomenon in 1858: "This is a young and growing nation," he stated in his Illinois state election debates with Abraham Lincoln. "It swarms as often as a hive of bees, and . . . there must be hives in which they can gather and make their honey. . . . I tell you, increase, and multiply, and expand, as is the law of the nation's existence." Moreover, the French diplomat and scholar Alexis de Tocqueville also observed the American lust for continental colonization westward in his two-volume *Democracy in America:* "not only for the sake of the profit it holds out to them, but for the love of the constant excitement occasioned by that pursuit." The new tone of commentary that emerged signaled the "second revolution" of sorts that America was undergoing. Immigrants—not muskets—poured into the country, and from infrastructure that included canals, steamboats, and turnpikes to permeating global commerce, this second revolution upended how Americans worked and lived all the same.

Anglo-Saxon Foot

We'll never be able to answer whether the Manifest Destiny of America made war with its neighbors inevitable. But it certainly made it much more likely. Nonetheless, we can't make a sweeping statement of all US public intellectuals or politicians at the time. John Quincy Adams, for example, is an important reminder of the occasional "reluctant imperialist" at the time. Adams failed to rally around the Louisiana Purchase and, decades later, opposed the acquisition of lands that became part of Texas. But most important, Adams demonstrates that not partaking in the furor of imperial ambitions didn't equate to complacency; he still had prophecy for America. Writing from St. Petersburg in 1811, Adams argued, "The whole continent of North America appears to be destined by Divine Providence to be peopled by one nation, speaking one language, professing one general system of religious and political principles, and accustomed to one general tenor of social usages and customs." And other challenges to this tide were intolerable. As McDougall wrote, "Without freedom to grow, the nation would not be free at all. Or, to put it the other way around, U.S. citizens saw barriers and restraints on expansion as intolerable assaults on liberty."

In addition to being majority expansionist, the US had a racial component to its national identity. O'Sullivan wrote in 1845 in "Annexation" that the United States could take California from Mexico since "the Anglo-Saxon foot is already on its borders. Already the advance guard of the irresistible army of Anglo-Saxon emigration has begun to pour down upon it, armed with plough and rifle, and marking its trail with schools and colleges, courts and representative halls, mills and meeting-houses." Yet some of Manifest Destiny's harshest critics, like South Carolina's John Calhoun, feared it would water down the nation's racial purity. Addressing the conquest of Mexico in a speech to Congress in January 1848, Calhoun said,

We have never dreamt of incorporating into our union any but the Caucasian race—the free white race. To incorporate Mexico, would be the very first instance of the kind, of incorporating an Indian race; for more than half of the Mexicans are Indians, and the other is composed chiefly of mixed tribes. I protest against such a union as that! Ours, sir is the Government of a white race. . . . We are anxious to force free government on all; and I see that it has been urged . . . that it is the mission of this country to spread civil and religious liberty over all the world, and especially over this continent. It is a great mistake.

So what to take away from all of this? We have seen that even when it was a relatively weak global, even regional, power the United States had a unique, outsized foreign policy that ran, first, into continental constraint and then into weak neighbors. To this end, we now turn to the overlapping episodes of Texas and the full-scale US invasion of Mexico to see Manifest Destiny expressed, as Mr. Calhoun's rhetoric reinforced, in its most controversial, lasting manner.

5 • A Lone Star Is Born

Sometime in the 1820s the decorated Mexican general Manuel de Mier y Terán expressed to colleagues his deep worry about Texas's "incoming stream of news of [Anglo-American] settlers unceasing" and its ramifications for the fledgling Mexican nation. For America, Mier y Terán lamented, was "the most avid nation in the world. The North Americans have conquered whatever territory adjoins them." On July 3, 1832, dressed in his most elegant service garb, the forty-three-year-old Mexican patriot stabbed himself. Written the night before, his despondent suicide note ended with: *En qué parará Texas?* What will become of Texas?

To get us up to speed on Texas, a bit of geography and history is in order. The Louisiana Purchase cost President Thomas Jefferson $15 million in 1803 and delivered 828,000 square miles of territory, reaching from the Mississippi River to the Rocky Mountains and from the Gulf of Mexico to Canada. The purchase doubled the size of the United States. Yet because these lands were transferred in spite of France's and Spain's unclear colonial boundaries in the region, the cagey Jefferson contended that Louisiana in fact held a section of what is now Texas. And due to Jefferson's successful imperial-style gambit, decades later the United States would directly rub up against Texas— and thus Mexico as well.

Years later John Quincy Adams made a similar argument during his border negotiations with Spain's Luis de Onís for the eponymous pact, the long-delayed Adams–Onís Treaty signed in 1819, which granted Florida to Washington and set the border between New Spain and the United States. Often with a nod and a wink from Washington officials, intrepid American settlers infringed on the critical buffer region of East Florida, the lightly defended Spanish frontier. In a series of skirmishes that came to be known as the First Seminole War, in early 1818 around three thousand troops led by General Andrew Jackson invaded the territory and basically "dared Spain to do something about it." Madrid chose negotiation.

Critically, in return for Madrid's ceding the Floridas and claims in the Pacific Northwest, Adams–Onís entailed Washington's acceptance of Madrid's dominion over its colony of Nueva España (which became Mexico after independence). Washington would also forgo any claims to Texas and pay several million dollars in debts owed to Spain by US residents. Yet even before the treaty was formally ratified in 1821, in September of that year Mexico gained its independence.

Washington and Mexico City nonetheless maintained the Sabine River as the demarcation point between US-held Louisiana and Mexico's Texas, which, together with neighboring Coahuila, constituted a single province. Up north, the treaty's architect, John Quincy Adams, was excoriated by messianic critics wedded to the notion that the Louisiana Purchase included Texas, and thus "signing away the U.S. claim to it was positively treasonous." For Mexico, however, though it might have inherited the border treaty from Spain, its right to rule in agriculturally fertile (read, cotton, tobacco, and sugar) Texas was sacrosanct.

A Risky Business

The number of Mexican nationals living in this remote stretch of the incipient Mexican nation paled in comparison to the Native American tribes: primarily Wichitas, Comanches, and Cherokees. This created problems for Mexico City and its already tenuous claim to the land. As the diplomatic norms of the time held, one country's hold on a particular province depended on their ability to actually control the land. And, as the historian Timothy Henderson keenly wonders, where were Mexico's soon-to-be-Texan settlers going to come from, given the country's sparse population? Or, as Henry Clay questioned in 1821, "By what race should Texas be peopled?"

Mexico's solution? Invite the Americans—on certain terms, of course. Spain had already laid the groundwork: after the Adams–Onís Treaty confirmed Spanish possession of Texas in 1819, colonial authorities had established a carefully regulated land grant system for American migrants that required new residents to practice Roman Catholicism and swear allegiance to the Crown. Upon winning its independence in 1821, Mexico adopted this *empresario* system, ultimately codifying it into the Colonization Law of 1824. Henceforth, immigration procedures and the distribution of public lands to settlers were delegated to individual Mexican states.

It was a risky gambit. Although Mexico needed Americans to populate Texas to help ensure its claim to the region and bolster its defense vis-à-vis the United States and native tribes, that same immigration also meant giving Washington a hook into Texas, arousing suspicions of the new settlers. Mexican sentiment held that the American settlers were "unassimilable, subversive, and untrustworthy."

First One, Then Thousands

In 1820 the Connecticut-born explorer and settler Moses Austin requested and received from Spanish officials access to Texan land. Austin was an early beneficiary of the empresario system and, given that he had previously resided in Louisiana as a Spanish subject, he seemed to be the very type of settler Spain was looking for. After receiving a massive land grant in eastern Texas, Moses Austin succumbed to pneumonia-related maladies in June 1821. The colonization onus passed to his son, Stephen F. Austin, now an empresario who inherited his father's holdings and subsequently negotiated with the now-independent Mexico to permit three hundred Anglo families to settle near the Brazos River, with an offer of Mexican citizenship not far off. It wasn't long before several other empresarios joined Austin in coordinating an immigration flood.

Within a few years upward of seven thousand white Americans had relocated to Texas; the population of thirty-five thousand white immigrants (including their African American slaves) towered over the "native-born *Tejanos* by a factor of ten." Though settler organizations declared their "firm and unshaken adherence . . . and our readiness to do our duty as Mexican citizens" into the early 1830s, most Anglo immigrants did not assimilate to Tejano culture, failing to pick up the Spanish language or convert to Catholicism. Thousands of illegal, that is, nonempresario-sanctioned, migrants also poured into Texas. Mexico City's envoy in Washington saw the handwriting on the wall: "The colonists in Texas will not be Mexicans more than in name." The Mexican secretary of state offered a keen take on American designs: "Where others send invading armies, [the North Americans] send their colonists." Nobody elucidated this reading of America better than Stephen Austin, who believed that "to dam out the North Americans, [would be as futile as] trying to stop the Mississippi with a dam of straw."

Whole Nation into Revolution

Prior to Stephen Austin, Texan settlers had mainly been part of unauthorized American filibusters, privately financed military expeditions that often operated in coordination with anti-Spain rebels and even managed to establish an abortive Republic of Texas in 1821. Austin, by contrast, was well read and had a fierce work ethic. As his father had done with regard to Spain, Austin initially served the Mexican government loyally; in fact, he even assisted in quelling a US-colonist-led insurrection called the Fredonian Rebellion in 1826.

One of Austin's personal sticking points was slavery. His father's grant did not specifically proscribe the practice, so the Americans proceeded to import slaves, which Austin viewed as "indispensable" to prosperity. In 1829, however, Mexico banned slavery. American settlements were suddenly called into question, even if the antibondage writ was largely unenforceable in Texas. As one Texas daily breathlessly stated, "[The effort is] to give liberty to our slaves, and to make slaves of ourselves." Mexican taxation, in addition to the proscribing of slavery, also irked the Anglo settlers. Delivering a final blow to American–Texan sentiment, the Mexican government banned immigration into Texas the following year.

By now Andrew "Old Hickory" Jackson was in the White House. Old Hickory had gained significant political capital by denouncing his predecessor, John Quincy Adams, for recognizing Spanish sovereignty over Texas in the 1819 Adams–Onís Treaty. One uncouth businessman, Anthony Butler, was even able to convince Jackson that Texas could be purchased for a cool $5 million. Jackson's efforts to buy it were not successful, but Mexico City felt the pressure nonetheless; their concern about not being able to hold Texas was now a full-blown anxiety. The Mexican border director, Manuel Mier y Terán, lamented to his colleagues that "the wealthy Americans of Louisiana and other Western states are anxious to secure land in Texas for speculation but they are restrained by the laws prohibiting slavery. . . . The repeal of these laws is a point toward which the colonists are directing their efforts. . . . Therefore, I now warn you to take timely measures. Texas could throw the whole nation into revolution."

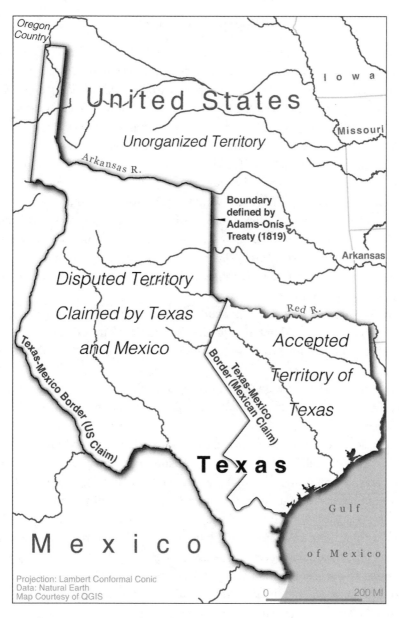

Map of Texas. (University of Wisconsin–Madison Cartography Lab. Christopher Archuleta, cartographer)

Renegade Province

In May 1834 the Mexican president Antonio López de Santa Anna established a dictatorship and attempted to quell the rebellious provinces. In response, the settlers declared the independence of the self-proclaimed Republic of Texas in March 1836, but the liberation movement was dealt an early blow when all of the two-hundred-odd fighters defending the Alamo Mission in San Antonio were killed by Santa Anna's men after a nineteen-day siege. The following month, at the Battle of San Jacinto, freedom fighters led by Sam Houston punched back, defeating the Mexican army in just eighteen minutes. (The deep irony is that their "freedom" would entail slavery.) Texan forces captured Santa Anna himself and quickly coerced him to sign a covert pact recognizing their autonomy. In the end, Santa Anna's diplomacy failed to change the standing of either side. Mexico City vehemently maintained that Texas was a renegade province, while in September 1836 Texans voted to request annexation by the United States.

In Washington, President Jackson, although welcoming the birth of the new sister republic, did not jump at the opportunity of annexation. It wasn't a question of desire for Jackson—he subsequently quipped, "We must regain Texas, peaceably if we can, forcibly if we must"—rather, he worried that annexation would lead to war with Mexico. As a result, over the course of the next decade, three US presidents would punt on the Texas annexation question.

Stephen F. Austin understood the US domestic opposition of those northerners who saw annexation as a thinly veiled scheme to add another slave state. "Threats and denunciations . . . ," Austin said, "will goad the North into a determined opposition and if Texas is annexed at all it will not be until the question has convulsed this nation for several sessions of Congress." Adding to the matter, the Whig Party's ideology of "internal improvements" posed yet another domestic obstacle to annexation. The Whig commentator Horace Greeley summarized succinctly: "A nation cannot simultaneously devote its energies to the absorption of others' territories and improvement of its own." No surprise, then, that the prominent Whig politician and losing presidential hopeful also came out against annexation.

Quakers and other abolitionists joined in blasting the idea of annexing Texas. In 1836 the Quaker Benjamin Lundy published a flyer titled *The War in Texas; A Review of Facts and Circumstances, Showing That This Context Is a Crusade Against Mexico, Set on Foot and Supported by Slaveholders, Land Speculators, &c, in Order to Re-establish, Extend, and Perpetuate the System of Slavery*

and the Slave Trade. It denounced Texas's independence as the "great deception." Yet the cold reality was that few Americans shared his critical view.
Many Americans considered the case of Texas to be not so much about slavery
but instead represented a "race war between brown Mexicans and white Texans." And in this conflict the latter needed to be supported. In fact, a Philadelphia mob smashed Lundy's printing press before he could publish a second
edition of the incendiary *The War in Texas.*

The fundamental assumption of the American colonists when revolting
from Mexico was that independence would entail automatic annexation. Under the stewardship of its first elected leader, Sam Houston, the independent
republic of Texas would instead have to wait more than a decade for annexation, achieved via a battlefield that stretched all the way to Mexico City.

6 · A Wicked War

I do not think there was ever a more wicked war than that waged by the
United States on Mexico. I thought so at the time, when I was a
youngster, only I had not moral courage enough to resign.
—Former president Ulysses S. Grant, 1879, a junior officer during
the Mexican–American War, 1846–48

[The US invasion of Mexico was the] most unjust war in history . . .
provoked by the ambition not of an absolute monarchy but of a republic
that claims to be at the forefront of nineteenth-century civilization.
—Mexican scientist and conservative intellectual Lucas Alemán

Mexican Influenza

America's war with Mexico—the first instance of Washington fighting a
war predominantly in a foreign territory, albeit right next door—was deeply
significant, scarring, and controversial on both sides. Yet perhaps most tragic
was the fact that it need not have occurred at all. Seeing as how most of the
massive territories seized from Mexico after the war—Nevada, Utah, sections
of Arizona, Colorado, Kansas, New Mexico, Oklahoma, and Texas—might
have been acquired through a more robust and credible diplomacy, compensation could have prevailed over battle scars as the lasting impact.

A wicked war it was indeed. The US experienced one of the highest casualty
rates (overwhelmingly from disease) in the history of American wars, at a rate
of 16 percent of the nearly eighty thousand soldiers deployed. Mexico fared

worse, suffering an estimated twenty-five thousand casualties, including civilians. Aside from the bloodshed, the Mexican–American War escalated political and social disputes, turning the protracted qualms over slavery into a full-fledged sectional conflict. If we look narrowly at how the war unfolded on the US side, we see American ignorance, racism, and belligerence. But it is crucial to acknowledge the forceful and anonymous American citizens who courageously opposed the war, and recognize the impact they made on the trajectory of the conflict, even if that impact couldn't stymie the prowar enthusiasts who drove the Mexican strongman Porfirio Díaz to later lament, "Poor Mexico, so far from God, so close to the United States."

This episode is also a reminder of the cliché—and, like most clichés, it contains more than a kernel of truth—that when Washington gets a cold, Latin America gets the flu. In this case, however, the United States, in the midst of Manifest Destiny hysteria, got a fever, and Mexico lost half its national territory.

Mr. Polk's War

In 1844 President John Tyler (1841–45) finally brokered a secret annexation settlement with Sam Houston's Republic of Texas, but the deal was met with strong criticism. In a January 23, 1844, letter, Daniel Webster of Massachusetts blasted the idea of annexation and the naked imperialism associated with it. "We have a republic, gentlemen, of vast extent and unequalled natural advantages," he lectured. "Instead of aiming to enlarge its boundaries, let us seek, rather, to strengthen its union." The Treaty of Annexation was initially voted down 16 to 35 by a Whig-majority Senate anxious about upsetting the slave/nonslave state equilibrium. Complicating matters, Mexico City had also severed diplomatic ties with Washington and thus US policy makers had to still consider that annexation meant war.

Battling the Whigs in the debate over annexation were proslavery southerners. In the early 1840s the Republic of Texas had one of the highest rates of enslavement in the Americas, but abolitionist sentiments in both Great Britain and Mexico threatened the Lone Star Republic's way of life. President Tyler, a Virginian aristocrat, claimed that annexing Texas was necessary in order to ensure that "slaves on both sides" of the Texas–American border were immune from "British abolitionists and Mexican armies alike." Southern Democrats thirsty for annexation were able to deny anti-annexation candidates the presidential nomination, handing it instead to James K. Polk, a slaveholding outsider candidate. To many a southerner's delight, Polk proposed annexing not only Texas but also a much greater part of Oregon Territory than had previously been proposed; Polk went on to win in a close vote against the anti-annexation Whig Henry Clay.

Polk, the "humorless, puritanical small-town lawyer," intuited the national zeitgeist of Manifest Destiny and turned it into a winning foreign policy. At the same time, it would be a mistake to chalk up Polk's stances to simple, cynical political calculus. Rather, Polk's ideology was genuinely one of American greatness and development, and thus continental conquest was a "perfect marriage of politics and conviction." His inaugural address was unabashed about America's moment in the sun: "It is confidently believed that our system may be safely extended to the utmost bounds of the territorial limits," he declared, "and that as it shall be extended the bonds of our Union, so far from being weakened, will become stronger."

Backed by the president-elect Polk, the lame duck Tyler managed to get vital annexation legislation, this time via joint resolution, passed (in a razor-thin 27 to 25 vote in the Senate) on Capitol Hill just days before he left office on March 4, 1845. This set the stage for Texas to enter the Union as the twenty-eighth state (and fifteenth slave state) after President Polk signed the legislation on December 29, 1845. There was still plenty of opposition to the resolution: the seventy-six-year-old John Quincy Adams, "his face grown haggard but his political will unbroken," fumed that Texas annexation would convert the Constitution into a "menstruous rag" and prompt the North to secede.

By 1846 Polk had abandoned his ambitious election claim of "Fifty-four Forty or Fight!"—referring to America's desired boundary for the Oregon Territory at the latitude of 54 degrees, 40 minutes—and settled with Great Britain at the 49th parallel. But Polk was by no means done, as he laid eyes on Cuba as the next logical candidate for incorporation. "As the pear, when ripe, falls by the law of gravity into the lap of the husbandman," Calhoun had previously observed, "so will Cuba eventually drop into the lap of the Union." But when Polk dispatched his diplomats to Madrid to broker a deal, Spanish officials retorted that they "would prefer seeing it sunk in the Ocean" than sell Cuba to the Americans.

Polk's attention returned to Mexico, although at first his approach was surprisingly restrained. Encouraged by the fact that Mexico City, also eager to avoid broader conflict, did not enforce its threat of war after Washington annexed Texas, Polk dispatched the New York lawyer John Slidell in late 1845 to secretly negotiate Mexican recognition of Texas's southwest border at the Rio

Grande for $25 million. He also hoped to buy California and New Mexico, which included Utah and Nevada and sections of four other states, for $30 million. The reasoning went along the lines of, Why should there be war when the mighty dollar could give America what it deserved? This effort failed as the Mexicans, sensing imperial machinations and already incensed about Texas annexation, refused even to meet with Slidell.

Greenback diplomacy proving futile, Polk dispatched soldiers in March 1846 under the command of General Zachary Taylor from an outpost in western Louisiana into the regions between the Nueces and Rio Grande Rivers: the lands not resolved via the Slidell talks. The land had scant practical use, being "so arid it could not even support a cotton crop until 1920," but Mexico considered the Nueces River the limit of its territory and an important buffer against *yanqui* incursions. General Mariano Arista accordingly interpreted Taylor's four-thousand-plus soldier expedition as an act of aggression, and on April 25 dispatched a small cavalry patrol across the Rio Grande. A skirmish ensued, and sixteen were killed or wounded; but more important for Mr. Polk was that he now had his cause for war. A belligerent Mexico had spilled blood on American soil—despite the fact only "fervent U.S. expansionists" believed this to actually be legitimate US territory. One US colonel, Ethan Allen Hitchcock, the grandson of the Revolutionary War hero, revealed his ambivalence: "the 'claim,' so called of the Texans to the Rio Grande, is without foundation. She has never conquered, possessed, or exercised dominion west of the Nueces." On the other hand, pro-Polk newspapers were blasting the Mexicans for their innate "insolence, stupidity, and folly."

A few weeks later, on May 8, news of the Mexican attack reached Washington. On May 11 the president notified Congress that a state of belligerence existed between the two countries and asked for a declaration of war. "Mexico," Polk told his legislative counterparts, "has passed the boundary of the United States, has invaded our territory, and shed American blood upon the American soil." Responding with alacrity and emotion, Congress days later voiced its support for Polk's declaration.

"Roused to the Most Earnest Vigorous Action"

The first two sizable battles—Palo Alto on May 8, 1846, and Resaca de la Palma, near present-day Brownsville, the next day—took place before President Polk had declared war and were won by Taylor's partial force against a larger enemy. Uplifted by these quick tactical wins, Taylor crossed the Rio

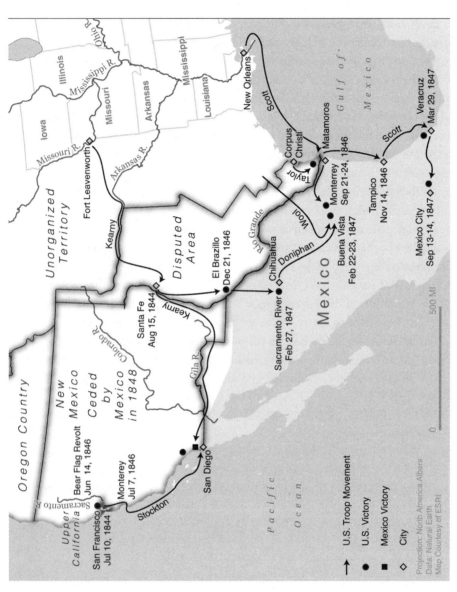

Mexican–American War, 1846–48. (University of Wisconsin–Madison Cartography Lab. Christopher Archuleta, cartographer)

Grande and brought the war to Mexican soil. He spent the next year winning many battles and gaining control over several northern Mexican states.

The American public was generally ecstatic with the news of the early victories. Taylor was fast becoming a war hero—the public dubbed him Old Rough and Ready—and he was seen as future presidential timber. Volunteers by the thousands signed up to fight. One recruiting poster's slogan promised national glory for those who would enlist: "Ho! For the halls of Montezuma." A newspaper, the *Union*, described the climate: "The general fact is well-known that the whole country is roused to the most earnest and vigorous action." Yet there were some holdouts. Henry David Thoreau famously spent time in jail for refusing to pay a one-dollar poll tax he believed went to fund the Mexican war. The incarceration also inspired him to write the classic essay *Civil Disobedience*.

By the fall of 1846 signs emerged that American support for the war was waning. Peace activists at home and disillusioned soldiers in the field—some having returned home—had begun expressing their opposition, or at least ambivalence. Pennsylvania's pro-Whig daily, the *North American*, had initially cheered "the spirit of the country . . . [where the leaders] can rely for its wars upon the volunteers . . . men abandoning a better and brighter future for the honor of striking a blow for the land of their love." Yet the same paper now admonished readers: "Should the lust of conquest, or the passions of revenge [manifest] public opinion will fall away as good men shrink from crime." The former two-time secretary of state Daniel Webster, who had criticized the proposal to annex Texas in 1844 and had presidential ambitions for 1848, told supporters, "The great objection of the war is that it is illegal in its character." Clearly influencing his thinking was the fact that Webster's son Edward, a volunteer soldier, was killed in the war.

Gringo Aggression

Sensing the need to bring the war to a quick conclusion, Polk shifted focus. On March 9, 1847, General Winfield Scott and twelve thousand troops landed at the coastal city of Veracruz and began the march east to Mexico City to finish the war once and for all. Scott's campaign tracked the same route as Spanish conquistador Hernán Cortés's 1519–20 trek to the Aztec metropolis of Tenochtitlán, present-day Mexico City—a fact not lost on either the American combatants or the invaded Mexicans.

However, as American soldiers spent more time fighting in Mexico and witnessed savagery on both sides, many came to see the war as unnecessary and immoral. Colonel Ethan Allen Hitchcock wrote, "I have said from the first that the United States are the aggressors. We have outraged the Mexican government and people by an arrogance and presumption that deserve to be punished. For ten years we have been encroaching on Mexico and insulting her. . . . But now, I see, the United States of America, as a people, are undergoing changes in character, and the real status and principles for which our forefathers fought are fast being lost sight of."

By August 1847 Scott's forces had reached the outskirts of Mexico City. At this point the Mexican leader Santa Anna was offering a truce but not surrender, which was the sentiment of some of his fellow generals. As a result, the Americans saw no choice but to seize the capital. With the advance beginning on August 20 in the city's southern environs with the Battles of Contreras and Churubusco, Scott's forces won two victories in the same day, decimating Santa Anna's army. Within a month US forces were attacking the formidable hilltop citadel Chapultepec Castle, which once was the Spanish viceroy's residency but was now a Mexican military school.

On September 13, America's siege of the fortress came to a close with the two sides engaging in brutal hand-to-hand combat. This short battle, however, created potent fodder for the Mexican nation. The taking of Chapultepec Castle quickly became a story of martyrdom. According to subsequent national lore, a Mexican cadet, rather than face imminent capture and humiliation, shrouded himself in a Mexican flag and, along with five of his compatriots, leaped to his death from the citadel's ramparts. The next day General Scott entered the central square, "resplendent in full-dress uniform, to accept the formal surrender of the city," while the American flag was flown over the National Palace.

The city had capitulated, but this did not end Mexican resistance to the conflict. Santa Anna encouraged the city's underclass—the *léperos* and just-released inmates—to conduct hit-and-run attacks on the gringo invaders. (This disparaging term for Americans may have been coined in this war, perhaps in reference to the Kentucky regiment's green coats or to a popular song sung by US soldiers ending in the phrase "green grow the bushes."]

"Make Mexico Do Justice"

In the fall of 1847 a provincial South Carolina paper, *Winyah Observer,* echoed much of the growing despondency surrounding the war when it described it as "probably the most unfortunate and disastrous war" in the nation's history. Or here is the social reformer Frederick Douglass writing in his own newspaper, *North Star:* "We beseech our countrymen to leave off this horrid conflict, abandon their murderous plans, and forsake the way of blood." He exhorted his countrymen, "Let the press, the pulpit, the church, the people at large, unite at once; and let petitions flood the halls of Congress by the million, asking for the instant recall of our forces from Mexico."

But General Scott's dramatic capture of Mexico City precipitated an about-face in US public opinion. The imperative now was not to bemoan America's thirst for conquest but rather to "make Mexico do justice" for the Americans killed in the war. And indeed, the hyper-expansionist All Mexico Movement swelled, clamoring for Polk and Scott to conquer and claim the entire Latin country. Significantly, there was a deep racial tinge to this movement. Even before Scott's conquest an author in the *Democratic Review* painted an apocalyptic picture of the fate of the Mexicans: "The Mexican race now see, in the fate of the aborigines of the north, their own inevitable destiny. They must amalgamate and be lost, in the superior vigor of the Anglo-Saxon race, or they must perish." A New York paper expressed similar sentiments: "There is a spirit abroad which will not long be stayed—a spirit of progress, which will compel us, for the good of both nations and the world at large, TO DESTROY THE NATIONALITY *of that besotted people.* It would almost seem that they, like the Israelites of old, brought upon themselves the vengeance of the Almighty and we ourselves had been raised up to overthrow AND UTTERLY DESTROY THEM *as a separate and distinct nation.*"

Ironically, many US slaveholders who initially backed the war did not line up behind the All Mexico campaign, for the very reason that should any of these massive new lands be acquired—thus destined to become states—they would be largely nonwhite possessions. The South Carolina senator and erstwhile expansionist John C. Calhoun most infamously made these points in an hour-long congressional address on January 4, 1848:

> [We have never] incorporated into the Union any but the Caucasian race. To incorporate Mexico, would be the first departure of the kind; for more than half of its population are pure Indians, and by far the larger portion of residue mixed blood. I protest against the incorporation of such a people. Ours is the government of the white man. . . . And yet, with this example before them, and our uniform practice, there are those among us who talk about erecting these Mexicans into territorial Governments, and placing them on an equality with the people of these States. I protest utterly against the project.

The celebrated poet and essayist Walt Whitman argued for a third way, where an independent Mexico would flourish under American guidance. He backed "placing 30,000 disciplined troops" in Mexico to oversee the installation of a new government there "whose efficiency and permanency shall be guaranteed by the United States. This will bring out enterprise, open the way for manufactures and commerce, into which the immense dead capital of the country will find its way." Others held that the war could be a chance to spread American republican ideals. US Navy Commodore Robert Stockton proclaimed, "If I were now the sovereign authority . . . I would prosecute this war for the express purpose of redeeming Mexico from misrule and civil strife. . . . I would with a magnanimous and kindly hand gather these wretched people within the fold of republicanism. This I would accomplish at any cost."

These moderate, idealistic voices were drowned out by the boisterous majorities. And while the dueling majorities seemed at odds—the All Mexico Movement which aimed to enfold Mexico into the United States and the complete rejection of said endeavor due to the feared impact on the institution of slavery—racial prejudice informed them both.

The Honorable Mr. Trist

The peace accord the United States negotiated with a vanquished Mexican government gave Washington "half of Mexico." To secure favorable terms, Polk tapped the Spanish-speaking attorney and expansionist Nicholas Trist, who had studied under the aging Thomas Jefferson and acted as President Andrew Jackson's aide-de-camp. With Polk's authorization, Trist dangled $20 million in front of his Mexican counterparts in order to secure the Rio Grande boundary as well as California and New Mexico.

Cash again failed to sway the Mexicans, and by October Polk had lost faith in Trist and ordered him recalled, although the severe time lag for the message's arrival meant the US diplomat did not get news of his dismissal until November 16. During the delay, however, Mexican moderates came to power, and, desperate as they were, Trist moved quickly, ignoring his commander in chief's instructions and negotiating a new treaty. While still a decidedly maximalist settlement, Trist omitted Baja California and the rights of crossing through the Isthmus of Tehuantepec in his offer. While Trist's notion of a just peace motivated him to ignore his president and pursue a less capacious land transfer, he came to believe that the "best part" of the Mexican population themselves (even if they might not readily admit this) wanted the gringos to take over.

By January 1848 real progress finally arrived in the form of a Mexican agreement to the Rio Grande border for Texas and the 32nd parallel for the rest of the border: El Paso to the Pacific Ocean. Washington would assume all the debts US citizens claimed Mexico owed them and would compensate Mexico $15 million for California and New Mexico (a total of 1.2 million square miles), $10 million less than Slidell had offered the Mexicans before hostilities erupted. Trist and the Mexican directors inked the treaty on February 2, 1848. It would come to be known as the Treaty of Guadalupe Hidalgo, after the hamlet in which it was signed, not far from the capital. The United States had expanded its size by just under two-thirds.

When the language of Trist's treaty landed in Washington in February 1848 the climate quickly became fraught. As the scholar Robert Malley has explained, Polk was pushing talks to consolidate the God-sanctioned land for his nation; Trist was trying to broker a deal "so he could terminate Polk's war." Polk faced a choice. He could ignore the rogue accord and attempt to get something greater, or he could appropriate the pact and call it a day, even if it was not on ideal terms. He chose the path of least resistance and successfully moved Trist's pact through the Senate in March. Texas became part of America. Together with his idol Thomas Jefferson, Polk was now one of the two most successful American expansionist presidents.

Texas Incorporated, A Country Divided

Texas was almost certainly the crown jewel of the South's foreign policy of slavery, but such a towering accomplishment, not surprisingly, came with much revulsion from the annexationists' political and cultural adversaries. To the New England writer Ralph Waldo Emerson, "The annexation of Texas looks like one of those events which retard or retrograde the civilization of the ages." Writing at the time, the British scholar T. B. Macaulay saw Washington's annexation of Texas as being about more than just an expanded national territory: "The United States Government has openly declared itself the patron, the champion, and the upholder of slavery," he wrote. "[I]t renders itself illustrious as the evil genius of the African race." And critically for Mexico, the war was decidedly a catastrophic humiliation; one that would come to condition the nation's testy relationship with the United States.

7 · California Conquest

As noted, the United States emerged from the Mexican–American War with possession of California, thanks to the 1848 Treaty of Guadalupe Hidalgo. But what is often left out of that story is how the United States effectively conquered California in 1846, just as the war was breaking out over Texas. The gringo conquest of California was a haphazard affair, the outcome anything but inevitable. The fate of this vast region was ultimately decided more by two intrepid men (and really one of these two) than by two countries.

Sutter's Eden

At the still-tender age of thirty-one, the German-speaking Johann August Sutter was an indebted husband and father of five children living in his native Switzerland. In 1834, desiring greater pastures and fortunes, he left Europe for New York City. Five years later the resolute immigrant, now known as Captain John A. Sutter (really a "counterfeit captain") was again westward-bound, this time aboard the *Clementine,* which landed at the Pacific coastal hamlet of Yerba Buena, today's San Francisco, in July 1839. Sutter proceeded to Monterey, the capital of Mexican-administered Alta California, where he sought the endorsement of the governor, Juan Bautista Alvarado, in order to legally settle the region's vast central valley.

At the time, Alta California housed a mere one thousand Europeans, compared to between one hundred thousand and seven hundred thousand Native Americans—this was not a land where gallivanting Europeans often trod. In granting permission for settlement, Alvarado hoped that Sutter's vision of a Central Valley colony would help buttress a wild-and-wooly frontier against the Russians, Americans, British, and, of course, Native Americans. In the multifaceted accord that evolved, Alvarado mandated that before Sutter could control a sprawling forty-eight-thousand-acre swath of river delta–infused lands, he must first live in the territory for twelve months and obtain Mexican citizenship, which Sutter did the following year.

But despite the governor's authorization, Sutter was still entering a territory whose level of administration is best described as a power void, as detailed by the author Mark Arax in *The Dreamt Land*. For around fifty years Spain had been an absent-minded landlord, to say the least. In 1822 Mexico inherited the New Spain colony—the modern-day states of California, Nevada, and Utah and parts of Arizona, Wyoming, Colorado, and New Mexico), but in practice Mexican rule was almost nonexistent. For many understandable reasons, both Spain and Mexico were not set on establishing dominion, despite the rumors of diamonds, gold, and silver. According to Arax, "Even a blinkered man could see that California, the idea of the place, the dimensions of the place, was a gigantic proposition. Who could blame the Mexicans, or the Spanish before them, for deciding to rule it with hands off and attentions fixed only on their own little fiefdoms?"

Undeterred, by August 1839 Sutter's New Helvetia (or "New Switzerland," in a nod to his native soil) was being constructed in the Central Valley. Once finished in 1841, he received the massive forty-eight-thousand-acre title from Alvarado. Sutter's grip on regional land, labor, and water made him the largest "farmer, storekeeper, innkeeper, distiller, miller, tanner, manufacturer" in California, and he also managed to assemble his very own fighting force.

Sutter was not one to rest on his laurels, however, and was soon eyeing more possessions, including a roughly one-hundred-thousand-acre site to the north of New Helvetia. Yet authorization for such a venture would no longer be decided by the supportive Alvarado. Sutter's expansionist fate now rested in the hands of his old colleague's replacement, Manuel Micheltorena.

Micheltorena had come north with an army of *cholos*—criminals that had been released from the prisons of northern Mexico—to help the new governor shore up Mexican power in California while Mexico's regular army was preoccupied with US incursions. While the Californios—often wealthy Spanish- or Mexican-blooded native-born ranching families in Alta California—were predisposed to resent the governance of an outside authority like Micheltorena, his reprobate troops all but guaranteed the Californios' rejection of Mexican rule. To bolster his military capabilities, Micheltorena offered Sutter a deal: if Sutter agreed to support Micheltorena militarily, Micheltorena would grant him the one hundred thousand acres. This promise of additional land, referred to as the surplus, or *sobrante,* proved irresistible to Sutter, and on February 5, 1845, he agreed to Micheltorena's terms.

A New Frontier?

Mexico's difficulties in asserting control over Alta California were viewed in a different light back east. Where Mexicans saw problems, the United States saw opportunity, chiefly through the eyes of the indefatigable, nomadic, and ambitious John C. Frémont. Born in 1813 in Savannah, Georgia, to a French father and American mother, Frémont was dispatched on several expeditions out West to examine the potential prize.

On March 1, 1845, just three days before James K. Polk's inauguration, Frémont returned to Washington from yet another probing mission to California and gave an assessment to the War Department that reinforced the value of these vast, rugged, but also thinly populated and weakly governed lands. This was also the very day that Congress passed the Texas annexation resolution (annexation ensued on December 29), which flared rumors of imminent war with Mexico. California suddenly seemed very vulnerable, especially as reports began to filter through about a sizable, menacing British armada sailing off the Pacific Coast in what could be part of a broader invasion of Mexico's inadequate and teetering hold on California.

Polk had a dilemma on his hands. Having won the presidency in part by stoking nationalist sentiments about an imminent British invasion in the West, he now faced the fact that it might actually be happening. US expansionists were terrified that, with American efforts centered on an invasion of Texas, London would swoop in to capture California outright or ally with Mexico City to fight the US. Having been in office for only a matter of weeks, a concerned Polk thus turned to the potent senator Thomas Hart Benton of Missouri and Benton's son-in-law and protégé Frémont to discuss the "Western problem." Frémont even met with two of Polk's key cabinet officials: Secretary of State James Buchanan and Secretary of the Navy George Bancroft.

Polk's solution: send Frémont back to California. Along with Buchanan, Bancroft, and Benton, the president worked furtively to devise a route for Frémont's mission, one that purportedly involved a civilian survey of a transcontinental trail for immigrants but, in reality, would serve as Polk's eyes and ears in California. In mid-May 1845 Frémont's hastily assembled contingent of "frontiersmen, scientists, soldiers, sharpshooters, and hunters" embarked on his supposed survey. By August, with war appearing imminent, Washington sent a coded letter to Frémont: "The time has come. England must not get a foothold. We must be first. Act; discreetly, but positively."

Frémont advanced to Sutter's Mill, near today's Sacramento. Sutter, however, was keen to play the part of a loyal Mexican citizen: he was hoping that the Mexican government would purchase New Helvetia. He received Frémont in his Mexican colonel's uniform and then relayed information regarding Frémont's progress to the Mexican authorities.

Frémont pushed on. In January 1846 he arrived at Monterey, the headquarters of the Californio leader José Castro, who had ousted Micheltorena. A month later Frémont's provocations, especially his unwillingness to obey Castro's restrictions on travel, led the Mexican governor to demand that they depart California immediately. The US contingent settled in at Gavilán (tellingly, now called Fremont), and Frémont indicated to Castro that neither he nor his nation would be dishonored. Frémont's men flew a hastily crafted US flag on a young tree—"a gesture that destroyed the last vestiges of Mexican goodwill."

Within weeks Castro had organized a force to repel the gringo invaders. After a less than stellar military performance at Gavilán Peak, Frémont was pushed further north, this time to US-claimed Oregon Country. What happened next has been the subject of heated historical dispute. While likely self-serving, the account Frémont wrote three decades later describes his belief that it had become necessary for him to unleash a "spontaneous" revolt in order to produce a pro-Washington outcome without Washington's fingerprints on the crime scene: "Absolved . . . from my duty as an explorer, I was left to my duty as an officer of the American Army with the further authoritative knowledge that the Government intended to take California. . . . [I]t had been made known to me now on the authority of the Secretary of the Navy that to obtain possession of California was the chief object of the President." Historians still are not fully sure who and what Frémont's superiors ordered or who exactly gave him the orders, but he, the sole US Army officer in California for the next nine months, nevertheless ordered his swelling band of fighters southward back into California. Many of the US settlers encountered along the way became ready recruits for Frémont's informal army.

"The Bear Republic"

On June 14, 1846, a thirty-odd-person corps of rebels led by William B. Ide and Ezekiel Merritta and made up in part of undocumented migrants and Frémont's own men took the lightly defended Mexican outpost of Sonoma, just north of Yerba Buena. Less than a day later the victors issued a declaration of independence and hoisted their flag. Designed by the insurrectionist William Todd, a nephew of Abraham and Mary Todd Lincoln, the almost comically primitive flag was made with a cotton sheet and red paint. It had two words, "California Republic," written on it and a grizzly bear facing a single red star (a reference to the earlier Lone Star Republic of Texas), giving the nascent uprising the name Bear Flag Revolt. Amid the heady atmosphere following the Sonoma raid, Frémont decided to go all in on the Bear Flag Revolt and accepted the role of commander of the insurrection.

It is often told that the rebels were not aware that the United States had declared war on Mexico a month prior and were instead motivated by more personal concerns. There is some truth in this: while total independence was the broader ambition, as covertly guided by Frémont, smaller grievances like not being permitted to buy land or threats of ejection were the more immediate and tangible factors leading the rebels to fight. But given that the Bear Republic rebels held a Fourth of July celebration in Sonoma, "complete with a reading of the Declaration of Independence," it was nevertheless clear which country they wanted to annex their newly liberated lands.

Their prayers were soon answered. The so-called Bear Flaggers learned that on July 7, the US naval commodore John Drake Sloat, relying on the oft-cited fear of an imminent British incursion into California, had directed the Pacific Squadron to take the thinly defended but still vital settlement of Monterey, a task accomplished without firing a shot. The force then raised the US flag and proclaimed, in both Spanish and English, that "henceforth California would be a portion of the United States." Two days later Joseph Revere's United States Navy forces took Yerba Buena and then Sonoma, raising the American flag in both locales. The navy also requested that a flag be raised at Sutter's Fort. The Bear Flag Revolt had ended to the rebels' complete satisfaction, and their pro-Washington stance would be duly rewarded in 1911 when the iconic Bear Flag was made the official California state flag. Like those of Hawaii and Texas, the California flag is distinct in that it honors a design first created by a formerly independent country.

Frémont's Rocky Road

After some months of low-intensity skirmishes, usually between Mexican soldiers and Californio ranchers assisted by settlers, the informal Treaty of Cahuenga in January 1847 ended the California theater of the US–Mexican

War. The war had lasted less than a year, erupting in late April 1846, with Congress declaring war on May 13. Amazingly, California had surrendered almost without bloodshed, something facilitated by the US commanders' (including Frémont) generous surrender terms that permitted the Mexicans to either return to Mexico or remain in California with the same rights and privileges as US citizens.

As news of Frémont's epic California conquest spread across the US, many citizens were euphoric over Manifest Destiny; others, especially in anti-expansionist New England and the Midwest—and not to mention Mexicans and Europeans—blasted the Polk administration for its imperial grab. After initially backing Frémont's moves, Polk now distanced himself from them. The US, Polk explained, wanted peace and prosperity, not acquisition through rogue campaigns. Buchanan publicly alleged that Frémont had acted well outside of his order; thus his record had a stain of insubordination of an "irregular junior Army officer," not the badge of wartime honor.

Still one of the nation's most renowned individuals, Frémont, on January 31, 1848, was convicted by a military jury of mutiny and disobeying orders, resulting in his dismissal from the army. Seven of the deliberators, however, sympathized with the accomplished expeditioner and asked that he receive leniency due to his outstanding service. Polk quickly responded affirmatively, commanding Frémont to "resume his sword." A betrayed Frémont instead offered his resignation.

Undaunted after being hung out to dry, Frémont, in 1850, the year California became a state, was elected as one of the state's first two senators. In 1856 he was the first presidential candidate of the embryonic Republican Party, running in an election in which he promised to lead the country out of the moral stain of slavery. He lost to the Democrat James Buchanan. He would later be distinguished for being the first Union Army general to issue an emancipation proclamation during the Civil War. He also served as the territorial governor of Arizona.

Following statehood, Sutter's fortunes differed from those of Frémont. Initially, he was celebrated as a pioneer and catalyst for the annexation of California. In 1853 he was commissioned as a major general in the state militia, a position he used to grant commissions to several friends of the great filibuster William Walker so that they could assist him in Nicaragua. Additionally, Sutter's son, Alphonse, went down to Nicaragua to lead a company of troops under Walker. But despite John Sutter's risk taking and shrewd dealings, the riches that he had left Switzerland to find so many years before continued to elude him. Rather ironically, the discovery of gold at Sutter's Mill was the beginning of the end for Sutter. When the lunacy of the California Gold Rush arrived in full force, squatters overran his land, and he was left nearly penniless, spending much of the rest of his life in Washington, DC, arguing for the recognition of the lands granted to him by Micheltorena.

The territory that the Mexicans had neglected soon became an economic powerhouse for the United States through the Gold Rush and the nineteenth-century agricultural boom (particularly the citrus industry), facilitated by transcontinental railroads. The Californio identity, however, persisted, with the 2010 state census reporting that almost 40 percent of the population was of Hispanic or Latino origin. It is a salient reminder that while borders may change overnight, a country's people can reflect a much deeper history.

8 · ¡Viva Grant!

Imperial Inklings

In the decades following Monroe's 1823 hemispheric promulgation, the self-imposed goal of the United States of keeping European powers out of Latin America was still largely aspirational. Contrary to what is often assumed, although the US was busy observing (and at times foiling) Latin American interventions by the European powers, Old World interests continued to pervade the hemisphere. From Napoleon III's attempt to impose a reactionary monarchical regime in Mexico and London's reassertion of sovereignty over the Falkland Islands in 1833 to Spain's imposition of colonial dominion in Santo Domingo, Monroe's writ rang hollow in the courts of Europe.

In these middle decades of the nineteenth century there was also an increasing societal acceptance of the Monroe Doctrine as a vital part of the US national fabric. As *Harper's Weekly* wrote, "The Monroe Doctrine is unquestionably a fixed principle of American political faith." The rub, though, was that while they expressed solidarity with the spirit, Americans differed as to what exactly the Monroe Doctrine entailed. Walter McDougall asks, "Was it meant only to be a protective mantle thrown over the republics of the hemisphere, or did it invite the United States to expand or otherwise intervene in them? Southern filibusters obviously argued the latter, while northern Free Soilers argued the former."

In the postbellum decades the United States would begin to veer toward more assertive action, giving the doctrine sharper teeth. In the case of Napoleon III's gambit in Mexico, General Ulysses S. Grant, the secretary of war at the time, worked in tandem with President Lincoln's secretary of state, William Henry Seward. Seward had been dismayed by the French incursion into Mexico during the US Civil War but had been unable to respond out of fear that Maximilian, the archduke of Austria who had been installed as emperor, would increase support to the Confederacy. But after Civil War hostilities ceased in 1865 Seward rattled his sabre, and Grant initiated covert assistance to the forces of the deposed liberal politician and Zapotec Indian Benito Juárez. For good measure he sent some fifty thousand soldiers to the Rio Grande border. Along with supplying guns to the anti-Maximilian forces, the Seward–Grant deployment helped precipitate the departure of French soldiers in early 1867, ushering in the way for Juárez's return to power. In fact, the threat of a US invasion contributed to Maximilian's backers abandoning his regime. As McDougall writes, "Thus did the United States employ the Monroe Doctrine as John Quincy Adams intended, as a robust but ultimately peaceful defense of republicanism in the hemisphere."

Not unrelatedly, the nation's territorial and imperial ambition was also increasing. Secretary of State Seward secured the 1867 purchase of Alaska from tsarist Russia for $7.2 million ($120 million today), inoculating the public with Washington's ambitions before the construction of a canal in Panama decades later. After France abandoned Panama amid mudslides and mosquito-induced yellow fever in the late 1880s, an American flag was raised there. Tellingly, President Rutherford B. Hayes declared that the "policy of this country is a canal under American control."

But there were also unexpected and, arguably, even idealistic ways of US hemispheric policy making in the latter half of the nineteenth century, as President Grant's novel approach to Cuba and Santo Domingo illustrates. In the latter case, the withdrawal of a European power, Spain, posed the question of what the US should do in the cases where the Monroe Doctrine did not apply. Grant's biographer Ronald C. White observed that, as was often the reality with US machinations in Latin America, it was "sometimes hard to differentiate between humanitarian concerns and imperialist swagger."

Cuba Libre?

Less than a week after Grant was sworn in as president in March 1869, the Civil War hero was confronted with a crisis in Cuba, where pro-independence insurgents, who had been pushing for greater autonomy and reform since the 1850s, fought a series of battles with Spanish colonial troops. Spanish forces responded with a flood of reprisal killings.

Government officials—Union and Confederacy alike—backed Cuba's fight for freedom. US dailies dispatched journalists to give their readers a blow-by-blow account of the revolt. Some Americans were also quietly or otherwise hoping that Washington would provide military assistance to tip the scales in favor of the rebels. While he was already predisposed to the insurgent cause, the newly inaugurated Grant was solicited by publishers of papers like the *New York Herald* and *New York Sun*, "which led the chorus for intervention."

Some of Grant's cabinet officials, including Secretary of War John Rawlings, who addressed the Cuba dilemma with "evangelical conviction," pressed for the commander in chief to recognize the insurgency and evict Spain from Cuba. Rawlings also convinced Grant to bolster the navy's operations in the region. On the other side of the equation, Grant's attorney general and secretary of the treasury argued that recognition of Cuba would violate international norms. Nevertheless, in April the House of Representatives voted to support any Grant initiative that recognized the insurgents. Grant, however, remained cautious. Applying his well-honed equanimity, Grant told his cabinet that "strict justice would justify us in not delaying action on this subject, but too early action might prejudice our case with Great Britain in support of our claims." The US insisted on being paid by the United Kingdom for the immense damage inflicted by Confederate Navy vessels built in British shipyards, known as the *Alabama* Claims for the CSS *Alabama*, the most notorious and feared raider.

But when news of a new wave of Spanish atrocities reached the US in the summer of 1869 the sensationalist domestic press had a field day. Writing in the *New York Sun*, the journalist Charles Dana argued that America had to "interfere in Cuba" to quell the bloodshed and injustice. Grant's fractious cabinet debated a variety of US responses, including buying the island from Madrid and then abolishing slavery. Leaks about US machinations with regard to Spain's Caribbean jewel sparked outrage on the Iberian Peninsula and dashed hopes for a Washington-brokered settlement to the fighting.

The insurgents' lack of usable ports and government institutions, however, left Grant equally inert militarily and diplomatically. Grant went on to stress his preference for self-determination: "These [Caribbean] dependencies are no longer regarded as subject to transfer from one European power to another. When the present relations of Colonies ceases they are to become independent powers, exercising the right of choice, and of self-control in the determination of their future condition."

"By Some Hook or Crook"

To Grant, Cuba was not the only Caribbean quagmire. Santo Domingo, comprising the eastern two-thirds of the island of Hispaniola, contained more arable land and the strategically enviable natural harbor of Samaná Bay. Accordingly, the Spanish colony had long been eyed by US officials. In the mid-1840s, for example, President Polk pushed the idea of surveying the bay for a future naval base and coaling station. In the 1850s President Franklin Pierce sent a special commissioner, William L. Cazneau, to Santo Domingo to pressure officials to lease or sell the harbor. Over the next twenty years the businessman Cazneau would lobby formally and informally for annexation. During the Civil War, Lincoln and Seward also pressed for establishing a naval base at Samaná Bay via lease or purchase.

As it turned out, the end of that very domestic conflagration in 1865 coincided with the Spanish departure from Santo Domingo, meaning that it was one of the few Caribbean locations not controlled by a European power. But despite having just gained independence, the Spanish-speaking creole (mixed-blood) elites on the island were not unwelcoming to leasing or annexation notions. The canny Seward, this time under President Andrew Johnson, made another gambit, electing Admiral David Dixon Porter and his son Frederick, "fortified by a boat-load of gold," to conduct the negotiations. And once in country, they were "entertained by that man for all seasons," William L. Cazneau, to push the plan.

Domestic proponents of annexation turned to the printing presses to paint Santo Domingo as the "the garden of the Antilles" and the "finest part of the whole West Indies." Critics, by contrast, were quick to dismiss the entire notion as a greedy scheme. To the *New York World*, "The signs are that there is a power-ful combination in this country to annex the [West Indian] islands by some hook or crook, not from considerations of public advantage, but merely as a large speculation in real estate and colonial debts." As journalists vied for clout, racism commanded a prominent role. As was the case with the Texas question a quarter century earlier, many Americans worried about the islanders' mestizo blood, Roman Catholicism, and backward Iberian-inherited political customs. But although this annexation attempt failed, the idea did not die.

Annexation Part Deux?

The Dominican strongman Buenaventura Báez had intermittently been in and out of the presidential palace since 1849. And in early 1868 he came into power again. "Slight of stature and long on political and economic scheming," in late 1868 Báez tellingly made it known he was once again amenable to the annexation whereby Santo Domingo would become a US territory and eventually a state. And Grant, the incoming White House occupant as of March 1869, soon came to obsess about Dominican annexation.

Only weeks after Grant's inauguration, Joseph W. Fabens contacted Secretary of State Hamilton Fish. A "Bostonian full of schemes," Fabens was associated with Cazneau, both of whom had "made a killing" in land speculation preceding the Texas annexation. Fabens then provided Secretary Fish with a glowing evaluation to present to the Grant administration, glamorizing the Caribbean nation's natural resources. "The annexation of this country to the United States should be an acquisition of great value," he said. Fabens even produced a putative document from Báez calling for "entrance into the United States as a free and independent state."

With Washington eyeing annexation once again, the press was quick to pick up on the issue. The *New York Herald* extolled a New York City assembly that May pushing for Santo Domingo to become a territory. For the *New York Sun*, it was "after Cuba, then Santo Domingo."

But whatever the merits of annexation, the truth remained that Fabens and Cazneau were, as the biographer Ron Chernow wrote, "shady operators" who had already accumulated vast tracts of land and "stood to pocket large profits" if Washington followed through with annexation. Fabens also gave Representative Ben Butler land on Samaná Bay in return for the congressman's pro-annexation advocacy. Butler assured Fabens that he would push Grant, then still the president-elect, to "secure his friendly cooperation."

Once in office, Grant quickly got the topic moving when he dispatched Colonel Orville Babcock, a Civil War general, engineer, and now the new president's private secretary, to Santo Domingo. Two months later Babcock was back stateside and had in his hands a draft treaty for annexation whereby Washington could buy Samaná Bay for between $1.5 million and $2 million or follow through on full annexation and assume the national debt of $1.5 million. The draft—already inked by Báez—also included language whereby Grant would deploy "all his influence" to get Capitol Hill to ratify the treaty. Grant asked Fish to draft a formal accord based on Babcock's on-the-fly version.

"A Congenial Home"

In early 1870 Grant brought the Babcock-brokered treaty, which now entailed two components, to Capitol Hill: a half-century lease on Samaná Bay and, dependent on a referendum, the gradual annexation of Santo Domingo into the union. Secretary Fish held a deep racial antipathy against the annexation of Santo Domingo. Further complicating matters, Grant's cabinet could freely discuss the Samaná Bay lease angle but was "sworn to secrecy" on annexation for the next year. The confidentiality was due to the fact that President

Báez was in a precarious political situation, one which he wanted to fix first to enhance his political bona fides in front of a skeptical US Congress. Grant, eager to help Báez, went so far as to deploy navy vessels to Hispaniola in order to bolster the Dominican leader's standing. Báez, in response, was working things on his end, as he himself was slated to benefit financially from eventual statehood. Again, in an effort to coax his Washington suitors, Báez rammed through a farcical plebiscite: 15,169 voting in favor and only 11 against. Chernow writes that Báez's vote was a "foolish act of bullying," seeing as "many observers agreed that the Dominican people genuinely favored an American union and would have delivered a safe majority through honest methods."

Grant's ambitions quickly ran into trouble in the shape of Senator Charles Sumner of Massachusetts, the Senate foreign relations chairman and now the president's nemesis regarding Santo Domingo. For starters, Sumner had no interest in humanitarian justifications for what was by definition imperialist annexation. He also had no patience for the strongman Báez, writing, "I know his history intimately. He is a usurper, whose hands have been red with innocent blood." The canny Sumner utilized his patented strategy of "delay and silence" to undermine the accord's chances.

In mid-March 1870, goaded to act by an insistent Grant, Sumner's committee delivered a major blow to the president's ambitions when it voted against the treaty 5–2. Now it was time for the full Senate to weigh in. In a move that was out of the ordinary for a commander in chief in this era, Grant personally lobbied scores of congressmen in a fashion the *New York World* cheekily deemed to be "somewhat in the style of [the towering English military and political chief] Oliver Cromwell."

An irate Sumner would have nothing to do with Grant's personal campaigning, which in his view was "as unconstitutional in character as that warlike intervention in the island." At one point Sumner unloaded a four-hour anti-Báez rant in a private session with his Senate colleagues. Race again came to the forefront of Washington's war-room talks. The Illinois congressman John Logan dismissed the Dominicans as "naked and half-savage people," while Senator Carl Schurz held that Dominicans were "lazy, shiftless, tropical people." In the popular press, a writer in the *Hartford Courant* lamented, " 'We don't want any of those islands yet, with their mongrel cutthroat races and foreign language and religion." As the treaty's opponents deftly exploited, annexation of brown peoples was simply beyond the comfort level of most Americans. When the Senate vote took place in late June, the 28–28 result was not even close to the two-thirds threshold.

But Grant was determined, unwilling to throw in the towel, and continued to praise the land, despite never having traveled there: "It possesses the richest soil, best and most capacious harbors, most salubrious climate and the greatest abundance of [most valuable] products of the forest, mine and soil, of any of the [West Indies] islands." He revisited the issue as part of his annual address to Congress in December 1870, saying, "The government of Santo Domingo has voluntarily sought this annexation." The president reinforced the point that this was not just about strategic natural harbors or lucrative export goods, but justice for freedmen: "The emancipated race of the South would have found there a congenial home."

In this, Grant was tactfully evoking a long-standing view among some Americans that the Caribbean and Central America were logical relocations for freed American slaves. Legions of racists wanted these peoples out of the United States, but it was also the case that abolitionists often supported what they believed would be an orderly and voluntary colonization. For example, a few years after Abraham Lincoln joined the leadership of the Illinois Colonization Society in 1858, he tried to get Capitol Hill to provide money for a colony outside the United States for freed slaves. And early in his presidency Lincoln's administration cemented diplomatic ties with Haiti and Liberia "with an eye to their being future destinations for emancipated slaves." A year or two after the war a few thousand freed slaves, backed by the American Colonization Society, left for Liberia.

There were also prominent African Americans like Frederick Douglass who were intrigued by colonization (and also annexation), especially in Santo Domingo. Grant saw annexation as a question of how to address the crime that was US slavery. Santo Domingo was judged to be "capable of supporting the entire colored population of the United States, should it choose to emigrate." As Chernow described it, Grant saw emigration as entirely voluntary and a "critical safety valve if white Americans refused to honor their [i.e., African Americans'] rights." In Grant's words, "The present difficulty in bringing all parts of the United States to a happy unity and love of country grows out of the prejudice to color. The prejudice is a senseless one, but it exists." Grant felt that blacks getting a new start in the Caribbean would ultimately lead to a renewed appreciation of sorts for their importance and value. He wrote, "If two or three hundred thousand blacks were to emigrate to St. Domingo . . . the Southern people would learn the crime of Ku Kluxism, because they would see how necessary the black man is to their own prosperity."

But once again Grant found himself opposed by the abolitionist Sumner. Sumner was of the mind that promoting freedmen's relocation to Santo Domingo would signal capitulation on the domestic justice issues. Grant set about building a case: the president persuaded the Senate to select a commission to visit the island. The commission was led by the former senator Ben Wade of Ohio, the activist Samuel Gridley of Massachusetts, and the Cornell University president Andrew D. White. Given that two of the three members were abolitionists of impeccable reputation, Grant was able to check "Sumner's critique that Santo Domingo was a racist enterprise." Grant then tapped Douglass to be the commission secretary, and the group sailed to the island in early 1871. Not surprising given its previous inclination to support such a move, the commission's report came out in support of annexation, even if it never really considered the preferences of the local population. Douglass, himself a slave before becoming an ardent abolitionist, wrote in his personal diary words that ended up in the formal publication, "Can't be worse off than they are." As part of the investigation, Douglass visited provincial reaches where he noted how "people . . . everywhere are raising the American flag."

But the commission's recommendation was not enough to convince Capitol Hill to act otherwise, and the Santo Domingo gambit came to naught. Douglass, however, was particularly motivated by the idea of annexation, spending the spring of 1871 whistle-stopping across the country to push for the plan. Writing in May 1871, he said, "The natural thing for Hayti, Cuba, and for all the islands of the Caribbean Sea is to come as soon as possible under the broad banner of the US, and conform themselves to the grand order of progress upon which this great Republic has now . . . earnestly entered." In Douglass's arresting oratory, Santo Domingo, "where Columbus first stood," was a "civilization . . . so feeble" and economically desolate that it required the United States' "restoring hand." Douglass even noted which of the island's resources, "timber, dye woods, sugar, coffee, cotton, and indigo," would yield lucrative returns to US investors. "The land was rich but the people poor," he remarked. They also did not enjoy the "comforts and conveniences of civilized life, that America would certainly provide them." As the Yale scholar David Blight put it in a smart biography of the American icon, on Santo Domingo, at least, Douglass "could sound like a standard-issue imperialist for American superiority."

Pan-American Spirit?

In an effort to promote a more harmonious interhemispheric climate, President Benjamin Harrison's secretary of state James G. Blaine, who had long dreamt of the first Pan-American conference, finally convened one in Washington, DC, from October 1889 to April 1890. At the end of the meeting, delegates from the eighteen hemispheric nations established the International Union of American Republics, choosing the US capital to house the union's secretariat, the Commercial Bureau of the American Republics. Interestingly, it was only a year prior that US newspapers and politicians had been using the term "Pan-Americanism." To Harrison and Blaine, Pan-Americanism was about securing better relations in order to bolster the robust free trade of the United States, which was already backed up by a potent American navy and the necessary coaling (fueling) stations. It was also about the use of US engagement to elevate the "standard . . . of civilization" in Latin America.

While undeniably paternalistic, especially as seen through twenty-first-century eyes, Blaine's vision represented a significant shift toward a more inclusive approach since Bolívar's original and ultimately star-crossed promotion of such interhemispheric consultation. Blaine clarified his country's role: "The principle of conquest shall not . . . be recognized as admissible under American public law." Within two decades, the Commercial Bureau of the American Republics had evolved into the Pan-American Union. Funded by a $5 million gift ($130 million today) from the Scottish-American titan Andrew Carnegie, an architecturally stunning (presumably a fusion of the key styles of union members) permanent edifice was completed, where the modern OAS resides. Many prominent Latin Americans were suspicious of Blaine's motives, fearful that such a customs union would advantage the United States at their expense. The seminal Cuban nationalist José Martí, who attended the conference as a journalist, was quite outspoken about this perceived imbalance.

To bolster the optics of this geopolitical strategy leading up to the first conference, Blaine orchestrated the appointment of Frederick Douglass to be the US envoy in Haiti, where he arrived in October 1889. After waiting several weeks to meet with the Haitian head of state, General Florvil Hyppolite, Douglass fired off a note to brief Blaine on the meeting: "Long lines of soldiers . . . saluted" the American ambassador. Haitian troops played the "Star-Spangled Banner" with "skill and effect." Douglass delivered a brief address at the National Palace and told his audience, "Mine has been a long and eventful life, identified with the maintenance of principles illustrated by the example of Haiti." As Blight explained, "The former slave from a backwater in a corner of the upper South did not have to put a name to slavery in front of men who had lived the history of Haiti."

During his tenure, Douglass led a failed bilateral negotiation to obtain rights to a coaling station. In a crystal-clear sign of the manifest racism of the time, the *New York Herald* contended that Douglass needed to go: "The remedy [to

"Keep off! The Monroe Doctrine must be respected." Cartoon depicting Uncle Sam as
armed soldier standing between European powers (Great Britain, France, Germany,
Spain, and Portugal) and Nicaragua and Venezuela, 1896. (Library of Congress Prints
and Photographs Division, Washington, DC)

reduce chaos in Haiti] is clear. Let the United States send to Hayti a Minister of
recognized force, ability, and above all, honesty. . . . He must be able to speak
the French language. To gain influence in the island he must be white" seeing
as how Haitians "look upon a colored man as one of themselves, whereas they
unwittingly recognize the superiority of the white race." That Douglass played
an outsized and unique role in nineteenth-century American history goes without saying. We see here that both latent and manifest racism were an essential
part of the American fabric, even when we have the remarkable occurrence of
this former American slave representing his nation in Port-au-Prince.

In part because Blaine wouldn't be written off on the basis of race, as Douglass was, his reframing of Pan-Americanism became associated with Washington's sharpening of the Monroe Doctrine's teeth. The country's swelling
diplomatic, and even military, might left Washington eager to strut across the
hemispheric and global stage, and no one exemplified hemispheric proctoring

more than the newly serving US secretary of state, Richard Olney. Referencing the Monroe Doctrine, Olney fired off a stern missive—some called it Olney's twenty-inch gun due to its length, twelve thousand words—to London insisting it submit a protracted boundary dispute between Great Britain and Venezuela to arbitration. (Back in 1876 Caracas, also citing the Monroe Doctrine, unsuccessfully solicited Washington's military support in what was a case of interhemispheric south-to-north.)

Now it was Washington's turn to not yield after Congress established a potent boundary commission, which precipitated the media's talk of imminent war with the European rival lurking in the Americas. Distracted by the exigencies of a global empire, mighty Great Britain agreed to cooperate with the boundary commission, as did Caracas, confident that the body would rule in its favor. In early October 1899 the commission produced a permanent border that, to Caracas's dismay, rewarded the British with the lion's share of the contested territory. But one key lesson from the Venezuela crisis of 1895 was not about the arbitration commission's delineation some years later but rather the patent example of Uncle Sam asserting himself, going eyeball to eyeball with John Bull and watching the former colonial master blink. The US was acting as a proxy of sorts: its bold, successful diplomatic move was enacted, at least in part, on behalf of a fellow New World nation.

PART II
EMPIRE TO AMIGOS, 1898–1940S

The period between Grant's attempt to annex Santo Domingo in 1870 and the sinking of the USS *Maine* in 1898 saw a diminished level of action in terms of Washington's involvement in the region. This drop-off was due partly to the simple fact that the United States was more preoccupied with post–Civil War internal reconstruction and consolidation, but the inactivity was undoubtedly also a product of Washington lacking what political scientists call state power: the federal power that underpins a more robust foreign policy. By the 1890s, though, the United States was showing signs of growing strength—and incipient major-power status.

Although the separation of history into eras can seem an artificial exercise, the sinking of the *Maine* inaugurated a definite sea change in America's approach to Central America and the Caribbean. During this era the US grew increasingly assertive in staging interventions in Latin America. There was a wide range of reasons for such contentious behavior, from anxieties surrounding political instability to advancing US ideals and sometimes economic interests. By the time of FDR's Good Neighbor Policy in 1933 a more cooperative approach had risen. Indeed, the period is often understood as the beginning of American hegemony in Latin America. That said, characterizing America's new posture in the period is a complicated task given the range of contexts, actors, and scenarios involved. It might be best to think of the initial years of this post-1898 era in terms of the imperfect label of protective imperialism, whereby America would use its power to foster or install stable governance in its sphere of influence; but banana wars or gunboat diplomacy are perhaps the more evocative, albeit sensationalist, terms for the period.

US ambition must also be seen in the light of the contemporary global context: although the United States unquestionably expanded its overseas economic and strategic footprint in this period, it did so in a less maximalist, more defensive manner than Germany, Great Britain, and France, or even Belgium for that matter. This is in no way to defend protective imperialism. Washington often found the deployment of customs officials, diplomats with outsized powers, leathernecks (read US Marines), and/or US naval vessels to be expedient ways of dealing with Latin American domestic instability or European machinations in what was becoming its geopolitical backyard. During the 1920s and 1930s and beyond there were multiple episodes in which, especially in the nearby Caribbean Basin, the United States took on the role of proconsuls, a kind of effective colonial governor. Despite the trend toward intervention, however, there were also instances of US ambivalence about meddling—or even cases of outright inaction.

One of the key challenges of evaluating the morality and success of policies conducted by the US protective empire is the extent to which US leaders, from William McKinley through Theodore Roosevelt and Woodrow Wilson to Franklin Roosevelt, were sincere in their rhetoric and actions about inter-hemispheric respect and consultation. One should not be surprised that US leaders' often lofty rhetoric was self-serving. But at times we may find instances when a sincere moral rhetoric was enacted, albeit with heavy-handed tactics. To pick an illustrative case, in the 1910s President Woodrow Wilson had a deeply felt and, in hindsight, moralizing sense of Latin American democracy, but he also ended up using the diplomacy of gunboats more than any of his White House contemporaries.

On the Latin American side, writers like the Nicaraguan poet Rubén Darío and the Uruguayan essayist José Enrique Rodó were publicly wary of the emerging US empire. In the case of Rodó, whose book *Ariel* was published in Uruguay in 1900, the critique of the United States was not just about Washington's foreign policies but also US materialist culture more broadly. For decades *Ariel* became a staple of Latin American pedagogy and also helped contribute to the formation of a pan–South American identity as defined against the perceived negative ideals of the United States. This age gives us some of our most compelling cases of Latin American agency and resistance through figures like the Nicaraguan nationalist Augusto Sandino, who went head to head with US soldiers in the late 1920s and early 1930s. But Sandino's actions weren't unheard up north. One of the notable features of the period is the rise in intergenerational solidarity movements and resistance against US interventionist policies domestically, in the shape of activist movements led by such figures as W. E. B. Du Bois.

Therefore, in evaluating this era—roughly the first half of the twentieth century—there are several things to bear in mind. While it is necessary to examine and reexamine well-known events, we must also cast light on forgotten, but important, episodes that may tell a more complex story. Second, although we should aim to understand the motivations for and consequences of American intervention in the region, we must be careful not to hold the United States to an anachronistically high moral standard that disregards the context of the era. And finally, the relationship between cause and effect with regard to American intervention in Latin America requires nuanced judgment to read between the lines of rhetoric. We should resist the temptation to ascribe all that went wrong during this time solely to the myriad intrusions of US soldiers, bankers, and diplomats. Activism and acrimony were all around.

9 • Yellow Fever

I should welcome almost any war, for I think this country needs one.
—Theodore Roosevelt, 1895

We have this war with Spain on our hands. William, don't lack the
moral courage. . . . Go in for action. Demand action. . . . Country
above all, William.
—William Randolph Hearst taunting President William McKinley in
his newspaper, the *New York Journal*, 1898

Remember the *Maine*!

On the night of February 15, 1898, Frank Weinheimer, a tourist, was walking along the colonial city's famed *malecón,* or esplanade, around 9:30 p.m. when he heard a "terrible roar" coming from the USS *Maine* anchored in Havana harbor. "It looked as though the whole inside of the ship had been blown out," Weinheimer later commented.

The mystery of the *Maine*'s explosion and rapid sinking, which took the lives of more than half of its five-hundred-odd sailors, has never been fully resolved, but it is almost certain that it resulted from a coal bunker fire or contact with a Spanish mine, not from Spanish perfidy. In fact, Spanish rescuers responded with alacrity, but there was little they could do.

Facts weren't the foremost consideration in the US reaction. To the historian Robert Merry, "The notion that it could have been an accident seemed inconceivable to many, and their ire wasn't assuaged by expressions from Madrid decrying the explosion and offering official condolences." Revealing his thoughts only to his diary, Secretary of the Navy John Davis Long analyzed how the destruction of the *Maine* was being interpreted in the country: "In this, as in everything else, the opinion of the individual is determined by his original bias. If he is a conservative, he is sure that it was an accident; if he is a jingo, he is equally sure that it was by design. . . . My own judgement is, so far as any information has been received, that it was the result of an accident, such as every ship of war, with the tremendously high and powerful explosives which we now have on board, is liable to encounter."

The nation's sensationalist newspapers—the infamous yellow press—had a field day as they used the presumed attack to beat the drums of war. Only days after the blast, the publisher William Randolph Hearst's daily, the *New York Journal-American,* dedicated prodigious ink to stories with headlines like "The *Maine* Was Destroyed by Treachery" and "The *Maine* Was Split in Two by Enemy's Secret Infernal Machine." It called on President William McKinley, a Republican, to draw blood, though the newspaper's sense of duty lay perhaps more toward its coffers than its country. The *Maine* represented a bonanza for the *Journal,* its circulation increasing from just under 420,000 copies distributed in early January to over 1 million after the sinking. Hearst quickly dispatched the illustrator Frederic Remington to Havana. Remington sent his boss a much-repeated but perhaps apocryphal update: "There will be no war. Wish to return." "Please remain," Hearst replied. "You furnish the pictures, I'll furnish the war."

Cynically or earnestly, most members of Congress alleged that Spain was responsible or at least abetted the attack and needed to be punished. Hawkish officials, like Assistant Secretary of the Navy Theodore Roosevelt, did not want their navy's "stupidity or incompetence" to be blamed for the attack and were unequivocal that the Spanish were behind the abomination. But while Roosevelt certainly wanted war with Spain, he sensed that his president did not. In mid-March he wrote to his colleague and naval-power philosopher, Alfred T. Mahan, "I fear the President does not intend that we shall have war if we can possibly avoid it."

Mr. McKinley's War

William McKinley, the twenty-fifth president, was one of the nation's most inscrutable heads of state, and his calculations in regard to the *Maine* are not easy to decipher. A combat veteran from the Civil War and deeply religious, McKinley was "high-minded, virtuous . . . something of a prude" and entered the White House in March 1897 promising "no jingo nonsense." On a spring day when the *Maine* crisis was still unfolding, his military aide Leonard Wood

USS *Maine*, Havana, September 23, 1911. In 1910 the US Congress directed the secretary of war and the chief of engineers to raise the wreck from Havana harbor and instructed that the remaining bodies be buried in Arlington National Cemetery. (Library of Congress Prints and Photographs Division, Washington, DC)

sat for a meeting with the commander in chief. McKinley attempted levity: "Well, have you and Theodore declared war yet?" Wood responded, "No, Mr. President, we have not, but we think you will sir." A suddenly somber McKinley offered this rejoinder: "I shall never go into a war until I am sure that God and man approve. I have been through one war; I have seen the dead pile up; and I do not want to see another."

The British scholar David Milne explains McKinley's innate aversion to belligerence: "Having fought on Virginia's bloodstained battlefields during the Civil War, he evinced little interest in military adventure of the type that Theodore Roosevelt—who was too young to have fought in the conflict—believed was natural and ennobling." Rather, McKinley wanted to use American diplomacy to stop the war which was then raging between the pro-independence rebels and Spanish colonial forces, with a view to orchestrating the latter's eventual departure from the island. In regard to the *Maine*, "The [United States] can afford to withhold its judgment and not strike an avenging blow until the truth is known."

There were voices backing the president's caution. Unlike his colleague Roosevelt, the naval officer Alfred Thayer Mahan thought a precipitous war with Spain over Cuba was strategically imprudent, and he was troubled by the Hearst-like warmongering engulfing the country. As he told a fraternal society audience in New Jersey, "We should be very cautious in forming hasty conclusions in reference to such things as this disaster. People are liable to jump to a conclusion at a great national crisis like this which might involve them seriously." The top French diplomat in Washington echoed this concern, writing of his dismay with the growing prowar sentiment: "A sort of bellicose fury has seized the American nation." The *Springfield Republic* of Massachusetts wondered in the aftermath of the *Maine* sinking if "the great majority of American newspapers do not share with Mr. Hearst the infamy of his patriotism for dollars."

But McKinley's measured response did not match the nation's "saber-rattling mood." Crowds from Denver to Virginia hung the impotent McKinley's image in effigy—and, invariably, the yellow press missed few chances to brandish these images in front of the eyes of millions of their readers. In this Victorian era when the elites were bedeviled by their "virility or lack thereof," the taunts were especially cruel. The *New York Journal* featured McKinley in a "bonnet and apron." Here is one by the lyricist Frank A. Putnam:

A mighty people proud and free, await their captain's battle call;
Their captain bends on coward's knee; his nerveless hand the sword lets fall.
The heroic deeds that reft our chains arouse in him no answering fire;

Trembling, he schemes for sordid gains and sees a race in rags expire.

The fraught domestic situation took its toll on McKinley, whose harried state is well captured by the journalist and historian Evan Thomas:

> McKinley was described by intimates as haggard, in his eyes bearing the dark circles of insomnia. There were suspicions that he was dipping into the patent narcotics used to treat his epileptic wife. Attending a musical at the White House one night, Herman Kohlstaat, a newspaperman friendly with McKinley, was summoned to meet privately with him in the Red Room. . . . McKinley rested his head on his hands, elbows and knees. He complained of not sleeping and vowed that Congress was trying to drive him into a war with Spain. "He broke down and cried like a boy of thirteen," Kohlstaat wrote in a memoir.

Behind his boss's back Roosevelt continued to quip that McKinley "has no more backbone than a chocolate éclair." He also borrowed Henry Adams's line of McKinley being "a jellyfish."

"The Cause of Humanity"

The bitter irony of McKinley's political trap was that he was not nearly as "weak and hapless" as the yellow press, Roosevelt, or future scholars would have us believe. In fact, since taking office in 1897, McKinley and his firm, diplomatic approach had gotten Madrid to make some compromises on Cuba, including moves toward greater self-autonomy. This was no small achievement in the context of what had been happening in Cuba since 1895, when Martí had restarted the pro-independence insurgence.

The situation in Cuba had become the cause of heated debate in the United States even before the sinking of the *Maine*, dividing opinion as to whether the United States should support the insurgence or not. McKinley was inclined to tread carefully in regard to what had become a savage and bloody struggle. Cuban insurgents (*insurrectos*), fighting against a superior force of more than two hundred thousand Spanish colonial troops, adopted a guerrilla strategy that involved the displacement of civilians and the brutal treatment of Spanish troops. "Determined to unfurl triumphantly, even over ruin and ashes, the flag of the Republic of Cuba," as the Cuban independence leader Máximo Gómez put it, the insurrectos believed that they merely needed to hold against the Spanish, as it would be only a matter of time before the Americans would intervene and effectively guarantee Cuban independence. Relations between

the US and Cuba were close given that before the war Cuba was tied economically to the United States: US investment in the sugar economy exceeded $50
million by 1898, and the lion's share of the island's imports and exports were
with the States, not Spain. But this did not mean that the Cubans wanted the
Americans to replace the Spanish as colonial keepers. In fact, while there were
elites like Tomás Estrada Palma (later the first president of Cuba) who were
accommodationists and pushed for annexation, most insurrectos, Martí included, were strongly opposed to Washington's entry into the war. In their
minds the US stole victory from the Cuban army and did so for self-serving,
that is, economic, reasons—not the altruistic ones most often trumpeted in
US accounts of the conflict.

Washington had urged Madrid to settle the internal war, but instead Spain
dispatched the infamous general Valeriano Weyler in 1896 to quell the insurrectos with an iron fist. Upward of one-third of the Cuban population were
hastily relocated to wretched concentration camps; hundreds of thousands of
civilians died. The ruthless approach against the rebels only further inflamed
the pro-independence sentiment in the Americas; it even sparked private
American citizens to join unlawful filibuster campaigns backing the renewed
Cuba Libre movement. One American who went to Cuba in 1897, Richard
Harding Davis, thought it inadequate to simply rebuke Madrid for its savagery: "Why should we not go a step farther and a step higher, and interfere in
the name of humanity?" One scholar noted that "millions of Americans
agreed." With the Cuban rebels demanding total independence and Spain unwilling to relinquish its perceived divine right to the island, direct American
action appeared to many as the only way to bring the conflict to a resolution.

Others, however, argued for noninterference, albeit often for rabidly racist
reasons as opposed to geopolitical principle. The midwestern editor William A.
White told his audience, "As between Cuba and Spain there is little choice. Both
crowds are yellow-legged, garlic-eating, dagger-sticking, treacherous crowds—a
mixture of Guinea, Indian and Dago. One crowd is as bad as the other. It is folly
to spill good Saxon blood for that kind of vermin. . . . Cuba is like a woman who
lets her husband beat her a second time—she should have no sympathy."

One factor staying McKinley's hand after *Maine* was his belief that Cuban
independence—the presumed result of any war with Spain—would be premature. As Thomas states, "It was all very well for the mob and their elected
representatives to clamor for Cuba Libre, McKinley believed; but it was his
responsibility as president to look beyond the war cries and calls for revenge
and ask, just what would Cuba, free of Spanish domination, look like? Were

the Cubans, about half of whom were recently freed slaves, capable of self-governance?" Equally skeptical, Secretary Long confidentially acknowledged to a friendly news reporter, "We can't recognize independence on the part of a people who have no government; no capitol; no civil organization; no place to which a representative government could be sent."

In some ways the *Maine* incident changed everything and nothing. Cuba had become a humanitarian nightmare before the *Maine* incident and the yellow press fury it unleashed. But for McKinley the sinking of the *Maine* did not mean that it was necessarily the right time for America to intervene. Instead, wanting to buy time for Spain to get a grip on the riotous climate in Cuba, he accepted Madrid's "official and seemingly heartfelt apologies" over the *Maine* incident.

Inevitable War

But McKinley's political calculations soon changed. In late March the navy issued its assessment ("presumptuously," according to one historian) that the *Maine* was sunk "by the explosion of a submarine mine which caused the partial explosion of two or more of the forward magazines." There was no direct mention of Spain. Yet still, as Milne explains, the national fever embodied in the battle cry "Remember the Maine! To hell with Spain!" was something McKinley could neglect only by tempting deep political peril. The historian Earnest May posits that McKinley even feared the overthrow of "what he conceived to be sound constitutional government."

As the weeks and months of the post-*Maine* era passed, McKinley came to better appreciate the humanitarian aspect of the Cuban independence struggle vis-à-vis its Spanish colonial masters. As the Kansas politico John Hames Ingalls put it, "A country nearly as large as England, with all the material conditions of opulent civilization, has been made a charnel house." Horatio Rubens, a New York lawyer representing the insurgents, met with McKinley at the White House. Deftly, Rubens showed the president vivid images of "emaciated and diseased" Cubans in Spain's infamous *reconcentrado* (concentration) camps. As Rubens later described the private scene, "I noticed tears began to course down his face. When he could trust his voice, he said 'I hope you say nothing of the effect of this sight on me.' "

On April 11, 1898, only two months after the *Maine* went down and despite his recent deep misgivings, McKinley addressed Congress and called for war. McKinley's belligerent petition was, however, predicated on humanitarian concerns, not vengeance for the *Maine*. It was America's imperative to safeguard vulnerable

Cubans, "a dependent people striving to be free," who were suffering from Spain's "cruel, barbarous and uncivilized practices of warfare." McKinley's lofty rhetoric claimed this would not be a war for the raw national interest but for "the cause of humanity and to put an end to the barbarities, bloodshed, starvation, and horrible miseries, now existing there, and which the parties to the conflict are either unable or unwilling to stop or mitigate." McKinley's address set off spontaneous celebrations in cities and towns, big and small. And as they did after Polk's 1846 call to war over Texas, American boys rushed to enlist as volunteers. Milne saw the declaration as doing the work of giving the US a common national project, and the young nation flexing its geopolitical muscle: "The United States, not McKinley's administration, stood up, puffed out its chest, and picked a fight with Spain, mainly because it could—it was cathartic. War also served the useful purpose of tying the North and South together in a patriotic embrace just thirty-three years after the end of the civil war. When Congress authorized McKinley's message and declared war on Spain . . . it disavowed the notion of imperial expansion."

On April 19, 1898, Congress demonstrated its strong support for the war with a congressional resolution granting McKinley the ability to use force and demanding an immediate Spanish withdrawal from the island. On April 25 Congress formally declared war on Spain. Incredibly, this declaration came in spite of a president who in many ways hoped to avoid war, although the extent of this reluctance remains disputed among historians; McKinley feared the bloodshed, the postconflict nation-building, and thus dedicated himself toward a nonmilitary solution. But his efforts were stymied by an intransigent Spain as well as by voices urging for war, including the Department of the Navy and influential press outlets eager for retribution for the *Maine*. When he did decide to prosecute the war, however, he did so very much on his own terms, although there was also an element of realpolitik involved, with McKinley harnessing prowar sentiments that otherwise might have destroyed him.

"Viva Cuba Libre! Vivan los Americanos!"

The war with Spain lasted 113 days. Overall, it was an easy victory for the rising American power against a declining European empire. Some have commented that the insurrectos might have won the war without the yanqui intervention. After a decade of naval expansion, the United States Navy greatly outweighed Spain's, allowing it to dominate the seas around Cuba. On the ground, though, it was a rather different situation, at least at first. US troops arrived on the island in early June, outfitted in blue, winter service dress. Numbering only 28,000

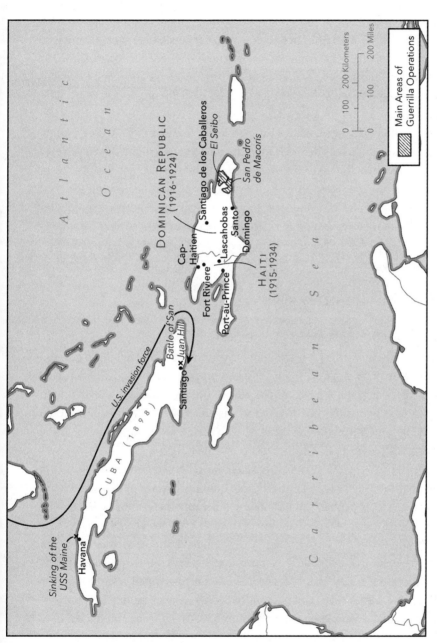

Map of the Caribbean showing US "Banana Wars" in Cuba, Haiti, and the Dominican Republic. (University of Wisconsin–Madison Cartography Lab. Christopher Archuleta, cartographer)

officers and troops at the beginning of 1898, the US invading force was woefully unprepared to face 150,000 Spanish regulars and 40,000 irregulars. But the US forces and Cuban rebels were united against the Spanish: US troops shouted, "Viva Cuba Libre!" when they first met up with Cuban insurgent forces and were met by Cuban cries of "Vivan los americanos!" (When US forces landed in Spanish-held Puerto Rico, "delirious" welcoming residents showered them with fruit, cigars, and flowers; frenzied locals even started using a new term to describe themselves: "Porto Rican, American.")

Despite their glaring shortcomings in training and numbers, within months the Americans decisively defeated their Spanish foes. Theodore Roosevelt even quit his day job as the assistant secretary of the navy so as not to miss out on his nation's noble crusade in Cuba, organizing the so-called Rough Riders, a nickname for the 1st US Volunteer Cavalry, one of three such regiments but the only one to see combat on the Caribbean isle. Famously, Colonel Roosevelt valiantly and successfully led men up an obscure Cuban slope on July 1, 1898. Dubbed the Battle of San Juan Hill, this exercise in bravado helped propel the flamboyant, redoubtable Roosevelt to become governor of New York in 1899, before being appointed as McKinley's vice president in 1901.

The conquering force, as expected, came with some words for the resident Cubans. Major General John R. Brooke told a Cuban audience when the last Spanish were departing the island that his country had intervened "to give protection to the people, security to person and property, to restore confidence . . . to resume the pursuit of peace, and to afforce full protections in the exercise of all civil and religious rights." Brooke's words broadcasting Washington's ostensibly noble and altruistic objectives in Cuba were reflective of an emerging American self-identity as a different sort of imperial power.

In April 1898 the US Congress enacted the Teller Amendment, which stipulated that the US could not annex Cuba, but only "pacify" it to leave "control of the island to its people." Soon, though, it became increasingly clear that the triumphant Americans were not going to hand over power to the insurrectos readily. The euphoria surrounding Washington's dramatic victory led US officials to believe that it should play a substantial role in the now "independent" Cuba. After the heady victory against the Spanish—which also brought the Philippines, Puerto Rico, Guam, and, indirectly, Hawaii under US control—the United States wondered whether empire was such a bad thing after all.

With Cuba now firmly under its military control, Washington needed to figure out how it would balance its stated position not to act as a "conventional" European-style colonial master with its equally strong desire to control events in

a manner favorable to US interests. The result was the Platt Amendment, legislation passed by Congress in 1901 authorizing the US president to grant sovereignty to Cuba only if several provisions were adopted. These conditions
included, among other things, the lease and sale of naval stations, including
Guantánamo Bay, through a related lease agreement in 1903 and a proviso en-
abling the US to intervene to restore order. US officials had told the Cuban nationalists that the American military occupation would not end until these
imperatives granting the United States exceptional powers were included in
Cuba's new constitution. This unyielding demand led the Cubans to incorporate
the Platt Amendment almost verbatim into the new constitution promulgated in
1902. Thus an extremely qualified Cuban independence was born right as Teddy
Roosevelt had ascended to the presidency and was solidifying his realist foreign
policy bona fides. This wave of confidence that arose from a war spun out of
tabloid outrage would influence the US posture in the region for decades.

10 • TR's Soft Talk and Big Stick

In a July 1901 letter to a German acquaintance, written only months before he would succeed the assassinated William McKinley as commander in chief, Teddy Roosevelt advised, "If any South American country misbehaves toward any European country, let the European country spank it." Yet as acute political and customs crises broke out in Venezuela in 1902, the newly installed US president acted with caution and balance. A president ordinarily perceived as a staunch proponent of the Monroe Doctrine (which forbade European meddling in the hemisphere) signaled a significant development in American foreign policy. It would come to be known as the Roosevelt Corollary.

Venezuela had been mired in a nasty civil war since 1898, leaving the door open for the strongman Cipriano Castro to gain control of the country. Castro inherited a financial disaster, including a morass of overdue payments on foreign debt. Foreign governments demanded they be serviced as they did compensation charges for damage to foreign-held assets in Venezuela. The US envoy in Caracas tried to get through to the dictator: "You owe money and sooner or later you will have to pay up." After Castro ignored a final ultimatum, on November 13, 1902, Kaiser Wilhelm II of Germany and King Edward II of Great Britain, agreed to an "iron clad" punitive plan, starting with the anchoring of naval vessels close to Venezuelan territory. Yielding unsatisfactory results from the European perspective, British and German diplomats told their American counterparts that diplomacy vis-à-vis Caracas had run its course, and, unless Castro caved, military force was imminent.

Although Secretary of State John Hay told his European counterparts that the United States "understood that European powers were bound to claim the right to defend their interests in South America," the Roosevelt administration urged Europe to proceed with caution and informally adopted a pro-Venezuela stance. Hay's comment that the United States "greatly deplored the intervention of a European power in the affairs of a South American republic" summed up Roosevelt's position on the matter.

Open to using lethal force to address the crisis, Roosevelt dispatched his own sizable fleet of navy ships—the US North Atlantic and European Naval Squadrons—to join up with the Caribbean Squadron off the coast of Puerto Rico. This newly formed armada was commanded by none other than Admiral George T. Dewey, famed for his annihilation of the Spanish fleet at the Battle of Manila Bay in 1898. Before the year was out, the naval presence of the United States cast a shadow on that of German and Great Britain combined, fifty-four ships compared to fourteen, not to mention that only the American side included battleships. Undeterred, on December 9, British and German ships, in an ostensibly peaceful operation, opened fire on multiple Venezuelan vessels. Within days Venezuelan coastal fortifications had been hit by the same force. Around this time Italy belatedly requested to be let in on the gunboat diplomacy and joined the Germano–British fleet.

Desperate, Castro placed his hope on the gringos, asking the US government to promote an arbitrated settlement. This proved to be a prudent move, as, influenced by US diplomatic pressure and bolstered by its large naval force, Berlin and London privately agreed to accept international arbitration, even if their naval blockade endured until February 1903, when the protocol was officially signed. Roosevelt's threats of war thus proved effective in convincing Wilhelm II to come to the bargaining table. After leaving office, Teddy Roosevelt self-servingly reflected on his strategy: "I succeeded in impressing upon the Kaiser, quietly and unofficially, and with equal courtesy and emphasis, that the violation of the Monroe Doctrine by territorial aggrandizement on his part around the Caribbean meant war, not ultimately, but immediately and without delay." TR saw this blunt, sober rhetoric and policy during this nearby crisis as helping ensure US credibility as a regional policeman. In helping to deescalate the Venezuela crisis, Roosevelt exhibited justifiable and necessary clear-eyed realism in pursuit of the US national interest of keeping European powers out of the hemisphere. Hence, the Roosevelt Corollary was born: a commitment by the United States to intervene as a last resort to ensure that its American neighbors pay their debts, thereby keeping Europe at bay as well as maintaining regional stability.

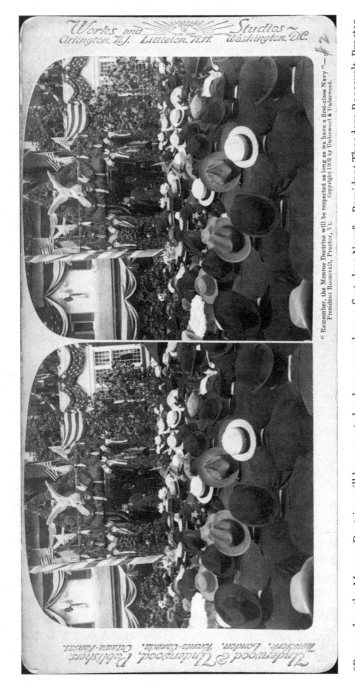

"Remember, the Monroe Doctrine will be respected as long as we have a first-class Navy."—President Theodore Roosevelt, Proctor, Vermont, 1902. (Library of Congress Prints and Photographs Division, Washington, DC)

Dominican Annexation Redux?

The Dominican Republic, a country described by the political scientist William Nester as being locked in a "vicious cycle of poverty, corruption, incompetence, violence, and authoritarianism," provided an almost immediate rerun of the situation in Venezuela as well as a fresh test for America's more muscular foreign policy. In late 1903 General Carlos Morales forced his way to power and "was as venal and inept as his predecessors." Making matters worse, Santo Domingo had over $30 million in largely European foreign obligations; default was likely. Observing the island's growing political instability, US investors began soliciting the Roosevelt administration to protect their property. For instance, a member of the Ansonia Sugar Company wrote to Secretary of State Hay in January 1904 urging that "surely it cannot be the purpose of the United States to abandon its citizens and their interests much longer to such a condition as exists in Santo Domingo!" This state of affairs was not helped by the fact that, although Morales was technically in power, other revolutionary groups continued to fight and, in turn, threaten US lives and economic interests. To provide security a detachment of US Marines came ashore at Puerto Plata, San Pedro de Macorís, and Santo Domingo in January 1904 to establish a no-fire zone and protect an American consulate. The situation continued to escalate in February, however, when a US service member from the cruiser USS *Yankee* was killed by Dominican forces. Roosevelt quickly ordered a small-scale amphibious assault on the offending party. "Santo Domingo is drifting into chaos after a hundred years of freedom," the twenty-sixth president stated, and "shows itself utterly incompetent for government work. Most reluctantly I have been obliged to take the initial step of interference there. I hope it will be a good while before I have to go further."

In an echo of the US annexation push by President Ulysses S. Grant three decades before, in February Morales instructed his diplomats to request that the White House annex the Dominican Republic. To Morales's disappointment, the sentiment in the White House had radically changed since Grant's days. In a letter to the newspaper editor and confidant Joseph Bucklin Bishop of February 23, 1904, TR vented, "I have been hoping and praying . . . that the Santo Dominicans would behave so that I would not have to act in any way. I want to do nothing but what a policeman has to do in Santo Domingo. As for annexing the island, I have about the same desire to annex it as a gorged boa constrictor might have to swallow a porcupine wrong-end-to. Is that strong enough?"

Matters were further complicated on February 24, when the Permanent Court of Arbitration ruled in favor of the Anglo-German belligerents in the Venezuela case. The court's decision granted the blockading powers preferential treatment in the debt collection process, thereby establishing a dangerous precedent for the Dominican Republic. This left little doubt in Roosevelt's mind that European powers would pounce on the Dominican Republic to extract payment, forcing him to devise an offer that followed the Monroe Doctrine yet satisfied the debt holders. His solution: set up a short-term customs receivership over the island. With the United States collecting the debts, the European nations would get paid and, critically, would not have to resort to methods which would infringe upon the Monroe Doctrine. That said, any intervention in the Dominican Republic, no matter how conciliatory, had the potential to be a politically unpopular move for Roosevelt, which is why he waited until after the 1904 election to pursue the customs receivership.

In early 1905 a bilateral accord between Washington and Santo Domingo gave Washington responsibility in the country's security situation but also customs revenue administration, including authority to name the head of the Dominican Customs Receivership. Within a few months Roosevelt's creativity would be put to the test: Italy demanded a payment, backing up its request by dispatching a gunboat to the country. Seeing as how Santo Domingo contended that it was unable to pay, leaving European assumptions about full payment aside, Roosevelt cleverly "arranged for American officials to collect the country's customs revenues, place them in a New York bank, and divvy out 45 percent of the money to the Dominican government and the rest to the foreign creditors in proportion to their claim." Now having a sum of $20 million housed in a US bank, Roosevelt appeared once again to be putting his weight on the scales in favor of a Latin American country and against European rivals. The Dominican government supported the deal, but the US Congress lacked the two-thirds necessary votes until 1908. The customs receivership existed for decades, not fully rescinded until 1940, when the FDR administration's secretary of state, Cordell Hull, referenced the "sore thumb" during the bilateral negotiations with the Dominican strongman Rafael Trujillo.

The Roosevelt Corollary

The Monroe Doctrine, as noted above, was a supremely self-confident yet naïve statement putting European capitals on notice that the United States would not take kindly to them exploiting the newly sovereign Latin American nations. In his Fourth Annual Message to Congress on December 6, 1904, Roosevelt sermonized on the importance of mutual respect: "It is our duty to remember that a nation has no more right to do injustice to another nation, strong or weak, than an individual has to do injustice to another individual; that the same moral law applies in one case as in the other." German machinations in Washington's near abroad lay behind Roosevelt's more aggressive stance to enforcing the Monroe Doctrine as well as protecting the future canal in Panama.

But Roosevelt didn't just propound the Monroe Doctrine; he also modified it, adding a circumstance which would justify US intervention in a formulation that would come to be known as the Roosevelt Corollary: "Chronic wrongdoing, or an impotence which results in a general loosening of the ties of civilized society may in America, as elsewhere, ultimately require intervention by some civilized nation, and in the Western Hemisphere the adherence of the United States to the Monroe Doctrine may force the United States, however reluctantly, in flagrant cases of such wrongdoing or impotence, to the exercise of an international police power." Although the United States now had provided itself with the ideological framework for foreign intervention, it is worth bearing in mind that the context surrounding the Roosevelt Corollary was not one of imperialistic expansion but of international arbitration and diplomacy. Indeed, contrary to what we sometimes assume about this emerging age of chest-puffing gunboat diplomacy—and Roosevelt's own previous hawkish stance circa 1898—Roosevelt's logic could be outright legalistic. For the sitting US head of state, the right of European powers to claim payments of debts from indebted states like Venezuela and the Dominican Republic was entirely within the realm of international law; more critically, to this unabashed American realist, was how and where European powers—above all, Germany and its designs on the Dominican Republic—would exploit this sanction to gain a toehold in the region so close to America's shores. And this thinking is what led to the practical strategy of imposing upon customs officials to ensure the foreign obligations were met—and by extension eliminate an excuse for European colonialism.

The outcome of the Venezuela crisis reinforced Roosevelt's self-proclaimed successful adherence to the aphorism "speak softly and carry a big stick; you will go far," which the then vice president attributed to a West African proverb but would now adopt as his own. This was undeniably Big Stick diplomacy: a stick primarily directed at European powers, not Latin American states. But guaranteeing freedom from European interference came at a price: TR's quid pro quo, as one scholar put it, was that "nations of the Americas would be expected to do as they were told."

The conditions under which the US would intervene under the Roosevelt Corollary were always subject to interpretation, and, again, we should be careful not to take the high rhetoric of leaders at face value. In September 1906 Roosevelt wrote to the Cuban ambassador in Washington expressing his reluctance to send in troops to quell an uprising in Cuba. "Our intervention in Cuban affairs will only come if Cuba shows that she has fallen into the insurrectionary habit, that she lacks the self-restraint necessary to secure peaceful self-government, and that her contending factions have plunged the country into anarchy." In reality, though, Roosevelt and his presidential successors appeared more than willing to send troops into Cuba and elsewhere. One cause of this enthusiasm was the enormous power imbalances between the continuously industrializing United States and its Latin neighbors. Using military force to determine favorable outcomes was all the more appealing when the prospects and potential rewards of success were so great. The rub was that overwhelming military advantage rarely translated into straightforward political success in the very countries where the gunboats were most active.

11 • Mr. Roosevelt's Canal

Since the 1600s, people had pondered the possibility of constructing a canal across Central America that would offer a shorter, safer route between the east and west coasts of the United States than the risky, months-long haul around Cape Horn and its fierce Antarctic storms. A successful canal would make its investors wildly rich—and this interoceanic El Dorado was an exceptional motivating force for politicians, engineers, and speculators.

The United States in particular had long recognized the potential of a transisthmian canal in Central America and made diplomatic moves to secure its place at the geopolitical table. With the signing of the 1846 Bidlack Treaty, the United States and Colombia began making coordinated efforts to maintain stability in Colombia's province of Panama, which was separated from the rest of the country by the inhospitable jungle of the infamous Darién Gap region. In return for these security guarantees, Bogotá promised Washington a right-of-way in Panama for a future canal.

The Californian Gold Rush, which kicked off in 1848, soon provided another reason for Washington to help maintain political stability in Panama. Since the US transcontinental railroad was not completed until 1869 there was a pressing need to shorten the long, exhausting trip between the east and west coasts. Into the breach stepped the transisthmian railroad in Panama, which was constructed soon after the gold rush began—it had an eye-popping initial fare of $25 in gold ($475 in today's dollars). Keeping this railroad open for business was vital, and the United States began to expend considerable resources to ensure its uninterrupted operation.

In the half century following Bidlack, Washington continually assisted in quelling armed insurrections by Panamanian nationalists. Hawks like

Roosevelt contended, perhaps cynically, that an uprising erupted on average once a year in this period. All told, Washington intervened in around a dozen cases, half of which entailed putting US boots on the ground. But despite his cynicism and the region's nagging rebellions, Roosevelt felt that the United States had the right and responsibility to monitor and control this volatile region. The US was not the only one to recognize the strategic value of Panama. Imperial Britain's sizable local footprint—deriving from its protectorate over the Mosquito Coast in modern-day Nicaragua, outposts in British Honduras, and the Bay Islands off the Honduran coast—was stepping on US toes, and regardless of the Bidlack Treaty it soon became clear that the bilateral relationship over the isthmus had to be regularized. Although the Bidlack accord outlined that the Colombian government keep an eye on British activity in the region on behalf of the US, in 1850 Washington nonetheless went for cooperation, signing the Clayton-Bulwer Treaty with London, whereby the two countries agreed to co-control any future Central American canal.

French Gambit

Despite the extent of American and British interest, it was France that made the initial attempt at constructing a canal in Central America, not surprising given the nation's nineteenth-century track record of engineering vision. In the mid-1870s Ferdinand de Lesseps, of Suez Canal fame, which opened in 1869, was the first to express an interest in a Panama canal. By 1881 the Compagnie Universelle du Canal Interocéanique, backed by over one hundred thousand small investors hoping the Frenchman would repeat his canal magic in Panama, had been established. World-class engineers were now at work on a sea-level route along the track of the 1855 Panama Railroad, which was officially Colombian territory.

By the late 1880s the French gambit had officially failed, de Lesep's company going belly up. Pestilential diseases like smallpox, yellow fever, and malaria; torrid heat and rain of biblical proportions; financial mismanagement; temperamental steam shovels, locomotives, and dredges; and the awesome Chagres River all took their toll. The campaign took twenty thousand to twenty-five thousand lives, mostly West Indians and local black workers, and billions upon billions of francs (about $290 million). Massive earthworks and rusting machinery were abandoned. As the canal catastrophe unfolded, critics had a field day. *Harper's Weekly* ran a caricature of the French director with the caption

"Is M. de Lesseps a Canal Digger or a Grave Digger?" Now the word "Panama" was associated with fraud and defeat.

A Volcano, Vote, and Canal

After President McKinley was assassinated on September 6, 1901, in Buffalo, New York, by an American anarchist, his successor Theodore Roosevelt wasted little time in raising the canal question. In his first Annual Message to Congress on December 3, he asserted that "no single material work which remains to be undertaken on this continent is as of such consequence to the American people." That November Congress ratified the US–UK Hay–Pauncefote Treaty, granting Washington the right to build and manage an interoceanic canal and annulling the 1850 cooperative agreement with London.

TR knew a canal must be built, as American power needed a potent American navy that in turn needed faster access between the two coasts, but there was still the burning question of where. Nicaragua, closer than Panama to the United States and posing fewer engineering challenges, had emerged as a more suitable candidate to host the canal. But here de Lesseps's top engineer, Philippe Bunau-Varilla, a "tiny Frenchman of charm and ingenuity," came into play. Bunau-Varilla very much stood to gain a financial windfall if the construction in Panama was resurrected, but he also deeply wanted to "vindicate French genius" with a successful restart and completion.

A private citizen of France and thus not negotiating in any official capacity, Bunau-Varilla became one of the "most successful lobbyists ever to hit Washington," according to the former US ambassador and historian Warren Zimmermann: he convinced Washington to choose Colombia–Panama over Nicaragua for canal construction. Bunau-Varilla hired the Brooklyn-born lawyer Wilson Nelson Cromwell to help lobby Capitol Hill on behalf of the New Panama Canal Company, which had land rights in Panama and equipment from de Lesseps's failed project in 1894. "Equally diminutive, fastidious in dress, devious, and highly articulate," Cromwell was a formidable advocate who also just happened to hold shares in the company. His goal? Sell the canal company and its assets to Uncle Sam while making a killing along the way. Warren Zimmermann described Cromwell: "Like Bunau-Varilla, he was a world-class lobbyist with a keen instinct for using money to buy influence. He even donated sixty thousand dollars to the Republican National Committee to sweeten its views on the Panama option, charging the contribution to his French clients. His greed, unlike Bunau-Varilla's, was unflecked by any particles of altruism."

By early 1902 the Rough Rider had come around to the Panama side, influenced in part by the preeminent bridge design engineer George C. Morrison's recommendation. With TR in their camp, Bunau-Varilla and Cromwell went to work on Capitol Hill and the State Department. Constructing the canal in Nicaragua made more sense because it was considered an easier construction challenge despite its greater length. It was also the conclusion of the 1876 report commissioned by President Ulysses S. Grant after extensive United States Navy surveys. But a Nicaraguan plan lacked such politically savvy agents to rival "these two Lilliputian giants." The redoubtable Bunau-Varilla deftly got the New Panama Canal Company to slash the going price for its Panama assets from a whopping $109 million to $40 million so that the route would be fiscally more attractive over its Central American competitor. He even published a propagandistic pamphlet entitled *Panama or Nicaragua* and distributed a circa 1900 Nicaraguan stamp depicting a smoking Momotombo volcano to all congressmen to reinforce the notion that Nicaragua was earthquake-prone. That a volcano in Martinique had killed over thirty thousand people just a few months prior was not lost on Bunau-Varilla and Cromwell—or likely many politicians on Capitol Hill.

History remains undecided regarding whether the Momotombo stamps were decisive in the final outcome, but on June 19, 1902, just days after the stamps were distributed, the US Senate voted overwhelmingly, 67 to 6, to support the Panama option. The United States would purchase the New Panama Canal Company and its assets for $40 million. President Roosevelt signed the Spooner Act authorizing the purchase nine days later. Cromwell's fee for the frenetic and wildly successful six-month lobbying effort was $800,000, or $20 million adjusted for inflation. In a fantastic harbinger of how potent the role of lobbying would come to be in Washington, Panama won out over Nicaragua for entirely political reasons: "money, investments, interests, and publicity, including that famous stamp."

Bogotá Rejects the Deal

With Panama getting the nod, the United States now needed to sell the deal to Colombia. Sensationalist critics advocated a direct approach, Hearst's *Journal* railing, "The only way we could secure a satisfactory concession from Colombia would be to go down there, take the contending statesmen by the necks, and hold a batch of them in office long enough to get a contract in mind." From the diplomatic point of view, the task of striking a deal with the Colombians certainly appeared daunting given the surge in diplomatic bad blood in the wake of TR's decision to unilaterally send US Marines to Panama to secure the rail connection only months after the Congress had passed the Spooner Act. It would be an understatement to say that the Colombians were not feeling friendly toward their northern neighbor.

Nevertheless, diplomatic discussions between the United States and Colombia took place in Washington, DC, in January 1903 and led to the Hay–Herrán Treaty later that month. For Washington, this was a fantastic development since it granted the United States a six-mile-wide canal zone with a one-hundred-year lease on a yearly rent of $250,000 ($6 million today), in return for a lump sum of $10 million ($250 million today). But in truth the Colombians were left with little option but to agree to the treaty.

Motivated by a combination of greed and patriotism, the US Senate ratified the pact on March 14. Its Colombian counterpart rejected it unanimously, possibly seeking to leverage more concessions from Washington or in pique at their diplomats, who had negotiated without proper supervision. This despite the fact that Secretary of State Hay, the top US diplomat who negotiated with the Colombian chargé d'affaires Tomás Herrán, had threatened Bogotá about making such an insolent move. An incensed Roosevelt unleashed a tirade, calling the Colombians "blackmailers," "homicidal corruptionists," "cut throats," and "jack rabbits." What's more, "talking with those fellows down there . . . is like holding a squirrel in your lap and trying to keep up the conversation." Here is Zimmermann's take: "Whatever their motives, the Colombians were short sighted in giving up certain profits for the uncertain prospect of greater ones. Still, it was the right of the Colombian Senate, as it was of the U.S. Senate, to reject a treaty negotiated by its government."

Hay advised his boss that there might be a way out of the impasse:

It is altogether likely that there will be an insurrection on the Isthmus against the regime of folly and graft that now rules at Bogota. . . . It is for you to decide whether you will (1) await the result of that movement (2) take a hand in rescuing the Isthmus from anarchy . . . . something we shall be forced to do in the case of a serious insurrectionary movement in Panama, to keep the transit clear. Our intervention should not be haphazard, nor this time should it be to the profit, as heretofore, of Bogota. I venture to suggest you let your mind play a little about the subject for two or three weeks, before finally deciding.

November 1903: A Fateful Month

Bogotá's summary rejection of the treaty had deep implications for Bunau-Varilla's legacy and Cromwell's New Panama Canal Company as well as for the independence fortunes of Panamanian nationalists. It was only logical that, united in frustration, the two silver-tongued lobbyists turned now to the Panamanians for support. The plan that emerged decided that the separatists would organize a revolt, which Cromwell and Bunau-Varilla would work day and night to ensure was backed by the United States. And like clockwork Cromwell was able to get one of the key revolutionaries, most of whom were from the local gentry, to meet with Secretary Hay in early September 1903. A month later the French lobbyist met with Roosevelt himself and came away with a strong impression that the US head of state would prevent Bogotá from quelling a revolt. Indeed, TR secretly began to aid the pro-independence forces, including via a clandestine visit by US agents to assess the extent of the pro-independence sentiment inside the isthmus. Their conclusion? Support was widespread, and a strong embrace of the revolution was all but inevitable. Roosevelt's team even provided the conspirators with a ready-made national constitution. Sensing the uprising was imminent, the Roosevelt administration, on November 3, dispatched ten navy vessels to the vicinity, but as it turned out, only one, the USS *Nashville*, arrived in time off the Caribbean coastal port of Colón on November 2 to be of any consequence.

The arrival of the *Nashville* did not prevent a five-hundred-soldier-strong Colombian expedition from landing the next day. A report back to Washington detailed a single skirmish with the Colombian soldiers, the sole casualties being "a Chinaman [killed] in Salsipuedes Street . . . and an ass in the slaughterhouse." A few dozen leathernecks were landed to protect the US-managed railroad, ensuring the Colombian forces could not exploit this essential transport. "Thus," writes Zimmermann, "the U.S. Navy, which had acted as guarantor of Colombia's sovereignty over Panama for half a century, assisted in the destruction of that sovereignty." Not lost in the translation, Roosevelt's gunboat diplomacy in Panama sent an unequivocal message to Bogotá: attempting to reassert its national sovereignty in Panama meant war. By the time a second US warship arrived on November 5, the Colombian forces had duly fled.

The November 3 revolution succeeded more quickly and fully than even the most ardent hawks like Roosevelt or hired guns like Cromwell could have imagined. On November 6 the newly established regime requested American recognition, which it received in about an hour. Here is Hay's dispatch to US diplomats in Panama City but intended "for all the world to see": "The people of Panama have, by an apparently unanimous movement, dissolved their political connection with the Republic of Colombia and resumed their independence. When you are satisfied that a *de facto* government, republican in form, and without substantial opposition from its own people, has been established in the State of Panama, you will enter into relations with it as the responsible government of the territory."

Back at the White House, Roosevelt deliberated the legal and ethical considerations for this precipitous military and diplomatic move that betrayed the half century of cooperation with Bogotá. "Have I answered the charges? Have I defended myself?" he asked. Secretary of War Elihu Root rejoined, "You have shown you were accused of seduction and you have conclusively proved that you were guilty of rape." Attorney General Philander Knox reassured the commander in chief, "Oh Mr. President, do not let so great an achievement suffer from any taint of legality!" Needless to say, TR's Washington was not pulling any punches.

The diplomatic situation quickly turned to farce. A week after the revolution Bunau-Varilla was in Washington, but now as the putative "envoy extraordinary and minister plenipotentiary" for the newly established Republic of Panama. It might have been because the true representatives from the new government were en route to Washington from Panama, but Bunau-Varilla pushed Hay to endorse a new treaty with "lightning rapidity of action." The true Panamanian delegation arrived in the US capital on November 18, but by now a bilateral accord had already been hammered out, and Hay was in no mood to tolerate any significant changes. Although furious at the Frenchman's machinations, the Panamanian diplomats were helpless to do anything about it.

The hastily assembled Hay–Bunau-Varilla Treaty was a facsimile of the Hay–Herrán accord, only this time there were greater concessions to the Americans. In fact, it was Bunau-Varilla who, to preempt any US Senate opposition, added them, most critically a new provision granting unilateral and perpetual control as if "it [the US] were the sovereign . . . to the entire exclusion of the exercise by the Republic of Panama of any such sovereign rights, power or authority" over a ten-mile-wide Panama Canal Zone. The price tag? More than the combined costs of purchasing Alaska, Louisiana, and the Philippines: $10 million outright, a $250,000 annuity to the new government, and $40 million to the New Panama Canal Company. The US Senate ratified the treaty 66 to 14 on February 23, 1904. That same year the Panamanian assembly hastily ratified the treaty only hours after it had arrived via sea. It is not clear if anyone in Panama even read the document before the vote was taken.

Cromwell's fee this time was a cool $2 million, or $50 million today. The author Mark Zwonitzer describes the zeitgeist: "The justifications for this explosive expansion of national aim and activity . . . were explicitly and loudly articulated by its projectors: the spread of democracy and Western Civilization, the opening of new markets for American business, the national defense, the supremacy of the white man, and even God's will. There was also much talk of abstractions such as patriotism, honor, and duty." The prospect of a US-controlled Panama Canal was inching closer to reality, but ahead lay the stupendous engineering challenge of crossing the "harsh terrain—a terrain in a tropical, malarial climate, one of the most challenging feats in history."

"I Took the Canal"

The first American steam shovel began work in Panama on November 11, 1904, and, despite the huge difficulties endemic to the terrain, construction progressed steadily. In 1906 the glowing Rough Rider made history when he visited the construction project and thus became the first sitting US commander in chief to venture overseas. Just months before the end of his presidency in late 1908, Roosevelt corresponded with a British newsman, Sidney Brooks. "This I can say absolutely was my own work," he wrote, "and could not have been accomplished save by me or by some man of my temperament." In 1911 the ex-president was equally boastful and unrepentant. "I am interested in the Panama Canal because I started it," he told an audience at the University of California. "If I had followed traditional, conservative methods I would have submitted a dignified State paper of probably about 200 pages to Congress and the debates on it would have been going on yet; but I took the Canal Zone and let Congress debate; and while the debate goes on the Canal does also." Roosevelt's braggadocio was a far cry from the universalist rhetoric he employed in his message to Congress two months after the November 1903 Panama revolution: "[It was in] collective civilization. If ever a Government could be said to have received a mandate from civilization . . . the United States holds that position with regard to the inter-oceanic canal."

Opened on August 15, 1914, the American canal in Panama was constructed with "consummate efficiency and singular brute determination," costing some fifty-six hundred lives and $352 million ($8.8 billion today). The crowning imperial (and engineering) success of the United States contrasted with the onset of war in Europe and the German invasion of Belgium. It would prove the truth behind the long-standing axiom of the United States Navy

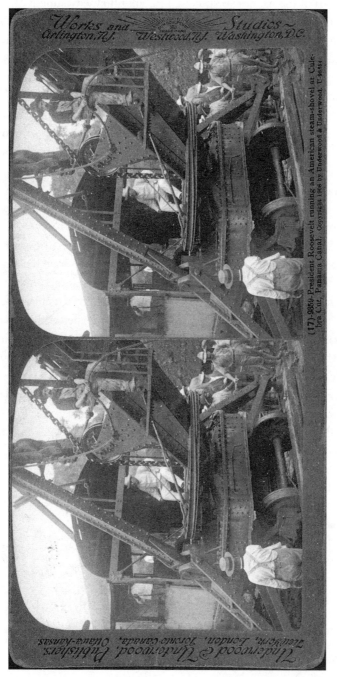

President Theodore Roosevelt running an American steam-shovel at Culebra Cut, Panama Canal construction, 1908. (Library of Congress Prints and Photographs Division, Washington, DC)

strategist Captain Alfred Thayer Mahan that an interoceanic canal was an indispensable part of the American strategic outlook into the twentieth century,
given that this was precisely the role the canal played during the Great War.
The canal cut the New York–San Francisco mileage by more than half, from
fourteen thousand to six thousand. As Milne wrote, "The United States now
had the ability to move its fleet swiftly between the Pacific and the Atlantic,
depending on the threats on either flank."

When the United States unleashed its total war campaign against the Axis
powers in the early 1940s, Washington was so paranoid about enemy incursions
against the canal that it constructed over 130 bases in Panama. But perceptions
of the strategic importance of the canal quickly changed, and by the time Harry
S. Truman was sitting in the White House in the latter part of the decade, the
perceived foreign security threat to the waterway had diminished to the point
where he considered handing over control of the canal to the nascent United
Nations. In the ensuing years and decades, reckoned the historian Daniel Immerwahr, every American commander in chief "sought to extricate the United
States from the increasingly irrelevant Canal Zone in various ways." It took until
the administration of President Jimmy Carter to formally produce a bilateral
diplomatic accord goal in the late 1970s, outlining the transfer of the canal to
Panamanian control in December 1999. Immerwahr notes that the canal itself
enjoyed growing levels of traffic after World War II but that control over the canal became less a strategic concern given the increased and improved means of
communication and transportation among nations. Hence, while the canal was
born in TR-era realism and Big Stick diplomacy, as technologies and advances
developed and its geopolitical importance diminished, the canal went out with a
style and intent far less imperialist.

12 • Imperial Idealism

Intervention must be avoided until a time comes when it is
inevitable, which God forbid!
—President Woodrow Wilson to his wife, August 1914

What to do with Mexico is the great problem.
—Josephus Daniels, US Secretary of the Navy, April 1913

When the Democrat Woodrow Wilson assumed the presidency on March 4, 1913, he could be forgiven for not anticipating the huge role Latin America would play in his foreign policy. It's also an aspect of his presidency that is often overlooked today. As the author Patricia O'Toole pointed out in her biography of the twenty-eighth president, the carnage of World War I has overshadowed Wilson's myriad other military interventions, most of which were in the backyard: Cuba, Haiti, the Dominican Republic, Panama (two times), Honduras (five times), and, finally and most critically, twice in Mexico, each time almost sparking a full-scale war.

The first crisis in Mexico can't be entirely ascribed to Wilson, as it had been incubating before he took office. Between the ninth and nineteenth of February 1913, about a month before Wilson's inauguration, Mexico City was rocked by a bout of violence known as the Decena Trágica (Ten Tragic Days). During that episode the nefarious opportunist General Victoriano Huerta ousted the democratically elected president, Francisco Madero. As David Milne writes, the US government's diplomatic stance toward these events was "one of studied indifference," but American businessmen with land and other interests in the country considered Madero's maverick reform agenda of social justice and democracy a threat. In full accord with this anti-Madero sentiment, outgoing president William Howard Taft's top envoy in Mexico City, Henry Lane Wilson (no relation to the incoming president), corresponded with Huerta.

At the end of the Decena Trágica, Wilson met with Huerta and signed the Pact of the Embassy, which established the commitment of the US embassy to install Huerta as interim president once Madero was out of the way. Madero was promised safe passage but was assassinated by Huerta's forces. That Ambassador Wilson did this without first establishing formal support from the Taft administration shows the oversized role he had in bilateral affairs. It would not be the last time that these sorts of US "viceroy diplomats" would significantly shape twentieth-century interhemispheric relations. Henry Lane Wilson sent several dispatches back to Washington lauding Huerta and his new government, but Taft left office before deciding to recognize Huerta's new regime—exactly what his top envoy was pleading for.

Into the breach came the new president, Woodrow Wilson, but from the beginning it was clear he had a different take on the Mexico crisis than Taft or Ambassador Wilson. Very much with an eye on the Roosevelt Corollary's legacy, on March 12, 1913, President Wilson issued a press statement explaining that respect and amity with the "sister republics of Central and South America" were rooted in the "orderly processes of just government based upon law, not upon arbitrary and irregular force." Wilson explained that his new team would "have no sympathy with those who seek the power of the government to advance their own personal interests or ambitions." Chatting with a European official, Wilson famously spelled out his broader hemispheric goals: "I am going to teach the South American republics to elect good men."

It is easy to discount Wilson's words as more patronizing rhetoric from a US leader, but one must not miss the earnestness of his attempt to forge a new policy path away from the Taft era's so-called Dollar Diplomacy, where big business helped US national security and vice versa. Wilson's approach to the region was genuinely idealistic, and he was an unabashed champion of what was dubbed constitutionalism, the idea that Washington would only support governments in power under constitutional means. In his address to a convention of southern business owners in Mobile, Alabama, in October 1913 the commander in chief announced what became known as the Wilson Doctrine toward Latin America, bashing degrading private profits and renouncing imperial expansion. "[The] United States will never again seek one additional foot of territory by conquest," he declared. One key Wilson administration official, Frank Cobb, put it this way: "The Wilson doctrine is aimed at the professional revolutionists, the corrupting concessionaires, and the corrupt dictators in Latin America. . . . [I]t is a bold doctrine and a radical doctrine." As Milne explains, "Wilson's aversion to anything that smacked of imperialism was shaping his geopolitical agenda. In his idealism and ambition, the president was opening a new chapter in the history of America's foreign relations."

President Wilson's equally moralizing secretary of state, William Jennings Bryan, was deeply serious and eager to put more teeth into his boss's foreign policy pivot. Bryan was described by one scholar as being "sanctimonious, dog-matic, and ascetic to a degree that made Wilson—who at least savored single-malt whiskey in small measures—appear bacchanalian in comparison." Here is Milne's analysis: "Like Wilson, Bryan was a foreign policy idealist who believed diplomacy served a higher function than pleasing big business; U.S. behavior should be exemplary, to persuade other nations to follow its example." Peace, America's top envoy believed, was the primary task for his tenure in office.

The unusual but potent executive branch foreign policy duo of Wilson and Bryan was committed to pushing the democracy line and not indulging vio-lent regimes even if they enjoyed the support of US business interests. To this end, Bryan and Wilson pursued a new pact with Colombia whereby the United States would issue a formal apology and an indemnity of $25 million "for the brutish manner in which President Roosevelt had detached Panama from Bo-gotá's control." Colombians, at least, considered this a necessary gesture to partially right a very clear moral wrong. Teddy Roosevelt was apoplectic, call-ing the treaty, which his ally Senator Henry Cabot Lodge of Massachusetts suffocated in the Senate before ratification, an unmitigated "crime against the United States." President Wilson had set out his stall clearly, but Mexico would prove the greatest test of his idealism.

What to Do with Mexico?

Unswayed by Ambassador Wilson's pleas, President Wilson didn't merely refuse to recognize the new status quo in Mexico but even pushed a novel nonrecognition angle, denouncing Huerta's "government of butchers." It's significant that President Wilson held deep misgivings about Ambassador Wilson for not only failing to stop Huerta's putsch but actually supporting the despot. President Wilson might have gone so far as to replace the emissary, but this was off the table, as in the president's eyes sending a new ambassador personally approved by him would be tantamount to officially recognizing Huerta's usurper regime. Although he'd suffered a severe slap on the wrist from the commander in chief, Ambassador Wilson was allowed to stay in place for the time being.

In early 1913 President Wilson's displeasure with the ambassador crossed a new threshold when he sent a handful of informal envoys to Mexico tasked with reporting directly to the White House. One of them, an erstwhile Episcopalian theologian named William Bayard Hale, assumed the identity of a foreign correspondent. Another, Reginald Francisco del Valle, was sent to judge whether the Constitutional movement was a viable alternative to Huerta. There were hiccups early on: del Valle not only wrote reports that were jumbled and inaccurate, but also showed a severe lack of discretion as he informed the media of his supposedly secret mission. While del Valle was soon recalled, the other diplomats proved more useful. It did not take long for Hale to send word back to Washington describing the chilling extent to which Henry Lane Wilson had been complicit in the illegal ouster of Madero. Hale was scathing in his assessment of the ambassador, writing, "It is no secret here that [the] fall [of] Madero was hastened by Ambassador Wilson. [It] is said freely [and] with great reason that the assassination never would have been ventured if [the] American Ambassador had made it distinctly understood [that] lives must be spared. Wilson is [a] vain busybody, [of] highly nervous temperament." Nor did Hale mince words in his evaluation of Huerta, painting him as "an ape-like old man" who "may almost be said to subsist on alcohol." These findings of President Wilson's extra-ambassadorial team proved to be the final straw with respect to Ambassador Wilson: he was recalled to Washington on July 16, 1913, and his resignation soon followed.

To fill the diplomatic void, President Wilson next dispatched another personal envoy, the former Minnesota governor and diplomatic neophyte John Lind, to the Mexican capital to broker a deal with the recalcitrant Huerta. The terms? A prompt cease-fire, clean elections, and Huerta's pledge not to run in the election. Huerta rejected the offer even after it had been sweetened to include a personal line of credit if he vowed not to jump into the election. A sham election ensued, and Huerta was duly elected, prompting Wilson to jettison his "watchful waiting." Indeed, the president was convinced that it was his "immediate duty to require Huerta's retirement."

If President Wilson had a horse in Mexico's chaotic political race, it would have been the revolutionary general Venustiano Carranza's constitutionalist forces. In April 1914 Wilson allowed materiel to be transferred to Carranza, but even this did not force out Huerta. The Wilson administration threatened the illegitimate regime with economic sanctions, but these also failed—and might have even emboldened the pitiless Mexican ruler to crack down even more severely on the disparate opposition.

Then, in early April 1914, Mexican security authorities inappropriately apprehended nine US seamen in the Gulf of Mexico port of Tampico who had been on land from the USS *Dolphin* searching for supplies. The situation was remedied quickly, with a Mexican apology included, but the vessel's commander insisted upon a twenty-one-gun salute and diplomatic apology from Mexico, "which he contended were necessary to fully restore American dignity." Initially refusing to agree to such terms, Huerta's regime offered a rejoinder of both Mexican and US gun salutes. An incredulous Wilson ignored the offer and moved quickly to prepare US military forces not just to settle the local Tampico affront but also to bring about regime change to oust the despised Huerta. Erring on the side of caution, Bryan was worried about the cost and justification for the military incursion, while hawks like Henry Cabot Lodge thought that Wilson's military plan was not nearly aggressive enough. *The Economist* magazine in London published an especially scathing critique of Wilson's impetuous response to the Tampico impasse: "If war is to be made on points of punctilio raised by admirals and generals, and if the Government of the United States is to set the example for this return to mediaeval conditions it will be a bad day for civilization."

One of Wilson's top policy advisors, Colonel Edward House (a ceremonial title) imagined the altruistic American armed intervention would be welcomed with open arms. "[If] Mexico understood that our motives were unselfish she should not object to our helping adjust her unruly household." And thus, on April 21, 1914, only twelve days after the Tampico affair, around twenty-three hundred US sailors and marines landed without encountering enemy fire in Veracruz, south of Tampico, and proceeded to capture key communication and customs facilities around the city. Eventually the force would number around five thousand troops.

The quiet was short-lived. The US force was soon embroiled in preliminary skirmishes that resulted in the deaths of over two hundred Mexicans and about two dozen Americans. Contrary to House's rosy predictions, the US soldiers that occupied the coastal city of Veracruz for a total of seven months were not welcomed as heroes and liberators but loathed as invaders. Anti-yanqui protests erupted in Mexico and then swept through the hemisphere, in Argentina, Chile, Costa Rica, and Guatemala. Even the most fervent anti-Huerta political and military forces, like Carranza's, called for the gringos to leave, but there was little the Mexicans could do to force the withdrawal. Back in Washington, Wilson began to realize that getting out of Veracruz would be far harder than getting in. "I cannot get it off my heart," he told an aide. "It was right. Nothing else was possible, but I cannot forget that it was I who had to order these young men to their deaths." By now Wilson's military planners were pushing him to call up as many as four hundred thousand reservists for a large-scale war, although he never approved this maximalist option. Those reservists who did get the call expressed the usual thrill of anticipated battle:

> Goodbye sister, goodbye sweetheart,
> Goodbye mother, too
> Don't be grieving for I'm leaving
> 'Neath the dear old red, white and blue
> Hark! I hear the bugles calling,
> Kiss me, I must go; to my country I'll be true;
> Think of me, I'll think of you, I'm off for Mexico.

In an early instance of hemispheric multilateralism, Argentina, Brazil, and Chile proffered their good graces for the so-called ABC conference in Canada, convening on May 20, 1914, to prevent a wider war between the US and Mexico. Both Wilson and Huerta accepted the third-party mediation, and as news spread that Wilson had agreed to the negotiations brokered by the ABC conference, pro-US goodwill erupted across the region. As one American living in South America described it, "The transformation was amazing; American flags were run up; the United States was cheered." According to the scholar Patricia O'Toole, Wilson "deemed it the duty of the United States to help the Mexican people until peace and constitutional government were restored. And for those who believed that Mexicans were innately unsuited to self-government, Wilson had a message: when properly directed, all peoples were capable of self-government."

Mere months after the conference Huerta fled Mexico and was replaced by Carranza. At least one of Wilson's Mexican policy objectives, regime change, had been met. Here is Milne's take: "Wilson's policy now appeared vindicated. A brutal leader had been dispatched and a better one had taken his place." Finally, in November 1914 Wilson pulled out American troops from Veracruz. Explaining his approach in a press briefing at the time of the US military withdrawal, Wilson underscored that "a situation arose that made it necessary for the dignity of the United States that we should take some decisive step; and the main thing to accomplish was a vital thing. We got Huerta. That was the end of Huerta. That was what I had in mind. It could not be done without taking Vera Cruz."

Yet Wilson's completion of his own goals should not obscure the fact that Carranza's strength was more critical to Huerta's departure than anything stemming from President Wilson's actions. In order to carry out the ouster of Huerta, Carranza had brokered alliances with members of the military, such as Alvaro Obregón, and regional strongmen, including Francisco "Pancho" Villa of Chihuahua and Emiliano Zapata of Morelos. Despite his efforts, Carranza's tenure as de facto president met immediate resistance. Zapata and Villa, his former aides, broke with the Constitutionalist movement, leading regional insurgencies against Carranza's central government. Zapata, intent on land distribution, waged guerrilla warfare in the South. Meanwhile, Villa blasted Carranza for "the sale of our country" to the gringos and excoriated Wilson as the "evangelical professor" intent on ensuring Mexico's descension to a "vassal" state.

The situation went from bad to worse. Villa warned Wilson that Mexican soil would be "a tomb for thrones, crowns, and traitors." As Villa and his vaunted División del Norte army broke away from Carranza's Constitutionalist movement, Villa would become increasingly violent and anti-American, especially in 1915 and 1916. Notably, Wilson had initially supported Villa until he was moved to take a new stance by brazen anti-US violence as well as División del Norte battlefield defeats by Carranza's forces like the one at the Battle of Celaya in April 1915. In one instance, *villistas* murdered American technical workers on a train in northern Mexico, leading Anglo-Americans in El Paso to riot against the city's Mexicans. In March 1916 the emboldened Villa and upward of five hundred of his men raided Columbus, New Mexico, just three miles from the US–Mexico border, the first such attack on American soil since 1814. The ambush killed roughly ten American soldiers and eight civilians, and the town was torched.

Punitive Measures

Soon after Villa's cold-blooded Columbus raid, "images of horror and chaos were splashed across the newspapers across the United States." As during the Veracruz spat two years prior, men volunteered to go south to protect US territory and honor. Under tremendous political pressure, President Wilson quickly approved General John "Black Jack" Pershing as the commander of the American Punitive Expedition into the northern Mexican state of Chihuahua in an attempt to catch the elusive Mexican bandit, a campaign that began in March 1916. While wary of the prospect of a general war with Mexico,

President Woodrow Wilson addressing a joint session of Congress in which he
sought authorization to use military force against Mexico after the Tampico Affair of
early 1914 during the Mexican Revolution. (Library of Congress Prints and
Photographs Division, Washington, DC)

which nonetheless almost erupted, the War Department did not set limits on
the depth of Pershing's penetration.

The patriotic fervor of an American contemporary, Mary Means Scott, can be
sensed as she witnessed the American military force heading across the border:

> Early, at the border, marked by a barbed-wire fence, families began to
> gather. . . . We watched for hours, it seemed, as the horses and riders
> passed in a giant parade: flags and guidons flying; pistols at the waist,
> sabres at the saddle, all enveloped in a canopy of dust. There was ap-
> plause, whistles, waves, and shouts of "goodbye" as friends came into
> view. Then men and boys volunteered much advice on what to do with
> Pancho Villa when caught. It was a great exodus—an historic hour. The
> might of the United States army departing on a punitive expedition to
> right a wrong visited upon an unsuspecting border town—the cavalry to
> the rescue! It was a thrilling sight to us.

It was perhaps inevitable that once the Punitive Expedition led by Pershing failed to quickly nab the wily Villa, the American invasion would cause a deep political row between Washington and Mexico City. This was largely because Mexican public sentiment was overwhelmingly opposed to the presence of American troops on their soil. As one observer put it, this nation much humiliated before the gringos was "about as eager to help the Americans in capturing their hero as were the people of Sherwood Forest to help the Sheriff of Nottingham capture Robin Hood."

As the campaign wore on, friction grew between the US troops and the Carrancistas, the federal government troops who at least initially had been tense allies. Following Pershing's orders, Captain Charles T. Boyd ordered an aggressive march through the town of Carrizal, Chihuahua, in mid-June 1916. The Carrancista commander of the town refused entry, knowing he had hundreds of men in well-defended positions to back up his intransigence, not including the numerous armed civilians who were also willing to take on the gringo invaders. Boyd ordered the inferior American forces to attack. In the ensuing fight on June 21, which lasted two hours, ten Americans, including all of the officers, were killed and twenty-three taken prisoner.

Inside the United States there was also a growing sense that US forces should not only capture the elusive bandit Villa but also expand the mission to teach the Mexicans a lesson. Echoing the jingoism of the USS *Maine* era, editorials pushed for a hard-line approach. Hearst's *New York Journal* was both indicative and causative of the rising American fervor: "Is it not the time for soldiers of the U.S. to do something PERMANENT? . . . Nothing worthwhile will be accomplished by occasional "punitive expeditions." . . . The way to IMPRESS the Mexicans is to REPRESS the Mexicans. . . . The way to begin is to say to them: 'We are no longer planning to catch this bandit or that. We are GOING INTO MEXICO. And as far as we GO, we'll stay.' "

In response to the demand to avenge the episode at Carrizal as well as other humiliations the War Department ordered General Frederick Funston to seize all international bridges across the Rio Grande in order to prepare for a full-scale US invasion of Mexico. But while he too was frustrated with Carranza, Wilson knew that an all-out war with Mexico was the last thing the United States needed at the time. Germany, not Mexico, was the real threat, and his military force needed to be ready to battle the European power. Thus the commander in chief ordered his men to effectively lie low to lessen the chance that the US troops would engage Carrancistas without appearing to have retreated in defeat. Thus while Pershing's force remained in Mexico for another seven months, the hunt for Pancho Villa had all but ended.

The Punitive Expedition lasted less than a year, from March 1916 to January 1917. Pershing's troops defeated the Villistas in the few major skirmishes or battles, but despite these tactical victories the campaign was a miserable failure. Instead of capturing or killing Villa, the Americans enhanced his strength and aura in Mexico. His depleted band of four hundred men swelled to perhaps five thousand fighters during that short period. What's more, Pershing's expedition repeatedly ended up clashing with Carranza's federal forces, which came close to sparking a broader war. And so while short-lived, the cat-and-mouse conflict had profound impacts on international relations and the internal politics of the Mexican revolutions. The Punitive Expedition's failure to capture Villa convinced Germany that the US Army was too weak to have an impact in World War I, emboldening the Germans to unleash unrestricted submarine warfare against the United States, What's more, they sent the infamous Zimmermann Telegram to Mexico in January 1917, which attempted to persuade Mexico to enter the fray on the side of the Axis powers and wage war against the United States.

Wilson had de facto recognized the government of Carranza in 1915, but the war in Europe and the Zimmermann gambit persuaded Wilson that he needed to go further to guarantee the neutrality of his southern neighbor. On August 31, 1917, Wilson set the relationship between Mexico and the US on a formal footing by a de jure recognition of Carranza's government.

How, then, should one understand the Wilson administration's policy toward Mexico? Wilson's desire to avoid intervention and find alternatives to war ultimately ran against his equally strong conviction that Latin American governments should be democratic. Rather than welcome the relative peace and stability that General Huerta provided, as many European countries did, Wilson failed to recognize the Mexican despot. The ultimate involvement by the United States in the removal of Huerta (albeit not the most important actor in his ouster) set off a series of events resulting in even greater US involvement in Mexico, driven in large part by Wilson's failed attempt to capture Pancho Villa. Indeed, this period reveals the oftentimes marked difference between stated policy and actions as well as between ideal goals and outcomes.

13 • Hunting Sandino

Goodness gracious. I don't think any time we've ever gone anywhere and
acted in the capacity of a policeman that we've been overly popular.
—Lieutenant General Edward A. Craig, USMC (ret.)

Intervention!

The three longest and most complicated US interventions in the period
under discussion here—Nicaragua (1912–33), Haiti (1915–34), and the Dominican Republic (1916–24)—started out as limited incursions to safeguard
US geostrategic interests: the United States Navy was under orders to control
the crucial shipping passages in the Caribbean Basin, including those to the
newly opened Panama Canal. Yet those incursions morphed into full-fledged
occupations. To varying degrees, US officers and diplomats took over key
functions of these three states—less so in Nicaragua, more so in Haiti, and
totally in the Dominican Republic, where the United States led a military government.

Contrary to how the story is sometimes told, a good number of locals, elites
and otherwise, initially welcomed the interventions or even believed the occupations were preferable to the chaos that appeared endemic to their societies. But there was also plenty of suspicion and pushback. One Haitian recalled
that he fled when he saw the USS *Washington* and the flotilla of launches un-
loading troops: "You only had to see them, with their weaponry, their massive,
menacing appearance, to understand both that they came to do harm to our
country and that resistance was futile." In 1920 Fabio Fiallo, a noted Dominican intellectual and the editor of *Las Noticias,* was sentenced to one year in

prison and fined $2,500 for his article "Listen All," which called the United States a "most cruel civilization that, bayonet at the ready, invaded our backyard on a dark night of betrayal, surprise, and cowardliness, and that has caused us countless tears, countless homes in ashes and countless starving orphans. . . . The order is RESISTANCE; RESISTANCE until victory or death!"

In addition to the numerous insurrections that rose to challenge US rule— or that of its domestic allies—the US occupations sparked international solidarity movements that were as central to the struggle as the armed insurgents. As one Dominican activist told a group in New York City, "On the international scene there has now appeared a new actor—solidarity. No nation, no people, can realize by itself its destiny." Haiti was a particular concern for a wide range of African American leaders, from communists such as Cecil Briggs of the African Black Brotherhood and the educator Robert Moton of the Tuskegee Institute to the founding feminists of the International Council of Women of the Darker Races, erected in 1919 to investigate the plight of Haitian women and children. Visitors to the "black republic" included some of the "brightest lights" of the Harlem Renaissance and 1920s civil rights movement—Langston Hughes, William Scott, and Zora Neale Hurston. The National Association for the Advancement of Colored People (NAACP) likely contributed most to making Haiti a domestic American cause. From 1915 onward the organization's cofounder, W. E. B. Du Bois, whose grandfather was Haitian, railed against the occupation. Du Bois even urged President Wilson to send African Americans instead of white troops if an occupation had to occur, and he called on "we ten million Negroes" to write the president.

Resistance rang through the government buildings of Washington as well. One senator, William Borah, who in 1913 had opposed the US troop presence in Nicaragua, spearheaded the anti-occupation movement. By the 1920s Borah had grown suspicious of "dark financial motivations" driving the US interventions. As he wrote to the civil rights leader Moorfield Story in 1922, "It is positively discouraging to know the things which are being done in the name of Americanism. In my opinion, there is very little difference between Japan's actions in Korea and our actions in Santo Domingo and Haiti."

Antipathy on the part of US occupiers themselves was also quick to take root once the complexities of administering a recalcitrant country became clear. One US customs administrator privately bemoaned to a superior, "All ideas relative to assisting or advising [Haitians] in running their own government, which ideas I was inclined to favor at first, I now regard as entirely hopeless. There is not a man in the Government who is concerned with anything except his private gain and finding places for his friends. Force and force alone can control the situation." Or, as the marine company commander William Upshur described conditions in a letter to his mother in March 1916, "The natives down here are all bad, and irresponsible and we are having trouble with them constantly."

Ultimately, the Dominican and Haitian insurrections against US rule failed, but in Nicaragua the tenacity of the guerrilla leader Augusto Sandino won out.

Boots on the Ground in Nicaragua

Nicaragua was the most protracted and controversial US occupation, lasting for more than twenty years, and was characterized by the hunt for Augusto Sandino in the 1920s. The search for Sandino was similar to the 1916 Punitive Expedition to nab the dastardly Pancho Villa in the remote lairs of Chihuahua, another instance in which America's huge, asymmetrical power advantage did not ensure success.

But US entanglement in Nicaragua had commenced much earlier than Sandino, a story that merits a description of the historical context. During the nineteenth century the potential for an interoceanic canal across Nicaragua got Washington's rapt interest, but when Washington picked Panama for the canal route in 1902, José Santos Zelaya, the fervently anti-American head of state, solicited Japan and Germany to dig a route through Nicaragua. Zelaya's move infuriated US officials, who were loath to see those two foreign powers gain any ascendancy in the isthmus (a case of protective imperialism in action).

The domestic context in Nicaragua itself was also tense. Zelaya's Liberal Party was locked in a bitter rivalry with the Conservative Party during the first few years of the new century, with arguments frequently erupting in violence. For better or worse, Washington often interposed US diplomats and marines to serve as purported judges to determine which side would emerge victorious in any particular dispute. The US officials were neither altruistic nor impartial in their officiating. Rather, they almost always intervened to resolve the events in a way that promoted US security and economic interests.

In October 1909 an anti-Zelaya revolt broke out in Bluefields, a port town on the country's Caribbean coast. Bluefields was the provincial center for banana, rubber, and gold-mining companies, most of which were controlled by US, British, and other foreign entities. Fed up with Zelaya's venality and virulent anti-yanqui-ism, US citizens in the locale backed the rebellion. Guided by an alienated Conservative Party official, Juan José Estrada, the rebellion soon had to confront the federal troops that Zelaya dispatched from Managua. In the subsequent fighting Zelaya's forces apprehended two American mercenaries working for Estrada as demolition experts. The two men, Lee Roy Cannon and Leonard Groce, were given a military trial and summarily executed.

Back in Washington, the Taft administration broke off relations with the recalcitrant Zelaya government. When it became apparent to the Taft administration, however, that Estrada was unable to hold Bluefields, it was forced to look again at the developing upheaval. Taft called in the United States Marine Corps, headed up by the formidable but at this point largely anonymous officer Smedley Butler. Soon after the arrival of the marines in Bluefields on May 27, 1910, Zelaya was forced from the presidency, and an interim Liberal regime took charge. In August Estrada's forces were in Managua, and he soon named himself *presidente*. US Secretary of State Philander Knox, the devout promoter of all things Dollar Diplomacy, quickly recognized the new Conservative administration. Needless to say, the United States had become firmly embedded in the country's affairs.

As early as 1911 the US-sponsored Estrada was forced to resign by the minister of war and political adversary Luis Mena, a situation that elevated Vice President Adolfo Díaz to power. But he too was confronted with Mena's threat. In another instance of the supposedly invaded asking for invasion, Díaz asked for US boots on the ground to confront the threat. Like magic, a force of twenty-seven hundred leathernecks landed on both the Pacific and Caribbean coasts and quelled the revolt in Managua and its surroundings. A legation of around one hundred marines was kept in the country for the next thirteen years. US military involvement in this era was protracted but limited, although Washington continued to influence outcomes in Nicaragua by, for example, promoting one politician over another in elections. Regarding the election of the Conservative Party candidate Emiliano Chamorro in 1916, Smedley Butler remarked, "Our candidates always win."

Exit, for Now

In the aftermath of the ultimately victorious but bloody and increasingly controversial involvement of the United States in World War I and with the occupations of Haiti and the Dominican Republic seemingly never-ending, US officials did not want to risk becoming embroiled in a quagmire in Nicaragua. Better to simply claim victory, remove the marines, and resist the temptation to resolve yet another Liberal–Conservative skirmish. Crucially, the Nicaraguans no longer owed large sums to US banks, a key factor in any withdrawal from "banana republics," the derogatory term used by O. Henry in his 1904 novel on Honduras titled *Cabbages and Kings*. But the question remained: How to exit in an orderly fashion? US thinking turned to the model used in the Dominican Republic and Haiti: hold elections and stand up an indigenous national guard.

Unfortunately, the success of this model regarding the national guards had been mixed, to say the least. These constabularies were intended to be apolitical, professional centralizing security forces which would break the grip of the regional *caudillos* (strongmen). But the reality often failed to meet the ambition. Marine trainers regularly complained that discipline would break down in the poorly funded ranks once a marine officer left. Many from the elite ranks were also loath to obey the fledgling forces. Most critically, the constabularies ignored repeated warnings against politicization. An American official characterized the Dominican Guard as an "absolute failure" and claimed that the main problem was that "every Dominican is more or less under the influence of some political party whose leaders would do anything to injure American prestige in the Island." Ultimately, the constabularies in all three countries became institutions of repression and tyranny that endured for decades following the US departure from each country.

The other proposal—holding elections—also proved problematic in Nicaragua's wildly unstable and polarized political environment. In 1925 the small legation of marines left Nicaragua, by which time Emiliano Chamorro was back in the presidency after a coup sent the Liberal president Juan Sacasa into exile. But Chamorro's dilemma was that he lacked Washington's support, so he wound up being replaced by another Liberal leader, Adolfo Díaz. Political instability ensued as various actors jockeyed for power, specifically Sacasa, who returned to claim his previous post. US forces were deployed at that point, once again to forestall Sacasa's ascension—Washington was not thrilled about Sacasa's cordial ties with the revolutionary regime in Mexico—and to protect US citizens and property. President Calvin Coolidge's secretary of state, Frank Kellogg, sent Colonel Henry L. Stimson to Nicaragua to find a way out of the Díaz versus Sacasa dilemma, which could easily have turned into a civil war. Kellogg told Simpson, "I want you to go down there, and if you can see a way to clean up that mess, I want you to do it."

By April 1927 Stimson had worked with Díaz to produce a compromise accord with the Liberal rebel forces. Stimsom met Sacasa's military guru, General

José María Moncada, near the Tipitapa River, which connects the country's two main inland bodies of water, Lake Nicaragua and Lake Managua. The deliberations produced a fresh accord, the Espino Negro, which addressed a multitude of issues intended to pacify the nation: Díaz would remain as president until US-supervised voting took place in 1928, while the Liberal generals would cease their insurrection and participate in a general amnesty. Díaz's conservatives were generally supportive of the accord as it kept them in power—at least for the moment. More vital, though, was the support Moncada lent to the agreement, which was no doubt assisted, in turn, by Stimson's thinly veiled threat to Moncada: "I have instructions to attain [peace] willingly or by force." Stimson's diplomacy seemed to have ended Nicaragua's political game of musical chairs—and, almost by definition, the deeper US military involvement that such continued fighting would have inevitably provoked. Eleven of Moncada's military lieutenants agreed to abide by the terms of Stimson's plan and lay down their guns. But one rebel commander, Augusto Sandino, did not cooperate.

Marines Meet Their Match

Sandino was likely born in 1895 as the illegitimate child of a middle-class coffee landowner and his indigenous maid. The young, bright-eyed Nicaraguan traveled across Central America during the 1920s "toiling at working-class jobs." His most ideologically salient time was probably in 1923 in the mightily capitalist Standard Oil refineries in the states of Veracruz and Tampico—sort of the Mexican version of Louisiana—where he "imbibed a variety of intellectual and spiritual traditions," embracing even yoga and vegetarianism. Sandino was also greatly influenced by anarcho-syndicalism, then the most prominent leftist ideology in a still-tumultuous Mexico. Sandino stole global syndicalism's colors, red and black, for his future flag in his campaign against the US Marines and their Nicaraguan toadies. After the oil fields and a return to his native soil in 1927, Sandino, coordinating with Moncada, began steering his own force against the central government in the mountainous Las Segovias. Over time, his military organization, the eponymous Sandinistas, resisted the US forces backing Managua; the US Marines were, to use his words, "blonde beasts," "degenerate pirates," "morphine addicts," and "the enemy of our race and language," among other epithets.

Between 1927 and 1932 US forces hunted for Sandino and his loyal forces to no avail, which prompted increasing scrutiny of the entire American effort back home, echoing the travails that plagued the Punitive Expedition. Senator

Burton K. Wheeler of Montana blasted President Coolidge for instituting a "dishonorable program of brutal bluff and bully." He added, "What right have we to send our boys into a foreign country to stamp out banditry? If we are to ask them to stamp out banditry, let's send them to Chicago to stamp it out there. As far as I'm concerned, I wouldn't sacrifice the lifeblood of one American boy for all the damn Nicaraguans." The noted satirist Will Rogers reflected the skeptical sense of many Americans with this pithy aphorism: "Why are we in Nicaragua and what the Hell are we doing there?"

Amid the brutal attacks on marines, Sandino fared surprisingly well in the US media, in part because he realized that he could sell his resistance as an American-style republican campaign. The itinerant journalist Carleton Beals was the first US newspaperman to interview Sandino, holed up in the rugged northern mountains. Here is one of Beals's dispatches:

> "Let me repeat," declared the General [Sandino]. "We are no more bandits than was [George] Washington. If the American public had not become calloused to justice and to the elemental rights of mankind, it would not so easily forget its own past when a handful of ragged soldiers marched through the snow leaving blood-tracks behind them to win liberty and independence. If their consciences had not become dulled by their scramble for wealth, Americans would not so easily forget the lesson that, sooner or later, every nation, however weak, achieves freedom, and that every abuse of power hastens the destruction of the one who wields it."

Such pronouncements were part of a conscious, effective public-relations strategy, Sandino commenting that "we learned the tremendous value of publicity in terms of world opinion." An acolyte of the guerrilla leader explained it this way: "Every time there is a battle, every time marines are killed, the attention of the United States and the world is drawn to what is going on in Nicaragua."

Glowing portrayals of Sandino in the media gradually motivated a shifting belief that it might actually be the US occupiers, not the Sandinistas, who were the true bandits in the conflict. In 1928 activists assembled near the White House to protest the occupation. Personal letters sent to marines sailing for Nicaragua urged them not to fight and instead join Sandino's forces. Sandino's half-brother, Socrates, made anti-US campaign speeches across the US. Some newspapers and magazines solicited funds for medical supplies or implored readers to "Enlist with Sandino" and "Defeat the War against Nicaragua." Senator J. Thomas Heflin of Alabama compared Sandino to the Founding Fathers.

US marines pose with Sandinista flag, circa 1932. (Library of Congress Prints and Photographs Division, Washington, DC)

"Sandino crying for liberty, begging for the deliverance of his country from the invader, sounds like the cries of our fathers made in the days of the Revolution," he argued. "We are seeking this man out to kill him for fighting for principles that we fought for in 1776." Sandino became a shining knight for the anti-imperialist, anticapitalist ideological left in the United States and around the globe.

Opposition to US involvement swelled in tandem with Sandino's popularity and the growing sense that the US forces were fighting a dirty war against him. In one account, the Coolidge administration had "used the armed forces of the United States to destroy human life, to burn villages, to bomb innocent women and children from the air." In truth, savagery was committed on both sides. In one episode, Sandino insisted upon an assortment of sentences for Nicaraguans caught collaborating with the marines or the National Guard. One punishment was the *corte de chaleco* (the "vest cut"), whereby victims' heads and arms were cut off and sword markings were carved on their chest. A Sandinista ode extolled beheadings and other forms of maiming; Sandino's seal, used on his letters and forged coins, featured a Sandinista beheading a marine.

Student audience listening to Peace Day address by General Smedley Butler, University of California, Berkeley, California, 1939. After more than thirty years as a marine with deployments to the Philippines, China, Central America, and the Caribbean, Butler became a vocal critic of US imperialist "Banana Wars." (Library of Congress, Prints and Photographs Division, Washington, DC)

US Withdrawal, Enter Somoza

President Coolidge sent Brigadier General Frank McCoy, "one of these iron-willed, super logical, single-track types whose stern jaw carried not an ounce of compromise," to oversee the key 1928 presidential election agreed in the Espino Negro accord. To preempt fraud and smooth the way for the much-desired US departure, just under a thousand marines and sailors observed the voting. Sandino wanted nothing to do with these sham elections, but he was not in a position to prevent the vote from taking place. Remarkably, the Liberal former rebel general José María Moncada won the vote.

Relatively free and fair only in relation to the nation's long-standing chaos, the much-anticipated presidential election gave Washington enough of a cover for an imminent withdrawal. Marine officers, however, feared that a precipitous departure would create a power vacuum and propound the cycle of chaos; it turned out they were right to be wary. After leaving Nicaragua in May 1929 for a year's recuperation in Mexico, Sandino returned, and in late December 1930 Sandinistas attacked a marine patrol outside Ocotal, killing eight leathernecks.

By this time President Herbert Hoover (1929–33) was in the White House and even more insistent on a full US withdrawal. This stance was part of his new "good neighbor" policy regarding Latin America, perhaps inspired by the seven-week tour he had taken of ten Latin American countries as president-elect in 1928. At a stop in Buenos Aires protestors against the Nicaragua occupation unfurled a banner that read, "Long Live Sandino! Long Live Nicaragua! Down with North American Imperialism!" In his State of the Union address on December 3, 1929, Hoover referenced US troops deployed in Haiti, Nicaragua, and China. "We do not," he said, "wish to be represented abroad in such a manner."

In this instance at least, Sandino's fortitude appeared to be weakening Washington's resolve to continue the fight in Nicaragua, which is what underpinned the decision for a phased withdrawal still in progress in 1932, when another Nicaraguan vote was slated to take place. Weighing on Hoover was an impatient Congress eager to cut off funding for the elections. In the end the marines and navy were still able to oversee the election, and, as in 1928, the US goal was to see the democratic election bolster the central government, embarrass Sandino politically, and expedite a *permanent* US withdrawal.

The Liberal Juan Sacasa and the Conservative Adolfo Díaz competed yet again in the election on November 6, 1932—and Sacasa won. But the clashes between Sandinistas and the marine-trained National Guard troops continued. Fatefully, Sacasa picked Anastasio "Tacho" Somoza García to be the new first commander of the Guard. US military trainers and diplomats were optimistic. The marine officer Matthew Hanna said of Somoza, "I know of no one who will labor as intelligently or conscientiously to maintain the nonpartisan character of the Guard or will be as efficient in all manners connected with the administration and command of the Force." Somoza subsequently commenced talks with Sandino, but Sandino's disdain for Somoza was no secret. At a dinner event in February 1934 Sandino was picked up by Guardia soldiers and executed per Somoza's instructions.

With the death of their vaunted commander the residual Sandinista rebels collapsed. In 1936 Somoza seized power entirely, setting off roughly forty years of autocratic rule. Far from being a pillar of the rule of law in Nicaragua, as US officials had hoped, Somoza soon instituted the Guard as his family's personal shock troops.

A Mixed Legacy

Evaluating the legacy of these interventions is a complex and fraught endeavor. At their respective heights, each of the interventions in Haiti, the Dominican Republic, and Nicaragua entailed a significant number, some two thousand to five thousand, of mostly Marine Corps troops, but they were certainly not occupations on the scale of the Philippines after 1898 or Vietnam or Iraq. Washington's costs were also relatively low: fewer than several hundred killed (several thousand on the resisters' side fell); but the $100 million ($1.5 billion in 2018) price tag for all three occupations far outweighed any profit from the investments they might have protected given that in 1913 the three countries received less than 1 percent of US investments in the Caribbean Basin. Indeed, while not precipitous, Washington's costs of occupation, both political and economic, grew over the 1920s. As one US ambassador remembered, "Armed intervention in Haiti and Nicaragua kept us in hot water not only with other countries of Latin America but also with a sizable sector of our own public." Even big business, usually predisposed to advocate for and benefit from gunboat diplomacy, began to catch on to the fact that the occupations were bad for the bottom line. One American corporate chief lectured President Hoover that "[Nicaraguans] do not want order maintained by marines any more than would Californians want order maintained by Japanese soldiers." The "expansive shift" in the US public's awareness, fueled largely by activism, likely helped end the occupations far sooner than would have been the case otherwise. This built on US officials' existing frustration with the chronic instability that Washington's enlightened handiwork could not correct.

From the occupied nations' side, there were a few positives. The US built roads, sewers, hospitals, and schools, and the national debt was managed responsibly. In fact, even some of the invaded acknowledged benefits of the

American occupation. A Dominican told a visitor in 1928, "You taught us how to work." As the Haitian president Sténio Vincent divulged, "The Occupation very sensibly marked Haitian mentality. She impressed upon it a tidier and more practical conception of life, a more developed and surer taste for material comfort, a greater need for peace, security, and work." But the costs were immense. Perhaps the most salient criticism of the occupations, according to the diplomatic historian Alan McPherson, is that the political culture in all three countries continued to be "anti-democratic, self-interested, and ruinous to the nation" and "largely unchanged from pre-occupation days." It might have been the case that the three nations were resigned to political chaos and tyranny with or without American occupations: it is impossible to say.

It is also problematic to generalize from the experience of these interventions to broader maxims about US foreign policy. McPherson's central lesson from the interventions in Haiti, the Dominican Republic, and Nicaragua is that "occupation is a folly to be avoided at all costs." But at the same time—and not denying the many ignominious parts of these three backyard episodes—the post–World War II occupations of Japan or Germany might argue for a more open-minded approach.

14 • Sumner Welles Goes to Havana

Uncle Sam as Good Neighbor

In his March 4, 1933, inaugural address, President Franklin D. Roosevelt made a declaration of a new approach to foreign policy that would have seismic implications for hemispheric ties: "In the field of world policy I would dedicate this nation to the policy of the good neighbor—the neighbor who resolutely respects himself, and, because he does so, respects the rights of others."

At a diplomatic conference in Montevideo, Uruguay, in December 1933, ironically just months after Washington almost intervened in Cuba, Secretary of State Cordell Hull, theretofore reluctant, came around to supporting a proclamation pushed stridently by other governments for the preceding decade: "No state has the right to intervene in the external or internal affairs of another." That same month FDR doubled down on Hull's Uruguay rhetoric: "The definite policy of the United States from now on is one opposed to armed intervention."

But the practical task of implementing the shift to the Good Neighbor Policy at times proved far more difficult than simply issuing the lofty rhetoric of hemispheric understanding and solidarity. Roosevelt oversaw the final withdrawal of US marines from Nicaragua in 1933—a very good neighborly thing to do—but transitions proved more challenging in the aforementioned Cuba crisis. And although many applauded the evolution from bygone eras of interventionism—especially that of protective imperialism after 1898—not all conditions proved malleable in the hands of history. Time and again, from the delicate handling of the 1933 Cuba crisis to the importance US officials gave to myriad interhemispheric conferences, the Good Neighbor Policy may have shaped US actions in Latin America, but it failed to push the US to relinquish its standing realist position of acting in its national security interests.

"Latin America." Editorial cartoon by Herblock shows Uncle Sam shaking the hand of a handsome man labeled "Latin America." The cartoon may reflect Herblock's approval of Roosevelt's Good Neighbor Policy, in which the United States renounced intervention in the affairs of the Latin American republics. (Library of Congress, Prints & Photographs Division, Art Wood Collection of Cartoon & Caricature, LC-DIG-ppmsca-07160)

Getting Rid of Machado

FDR had a problem. The new president, fresh off the campaign trail where he promoted his Latin America strategy through his inauguration speech to the country, was immediately faced with the question of yet another gunboat diplomacy–style hostile intervention. Cuba was under the tyrannical grip of the despised dictator Gerardo Machado y Morales. Born in 1871, Machado was the youngest general in the Cubans' independence battle against Spain, which culminated in the invasion of Cuba by the United States in 1898 and in the subsequent occupation, which formally ended with the 1901 Platt Amendment. Running on a clever platform of "Water, roads, and schools," Machado was elected and took office in 1925 with a campaign promise of modernizing the poverty-stricken country. This project included a series of sizable public works such as the seven-hundred-mile highway connecting Pinar del Río in the west of the country with Santiago de Cuba on the distant eastern tip.

In 1928 the increasingly corrupt Machado was reelected in a vote in which he was the only candidate. His abominable secret police, La Porra, hunted down political opponents. But that did not forestall the growing radicalization of assorted groups of students, trade unions, and even clandestine networks of well-educated Cubans, notably one called the *abecedarios* (ABCs).

When combined with the island's catastrophic economic climate—the Great Depression had caused a plunge in the vital export of sugar—Machado's repression and the growing insurrection against this iron-fisted rule was pushing Cuba toward outright war. That eventuality was not lost on an increasingly alarmed US public. So how to help ensure a favorable outcome in Cuba without resorting to landing the marines? The commander in chief's twofold strategy was hatched by his secretary of state, Cordell Hull: bring stability to Cuba through a new trade pact to jump-start sugar exports and by extension save the desperate sugar plantation workers whose already pitiful wage had plunged by half since 1929; and get rid of the thug Machado through diplomatic means.

Fortuitously, Roosevelt had the perfect individual to dispatch to Havana to fix the mess and preclude an embarrassing and potentially very costly relapse of gunboat diplomacy: Benjamin Sumner Welles, a seasoned Latin American diplomat educated at the patrician New England schools of Groton and Harvard and a personal friend of the First Couple. Before Roosevelt entered the White House, Welles had sent the president-elect a note outlining his notions for a new, Good Neighbor–style approach to the region: "The creation and maintenance of the American Continent must be regarded as a keystone of our foreign policy." This lofty ideal would be accomplished by shunning endemic interventionism and embracing lower tariffs to boost trade. The approach opposed the protectionism most notoriously embraced in the 1930 Smoot–Hawley Tariff Act, which had set the price for imports of Cuban sugar at the pitiable level of two cents per pound.

In early May 1933, less than a month after being appointed as Roosevelt's top envoy to Latin America, Welles was reassigned as the American ambassador to Cuba, instructed to immediately assuage popular unrest. Roosevelt's envoy was sobered by what he encountered: "The situation [in Cuba] frankly is rather more precarious than even I had anticipated," he wrote to a colleague. "There is a tension in the atmosphere and a bitterness of feeling generally which I have not previously experienced except during the brief weeks I was in Honduras at the time of the revolution in 1924."

Welles wasted little time before sitting with Machado to negotiate sensitive bilateral issues the US envoy hoped would result in a "gradual return to the Cuban people [of civil rights]" and to lay the groundwork for "fair and uncontrolled elections" the following year. The carrot was the US offer of a reciprocal trade agreement, which Welles explained could not be granted "so long as this political unrest continues." This did little to sway the headstrong Machado, himself appearing implacable. Responding to one of Welles's late July proconstitutional reform pleas, the Cuban head of state said, "The re-establishment of the guarantees [suspended by Machado] is a prerogative of the President of Cuba and will be done when the President considers it necessary."

Welles's magnanimity didn't entirely define his talks with Machado; he repeatedly waved the big stick of a yanqui intervention, even if privately Welles had reservations about wielding military force: "I cannot admit the policy of intervention. . . . Intervention would at once create suspicion and distrust." Interestingly, while Welles had adopted a hard-line stance directly with Machado, Roosevelt was more cautious, worrying that a heavy-handed approach could backfire: "We cannot be in the position of saying to Machado, 'You have to get out.' That would be obvious interference in the internal affairs of another nation."

As the scholars Philip Dur and Christopher Gilcrease have written, the genius of Welles's Cuban gambit is that "under the cover of mediation" he had "encouraged disaffection among politicians and army officers." The covert strategy of fomenting dissent via key Cuban political, military, and economic actors was a spectacular success. On August 12, only a few months after Welles had presented his ambassadorial credentials to Machado, the dictator was toppled through the combination of a wide-scale strike and military defections by soldiers like Fulgencio Batista. Machado departed for the Bahamas and never returned to power in Cuba. Welles, described by a relative as "subsisting mainly on coffee and cigarettes," was ecstatic, and the New York Times sung his praises, "At the age of 41 . . . [he] has brought off a difficult job with the aplomb of veteran."

Eager to place the stability of Cuba in the hands of what he considered capable leaders, Welles worked to ensure that his long-standing acquaintance, the pro-Washington Carlos Manuel de Céspedes, succeed Machado. Here one can see the extent of US hegemony as well as the authority of a single emissary: Welles was effectively governing Cuba alone in these pivotal weeks and months. "Owing to my intimate personal relationship with President Céspedes," he cabled to Washington, "and the very close relationship which I have formed during these past months with all the members of this Cabinet, I am now daily being requested for decisions on all matters affecting the Government of Cuba. These decisions range from questions of domestic policy and matters affecting the discipline of the Army to questions involving appointments in all branches of Government."

But Welles's bet on Céspedes proved to be a losing one. On September 4–5, 1933, a coup, the so-called Sergeants' Revolt, by junior military officers and, quickly, trade unions and student groups led by the University of Havana's Ramón Grau San Martín, ended Céspedes's brief presidency. It did not help Céspedes's fortunes that he was often photographed alongside Welles, the yanqui empire's controversial proconsul. Protestors in the Cuban capital burned the US envoy in effigy and chanted, "Down with Welles!"

Welles urged Washington to withhold recognition in order to signal to the island's opposition that Grau did not enjoy US support. Then Welles went further, echoing the calls of his pre–Good Neighbor predecessors. It was time for American boots on the ground, and Welles believed such action could be justified as part of the 1901 Platt Amendment. He cabled Washington on September 6: "What I propose would be a strictly limited intervention" entailing "the landing of a considerable force at Havana and lesser forces in certain of the most important ports of the Republic."

Yet Welles was acting under a president committed to pragmatism and nonintervention. FDR and Hull were not swayed by Welles's position, and the intervention never took place, although United States Navy ships did patrol menacingly off Cuban waters. Roosevelt explained to Welles the following day: "We feel very strongly that any promise, implied or otherwise, relating to what the United States will do under any circumstances is impossible; that it would be regarded as a breach of neutrality, as favoring one faction out of many, as attempting to set up a government which would be regarded by the whole world, and especially throughout Latin America, as a creation and creature of the American government. . . . [S]trict neutrality is of the essence."

The invasion debate was made moot when after a few months Grau resigned under relentless pressure from Welles-backed Fulgencio Batista, who

The dictator from Cuba arrives in Washington, DC. Colonel Fulgencio Batista was
met at Union Station by General Malin Craig, chief of staff of the US Army, who
invited the Cuban leader to the Capitol, and Undersecretary of State Sumner Welles.
Left to right: Welles, Batista, Craig, and the ambassador of Cuba, Pedro Fraga.
November 10, 1938. (Library of Congress, Prints and Photographs Division,
Washington, DC)

by then was already the real power behind the scenes. Batista was elected president in 1940, governing as a social reformer and even enjoying the support of
the Communist Party of Cuba. When his term ended in 1944, he relocated to
the United States but in 1952 returned to Cuba and seized power in a military
coup. He ruled as an autocrat until he himself was toppled by Fidel Castro's
Cuban Revolution.

Welles returned Stateside, where he spent the next few years trying to play
down the reputation that he was an interventionist. Keen to be perceived as
truly committed to the Good Neighbor approach, Washington sent Welles in
1934 to negotiate with Havana in order to remove the humiliating components of the bilateral relationship, such as conditions allowing US intervention outlined in the 1903 bilateral treaty (mandated by the Platt Amendment).

Secretary Welles was also a visible figure in hemispheric conferences through the Good Neighbor decade. He worked with Panama to consider adjustments to the infamous (at least in Latin America) 1903 Canal Treaty. The so-called Chaco War in 1935 that pitted Paraguay and Bolivia was mediated by a hemispheric peace meeting in Argentina the following year, Welles once again assuming a key diplomatic role. But his prior and subsequent multilateralism does not change the fact that in September 1933 Welles was urging his superiors to invade Cuba. If we are ever tempted to assume that Washington, either yesterday or today, always acts with a single voice and desire, the Welles versus Roosevelt/Hull disagreement will quickly disabuse us.

15 • Nuestro Petróleo

Today, just as seven decades ago, oil is the patrimony for all Mexicans, a
symbol of our sovereignty and an emblem of nationalism.
—Felipe Calderón, president of Mexico, 2008

Cuba wasn't the only nation to poke at President Franklin Roosevelt's Good
Neighbor Policy; Mexico also put FDR to the test when the populist president
Lázaro Cárdenas moved to nationalize US- and European-controlled petroleum assets inside the country. If Polk's actions toward Texas in the nineteenth century or Roosevelt's Big Stick policy in the early twentieth century
were to contribute to FDR's decision, conflict was sure to unfold. But FDR
was determined to make the Good Neighbor Policy salient, and that required
demonstrating that the US hegemonic presumption in the hemisphere was
over.

Prior to Cárdenas, Mexico was still emerging from the calamitous revolu-
tion that had begun in 1910 and involved two Wilsonian interventions: landing troops at the Gulf Coast port city of Tampico in 1914 and chasing after
Pancho Villa in 1916. For any self-respecting Mexican leader at the time,
Cárdenas included, building a one-party nationalistic regime—which would
eventually come to be known as the Institutional Revolutionary Party, or
PRI—to stand up to the United States was a cornerstone of political rhetoric.
In addition to political centralization, both petroleum and labor were inextricably linked to the revolution's consolidation in the 1920s and 1930s and
would prove to be more galvanizing than the most talented orators.

Mr. Cárdenas's Neighborhood

One of the myriad bitter facts of Mexico's decade of chaotic, destructive revolution was that it overlapped with an oil boom in the so-called Golden Belt near Tampico. After Edward L. Doheny discovered "black gold," he drilled his first hole in 1901. Rumor has it that the enterprising gringo from Los Angeles offered five pesos to any local who could successfully steer him to the tar pits, as every prospector worth his salt knew that pits meant oil. Here is one of Doheny's reflections: "We found a small conical-shaped hill . . . where bubbled a spring of oil, the sight of which caused us to forget all about the dreaded climate—its hot, humid atmosphere, its apparently incessant rains . . . the dense forest jungle which seems to grow up as fast as cut down."

By the mid-1920s, and despite the nation's ongoing political and social turmoil, Mexico was the world's second largest oil producer and held the largest reserves in Latin America. Still predominantly an agrarian country, almost all of the oil was sold to foreign markets, including the US, where in the early 1920s Mexican crude served one-fifth of the domestic market. During this time the Mexican Eagle Oil Company, owned by Royal Dutch/Shell after 1919, emerged in Mexico under the British industrialist and engineer Weetman Dickinson Pearson. Pearson wasn't entirely a foreigner. Active during President Porfirio Díaz's protracted autocratic era (1876–1911), the engineer had been enlisted by Díaz in 1889 to construct the Tehuantepec Railway linking the Pacific and Atlantic coasts. The railway ended up supporting key US-owned interests, including Standard Oil Company of New Jersey, today's ExxonMobil, and Standard Oil Company of California, today's Chevron. During the 1920s more than one hundred foreign-owned outfits were responsible for producing and selling over 90 percent of Mexico's nonrenewable natural resource.

Fine and dandy as it was for foreigners to exploit the rails and make a killing, the rub remained that Article 27 of Mexico's Constitution of 1917 explicitly gave ownership of subsoil to the nation. Both the Mexican government and corporations backed by the government finally came together with a late-1920s agreement whereby the foreign entities, unsettled by Article 27, maintained their rights in fields controlled before the 1917 promulgation. Despite the government's seeming pandering to foreign interests, the heightened nationalism of postrevolutionary Mexico further complicated matters. Widely loathed for their rapacious practices, foreign corporations became the target of labor organizations and strikes starting in the mid-1920s, specifically plaguing the refineries owned by the Mexican Eagle Oil Company. Factor in the Great Depression in the 1930s and a dampened international demand for petroleum—which, not surprisingly, depressed Mexico's production—and doing business in Mexico looked anything but enticing.

Enter Lázaro Cárdenas. Born on May 21, 1895, in the state of Michoacán, he was promoted quickly through the ranks during the revolution to become a general in the so-called Constitutionalist Army. Lieutenant Colonel Cárdenas spent a few years in Tampico during the war and witnessed paramilitaries organized by the oil company terrorizing the local population. Years later he rhetorically asked his Mexican compatriots, "In how many of the villages bordering on the oil fields is there a hospital, or school or social center, or a sanitary water supply, or an athletic field, or even an electric plant fed by the millions of cubic meters of natural gas allowed to go to waste?"

Fueled by injustices witnessed, Cárdenas wasted no time after assuming the presidency in 1934 in boldly moving on the nationalist card, not by oil but by land. His policies confiscated tens of millions of privately held lands, including massive estates and foreign-owned properties, given to the landless as *ejidos,* or communal land plots. By August 1935, with the full backing of Cárdenas's government, almost two dozen disparate labor syndicates organized into the National Petroleum Workers Syndicate. Oil workers, now in a better negotiating position vis-à-vis the mighty oil firms, acted accordingly, effectively striking in 1937 until Cárdenas brokered a deal to address the impasse. The Mexican labor bureau set a deadline of March 7, 1938, for the foreign outfits to conform to the higher pay advocated by the militant unions: a decision recently upheld by the Mexican Supreme Court.

When the multinational companies dismissed the terms and the deadline passed, Cárdenas took the crisis into his own hands. Terrified that the oil sector might disintegrate, Cárdenas, in a fit of patriotic fervor, declared on March 18 the expropriation of almost all the private- and foreign-owned petroleum corporations active in Mexico, in effect nationalizing Mexico's oil. In the president's words, "It is the sovereignty of the nation which is thwarted through the maneuvers of foreign capitalists who, forgetting they have formed themselves into Mexican companies, now attempt to elude the mandates and avoid the obligations placed upon them by the authorities of this country." The headline in the influential newspaper *El Nacional* read, "OIL COMPANIES REFUSE TO ABIDE BY SUPREME COURT DECISION, THE GOVERNMENT WILL FOLLOW THE PATH OF THE LAW." Cárdenas also created the new state-run Petróleos Mexicanos, or PEMEX. Mexicans took to the streets to celebrate.

"For Sale. Gracias!" In 1938 President Lázaro Cárdenas of Mexico nationalized the foreign oil companies. Many countries, including the United States and Great Britain, retaliated by boycotting Mexican oil, but the onset of World War II resulted in the abandonment of the boycotts and an agreement by Mexico to provide compensation. (Library of Congress, Prints and Photographs Division, Washington, DC)

In an effort to placate the foreign oil companies Cárdenas emphasized that expropriation entailed not confiscation but compensation. To help fund the nationalization, Mexicans of all social classes rushed to donate money, jewelry, "even homely domestic objects, chickens, turkeys, and pigs," wrote the historian Howard Cline. Here was Cárdenas's encouragement: "I ask the nation to furnish the necessary moral and material support to face the consequences of a decision which we, of our own free will, would neither have sought nor desired." March 18 is now one of the nation's most unusual holidays: Oil Expropriation Day.

Mexican Standoff

The oil companies did not want to play ball with Cárdenas on the matter of compensation. Spoiling for a fight, they acted as though he had indeed confiscated their assets and, in return, summarily boycotted the now-nationalized Mexican crude in international markets. Moreover, they began planning to take their Mexico-based assets with them as they hastily departed, another attempt to mount pressure and force *el señor presidente* to reverse his move. For Washington and Big Oil in particular the loss of control over relatively nearby sources of oil was a national security calamity that would only escalate if other Latin American countries followed suit. As one US diplomat explained to Secretary of State Cordell Hull and President Roosevelt, "Should the government of Venezuela follow the government of Mexico and expropriate the foreign owned oil properties . . . without adequate payment therefor, the proper interpretation of the Monroe Doctrine will become the gravest problem the State Department will have to face." The issue of Mexican compensation therefore became a matter of regional coercion. To this end, the oil companies demanded levels of compensation far above what Cárdenas was either able or willing to offer. The companies also worked to influence public perception. They urged a boycott of US tourists heading south, which cut the foreign visitor trade by a third. Standard Oil of New Jersey took to the papers, disseminating editorial cartoons depicting Cardenas's gambit as entirely anti-American. But despite the corporations' many efforts, Americans never quite caught the fervor. The notion that expropriation was a serious offense—the foundation of the anti-Mexico effort—failed to catch hold.

Futile in their efforts to persuade the public to back their anti-Cárdenas case, oil firms turned to national governments to do their bidding. At least in Washington, however, key Roosevelt administration officials were inclined to caution due to the Roosevelt administration's self-proclaimed Good Neighbor spirit and the worry that the oil boycott could launch Mexico into chaos, into the hands of the Axis powers, or into a communist revolution. US secretary of the interior Harold Ickes drafted a note: "If bad feelings should result in Central and South America as a result of the oil situation that exists just now with Mexico, it would be more expensive for us than the cost of all the oil in Mexico." Notably, in 1937 Bolivia expropriated the assets of Standard Oil, and while the amount of US investment at stake was a fraction of that in Mexico, FDR once again declined to intervene.

By contrast, Secretary of State Cordell Hull initially backed a more aggressive stance on the Mexican compensation issue. Cárdenas's negotiating maneuvers had convinced the top US diplomat on "the need to punish Mexico economically to gain its respect for American business" before the bilateral relationship could be healed. Hull even sent a note to Cárdenas raising the notion that the United States could stop purchases of Mexican silver. In an instance where an imperialistic approach lost out to moderation, Hull's State Department lost the bureaucratic fight to the Interior and Treasury Departments.

FDR's team finally came up with the policy of continuing to back the US private claim while not opposing Cárdenas's right to take over the assets. In April 1938 FDR used a folksy example from the Little White House in Warm Springs, Georgia, to expose Big Oil's exaggerated indemnification numbers. "If I have a piece of land at Warm Springs that is worth $5,000, and the Government, or the state of Georgia wants to take it over, I ought to get $5,000 out of it," the commander in chief said. "I ought not to be able to say, 'In a few years this is going to be worth $20,000, so you have got to pay me $20,000.' "

Over the next few years the oil firms continued to demand large compensation sums—each time dismissed by Cárdenas. But when World War II broke out and national interests outweighed whatever fidelity FDR's administration felt to the private companies, the US government pressed assertively for a settlement. It occurred in April 1942, when Mexico granted $29 million ($540 million in 2018) to the participating US firms. Also in 1942 Mexican production finally returned to its pre-1938 levels. FDR dispatched engineers to help ensure that the Mexican crude flowed straight into the Allied war-making machine. FDR's preference to be a Good Neighbor in Mexico was challenged by his own country's corporate interests, a spat eventually eclipsed by global threats and imperatives.

16 • The Shadow War

Picture Germans at a café discussing Nazi politics and enjoying *apfelstrudel*. Naturally, one would assume this scene was taking place in Germany or near Western Europe at the least. Remarkably, however, it played out just as often in towns across southern Brazil or Córdoba, Argentina, where over a million Germans lived circa the 1930s and early 1940s. Germans weren't alone either: Latin America also hosted populations of ethnic Japanese and Italians, and, as we know, the three diasporas' homelands would share a destiny of becoming US enemies in 1941.

Throughout the 1930s the mere prospect of a Nazi threat originating in the geostrategic backyard of the United States both terrified President Franklin Roosevelt's foreign policy team and shaped the strategic imperatives of a global war for the American people. With war on the horizon, Roosevelt, in an October 1941 speech, invoked a "secret map," provided by British agents who came into possession of it while spying in Argentina. It purported to show official and classified Nazi plans to conquer and partition Latin America, take over the Panama Canal, and bring the war to the southern border of the US. As we know today, an overlooked "shadow war" did indeed bring the world's war to the Western Hemisphere, pitting the Allied and Axis powers against each other for control between the Rio Grande and Tierra del Fuego.

Today it is easy to underplay the perceived security threat of the Nazis in Latin America, simply because we know how the war turned out. "It is difficult to imagine how strong the Reich was before 1943, how grievous a threat to the Allies, how unsure anyone was about which way the conflict would go," the scholar Mary Jo McConahay put it. "In the run-up to the war and during the hostilities in Europe and the Pacific, the Latin American region was up for grabs."

Latin America was central to US strategy during World War II: the executive branch's Joint Planning Committee held hundreds of national security meetings in 1939 and 1940, all but six of which had Latin America as a key subject. Allies weren't alone in their interests; Axis powers also vied for popularity within various Latin nations, also as keen as their Allied enemies to procure the raw materials of war: rubber and oil, the obvious candidates, but also hemp for rope, tin for munitions, and cinchona for quinine as well as the shipping lanes themselves, which would "feed their war machines." Illustrating Latin America's role, coffee from Latin America, the most worshiped item in the ration kit, constituted almost 10 percent of all US imports between 1941 and 1945.

A remarkable development of this era was the geopolitical importance of the Axis countries' diaspora within and across national boundaries in Latin America. For example, Washington pressured Latin American governments to kidnap and relocate thousands of Japanese, Italian, and German residents as a national security measure. Entire families were abducted in the middle of the night and whisked off to the United States to serve as bargaining chips in clandestine prisoner swaps with Japan. In the immediate postwar years a system known as Ratlines relocated fascist war criminals from Europe to Latin America, and officials within the Roman Catholic Church used international church networks to facilitate the escape of Nazi war criminals like the concentration-camp physician Joseph Mengele and the Gestapo officer Klaus Barbie to South America. Perhaps most well known is Adolf Eichmann, who escaped to Buenos Aires with help from an Austrian cleric and lived and worked there for a decade until his capture in 1960.

Anti-Axis Allies

To characterize Latin America as a hotbed of Nazi sympathy united in its hostility to the Allied cause would be purblind. Around twenty-five thousand Brazilians served in the European theater in the fight against fascism, and Brazil had a close strategic partnership with the US, as evidenced by the scaling-up of a US Army base close to the coastal city of Natal in remote northeast Brazil. Part of the "Brazilian bulge," Natal was enticingly close to Africa, where the distant US expeditionary military was active. Brazil helped bring Africa in range in an era when transatlantic flights had commenced only in 1939 and short-range flights were overwhelmingly the default. Indeed, the reliably sunny climate facilitated Natal's utility as a lily pad base airport for cargo and

President Franklin Delano Roosevelt's "Secret Map." Perhaps given to US officials by Allied agents in Argentina, the map was supposed proof of Nazi Germany's nefarious plotting in the Western Hemisphere. The handwritten notes, in German, related to petroleum production and storage issues. Some scholars have contended it was a British forgery. (FDR Library, "Franklin D. Roosevelt, Papers as President: The President's Secretary's File [PSF], 1933–1945," PSF Safe File [Box 3], Safe: Germany, Map "Luftverkehrsnetz der Vereinigten Staaten Süd-Americkas Hauptlinien." (FDR Library, Hyde Park, NY)

soldiers moving back and forth from Africa. This vital role is precisely why FDR called the Natal base the "Trampoline to Victory."

At various points during the war around twenty thousand US military personnel, compared to a prewar population of forty thousand, were stationed at the airstrip at Natal, handling as many flights as the busiest airports anywhere, with planes landing or taking off every few minutes. The Natal native and historian Rostand Medeiros described the base's legacy with regard to the city: "It was the principal event for Natal in the 20th century . . . for the economy, for the population." (The closeness of US–Brazilian ties in that period was revived in 2019 when the right-wing nationalist Brazilian president Jair Bolsonaro suggested that his government might be open to hosting a US military facility to check Russian meddling in the region, especially in Venezuela. "My approximation with the United States is economic, but it could also be warlike," Bolsonaro told a reporter.)

Even Mexico set aside its fraught century of relations with the United States during the World War II era. To explain such a reversal, one must look back to a visit by President Roosevelt in April 1943 to Monterrey, Mexico, where the president consulted his counterpart, Manuel Ávila Camacho, a military veteran. By November Camacho was on board with supporting the Allied cause, under the condition that its force contribution would be limited and commanded by a Mexican. To help rally his beloved Aztec nation, Camacho had the Mexican Air Force (FAM) conduct air maneuvers over Mexico City on March 5, 1944, which tens of thousands of residents observed. Soon enough three hundred Mexican pilots, known as the Aztec Eagles, and crew members of the underfunded, undermanned FAM flew combat missions throughout the Pacific. Under US guidance the Aztec Eagles maneuvered in the Philippines and carried out long-distance sorties over Taiwan, gaining medals from US and Mexican generals alike.

Old tensions hadn't entirely dissipated, however. While in training camps in Texas and Idaho the Mexican service members were not free from bigoted attitudes on the part of their US comrades. As Captain Reynaldo Gallardo reflected decades hence, "The Americans looked down on us at least a bit. They didn't say so, but I noticed it. We made up our minds that we wouldn't say anything but instead would show their people what we had." When the Aztec Eagles finished their service they were greeted as heroes by cheering compatriots in Mexico City. Later, during the Cold War, the PRI was not enamored by Mexico's military collaboration with the yanqui empire, and the legend began to fade.

The Argentine Hemispheric Holdout

Following the December 7, 1941, Japanese Imperial Navy's strike on the US Pacific fleet at Pearl Harbor, Hawaii—an attack that precipitated America's involvement in the global conflagration—Washington pushed for a meeting of hemispheric foreign ministers, which took place in Rio de Janeiro in January 1942. FDR's goal for the conference was nothing less than a resolution committing all the American nations to cutting their ties with the Axis powers of Germany, Italy, and Japan. Before the ministerial assembly was over, eight Central American and Caribbean countries had joined Washington in declaring war on the Axis powers, while Colombia, Venezuela, and Mexico had cut diplomatic ties with them.

Argentina and Chile refrained from declaring war, and even though Argentina accepted the resolution, they would not comply, refusing to sever commercial and financial ties with Axis countries. Neutrality in World War I had benefited Argentina economically, and, besides, the country saw itself as a southern counterweight to the US that didn't like being told what to do by its northern neighbor. Moreover, Argentina's German population was economically important, controlling large segments of the country's pharmaceutical, chemical, and electrical goods production. However, there was nothing necessarily ideological or pro-Nazi in the Argentine government's unwillingness to declare war: theirs was a pragmatic decision based on economic and domestic political calculations. Furthermore, it is revealing that while Argentina is known as a Nazi refuge in the immediate postwar months and years, the country also received twenty-five thousand to forty-five thousand Jewish refugees during the war period, more than any other country in the Western Hemisphere.

None of this is to say Washington officials were done worrying about the southern heavyweight's apparent slippage. Concerns remained in the US government that Argentina's vibrant German business community was facilitating the transfer of supplies and money to the Third Reich or, as catastrophists feared, that a Nazi outpost was forming in their own hemisphere. These fears were not without merit: the State Department confirmed that German banks and firms operating in Argentina had transferred US dollars to Germany and were sending supplies like platinum, insulin, iron, and industrial diamonds. FDR reacted to the news by increasing pressure on Argentina through economic sanctions. A separate concern that developed by 1944—that Germany was attempting to move assets to neutral countries like Argentina to both finance a Nazi resurgence after Hitler's defeat as well as minimize reparation payments—also worried US officials when it came to changing Argentina's wartime neutrality.

Argentina would become the last South American country to commit to the Allied cause, breaking ties with the Axis powers in January 1944. This decision generated internal unrest in Argentina, leading to a takeover of power by General Edelmiro Farrell following a presidential putsch led by Colonel Juan Perón. Still convinced that Buenos Aires was pro-Axis, the Roosevelt administration called home its ambassador in July 1944 and did not recognize the new administration. It also froze Argentine-held gold deposits in the United States, believing they may have been Nazi gold looted from the central banks of conquered countries and laundered in friendly or neutral countries like Argentina.

Real progress wouldn't ease this simmering US–Argentina bilateral saga until the end of March 1945, when the Farrell regime officially declared war on the Axis powers. At the same time, it supported the 1945 Act of Chapultepec, a Mexico City–brokered agreement calling for a formal multilateral approach to hemispheric security, and later that year signed the charter for a new international body, the United Nations. From 1945 to 1948 the Good Neighbor model helped spur the creation of an assortment of global institutions in addition to the UN, for example, the World Bank, North Atlantic Treaty Organization (NATO), International Monetary Fund (IMF), and the General Agreement on Trade and Tariffs (GATT). US diplomatic pressure on the nascent Farrell government coupled with economic sanctions had their intended effect. But just as important in Argentina's geostrategic decision was Hitler's inevitable and impending military decline; indeed, a mere two months after Argentina declared war against Germany and Japan, Nazi Germany was defeated.

The (Protective) Empire's Intellectual Apologist?

One of the most influential US diplomatic historians of the first half of the twentieth century, the Yale professor and two-time Pulitzer Prize recipient Samuel Flagg Bemis wrote numerous books on American foreign policy, including the innocuous-sounding *Jay's Treaty: A Study in Commerce and Diplomacy* (published in 1924). In 1943, when the United States was over a year into the world war, Bemis came out with what at the time was a largely noncontroversial book, *The Latin American Policy of the United States: An Historical Interpretation.* Bemis's thesis on the post-1898 US hemispheric record merits revisiting. As he frames it, Washington was unquestionably an imperialist power in the two decades after the defeat of Spain (read: McKinley through Woodrow Wilson); but "[this] comparatively mild imperialism was tapered off after 1921 and is fully liquidated now." Bemis viewed FDR's Good Neighbor Policy as the crowning moment of US policy in Latin America because it simultaneously repaired Uncle Sam's frayed image in the region and helped check a potent Nazi threat.

Even more significantly, Bemis reckons that the special US variant of imperialism, "protective imperialism" (our use of the term throughout this book is not meant to endorse his arguments), was "designed to protect, first the security of the Continental Republic, next the security of the entire New World, against intervention by the imperialistic powers of the Old World. It was, if you will, an imperialism against imperialism. It did not last long and it was not really bad."

Bemis's interpretation of benevolent US protection was decidedly mainstream in its time but by the 1960s had fallen out of favor for its perceived US chauvinism. Some students jokingly called him American Flagg, whereby the Yale historian was supposed to have rejoined, "I wouldn't want to be called by any other flag." Bemis's style is decidedly politically incorrect by today's standards. But while it could very well be the case that Bemis's bombastic interpretations are needlessly self-serving and narrow and that he overstates American virtue in these post-1898 decades, one should ask: if the Good Neighbor years were not the gold standard of Washington's approach to the hemisphere, then what would such a distinguished period look like?

Whether we agree with Bemis's assessment or not, that the period surrounding World War II formed a high-water mark for hemispheric solidarity is undeniable in light of what was to follow. The very different dynamics of the Cold War completely reshaped relations between the United States and the rest of the hemisphere, with drastic consequences.

PART III
HOT COLD WAR, 1950–1991

As the historian Hal Brands notes, while the contest between Washington and Moscow is universally referred to as the Cold War and while the two countries never engaged in direct conflict or drew on their nuclear stockpiles, the wars experienced by their respective proxy countries were actually quite hot. Latin American nations weren't immune to the superpower rivalry and foreign meddling of Washington and Moscow, subject to interference from Havana, and riven by ideological polarization, rapid swings between dictatorship and democracy, and wanton violence. This lethal cocktail of factors ensured the "relentless intensity" of Latin America's Cold War. President John F. Kennedy called Latin America "the most dangerous area in the world" in the early 1960s.

Faced with such turmoil, often the result of their own actions, US policy makers during the Cold War came to fixate on the concept of *security*. They frequently justified US intervention by claiming that the possibility of a communist takeover in Latin America constituted an existential threat to the US. Whether US claims of a "red peril" were credible is a pertinent question, but certainly there were true believers and probably none more so than the executive branch foreign policy practitioner Henry Kissinger. A central player in both the Richard Nixon and Gerald Ford administrations, Kissinger was especially associated with this realist school. The US accordingly began to ascribe increasing importance to the region over the course of the Cold War, despite its many involvements elsewhere, not least in Vietnam. Toward the end of the Cold War in the 1980s, during the height of the controversy over US strategy in Central America, the polarizing US ambassador to the United Nations Jeane Kirkpatrick claimed that the Caribbean and Central America had become "the most important place in the world for us."

There is no question that Washington used its enormous military and economic might during the Cold War as a Big Stick to determine outcomes, although in some instances, including the 1961 Bay of Pigs invasion of Cuba, this approach failed horribly. The US also used more oblique means, such as President Dwight D. Eisenhower's covert overthrow of the leftist, democratic Guatemalan president Jacobo Árbenz in 1954. Critics deplored such actions, claiming that Washington had relinquished its moral authority by engaging in activities antithetical to the country's democratic principles. It didn't help that hard-line policies were fodder for critics to paint them as counterproductive, creating as many enemies as friends in the region.

However, it's equally misguided to hold that Washington relied solely on threats and raw power to promote its policies; rather, it also encouraged economic development and democracy as a means to promote communist-free ends. The first significant type of this approach was President Kennedy's Alliance for Progress and Peace Corps programs, hatched in the early 1960s and flooding the region with droves of idealistic volunteers and massive capital sums (over $11 billion in today's money) before the program ended late in the decade.

Cold War Twilight

The latter Cold War years are often portrayed as simply a continuation of the previous era, rife with heavy-handedness and covert intervention, but the Watergate scandal in 1972–74 fundamentally changed that. Public outrage over Nixon's criminal conduct brought an end to the period of secret White House machinations, a shift codified in the 1974 Hughes–Ryan Amendment to the Foreign Assistance Act of 1961. Going forward, a president who wanted to use the CIA to conduct a covert operation would have to get Congress to sign off on it, a process known as the presidential finding. Congress also added section 502B, which prohibited the provision of security assistance to any government engaging in a "consistent pattern of gross violations of internationally recognized human rights." Even though the Cold War was at its height, US policy was broadening beyond the simple obsession with tackling the communist threat at all costs. And it wasn't enough to prepare for the future; the nation also had to tackle the pile of dirty laundry that constituted its past. In 1975 the US Senate's Church Committee conducted public congressional hearings and published reports on CIA involvement in Latin America. Americans could now read for themselves about US plotting in, say, "Covert Action in Chile: 1963–1973."

Adding momentum to this shift, the former Georgia governor Jimmy Carter came into office in 1977 believing that the best way to deal with the dilemma of armed revolution in Latin America was to stop backing the pro-American rightist dictators whose tyranny and injustices led citizens to revolt in the first place. Instead, the United States would now be a vocal champion of human rights around the globe, even if that meant criticizing some of its reliable allies (read: tyrants) in Cold War flashpoint states. Carter urged Americans to rid themselves of their "inordinate fear of Communism which once led us to embrace any dictator who joined us in that fear." Deputy Secretary of State Warren Christopher promised that human rights would be "woven, we are determined, into the fabric of American foreign policy."

Nicaragua's successful anti-Somoza rebellion, led by the Sandinistas in 1978–79, was a sobering development for the United States; while Carter did not jettison his human rights agenda, his Democratic administration undoubtedly became more hawkish. As Carter was leaving office in January 1981, many voices on the US political right (the so-called neoconservatives) were clamoring for a more muscular anti-Moscow, and, by extension, anti-Havana, stance. Ronald Reagan's entrance into the White House swung the pendulum away from Carter. Reagan preached that the United States had an almost God-given responsibility to stop, even to roll back, perceived communist gains throughout the world. Reagan also believed he was elected in large part to restore the prestige and self-confidence of the United States, but no one wanted to repeat the mistakes of Vietnam. Instead, Reagan adapted to a smaller military training footprint to ensure that the US did not assume too much of the responsibility for winning a war but would still work to prevent other hemispheric communist dominoes from falling. The precipitous collapse of the Soviet Union in 1991 surprised many in the US, but even in the dying days of the Cold War a new threat was emerging that would come to take the place of communism as the central preoccupation of US foreign policy in Latin America: drugs.

In the introduction we contended that it was important not to let the Cold War era overwhelm our broader study of the two-century hemispheric relationship. We also must not reduce US Cold War policy to only the most damning instances—no matter what they might singularly or collectively teach us—given there are other occasions when US policies had a more positive impact. The Reagan administration, for instance, funded the democratic opposition that ultimately defeated the Chilean dictator, formerly a US ally, in a 1988 national referendum.

Still, no matter how we evaluate the legacy of Washington's actions in Latin America during the Cold War, the period undeniably fomented an antipathy toward the United States in several Latin American countries such as Guatemala and Nicaragua, an antipathy that would have significant implications for hemispheric relations after the fall of the Soviet Union. In other words, regardless of how we want to apportion blame (or credit), the fact is that relations between the United States and Latin America for the most part got worse. The period of the Good Neighbor was a fantasy of the past; suspicion and intrigue flourished.

17 • Mr. Kennan Goes to Latin America

The Good Neighbor spirit of multilateralism remained potent through the initial post–World War II years. By September 1947 Washington was front and center as the sole hemispheric superpower at the establishment of a multilateral security accord known as the Rio Treaty (formally the Inter-American Treaty of Reciprocal Assistance), which committed to "prevent and repeal threats and acts of aggression against any of the countries of America." In 1948 what in its first rendition was the James Blaine–led conference of the Pan-American Union became the interhemispheric Organization of American States, or OAS, established in Bogotá, Colombia.

In these early postwar years the US and Latin America seemed to be singing from the same hymn sheet when it came to tackling the new danger of communism. At the 1948 Bogotá meeting the OAS adopted Resolution 32, the first official multilateral statement to, in its own words, "safeguard peace" and "prevent serving international communism," including, in a significant modification by Latin American delegates, "any other totalitarian doctrine." So, while the ensuing almost half century of the Cold War is appropriately associated with Uncle Sam's meddling and heavy-handedness, multilateralism, or at least the appearance of it, was also part of the story at the beginning.

Mr. Kennan's Tour of the Backyard

By 1950 the Good Neighbor spirit was giving way to a far more anxious and confrontational US posture. North Korea's invasion of its southern neighbor brought the Cold War from Europe to Asia, and the United States had begun to formulate a more direct approach to countering the communist threat in its own backyard than multilateral resolutions.

Much of the ideological groundwork for the new US approach was laid by the US diplomat and seasoned Russian hand George Kennan, whose ideas about containment would shape US strategy for decades. Perhaps surprisingly, Kennan was something of a dove. Even when composing his famous five-thousand-word State Department cable on Soviet communism in February 1946, the so-called Long Telegram, Kennan urged Washington to agree that active public diplomacy—what today is called soft power—needed to be part of the anti-Moscow arsenal. "We must," he asserted, "put forward for other nations a much more positive and constructive picture of [the] sort of world we would like to see than we have put forward in [the] past." Still, Kennan's insight that Joseph Stalin's postwar Soviet Union was founded on an inherently malevolent communist ideology that needed to be contained had seismic consequences for US foreign policy. Kennan eventually came to rue how various successive US administrations implemented his strategy.

While Kennan's role as the architect of the anti-Moscow strategy is well known, his assessment of the situation in Latin America is also revealing of the hardening US approach. His brief but not insignificant foray into Latin American policy began in February 1950, when he undertook a trip to meet US diplomats from Mexico to South America—coincidentally right before Kennan temporarily left government service. He kicked off his hemispheric tour in Mexico City, where he was impressed by the national monuments and wide, European-style *avenidas* but disgusted at seeing the locals "living, eating, and begging on slimy sidewalks." He found the Mexican capital to suffer from an "ostentatious, anxious demonstration of wealth by an ever-changing *nouveau riche*." Moving on to oil-fueled Venezuela, the American diplomat was shocked by the exorbitant local prices. Presciently, he warned that when the nation's "morphine" (read: oil) ran out, a "terrible awakening would follow." In Brazil hostile local communists brandished signs declaring "Death to Kennan." (While Kennan was in Buenos Aires, the Argentine leader Juan Perón thought he ran the CIA.) While occasionally rattled by the vocal protests against his visit and, by extension, Washington's strategies, Kennan revealed in his diary how enlightened he found parts of Latin America, describing Brazilian society as a "vast panorama of racial tolerance and maturity which could stand as a model for other peoples."

But even Kennan was not immune from making sweeping judgments and recommendations in the especially anxious times of the early Cold War. This is evident in his lengthy report to Secretary of State Dean Acheson on March 29, 1950, soon after his visit to the region. In his telling, the Iberian conquistadors landed in Latin America "like men from Mars," with devastating effect: "History, it seems to me, bears no record of anything more terrible having been done to entire peoples." And from this point forward, Kennan told his boss, it was "unlikely that there could be any other region of the earth in which nature and human behavior could have combined to produce a more unhappy and hopeless background for the conduct of human life than in Latin America." According to Kennan, the Ibero-Catholic legacy had been one of "religious fanaticism, a burning, frustrated energy, and an addiction to the most merciless cruelty," and the mixing of the European invaders with the indigenous blood ensured that the Iberians "came to share the scars and weaknesses which they had themselves inflicted."

After these pop anthropological observations, Kennan got to the point of his memo: communism in the region. He explained how Latin America was not vital in terms of US military bases but instead as a source of raw materials like oil and metals for use in a major conflict. Furthermore, he declared that a widespread communist political revolution would bar the US from obtaining these critical resources. To his credit, Kennan pointed out that he regretted having to elevate the communist question, given that the "emphasis of our policy must continue to be laid on the constructive, positive features of our relationship; and no more here than in any other part of the world can a successful policy be founded exclusively, or mainly, on just a negative combatting of communist activities."

Kennan assessed that direct subversion from Moscow was not a significant factor in Latin American communism; the threat lay in homegrown party members:

> [Local communist leaders are] fanatical, disciplined, industrious, and armed with a series of organizational techniques which are absolutely first rate. Their aim is certainly not the acquisition of power by democratic means. . . . Their present aim, after all, is only the destruction of American influence in this part of the world, and the conversion of the Latin American peoples into a hotbed of hostility and trouble for the United States. And in this their activities tie into the formidable body of anti-American feeling already present in every one of the Latin American countries, without exception.

Kennan explained to his superior that the imposition of European "political system[s]" had prompted Adams and Monroe to issue the Monroe Doctrine. This stance, he observed, should apply to communism as well, "a system certainly no less hostile to us than that of the European courts of the early 19th Century, and one which, if given its head, would not only 'oppress' the Latin American peoples, but would certainly control their destinies in a number of ways." Kennan reminded Acheson that in 1928 the US senator and statesman Frank Kellogg had called the Monroe Doctrine "simply a doctrine of self-defense." And it was "precisely the principle of self-defense," Kennan told Acheson, "which is involved today in our attitude toward communist activities in the hemisphere."

So what needed to be done? Kennan was belligerent: "We cannot be too dogmatic about the methods by which local communists can be dealt with. These vary greatly, depending upon the vigor and efficacy of local concepts and traditions of self-government." Outside of places like the United States, where there were enough institutional checks against the "virus of communism," aggressive measures were permissible: "[W]here the concepts and traditions of popular government are too weak to absorb successfully the intensity of the communist attack, then we must concede that harsh governmental measures of repression may be the only answer; that these measures may have to proceed from regimes whose origins and methods would not stand the test of American concepts of democratic procedure; and that such regimes and such methods may be preferable alternatives, and indeed the only alternatives, to further communist successes."

Most scholars would agree that Kennan overstated the communist threat in Latin America. Most national communist parties were very small, and their credibility had been eroded by their association with dictators. Yet despite the notoriety Kennan's report subsequently achieved (it was fully released in the mid-1970s), it is important to note, as the biographer John Gaddis has pointed out, that it was never translated into policy, being considered by Acheson too incendiary to distribute even within the State Department. And even if they had perused the report, Gaddis adds, "they would have found it recommending a far more cautious policy than those carried out by the Eisenhower, Kennedy, Johnson, Nixon, and Reagan administrations, all of whom intervened in Latin America in ways well beyond anything Kennan recommended."

Two decades later, in his memoir, Kennan explained that Acheson, recognizing the provocative potential of Kennan's Latin American report, had all the existing copies put under lock and key, "hidden from innocent eyes." In later times his about-face in regard to Latin America became even more pronounced, with Kennan calling for the United States to give the Panama Canal to Panama and normalize diplomatic relations with Cuba.

George Kennan testifying before the US Senate Foreign Relations Committee, February 10, 1966. (Library of Congress, Prints and Photographs Division, Washington, DC)

"Militarizing the Good Neighbors"

In 1953 President Eisenhower's secretary of state, John Foster Dulles, warned Congress about communism's potential reach in Latin America: "Conditions in Latin America are somewhat comparable to conditions as they were in China in the mid-thirties when the Communist movement was getting started. They were beginning to develop the hatred of the American and the British, but we didn't do anything about it. . . . It came to a climax in 1949 [with the victory of Mao Tse-tung's communist revolution]. Well, if we don't look out, we will wake up in South America the same kind of thing that happened in China in 1949." We must not avoid the searing influence of seminal global episodes like the Chinese communist revolution in 1949 and the Soviet domination of Eastern Europe. US policy makers seemed to draw straight lines from Mao and Stalin to Latin America. To critics, this "seeing Red" was hyperbole that might have simply been pretext to allow the United States to dominate the hemisphere, especially ensuring corporate profits. But we also have to understand how elevated—at times hysterical—the anticommunist sentiment was in the United States at the time, and how this fever influenced US policy makers and policies to hold this hawkish, militarized regional outlook.

The United States made a fateful decision in these early years of the Cold War: equip and train Latin American militaries to check communist subversion. The rub, though, was that one person's revolutionary, Cuba-financed communist subversion was another person's domestic, leftist freedom fighter movement. Yet Uncle Sam would nonetheless proceed. In 1951 the US Congress passed the Mutual Security Act, which combined with the Mutual Defense Assistance Act of 1949 to fund a strategy of providing military aid to "free peoples" to stem the spread of communism. It was a decision that would have deep and at times wholly unexpected ramifications for the region over the next four decades.

18 • Getting Jacobo

Guatemalan Spring

In the late 1940s and early 1950s the small Central American country of Guatemala was enjoying an unprecedented period of democracy and social reform, the so-called Ten Years of Spring, after decades of strongman rule and oligarchic control of the economy. Brought on by teachers, students, and civilians protesting in the summer of 1944, the departure of the repressive dictator Jorge Ubico demarcates the onset of this decade of reforms. Within months of Ubico's ousting, young army officers revolted against the military junta which replaced Ubico, sparking Guatemala's own reformist October Revolution. The intellectual Juan José Arévalo returned from exile to win the presidency with the freest vote in Guatemala's history. Arévalo cited Franklin Roosevelt's New Deal and the Four Freedoms—freedom of speech and religion and freedom from want and fear—as the inspiration for his administration in Guatemala. His March 15, 1945, inaugural address has a very FDR-like tone: "There has in the past been a fundamental lack of sympathy for the working man, and the faintest cry for justice was avoided and punished as if one were trying to eradicate the beginnings of a frightful epidemic. Now we are going to begin a new period of sympathy for the man who works in the fields, in the shops, on the military bases, in small businesses. . . . We are going to add justice and humanity to order, because order based on injustice and humiliation is good for nothing."

Arévalo's new constitution kick-started his agenda, greatly expanding enfranchisement (but still excluding illiterate women) and banning military officials from holding office. Arévalo's government also gave new liberties to labor unions, allowed freedom of the press, and promoted literacy campaigns, especially in the mountain highlands dominated by the indigenous Maya people.

Despite his unprecedented social reforms, including instituting a labor code and establishing social security and education programs, Arévalo was unable to meet many of the expectations associated with his historic presidency. But the fact of the coup and subsequent election of a progressive president was enough to make the US press begin to worry. The October Revolution, combined with the worldwide proliferation of leftist activism and revolutions, ignited some to panic over the presence of Reds in the Guatemalan government.

US anxiety levels rose further following the 1950 election of Jacobo Árbenz, a quiet, bright, left-leaning army colonel who won 65 percent of the vote and succeeded Arévalo. Árbenz had served as Arévalo's defense minister for six years after participating in the 1944 putsch. Following his election, the patriotic, thirty-seven-year-old son of Swiss immigrants Árbenz unapologetically promised to "convert Guatemala from a backward country with a predominantly feudal economy into a modern capitalist state," approaching reform more aggressively than his predecessor. Árbenz's sweeping Agrarian Reform was approved by the national assembly and launched the year after he took office, the first attempt at land reform in the region's history. Árbenz's urgency was understandable: even by Latin America's historically skewed standards, land distribution in Guatemala was highly unequal: 2 percent of owners held three-quarters of all arable land, while more than half of all farmland was locked in large plantations (of over 1,100 acres), much of it fallow. The reforms initiated by Árbenz in his Decree 900 impacted unused land larger than 223 acres in area. Compensation was provided in interest-bearing bonds based on the land's *declared* tax value. In only two years a million acres were distributed to roughly 100,000 families. By 1954 the Árbenz government had expropriated roughly 1.5 million acres.

Going after land instantly brought Árbenz into conflict with the United Fruit Company (UFCO), the largest landholder in the country. Árbenz called for the expropriation of roughly four hundred thousand acres of United Fruit land, around 40 percent of its holdings (one-fifth of total arable land) in Guatemala. Almost 85 percent of this land was fallow, ostensibly to guard against any outbreaks of banana diseases or natural disasters. In 1936, hiring the New York–based law firm Sullivan & Cromwell to negotiate the details, United Fruit had acquired a ninety-nine-year concession over a large area of jungle from Jorge Ubico. This deal gave the Boston-based company the right to construct and operate a railroad to the Caribbean coast through its subsidiary, the International Railways of Central America (IRCA). United Fruit's port at Puerto Barrios was the country's only Atlantic port, while its railway was the only way to move freight to and from the port. Árbenz's government offered compensation of $1.2 million for the property, far below UFCO's claim that the land was worth $16 million. By making such a large claim, United Fruit inadvertently revealed the extent of its previous tax evasion.

"Walks Like a Communist . . ."

With approval from the Truman administration, United Fruit officials collaborated with the CIA in an operation to plot a coup against Árbenz in 1952. However, upon learning of the conspiracy, Secretary of State Dean Acheson set to stop the plot out of concern that it would damage the US image as a member of the newly formed OAS. United Fruit would have to wait for the election of Eisenhower, who came to office in 1953 and who was far more anxious about the potential communist threat in Latin America and Árbenz's leanings in particular. Although Árbenz always claimed he was not a communist he was undeniably influenced by communist ideology, and key members of Guatemala's communist party entered his government. For the Eisenhower administration the composition of Árbenz's cabinet reinforced the fear that Guatemala could become a "Soviet beachhead in the Western Hemisphere." What is ironic about Eisenhower's stance against Árbenz is that within several years Washington would be promoting the very type of land reform throughout Latin America and Asia that it had condemned as communism in Guatemala.

Big Business threw its weight behind the growing anticommunist sentiment. The US entity with the most to lose in Árbenz's reform program, United Fruit, once again exerted considerable pressure on Washington to act. As everyone knew, the banana giant had extremely close contacts with the Eisenhower administration: the brothers Allen and John Foster Dulles, for instance, were directors of the CIA and secretary of state, respectively, and both had ties with United Fruit through their work with the Sullivan & Cromwell law firm. Moreover, the family of the State Department's top diplomat for Latin America, John Moors Cabot, owned shares in United Fruit, and brother Thomas had been the corporation's president. Another relative, Henry Cabot Lodge, was such a strident defender of UFCO's interests as a Massachusetts congressman, he earned the moniker "the senator from United Fruit." Ann Whitman, Eisenhower's personal secretary, was the spouse of the company's public relations director, who had produced the film *Why the Kremlin Hates Bananas*. The author Stephen Kinzer sums it up: "No American company has ever been so well connected to the White House."

With such machinations going on behind the scenes, the central question surrounding the Guatemala episode is to what extent Eisenhower and the Dulles brothers truly saw Árbenz as an ideological threat; the antithesis is that he was simply used as a pretext to protect UFCO's bottom line. Many leading scholars, including Richard Immerman, argue persuasively that the US government's main reason for opposing Árbenz was genuinely rooted in concern about the spread of communism into the Americas. The Eisenhower administration held no truck with the notion that Árbenz could not be a communist while being surrounded by communists and enacting communist-style land expropriations. In 1950 Richard Patterson, the US ambassador to Guatemala, boiled down the question of Árbenz's communist leanings to the infamous "duck test": "This bird wears no label that says 'duck.' But the bird certainly looks like a duck. Also he goes to the pond and you notice he swims like a duck. Then he opens his beak and quacks like a duck. Well, by this time you have probably reached the conclusion that the bird is a duck, whether he's wearing a label or not."

Therefore, as the historian Stephen Streeter states, "Because Árbenz talked, thought, and acted like a Communist, he had to be one." The idea was not a crazy one; after Árbenz's legalization of the country's communist party, its membership grew from one hundred in 1950 to five thousand in 1954; it even won a mayoral race in Escuintla in 1953.

Some US officials dissented from the Eisenhower team's rigid interpretation. One foreign service officer suggested that Árbenz might in fact be a domestic nationalist and reformer, not an agent doing Moscow's bidding. The senior diplomat Walter Bedell Smith would have none of this apostasy. "You don't know what you're talking about," he told his subordinate. "Forget those stupid ideas and let's get on with our work."

Coup

By the end of 1953 tensions between Washington and Guatemala City had not only escalated dramatically but also evolved into a multinational affair. Leaders in Guatemala's neighboring states—including the pro-US strongman Anastasio Somoza in Nicaragua and the civilian president Juan Manuel Gálvez in Honduras—were now also concerned about communist infiltrations into their countries. The CIA had been hatching a covert operation, authorized by Eisenhower in August 1953, to address the threat in Guatemala, and by January 1954 the operation had a code name, PBSUCCESS. An undistinguished Guatemala ex-army colonel and furniture salesman named Castillo Armas was picked to lead the anti-Árbenz Liberation Army, and his paramilitary force began to be armed and trained in Somoza's Nicaragua. Right before the coup Castillo Armas was given housing and food on United Fruit property in Honduras; this was also where the invading troops assembled.

Washington dispatched a new ambassador to Guatemala City, John Peurifoy, who had been selected to coordinate PBSUCCESS on the ground. The fiercely anticommunist Peurifoy had worked in Greece in the late 1940s during the successful effort to support the anticommunist regime in Athens. Indeed, the relatively easy counterinsurgency win in Greece contributed to the Eisenhower administration's belief that a similar outcome could be achieved in the mountains of Central America. This time, though, it would entail removing a procommunist government rather than, as in Greece, keeping communists from overthrowing an American-backed government. Once again there were dissenters within the US intelligence community against the idea of launching a coup. The CIA's Latin America hand, Colonel J. C. King, feared a long-term backlash, arguing that "[we'll] be starting a civil war in the middle of Central America!" Assistant Secretary of State for International Organization Affairs Robert Murphy got wind of the covert plot by happenstance and wrote a blistering memo to his boss, John Foster Dulles, stating that it was wrong and likely to be "very expensive in the long term." The CIA chief Allen Dulles, by contrast, had this instruction to the intelligence agency's top operational man in the plot, "You've got the green light!"—and this meant direct approval and support from the White House.

US government officials continued to deny the veracity of published reports of secret armies and unfolding plots. Then, in March 1954, at a meeting of the OAS in Caracas, Venezuela, John Foster Dulles invoked the Monroe Doctrine and was able to obtain a majority resolution that effectively justified armed intervention in any member state that was "dominated by Communism" and was therefore a "hemispheric threat." With its diplomatic backing enhanced, the CIA proceeded with the training of Armas's paramilitary force in Nicaragua. A variety of psychological operations were planned, including taped recordings of disinformation for broadcasting and printed leaflets to be dropped over Guatemalan cities. Soviet-issue weapons were purchased, to be planted in Guatemala as purported evidence of Árbenz's strong ties with global communism. In April Eisenhower used aggressive language in an address to Congress, warning that the Reds were already in power in Guatemala and were now eager to spread their "tentacles" to other Central American republics.

Soon thereafter Árbenz's government accepted delivery of a cache of arms from Czechoslovakia. The clandestine shipment, intended to circumvent the Washington-imposed arms embargo in place since 1948, had originated in the Polish port of Szczecin, packed inside the Swedish freighter *Alfhem*. It arrived in Guatemala's Atlantic port of Puerto Barrios on May 15, 1954. The CIA, which had tracked the freighter as it crossed the Atlantic, altering its course repeatedly, the delivery was proof positive of Árbenz's communist bona fides. Allen Dulles quickly convened senior administration officials and was supported in his plan to set the invasion date for the following month.

Over the ensuing weeks the CIA placed alarmist articles in newspapers across the region and handed out booklets warning of the growing communist threat in Guatemala. On June 2 a coup against Árbenz was foiled, but as the pressure continued Árbenz suspended constitutional guarantees for thirty days. Later that month US mercenaries began bombing missions over Guatemala, and Castillo Armas soon led his 480-man army across the Honduran border into Guatemala. At first it appeared as though Árbenz would be able to repel the invading forces, as his army largely remained loyal and fought back against the invaders. While Castillo Armas managed to enter the provincial city of Esquipulas, he had difficulties elsewhere. As his advisors grew concerned about the possibility of failure, Eisenhower authorized the use of two more fighter-bombers to strike targets throughout the country.

At the same time, psychological and propaganda efforts made the revolt appear to be much more widespread than it actually was. The CIA filmed anti-Árbenz propaganda in a studio in Miami and then broadcasted it from Nicaragua after falsely claiming that the studio was located "deep into the jungle." Castillo Armas's planes buzzed over Guatemala City dropping leaflets intended to convince army troops to defect to the rebel side. Written on the pamphlets were such slogans as "Struggle against Communist atheism, Communist intervention, Communist oppression. . . . Struggle with your patriotic brothers! Struggle with Castillo Armas!" Richard Bissell, a CIA official, hatched the inventive ploy of using a small, ragtag air force to drop relatively harmless Coca-Cola bottles over Guatemala City, which sounded like artillery shells when they exploded. The psychological operations were highly effective in spreading fear and uncertainty throughout the country.

On June 25, having seized the town of Chiquimula, Castillo Armas proclaimed it the capital of his "provisional government." The momentum had shifted away from Árbenz. Further sealing the Guatemalan president's fate, Washington won a United Nations vote 5 to 4 against an official inquiry into the events unfolding in the Central American country, delaying a UN investigation until after Castillo Armas's dictatorship had been installed.

This CIA-hatched episode of regime change never sparked a wide-scale insurrection against Árbenz. Yet within less than two weeks of US bombings and Armas's invasion, Árbenz was unable to rely on his military's loyalty, forcing the Guatemalan president to flee into exile in Mexico in late June. Over the next two weeks three provisional governments attempted to restore some semblance of order. As the dust settled, Castillo Armas himself assumed the interim presidency. Only days into his dictatorship he outlawed political parties and peasant and labor cooperatives and suspended the agrarian reform law. Several months later his regime was endorsed in a dubious plebiscite in which he won 99 percent of the vote: 485,531 to 393. Just a few weeks after the operation President Eisenhower attended a reception for senior CIA officials and commented, "Thanks to all of you. You've averted a Soviet beachhead in our hemisphere."

Árbenz did not step down without getting in one last word about the United States and its investors. The former president fearlessly gave his final thoughts on the coup in his resignation speech: "We are indignant over the cowardly attack by mercenary US fliers. They know Guatemala has no adequate air force so they try to sow panic. They bomb and strafe our forces[,] preventing operations. Today they sank a ship taking on cotton in San José. In the name of what do they do these things? We all know what. They have taken the pretext of communism. The truth is elsewhere—in financial interests of the United Fruit Company and other US firms that have invested much in Guatemala."

In the months immediately following Árbenz's ouster, police, military, and ad hoc vigilante militias killed three thousand to five thousand Arbencistas. Within three years the share of Guatemala's lands that had been redistributed during Árbenz's tenure had all been taken away from the beneficiaries. For the next three decades military generals and their civilian lackeys maintained power in Guatemala. The Ten Years of Spring Guatemala experienced from 1944 to 1954 were over, yet Washington's lesson from Guatemala was that targeted covert operations could help check communism in the hemisphere without the deep commitment or risk of putting American boots on the ground. Not forgotten, however, was the high price Washington paid in public esteem throughout Latin America for its blatant involvement in the ouster, as shown by protests outside US embassies in several Latin American capitals.

Coda: The Bolivian Exception

One of the deep historical paradoxes of the Eisenhower administration's secret toppling of Árbenz is that the administration was openly backing the leftist
reforms of a newly installed government in Bolivia. Known as the Bolivian National Revolution, in 1952 it toppled a military regime and proclaimed the time
had come for a radical redesign of Bolivian society, most critically national land
reform and nationalization of tin mines. As in Guatemala, US officials worried
about the possibility of communist infiltration of the new government: in a
1953 classified cable that reads as though it could have been written by George
Kennan, the US embassy in the capital, La Paz, informed the State Department
in Washington that the new leaders, like the Bolivian president Víctor Paz Estenssoro, were communists and that there was "little doubt [of their] totalitarian ori-
entation." But Eisenhower's approach to Bolivia was very different.

There were certainly a variety of factors behind Eisenhower's dovish line on
Bolivia, not least of which was his belief that bolstering La Paz would help the
broader anticommunist stance in the Americas or at least preclude more radical elements and policies inside Bolivia. Bolivia's remoteness was also a factor.
Unlike Guatemala, which lay in the American hegemonic region of the Caribbean Basin, Bolivia was far enough away not to pose a direct threat and therefore could be icily tolerated. But interestingly Eisenhower went further,
showering Paz Estenssoro's revolution with foreign aid, as much as one-third
of Bolivia's national budget by 1957, the highest per capita recipient of US foreign aid in the latter half of the 1950s. Was Washington offering Bolivia diplomatic carrots despite its hemispheric predilection for sticks, as in Guatemala?

That the similar contexts of Bolivia and Guatemala drew wildly different reactions from the Eisenhower administration should give one pause for thought.
Many scholars have debated the possible motivations behind the divergence,
but one thing is clear: there was no Machiavellian logic trying to undermine
every single reformist government in Latin America that hosted US business
interests. As discussed above, the political power of UFCO was integral in
pushing the United States toward intervention. Conversely, the low number of
US investors in the Bolivian tin industry made Eisenhower's nonintervention-
ist course of action more palatable. The lack of powerful US businesses scream-
ing in his ear meant he could afford to let the situation play out.

More subtle factors, which might seem paper-thin today, may also have
made an important difference in the divergence of policy. For example, Paz
Estenssoro had previously been branded a fascist, which may have helped

challenge the attempt to identify him as a communist duck. Such fine grain may have motivated Eisenhower's actions when considering countless other factors in play at the time, from the differences in the nature of reforms in the two countries, the previous relationship each had with the US, and the different perceptions that were channeled back to the White House through embassies and business interests. Whereas in Guatemala high-level policy makers like Eisenhower and the Dulles brothers took decisions, in Bolivia low-level officials had to push their message through the slow-moving bureaucracy. Finally, perhaps Eisenhower simply wanted to try a different approach in Bolivia, making the region a laboratory in which different ideas of containment could be tested. Bolivia was a safe distance away in case things went wrong.

In the end, the fact that there was no "Guatemala 1954" in the administration's stance toward Bolivia does not mean Eisenhower's relatively dovish response to leftist revolution in South America should be ignored. In Bolivia left-leaning governance was met not with a military response but with economic support. Indeed, sometimes what doesn't happen is as significant as what does.

19 • Containing Cuba
A Perfect Failure

Cuba will not be Guatemala.

—Ernesto "Che" Guevara

In the early 1950s Fulgencio Batista was busy consolidating his grip on power in Cuba. A former sergeant in the Cuban army who had served as president in 1940–44, Batista had become the region's newest strongman through a bloodless coup in 1952. Over the next six years he ran the country with a heavy and increasingly corrupt hand, suspending the 1940 constitution, censoring the media and public expression, and banning labor mobilization. His regime's secret police, known for their clandestine kidnappings and torture rooms, are estimated to have killed upward of three to four thousand Cubans, although some estimates are far higher.

The Eisenhower administration, seeing Cuba as the strategic anticommunist pearl of the Caribbean, was nevertheless willing to live with the authoritarian tendencies of the Batista regime in exchange for its reliability in fighting the red threat. Cuba's economy was also very much geared toward satisfying American needs, albeit of a less ideological kind. Unflatteringly labeled as the "whorehouse of the Caribbean," mid-1950s Cuba was a place that encouraged American tourists to drink, gamble, and carouse. This seedy economy, and indeed the island as a whole, was sustained by the cozy relationship between Washington and Batista's Havana. On the side, Batista personally established a highly profitable rentier system with US corporations.

Batista's autocratic rule soon began to antagonize Cubans. Some in Cuba's aristocracy were openly racist toward the dark-skinned Batista, rejecting his bid for membership at one of Havana's most exclusive whites-only country clubs. But larger wheels had also begun to turn. Swaths of Cuban intellectuals, inspired by the teachings of Marxism and the revolutionary exploits of Vladimir Lenin and Mao Zedong, were growing resentful of Cuba's cozy and docile relationship with the imperialistic Colossus of the North, perceiving the Cuban leader as a puppet for US interests on the island. One young, idealistic, and highly charismatic and precocious Cuban named Fidel Castro considered running for a seat in Cuba's congress, but Batista's return to power prompted him to abandon the crooked political system for a quixotic attempt to seize power through the force of arms.

The infamous Moncada Attack on July 26, 1953, was a slapdash attempt by Fidel Castro and 160 of his Orthodox Party members to ignite revolution on the island by assaulting a military outpost in Oriente province. The operation fell apart upon first contact with Batista's troops, and Fidel was captured and put in prison. But the aftershocks of the failed attack would be felt for decades to come. During the Moncada trial Fidel delivered the now-legendary "History Will Absolve Me" speech, in which he condemned the Batista regime and introduced his ideology and proposed reforms. His antics did little to sway the judge in his favor, and he was sentenced to fifteen years in prison. Under public pressure, however, Batista released the prisoners convicted for the attack in 1955. Fidel and his brother Raúl and other members of the newly inaugurated M-26-7 movement (named to commemorate the Moncada Attack) were quick to flee to Mexico City, a well-known haven for leftist exiles. Here they would recoup and reorganize in preparation for their fateful return to Cuba.

Becoming Che

Meanwhile, a young, utopian Argentine doctor named Ernesto Guevara was living in Guatemala at the time of the Eisenhower-hatched coup that deposed the leftist president Jacobo Árbenz in 1954. Although Árbenz's Guatemala did not fulfill all of Guevara's high expectations about what a communist revolution should look like, the biographer Jon Lee Anderson has noted that Árbenz's reformist aspirations made the country "a compelling place to be in 1954." Almost daily Guevara socialized with revolutionaries and communists from across Latin America, including well-respected Cubans, who stood out from the other political expatriates. Some of them were veterans of an armed uprising against Batista in 1953. While they had failed to dislodge the dictator, they had gained considerable admiration among these exile circles.

For the first time in his life Guevara openly identified with a political cause. The Argentine wrote to his family that in Guatemala he could breathe the "most democratic air" in Latin America.

Watching the dramatic events unfold before his eyes, Guevara became convinced that Washington's intervention in Guatemala was only the "first skirmish" in what would be a global confrontation between the United States and communism. Guevara wrote that Árbenz "could have given arms to the people, but he did not want to . . . and now we see the result." Only by taking the fight directly to rapacious Latin American elites and imperial Washington could the region liberate itself from the "hostile governments and social conditions that do not permit progress."

After the coup against Árbenz, Guevara was lucky to escape from Guatemala with his life. He sought asylum in the Argentine embassy and then fled to Mexico, where the government, led by the PRI, was admired by leftists worldwide for its willingness to harbor revolutionaries and dissidents fleeing rightist governments. In Mexico Ernesto Guevara—later universally known as "Che" Guevara—first met and subsequently joined Castro's growing band of revolutionaries. The Castro brothers Fidel and Raúl were laying plans to overthrow the despised Cuban dictator once again, and Che was to be their doctor. Guevara wrote in his diary in July 1955, "A political occurrence is having met Fidel Castro, the Cuban revolutionary, a young man, intelligent, very sure of himself and of extraordinary audacity; I think there is a mutual sympathy between us."

In November 1956 Che, the Castro brothers, and roughly eighty other fighters harboring radical ideas for Cuba's future cast off from the Mexican port of Tuxpan, Veracruz, on the creaky yacht *Granma*. Despite the high spirits of the *barbudos*—a nomenclature for the bunch that arose from their unkempt appearance—their quest initially appeared destined to fail. An uprising in the provincial city of Santiago that was slated to coincide with the *Granma's* arrival started prematurely and was quickly extinguished. Seasickness and the abandonment of a majority of their supplies during a storm debilitated the force. Their modest yacht was also spotted nearing Cuban waters by a coast guard patrol, which alerted the Cuban military. The revolutionaries were then fired upon as they attempted to disembark at Playa Las Coloradas, a beach on the eastern part of the island. Absent vegetation—or any coverage for that matter—Batista's air force picked off Fidel Castro's men as the exhausted revolutionaries scrambled for safety to the mountains. Fewer than two dozen revolutionaries made it from the beach to the rugged Sierra Maestra mountains.

Batista's forces claimed that Fidel was dead, a claim that would later come back to haunt the dictator.

The guerrillas' ordeal continued, as subsequent military operations all largely failed. Disorganization and an inability to communicate between scattered groups plagued the early movements of the barbudos, slowing their planned sprint through the mountains to an incremental, maddening crawl. Fidel Castro, the insurgency's leader, had derived tactics from the major revolutionary trends of the era. As was practiced in China and Vietnam, the Cuban rebels sought to educate the local populations about the revolution and thus foment a rural insurgency, the goal being to produce a tidal wave of support that could swell the twenty-odd revolutionaries to a force of thousands.

Considering the guerrillas' many travails, they were lucky to confront a Cuban army generally reluctant to engage. After less than a year of hunt-and-be-hunted in the Sierra Maestra, the Cuban army had effectively conceded the mountains to the rebels. Although in 1957 the rebel force was a fraction the size of that which had boarded the *Granma* only a year earlier, the initial phase of securing a foothold in the mountains was complete.

In February 1957 Herbert Matthews, a senior *New York Times* reporter, arrived in the rebels' clandestine camp. A press veteran of the Spanish Civil War, Benito Mussolini's Abyssinian campaign, and World War II, Matthews was a symbol of status in itself to the guerrilla force, and Fidel Castro was determined not to squander the opportunity. The bearded revolutionary, acutely aware that his fighters were exhausted and disillusioned by the arduous campaign, knew he needed to write his own narrative via Matthews. Thus Castro instructed a soldier to barge into his meeting with Matthews relaying "a message from the Second Column." The ploy worked: Matthews concluded that Castro had large numbers of guerrillas under his control and reported a rebel force well beyond the real number of twenty or so fighters. Castro "is alive and fighting hard and successfully in the rugged, almost impenetrable vastness of the Sierra Maestra, at the southern tip of the island," Matthews wrote. "[T]housands of men and women are heart and soul with Fidel Castro. . . . Hundreds of highly respected citizens are helping Señor Castro . . . [and] a fierce Government counterterrorism [policy] has aroused the people even more against General Batista. . . . From the look of things, General Batista cannot possibly hope to suppress the Castro revolt."

Matthews went on to portray the "Rebel Army's" political leanings as an analogue to Rooseveltian liberalism: "It is a revolutionary movement that calls itself socialistic. It is also nationalistic, which generally in Latin America means anti-Yankee. The program is vague and couched in generalities, but it amounts to a new deal for Cuba, radical, democratic, and therefore anti-Communist. . . . [Castro] has strong ideas of liberty, democracy, social justice, the need to restore the Constitution, to hold elections." The *New York Times* continued by publishing a photo of Matthews with an unmistakable, fatigue-sporting Fidel Castro. Batista's claims that the encounter was fake resounded hollow.

By the end of 1957 the now globally known rebels were back on their feet, able to establish an operable, albeit unpolished, civil administration in the Sierra Maestra mountains. It was no coincidence that the rebels had set up shop there; the dense vegetation of the Cuban mountains was a crucial tactical advantage for the barbudos in their fight against the army. Small guerrilla groups careened through the lush forests and deep ravines that stymied the Cuban army's movement, thwarting its strategy of steadily tightening the noose around the rebels. The guerrillas also executed hit-and-run attacks in the mountains, wearing away Batista's larger force. Simultaneously, the sagacious Fidel Castro publicized his men's relatively benign treatment of captured Cuban army soldiers to cement their reputation as humane fighters. Early the following year the rebels established Radio Rebelde, a clandestine radio station that broadcast prorevolutionary propaganda. What is more, a new urban insurgency created problems in cities, demanding Batista's attention as well as a diversion of his forces. The rebellion was swelling into a full-blown revolution.

Adding to the revolution's growing momentum, Castro's movement soon expanded beyond the confines of the island. In early 1958, fed up with the teetering Batista, the Eisenhower administration stopped the pipeline of military supplies Batista had depended upon. From late June to early August 1958 a desperate Batista ordered a large number of raw recruits and reservists into Operación Verano (Summer Operation), but these new troops made few gains against the self-assured, seasoned, popular guerrillas. The offensive ended in a humiliating failure, and by New Year's Eve 1958 the despised Batista was on a plane bound for the tyrant Trujillo's welcoming Dominican Republic. Castro, by comparison, was riding victoriously into Havana on a tank as the rebels and throngs of Cubans celebrated the end of a harrowing two-year campaign.

The 26 of July Movement, founded in 1955 and named after the July 26, 1953, Moncada attack, had officially evolved from an underfunded catalogue of antiregime forces into the predominant political movement in Cuba. Two key rebel leaders, the Argentine Che Guevara and the Cuban Camilo Cienfuegos,

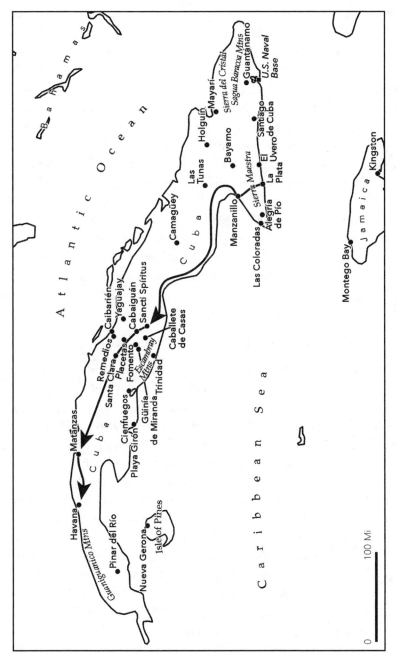

Ernesto "Che" Guevara's route to Havana. (University of Wisconsin–Madison Cartography Lab. Christopher Archuleta, cartographer)

were the first to enter Havana, securing military facilities. A week after swearing in the "revolutionary government's" first president, Judge Manuel Urrutia, Castro himself entered the capital in triumph. His guerrillas had fought an uphill battle and against the odds had succeeded. Yet contrary to the apocryphal narrative of Castro's fatigued idealists defeating a *mano dura* (strong hand) strongman in David-versus-Goliath fashion, Castro's band of barbudos wasn't solely responsible for toppling the Batista regime. In fact, the mountain-based fighters received significant support from the *llano,* the urban underground, who bitterly opposed the dictatorship. In fact, it was the middle and working classes in Havana and other cities that took the brunt of Batista's repression. After the Revolution, Fidel and Che downplayed this support after 1959 to gild their interpretation that their role in the Sierra Maestra was critical to the revolution's success.

By the time he fled into exile Batista was the island's most reviled figure. More than any devastating defeat on the battlefield—only two hundred government troops were killed between December 1956 and January 1959—Batista's total loss of political credibility, including with his former US backers, led to his fall from power.

Havana Honeymoon Turns to Hardball

For a brief period of time after the ouster of Batista the United States and Cuba enjoyed a honeymoon phase. In April 1959, four months after seizing power, Fidel Castro embarked on a remarkable trip to the United States. More than fifteen hundred well-wishers greeted him at the National Airport in Washington; two thousand were waiting at Penn Station in New York; ten thousand more heard him speak at Harvard. At the Bronx Zoo the youthful and charismatic Cuban guerrilla leader *cum* supreme ruler stuck his hand into the tiger cage to play with the cats—a bold move that was "quintessential Fidel." At Princeton Castro met former secretary of state Dean Acheson, who saw the Cuban as someone who "really knows what he is doing" even if he was "going to cause us some problems down the road." In Cambridge Castro dined at the Faculty Club with the dean of Arts and Sciences, McGeorge Bundy. (As John F. Kennedy's national security advisor Bundy would help plot Castro's overthrow through the Bay of Pigs operation two years later.) Castro also sat down for a two-and-a-half-hour, closed-door talk with Vice President Richard Nixon. To the surprise of the Eisenhower administration Castro did not ask for any military or economic assistance on his trip.

Fidel Castro at MATS Terminal, Washington, DC. April 15, 1959. (Courtesy of the
Library of Congress, Prints and Photographs Division, Washington, DC)

During his visit Castro employed the Madison Avenue public relations firm
Bernard Relin and Associates, at the cost of $75,000 a year, to improve his pub-
lic image. The Cubans, however, ignored the firm's advice to shave their scruffy
beards and replace their olive-green fatigues with business suits. Surprisingly,
this helped solidify Castro's image as a moderate nationalist as opposed to a
Moscow-loving comrade in the eyes of the American public and media. Castro
said to an American journalist, "We are not communists" and added that his
government would not expropriate private property. US newspapers and television broadcasts were replete with stories about the larger-than-life Cuban leader.

Meanwhile, even decidedly "imperialist" US conglomerates such as Texaco and Esso ran advertisements in *Revolución,* the new pro-Castro Cuban daily. Back in Cuba, companies like Bacardí paid their taxes in advance as a patriotic gesture.

But the bilateral relationship soured soon after Castro's historic visit. Few at the time could have foreseen that deterioration or have guessed it would persist through eleven US presidential administrations. How and why the relationship imploded so quickly remains a debated question, but it is clear that mutual perceptions rapidly changed. Washington increasingly saw Castro as a communist, while the Cuban leader increasingly believed that the United States was out to get him. Both were mostly correct. Only a month after Batista had fled, Daniel Braddock, the acting US chargé d'affaires in Havana, sent out a classified memo to the CIA and State Department titled "Cuba as a Base for Revolutionary Operations against Other Latin American Governments." It read, "A number of leaders of the successful revolutionary movement in Cuba consider that efforts should now be undertaken to free the people of some other Latin American nations from their dictatorial governments." While Che was generally regarded as the principal ideological and operations force behind the unleashing of revolution across the Americas, Fidel Castro had also reportedly made remarks along such lines, particularly during his visit to Venezuela in January 1959. As Braddock noted presciently, "It can be expected that Cuba will be a center of revolutionary scheming and activities for some time, with consequent concern and difficulties for various governments including our own."

Reports of Cuban efforts to actively foment leftist revolution in Panama, Haiti, and Venezuela helped convince the Eisenhower administration that a tougher approach was necessary. Eisenhower said Castro was a "madman" and considered erecting a blockade of the island to cut the Cuban people off and thus encourage them to "throw Castro out." Vice President Richard Nixon issued a memo soon after Castro's visit to *gringolandia* that rejected attempts to get along with and understand Castro. Soon the CIA group that had overthrown Jacobo Árbenz in Guatemala in 1954 was reconstituted to replicate its magic in Cuba.

Sympathy toward Castro and his cause wasn't entirely absent in the US. Then Senator John F. Kennedy wrote a book, *The Strategy of Peace,* in which he accused the Eisenhower administration of stoking antipathy toward Cuba. He bravely claimed that had the White House given Castro a "warmer welcome," Washington could have encouraged "a more rational course." Yet even Kennedy had his limits, and that year's presidential campaign confirmed that any potential Kennedy administration would aid anti-Castro groups in exile. A step ahead, the Republican candidate Richard Nixon had privately been doing exactly that and so, reluctantly, tried to vilify Kennedy for being reckless in risking a World War III over Cuba. Behind the showmanship of politics, however, the planning for a secret invasion of Cuba continued. General Lyman Lemnitzer, the chairman of the Joint Chiefs of Staff, assured Eisenhower that the Cuban exiles in training were "the best army in Latin America."

To borrow a sports metaphor, by 1960 US policy toward Castro had turned to hardball. As the US diplomat Richard Rubottom put it, it was time to move from "the testing phase in which Castro had failed practically every test we had given him to the pressure phase." Coexistence with Castro was dead.

"Undeclared War"

Whether it was a conflict over political ideologies or simply a response to an aloof Eisenhower administration, Castro read the unfriendliness of the US as cause for conflict. On January 2, 1961, speaking at a rally to celebrate the second anniversary of the revolution, a scorching Castro labeled the US embassy a "nest of spies" and demanded that the staff be cut from eighty-seven to eleven in two days' time. In response, Eisenhower skipped cutting back on US personnel and jumped straight to breaking diplomatic relations with Cuba the very next day. Only two years into what would be Fidel's nearly half-century tenure as Cuba's leader, Washington and Havana were in a state of "undeclared war," choosing finger-pointing instead of resolving the recently arisen differences.

By this time Washington viewed Castro as a serious threat to its interests in the hemisphere. Adding to US officials' paranoia, an influx of Soviet and Eastern Bloc arms bolstered the Cuban armed forces and sparked a sense of urgency. Having criticized Eisenhower's apparent apathy toward Castro as the root of soured relations, Kennedy entered the White House less than three weeks after the break in diplomatic relations with Cuba. He was feeling pressure to carry out Eisenhower's planned clandestine operation and rid the hemisphere of Cuba's Marxist leader.

¡Viva Zapata!

In early April infantrymen of the Cuban Expeditionary Force—Brigade 2506, as the men called themselves—flew into Nicaragua to rendezvous with CIA strategists in training camps near Guatemala's Pacific coast. After transferring to the coastal town of Happy Valley on April 13, four hundred trained insurgents, many of them Cuban exiles, boarded rusty old frigates and set off for Cuba. Ringing in their ears was the Nicaraguan dictator, and son of Tacho, Luis Somoza's flippant command to "bring him some hairs from Castro's beard."

The CIA had also cobbled together a fleet of eight Douglas B-26 Invaders at Happy Valley, recently acquired from a US air force boneyard near Tucson, Arizona. The secondhand fighters had been repainted to match the B-26s in Castro's air force, which bore Fuerza Aérea Revolucionaria markings on their fuselages. The ploy was intended to confuse the defending forces and make it appear as if the attacks were initiated by Cuban defectors. On April 15 this improvised air arm took off to conduct a bombing raid against the Cuban air force in support of the planned land invasion, but it was already under strength. After the last of the eight planes had taken off and ascended into the sky, an American pilot, Albert C. Persons, reportedly asked, "Is that all?" The plans had originally called for sixteen planes.

As the operation proceeded, US periodicals grabbed readers with such headlines as "Castro's Pilots Bomb Their Own Bases" and falsified claims that Cuba's air force had been destroyed. Deepening the CIA-crafted narrative, one Cuban-exile pilot, Mario Zúñiga, landed a "distressed" plane at Miami International Airport with a rehearsed story: he was a Cuban air force officer who had perpetrated the reported attacks from within and since defected from Cuba. Perhaps the story was too well rehearsed, as reporters immediately questioned Zúñiga's account, in part due to the machine-gun barrels mounted on his plane's nose as opposed to being on the wings, like Castro's B-26s. It became clear that Zúñiga was backed by the CIA.

Meanwhile, the invasion campaign, known as Operation Zapata, had identified three landing points adjacent to the Bay of Pigs, the most important of which was Playa Girón, known as Blue Beach in the circle of CIA planners. Despite the popular narrative that Operation Zapata plotted a complete military takeover, the goal was instead to simply use the fourteen-hundred-man force to occupy part of Cuban territory long enough to permit the eruption of a nationwide anti-Castro uprising. Unbeknownst to the CIA, however, was the dearth of native Castro naysayers; the majority of these individuals, whom the CIA assumed would lead the uprising, were already in prison.

On the morning of April 17 the invasion force landed in Cuba, but things quickly began to go wrong. A day into the invasion the ground forces had done their part by gaining a foothold on the beach, but the problem of low ammunition grew more and more critical after the invasion transport fleet carrying supplies and materiél came under attack by Castro's planes. McGeorge Bundy, the US national security advisor at the time of the invasion, warned Kennedy that "the Cuban armed forces are stronger, the popular response is weaker, and our tactical position is feebler than we had hoped." A mere three days after landing on the island the CIA-trained taskforce was overrun by Castro's forces and more than a thousand insurgents were captured. In a matter of five days the CIA operation blew through $46 million and was responsible for over one hundred lives lost (some of whom were US citizens), not counting the untold number of deaths among Castro's troops. Repelling the so-called American imperialists in the Bay of Pigs fiasco not only emboldened an already self-assured Castro but also made total his dictatorial grasp on the island's future.

Why did the Playa Girón invasion, as the Cubans call it, fail so quickly? Contributing to the invasion's precipitous failure were several grossly incorrect assumptions. Fatefully, the anticipated popular uprising across the island never materialized. Another false assumption was that the Cuban air force would be a graveyard of dislodged engines and contorted steel by the time invading forces hit the Cuban beaches, but US B-26s had been directed to provide air cover rather than striking parked Cuban planes. Demonstrating his superior military discernment, Castro made no misstep in his response to the invasion by sea; via the destruction of exiles' transport ships Cubans cut their invaders' supply line and repelled the offensive by preventing any formidable beachhead. Finally, the Soviets provided timely intelligence in the run-up to the operation as well as training and organizing the Cuban intelligence service in the early years of the revolution.

As the invasion began to fall apart President Kennedy's advisors recommended bolstering military support to the fighters on the ground. This left the president, who had originally rejected the plans mandating the destruction of Castro's air force, with a difficult choice: either introduce greater force to save the crumbling brigade at the cost of a potentially larger conflict or accept defeat and cut his losses. Although Kennedy did approve limited, highly restricted military operations over the Cuban beaches, he effectively opted to step back and write off the operation.

Part of Operation Zapata's immediate failure undoubtedly stemmed from Kennedy's hesitancy to entirely commit US forces. Yet success would have necessitated a massive invasion force to stand toe-to-toe with Castro's army. Secretary of State Dean Rusk alluded to the White House's miscalculation when he commented, "It doesn't take Price Waterhouse to figure out that fifteen hundred Cubans aren't as good as twenty-five thousand." And although it is easy to criticize Kennedy for approving an underwhelming fourteen-hundred-man insurgency to usurp Castro, there was logic to the plan. After all, it was approved by the White House and the Joint Chiefs of Staff. From the painted planes to the use of Nicaragua as a base, great care was taken to distance the US from allegations of direct involvement. The operation was designed to appear as an entirely Cuban-on-Cuban affair, which would have allowed an exile-led provisional government to declare itself the authority in Cuba and keep the US out of the equation. Washington saw its role, in the best-case scenario, as a lender of aid in an unfolding Cuban civil war.

There were others in the plentiful cast of characters behind the Bay of Pigs invasion who likely took active delight in the kind of subterfuge employed. Richard Bissell, the CIA's deputy director for plans regarding the anti-Castro operation, had cut his teeth in America's covert operation against the Guatemalan leftist reformist Jacobo Árbenz, where he had come up with a host of psychological warfare tactics. The Guatemalan affair gave men like Bissell the opportunity to "lead armies and install governments, to create small air forces and devise wondrous chimeras, to break and make rules as needed, and to do all of this in the name of a cause they sincerely believed to be noble and just." It is therefore not far-fetched to assume that these same men watched with glee as Kennedy signed off on the Bay of Pigs mission.

Whatever the strategy behind the operation, the outcome was a public relations nightmare for Washington. The Kennedy administration's initial denial of US involvement was quickly exposed, and they became known liars. Even more humiliating for Washington was the open defeat they suffered at the hands of an infinitely weaker communist foe. In the words of the historian Theodore Draper, it was "a perfect failure." But surprisingly, Kennedy continued to challenge the Castro regime after the Bay of Pigs catastrophe. Aiming to "stir things up on [the] island with espionage, sabotage, and general disorder," Kennedy approved Operation Mongoose in November 1961, another overly ambitious and morally questionable attack on the Cuban leader that would once again tarnish the CIA's image. Attorney General Robert Kennedy informed the CIA that Mongoose was to be "the top priority in the United States government—all else is secondary—no time, money, effort, or manpower is to be spared." Robert Kennedy envisioned a multiple-pronged covert program of action including industrial sabotage, the burning of sugarcane crops, even the concocting of rumors that Castro was the Antichrist—all synchronized to dethrone Castro. When Mongoose finally materialized, its overtly aggressive elements later led then President Lyndon Johnson to title it "a damned branch of Murder, Inc. in the Caribbean."

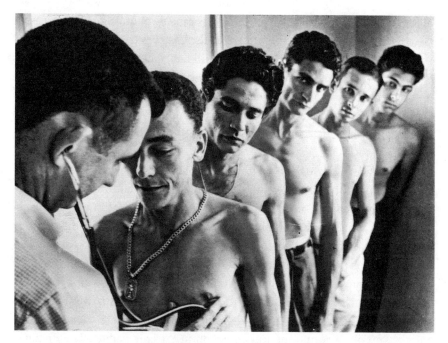

Recruits, possibly Cuban refugees, line up for physical examination in
Miami, Florida, prior to the Bay of Pigs invasion. April 17, 1961. (Library of
Congress, Prints and Photographs Division, Washington, DC)

What was quite possibly Kennedy's greatest achievement in the bilateral
relationship came in December 1962, when his administration bartered
food and medical supplies for the release of more than eleven hundred men
captured during the Bay of Pigs operation. Robert Kennedy came to the president's side in front of business representatives: "My brother made a mistake.
. . . These men fought well; the disaster was no fault of theirs. They are our
responsibility."

"Ready to Make Peace"

That the Kennedy administration was able to secure the prisoner release is
doubly remarkable, coming as it did so soon after the Cuban Missile Crisis.
On the morning of October 14, 1962, only two months before the release of
the prisoners, an American U-2 plane flying high above Cuba took a series
of photographs that would, within a matter of days, lead the CIA's National
Photographic Interpretation Center to confirm the presence on Cuban soil of

at least two medium-range ballistic missiles capable of hitting US cities east of the Mississippi River with nuclear payloads. Castro was absolutely convinced that after the failure of the Bay of Pigs, a full-fledged US military invasion was imminent. Given the climate at that moment—Cuba's aligning itself with the Soviet Union, the embarrassment of the Bay of Pigs, history, and Operation Mongoose—it was not an unreasonable assumption to make. This helps one understand why Fidel asked Premier Nikita Khrushchev of the USSR for the missiles.

The president convened a group of senior advisors known as ExComm (Executive Committee) to determine how the United States should respond. While the internal ExComm deliberations are well known, the authors Walter LeoGrande and Peter Kornbluh have used the declassified documents to reveal that Kennedy also pursued a "complicated clandestine" approach to Castro through Brazilian intermediaries. Kennedy approved sending Castro a message disguised as a Brazilian communiqué, asking Brazil's ambassador in Havana to transmit the message as if it were a Brazilian initiative. This veiled message was to have told Castro that the presence of the Soviets' offensive nuclear missiles had put the Cuban nation in extreme danger. The Brazilian would then offer the diplomatic carrot of warmer ties with Washington if Castro would kick out the Russians and stop supporting revolutionary movements in Latin America. This Washington–Havana (via Brazil) track went nowhere, however, as it was overshadowed by the Washington–Moscow bilateral correspondences over the missile issue.

President Kennedy's steady performance during the Cuban Missile Crisis likely had much to do with the bitter lessons he had learned from the Bay of Pigs, not least to take the advice of aggressive military advisors with a healthy pinch of salt. In this instance Kennedy opted for a quarantine of the island nation despite the riskier call of the Joint Chiefs of Staff for aerial bombing and a subsequent ground invasion. At this fateful point in the Cold War, it is unlikely that either Kennedy or Castro was thinking about the seemingly inseparable bonds that had tied the two countries together only a few years before.

On November 18, 1963, only a few days before his assassination, Kennedy gave a speech in Miami in which he claimed that Cuba had become "a weapon in an effort dictated by external powers to subvert the other American republics. This and this alone divides us. As long as this is true, nothing is possible. Without it, everything is possible." Kennedy's trusted White House aide Arthur Schlesinger Jr. helped draft the speech and later claimed that its language was intended to show Castro that normalization was possible. Yet this putative olive branch was so well disguised that the following day the *Los Angeles Times* ran a headline reading, "Kennedy Urges Cuban Revolt."

Around this time Kennedy met privately with the French journalist Jean Daniel, who was en route to Havana. More explicitly than in his Miami speech, Kennedy told Daniel that he was willing to lift the trade embargo if Castro would cut his support of revolutionary movements in the region. According to Daniel, Kennedy also expressed some empathy for Castro's virulent anti-Americanism, stating that Washington had committed a "number of sins" in Cuba. After conveying Kennedy's message to Castro a few days later, Daniel reflected that both leaders "seemed ready to make peace."

The assassination of President Kennedy put to rest any gestures of peacemaking between the two countries. America, shocked and reeling, would soon fall deeply into the morass that was Vietnam, while Castro's rule over Cuba would grow ever more authoritarian and inflexible. Over the subsequent years US–Cuba relations degenerated into a pantomime of plots and stratagems, including "exploding conch shells, poison pens, poison pills, sniper rifles, toxic cigars." But while Castro remained seemingly invincible, his revolutionary second-in-command, Che Guevara, was not.

20 • Washington and the Dominican Republic
Part One: Our S.O.B.

"Sure, he's a son of a bitch, but he's *our* son of a bitch." Some variant of this phrase is usually attributed to President Franklin Roosevelt or his secretary of state Cordell Hull, with the "son of a bitch" in question generally being understood as either Nicaragua's Anastasio Somoza or the Dominican Republic's Rafael Trujillo (General Francisco Franco of Spain has also been cited). Although the phrase might be apocryphal, its tenacity in the historical imagination reveals US perspectives in the late 1930s and 1940s. Even though its public rhetoric remained very much in the multilateral spirit of the Good Neighbor Policy, Roosevelt's administration privately understood that it could not jettison even the most unsavory actors if they might have a utility in the broader antifascist struggle. This was Realpolitik 101.

In this chapter we look at this subject through the rise and fall of Rafael Leonidas Trujillo Molina, the "archetypal Latin American dictator" who ruled the Dominican Republic from 1930 to 1961 and served as Washington's S.O.B. leading up to and during World War II. After a period in the sun Trujillo wound up on the wrong end of US policy preferences, and ultimately the CIA conspired in his assassination. Trujillo's downfall, which came not long after the Cuban Revolution in 1959, set the stage for a sizable US effort to back left-leaning democratic reform; and when that failed it led to US boots on the ground to preempt what US officials believed was the real threat of the Dominican Republic falling into communist hands.

Exit US . . .

Understanding how and why the US and Trujillo became bedfellows requires a short discursion into the history of US involvement in the Dominican Republic. The United States militarily occupied the country from 1916 to 1924 in order to quell a brutal guerrilla insurgency in the eastern provinces of El Seibo and Marcorí. In the initial years of the occupation many of the key US diplomatic appointments on the island were held by political appointees who often had only a rudimentary understanding of its culture and language. Complicating matters, the Dominican National Guard, created by the United States in 1917 and responsible for counterinsurgency and stability after an American withdrawal, was an unmitigated disaster.

By the early 1920s, though, savvy policy makers like Sumner Welles (of Cuba fame) started getting a handle on the political and economic administration. In 1922 Welles was named commissioner to the republic with the rank of envoy extraordinary and minister plenipotentiary. In the post–World War I climate, when foreign wars and involvement had lost their luster, Sumner had one fundamental task: secure the end of the US intervention. One pillar in the American withdrawal strategy was to revamp the Guard to stand up and prevent a security vacuum in the postwithdrawal era, a task accomplished in only eighteen months. But the main obstacle, at least as US officials saw it, was the protracted infighting among various Dominican political factions. Washington thus decided that its way out of the Dominican Republic would be through elections, scheduled for March 1924. However imperfect the vote, the election of the aged general Horacio Vásquez marked the first instance in the nation's tumultuous history that the losing candidate actually congratulated the victor. US officials were bullish about the country's prospects. Welles wrote that "a new era of liberty and independence had commenced." This optimism was bolstered by the American expectation that all of the roads, schools, post offices, piers, and telegraph, finance, and sanitation systems built or designed by American administrators and American taxpayer dollars would ensure continued progress. Mission accomplished, it appeared.

. . . Enter Trujillo

Trujillo joined the newly formed Guard in 1918 in his late twenties and quickly capitalized on the social mobility that such an affiliation granted a mulatto, or mixed-blood Dominican, like himself. The socially and politically deft Trujillo wasted little time ingratiating himself with US officers and maneuvering his way up the career ladder. In 1924, on the eve of the American departure, he was promoted to major, being described by a US official as "calm, even-tempered, forceful, active, bold, and painstaking . . . one of the best in the service." In December of that year Vásquez, the newly elected democratic president, promoted Trujillo to lieutenant colonel and chief of staff of the national police. It took Trujillo less than a year to become the commander of the force.

By the end of the decade the Dominican Republic had a newly constituted army and secret police—and Rafael Trujillo was in charge of both. It was time for him to turn his power against his benefactor, Vásquez. Despite his victory in an election in 1924, Vásquez was now organizing a dubious constitutional maneuver to allow himself to remain in office until 1930. In February of that year, just a few months before the elections for which Vásquez had declared his candidacy, an uprising against his increasingly autocratic rule broke out in the city of Santiago de los Caballeros. US diplomats in Santo Domingo mediated the conflict between the insurgents and the national government that led to a cessation of hostilities. After talking with US officials and seeing the handwriting on the wall, Vásquez agreed to step down. Rafael Estrella Ureña, a leader of the revolt, was named provisional president before the scheduled elections and was quickly recognized by Washington.

The cagey Trujillo had initially supported Estrella Ureña's revolt, anticipating that it would loosen Vásquez's grasp on power, but once that threat had been neutralized he wasted no time pushing Ureña aside to emerge as the presidential candidate. Trujillo won the May 16, 1930, vote by the overwhelming—and highly fraudulent—margin of 223,731 to 1,883. The US minister wrote back that the number of votes "far exceeds" the number of voters in the country. Although US officials were well aware of Trujillo's electoral malfeasance, it did not take long for the Hoover administration to grant him recognition. This time there was little appetite in Washington for foreign intervention. Pretending that Trujillo was democratically elected was preferable to getting involved. And even if Hoover had the desire and political capital necessary to mount an intervention, as history had shown, there was no guarantee that Trujillo's hypothetical replacement would be an upstanding character. With this in mind, Hoover cabled his recognition in August, commemorating the "auspicious occasion of your [Trujillo's] elevation to the high office of President of the Dominican Republic" and sending "best wishes" for "the happiness of the people of the Republic under your wise administration." The decision to recognize Trujillo was not an isolated instance. In 1930 alone the Hoover administration recognized seven military or personal dictatorships that overturned democratic governments.

Scholars often portray Trujillo's rise to power and iron-fisted rule as a direct result of the US military's establishment and training of local police forces that, after the American departure, turned into institutions of political repression and autocratic rule. For example, the political scientist Peter Smith writes that in the US occupation of the Dominican Republic (as well as Haiti and Nicaragua), "Washington supervised the creation of local constabularies that would eventually become the agents of dictatorial repression. Not only did the United States fail to promote democratic development in Latin America; it could even be argued with considerable reason that U.S. military interventions tended to retard the prospects for political democracy." Yet Smith overlooks that the Dominican Republic pre-1916 did not enjoy even the semblance of "political democracy" that could have been retarded by the US occupation. A more balanced and accurate interpretation might be that US indifference following the 1924 withdrawal—such as its unwillingness to intervene in the fraudulent 1930 elections—helped allow a schemer like Trujillo to take advantage of the still-fragile political situation. In this sense, keeping a figure such as Trujillo at bay could have actually necessitated more US involvement and meddling, not less.

Perhaps sensing the need to counterbalance his antidemocratic seizure of power with a diplomatic charm offensive, Trujillo, once in office, focused the Caribbean nation's policies on winning US favor through trade pacts and greater US foreign investment. Over the ensuing decades Trujillo spent vast sums of money employing top-level political lobbyists in Washington and entertaining the endless procession of US congressional delegations that came to Santo Domingo to view the professed Trujilloist Miracle of a dirt-poor nation modernizing into a Caribbean power. By renegotiating the Dominican Republic's sovereign debt Trujillo was able to direct money toward infrastructure projects as well as his military and won acclaim by creating a favorable investment environment for foreign capital. The *New York Times* went so far as to say that Trujillo was on par with "the President of the United States as an economist and reformer." Trujillo even sought to lock arms with Washington in the fight against European fascism leading up to World War II; the Dominican despot was well aware of the continued influence that the United States had in the Dominican Republic and the region more broadly.

On the domestic side, however, Trujillo was a brutal steward of the country. Almost all political opposition was banned, and the Dominican Republic was transformed into an authoritarian, conspiratorial society. The regime used violence, fear, and terror as ends in themselves. Relying on an intricate espionage

General Rafael Trujillo was accorded a luncheon at the US Capitol by Senator
Theodore Green of Rhode Island. Avidly talking to the general, who spoke no
English, are Senators Green and Guy Gillette while Minister Andrés Pastoriza rapidly
interprets. *(Left to right)* Trujillo, Green, Pastoriza, Gillette. July 7, 1939. (Library of
Congress, Prints and Photographs Division, Washington, DC)

network, Trujillo set out to consolidate his rule throughout the cities and countryside. In one particularly heinous episode, in early October 1937 Trujillo ordered his military to massacre the Haitians, including Dominicans of Haitian
descent, who lived along the binational border. These killings, carried out over
roughly a week, were executed by machete "in order to sell the regime's official
account that the massacre was a spontaneous uprising of patriotic Dominican
farmers against Haitian cattle thieves." Estimates of the number killed in what
is known as the Parsley Massacre range from ten thousand to thirty thousand.

Throughout the thirties, forties, and fifties Trujillo continued to be either
reelected or supposedly succeeded by a puppet president, but he was never
content to be merely another venal strongman. A true totalitarian, he wanted
to forge the country in his image, and he set out to establish himself as the
sole figure controlling not only Dominicans' political and economic activities

but also their social and cultural ones. A province was soon named after him, and the congress passed a resolution declaring him "Benefactor of the Fatherland." In 1936 Santo Domingo, the oldest of European capitals in the Caribbean, was renamed Ciudad Trujillo. Trujillo held over forty different titles, including Genius of Peace, Father of the New Fatherland, Protector of Fine Arts and Letters, and The First and Greatest of Dominican Chiefs of State. One figure put monuments to Trujillo in Ciudad Trujillo at eighteen hundred. It has been estimated that the Trujillo family held nearly two-thirds of the national wealth.

Communist Cuba Changes Everything

Initially, Trujillo was able to successfully pivot from being an anti-Axis S.O.B. to an anticommunist one when the Cold War began in the late 1940s. After Vice President Nixon toured the country in 1955, he extolled the national president: "[Trujillo is] one of the hemisphere's foremost spokesmen against the communist movement." But regardless of its impeccably cultivated reputation as fiercely anticommunist, the Trujillo administration was rampantly corrupt. The regime's image deteriorated during the latter half of the 1950s, presenting a dilemma for Ike and his foreign policy team, who were ostensibly committed to spreading liberty among the global communist oppressors. In 1956 Colonel Johnny Abbes García, a "violently anti-American, anti-clerical thug," became head of the secret police and the "principal confidant" of Trujillo, who was then in his mid-sixties and "whose behavior was increasingly erratic." Like leftover seafood, Trujillo was beginning to smell bad.

Moreover, the Trujillo regime's method of rallying US congressmen—supplying prostitutes and over $5 million in bribes—became increasingly known and was becoming a public relations nightmare for the Eisenhower administration. After his ill-fated trip to the region in 1958—during which anti-American activists pelted him with "rocks, bottles, eggs, and oranges" in Peru and a mob tried to overturn his car in Caracas—the anticommunist hawk and then vice president Nixon came to see the US relationship with regional despots as counterproductive and that addressing poverty should be the real focus of US policy. Immediately after the trip Nixon told the National Security Council that the US government "must be dedicated to raising the standard of living of the masses," offer only a "cool handshake" to strongmen, advice mocked by moderates and leftists alike throughout the region, and champion democratic leaders. If key officials like the Dulles brothers were inclined to

stick with strongmen, Eisenhower's team was talking with democratic reformers such as Costa Rica's José Figueres and Venezuela's Rómulo Betancourt. In
turn, these reformers urged Washington to distance itself from strongmen,
above all, Trujillo.

Then, in 1959, when Fidel Castro and his motley band of bearded revolutionaries came to power, Trujillo was suddenly faced with an ideological and
regional rival. It was admittedly a difficult start for the two in that the former
Cuban strongman Fulgencio Batista had fled into exile in Trujillo's Dominican Republic. The countries' relationship worsened when Trujillo emerged as
one of Castro's principal ideological enemies. Representing a bold move considering that his own revolution was only six months old, in June 1959 Castro
ordered an invasion of the Dominican Republic by groups of insurgents of
various nationalities. Trujillo's forces soon apprehended the invaders and
killed them in what Trujillo labeled a "rabbit hunt." Some insurgents who
were not immediately killed were taken to the San Isidro Air Base, where Trujillo's son Ramfis tortured them. Only five guerrillas survived the invasion.
Although he easily stomped Castro's plot, Trujillo didn't miss an opportunity
to play up the threat of a communist insurrection to his "increasingly concerned American counterparts."

In 1960 it was Trujillo's turn to attempt regime change. This time the Great
Benefactor, as he liked to be referred to, backed a plot to assassinate his longtime regional rival, Venezuela's Betancourt. But Betancourt was only wounded
in the bombing of his vehicle. In response, the OAS, backed by Eisenhower,
slapped sanctions on Trujillo, including suspending diplomatic ties. Trujillo
did not take it lying down and, through Colonel Abbes, initiated a series of
maneuvers in response to the tougher stance of the US, easing tensions with
Castro's Havana, reaching out to Moscow, and legalizing the Dominican Communist Party. Utilizing his propaganda network housed in a whopping fifty-
four consulates inside the United States, Trujillo "[took] out advertisements in
newspapers and planted stories with friendly journalists." These stories sought
to reinforce Trujillo's anticommunist stance in the minds of American readers, the implicit message being that the excesses of the regime should be ex-
cused in the name of blunting the Communist advance. However, they did
little to return Trujillo to the good graces of the US government, which had had
enough of the shocking abuses of power on the island.

That same year an exasperated Eisenhower approved a State Department
paper on policies to be enacted "in the event of the flight, assassination, death,
or overthrow of Trujillo" in order to prevent a Castro-type government or one

sympathetic to Castro. Mooted options included sending a US naval force or even devising an armed intervention. On orders from the White House, Ambassador Joseph Farland, Senator George Smathers of Florida, and former ambassador to Peru and Brazil William Pawley all made the futile voyage to Santo Domingo, each returning with the same message from Trujillo: "I'll never go out of here unless I go out on a stretcher."

Regime Change

As the historian Stephen Rabe has chronicled, between September 1960 and May 1961 State Department and CIA officials labored over the question of whether and how to get rid of Trujillo via covert means. Eisenhower's thinking was that Washington would never be able to garner hemispheric diplomatic support for the (still secret and soon-to-be calamitous Bay of Pigs) anti-Castro invasion if Trujillo was still in power. There were also hesitations about a power vacuum in the Dominican Republic after Trujillo was dead. Here is Under Secretary of State C. Douglas Dillon to Eisenhower in October 1960: "We do not want to take concrete moves against the Dominican Republic just at present, since no successor to Trujillo is ready to take power, and the result might be to bring an individual of the Castro stripe into power there."

Per Eisenhower's request, the US ambassador in Santo Domingo, Joseph Farland, contacted Dominican anti-Trujillistas interested in removing the dictator; the putative insurgents requested twelve sniper rifles. (It might appear curious to modern readers why the insurgents requested low-tech weapons, but it must be remembered that weapons were not readily available, as the National Guard had a monopoly over lethal force in the country.) Farland's tenure as ambassador came to an end in 1960, but he introduced his successor, Henry Dearborn.

Dearborn was very much left alone to run the operation, as all CIA personnel departed the Dominican Republic following Eisenhower's suspension of diplomatic relations with the Caribbean nation in 1960. Negotiations over the operation dragged on as the dissidents consistently changed their request, from firearms to antitank weapons and delayed lethal chemicals, whereby a handshake would transmit the lethal chemicals into Trujillo's system. It was likely this indecisiveness and disorganization that led Dearborn to cable Washington that the dissidents were "in no way ready to carry out any type of revolutionary activity in the foreseeable future, except the assassination of their principal enemy [Trujillo]."

As 1961 commenced, the reins of operation were passed from Eisenhower to the newly elected president, John F. Kennedy. Under the inexperienced Kennedy, in early 1961 a supply of pistols and carbines was delivered to the Dominican dissidents via Dearborn. Shortly thereafter the world witnessed a catastrophic uncovering of CIA operations in Cuba: the April 1961 Bay of Pigs invasion. Kennedy's attempt to oust the communist Fidel Castro from Cuba was such a disaster that the president reached out to Dearborn in the Dominican Republic to call off the assassination of Trujillo, but with arms already in the hands of the dissidents it was too late to change tack.

On May 30, 1961, after the sun had set, Antonio Imbert Barrera and Antonio de la Maza, both former military loyalists, orchestrated and executed the assassination of Rafael Trujillo. As Trujillo rode in his snazzy Chevrolet along an abandoned strip of road between Santo Domingo and San Cristóbal (the locale where he regularly met with a mistress) the assassins blocked the path of the tyrant's car and, in the ensuing gunfire, emptied twenty-seven rounds into his body. With Trujillo dead and no immediate plan for new governance, the Caribbean nation fell into disarray. The United States removed itself entirely from the situation, pulling Dearborn from Santo Domingo, partly to save face: how would it look if the CIA was outed as being involved in the Dominican plot only weeks or months after Kennedy's covert Cuba operation had blown up in his face?

In the mid-1970s a congressional investigation into secret CIA programs—known as the Church Committee after the chairman, Democratic senator Frank Church of Idaho—concluded that the CIA provided "material support" to the Dominican plotters who killed Trujillo, and the covert program, as the Ohio Democratic representative James V. Stanton put it, represented a "successful assassination attempt." But decades after the assassination many Dominican voices disputed the accounts depicting consequential CIA involvement in Trujillo's murder. Given how much suffering and political and social retardation had occurred under Trujillo's rule, it was a point of pride for many that Dominicans alone had been able to kill their tormentor. Antonio Imbert Barrera, the only plotter out of the seven who survived the initial post-Trujillo retribution phase, described the Church Committee's assessment as "a cowboy picture without any basis in reality. . . . The men who participated in that historic act did not need help. We had our own arms, we had our own cars, we had our own reasons. My friend, I challenge anybody to find the aid of any foreign organization in what we did."

The extent of US involvement in the operational components of the Trujillo assassination might never be fully known, yet it does appear that US "secret squirrel" spies, so often associated with unsavory or outright immoral actions like the 1954 Guatemala and 1973 Chile cases, were, in this instance, on the side of anti-tyranny. Either way, the role the US played in the killing of Trujillo would pale in comparison to Washington's infinitely more maximalist campaign in the Dominican Republic in 1965.

21 • Washington and the Dominican Republic

Part Two: Intervention

With the recent failure in Cuba very much in mind, in May 1961 President Kennedy made it patently clear that preventing the spread of communism into the Americas was his country's overriding priority: "Should it even appear that the inter-American doctrine of non-intervention merely conceals or excuses a policy of nonaction—if the nations of this hemisphere should fail to meet their commitments against outside Communist penetration—then I want it clearly understood that this government will not hesitate in meeting its primary obligations which are to the security of our nation." Kennedy's fighting talk betrayed his anxiety about the postassassination period in the Dominican Republic, which he saw as terrifyingly ripe for communist subversion. Trujillo's murder in May 1961 had plunged the country into chaos, setting off a series of reprisals that could be called Trujillismo without Trujillo. Security forces rounded up or killed critics of the regime, including most of the assassination plotters. Then Trujillo's erratic son Ramfis seized power. This action was not the preferred outcome of the US, given that the CIA almost certainly played a role in his father's death. But while the desired democratic outcome wasn't forthcoming in the immediate aftermath of Trujillo's death, perhaps the regime's continuity would nullify any communist influence. At this point Kennedy outlined the three paths the Dominican Republic could take: "In descending order of preference: a decent democratic regime, a continuation of the Trujillo regime, or a Castro regime. We ought to aim for the first but we can't really renounce the second until we are sure we can avoid the third."

Ramfis's tenure was short-lived. In November 1961 two of the elder Trujillo's brothers, Héctor and José Arismendy, returned from exile and challenged Ramfis's control over the military and family wealth. Kennedy immediately dispatched a naval task force to anchor off the coast of Santo Domingo, send-ing a strong message to Trujillo's "wicked uncles" that to move against Joaquín Balaguer, once Trujillo's figurehead president but now officially in charge, would not be tolerated. As always, Kennedy was on the watch to see if com-munists would exploit the situation. Kennedy instructed Balaguer that the United States was interested in "progress of anti-communist laws in [the] Do-minican Congress, measures taken [to] exclude [the] return [of] Communist and Castroist exile, and other actions taken [to] prevent infiltration and agita-tion by Communist–Castroist elements."

"Pearl of the Caribbean"

Political instability continued unabated in the country. On January 15, 1962, Balaguer was forced into exile by forces led by General Rafael Rodríguez Echevarría of the Dominican air force. Kennedy countered by once again dis-patching a task force off the coast, which helped lead to Echevarría's arrest. Captain Elias Wessin y Wessin presided over a so-called Council of State until elections took place that December, the first democratic election in the Do-minican Republic since 1924, the year the marines left the island.

Enter Juan Bosch, the hypnotic leader of the social-democratic Dominican Revolutionary Party (PRD), who had returned to the Dominican Republic in 1961 after twenty-five years in exile. Bosch duly won a landslide, taking 648,000 votes out of roughly a million votes cast and beating his closest com-petitor by a two-to-one margin. The PRD also garnered twenty-two of twenty-seven seats in the Chamber of Deputies. President-elect Bosch visited the Kennedy White House, and Vice President Lyndon Johnson attended Bosch's inauguration on February 27, 1963.

Praying that Bosch would be able to transform the Dominican Republic into a "showcase for democracy," the Kennedy administration quickly poured over $100 million in US assistance into the country. Hundreds of US techni-cal experts and young, idealistic volunteers from the newly created Peace Corps went to the country during Bosch's tenure as president. Yet despite these efforts Bosch turned out to be a disappointment to many, as he was unable to follow up on the many promises he made during his idealistic cam-paign.

Part of Bosch's problems stemmed from the fact that he was the first demo-cratic president in a country more accustomed to mano dura leadership than democratic politics. Bosch's standing in this postdictatorial ecosystem was undermined when he allowed communists to operate openly in the country—at least from the perspective of conservative and military circles. Not himself a communist, Bosch's approach resembled that of Árbenz in Guatemala, whose tolerance for communist activity contributed to the rationale the Eisenhower administration used to covertly get rid of him. That said, US ambassador John Bartlow Martin was originally a strong supporter of Bosch, hoping that he could be the president who would unite Dominicans behind a progressive, but non-Communist government. Yet like his boss John Kennedy, Martin remained doubtful that Bosch was indeed the type of reformer Washington had hoped for. For example, Martin recalled that with respect to Bosch, "in our own interest, we could not ignore several possibilities—that Bosch himself was a deep-cover Communist (I did not and do not believe it); that he would lose cover control of his PRD to the Castro/Communists; that if he failed to meet the people's expectations he might be overthrown."

Over time the Kennedy administration moved from a policy of cautious support to one of damage control. Policy decisions were increasingly focused on ensuring that Bosch's tenure did not lead to another military coup or, much worse, a communist takeover. Years later Vice President Johnson outlined the progress of US disenchantment with Bosch: "We continued to hope that Bosch would be able to do for this people what President Rómulo Betancourt had done for Venezuela after dictatorship had been overthrown there. But Bosch was no Betancourt. While his aspirations were admirable, his performance was weak. . . . He lacked the capacity to unite under his leadership the various elements that wanted progress and constitutional government— elements of the non-Communist left and center. Nor was he able to control or satisfy the rightists, including powerful elements in the military, who looked on him with suspicion." One of Kennedy's top officials, George Ball, was a little less diplomatic than Johnson in his description of Bosch but perhaps closer to the administration's consensus view. To Ball, Bosch was "unrealistic, arrogant, and erratic. I thought him incapable of running even a small social club, much less a country in turmoil. He did not seem to me a Communist . . . but merely a muddle-headed, anti-American pendant committed to unattainable social reforms."

With rumors of a conservative coup circulating throughout Santo Domingo, on September 24, 1963, a desperate Bosch asked Ambassador Martin to request immediate military assistance from Washington. Bosch wanted not a full-scale invasion but a naval force off the coast, similar to what Washington had done against Trujillo's family in November 1961 and the Echevarría coup in January 1962. Martin went ahead and asked that the United States "alert a carrier as requested," but Washington rejected his recommendation. Martin was then told that "little more can be done by us to maintain [Bosch] in office against the forces that he himself has created." Privately, Martin agreed with Washington's decision. Although he publicly opposed the coup against Bosch and had requested a task force, he nonetheless cabled Washington that "I have no desire to return him . . . to power."

On September 25, only seven months after taking office, Bosch was overthrown, and he escaped into exile in Puerto Rico. The Dominican army, supported by some conservative political groups, led the bloodless coup that ousted Bosch, who they claimed was insufficiently tough on communism on the island. The coup leaders immediately banned communist groups, promised to hold free elections, and declared Bosch's 1963 constitution, a highly progressive one by Dominican standards, nonexistent. A year later Donald Reid Cabral, who had earlier served in the governing mechanism before Bosch's 1962 election, became the head of a three-person civilian junta.

Back at the White House, Kennedy was unhappy. The coup had damaged Washington's policies of promoting democratic social change, and he did not want to see the country revert to the Trujillistas. Washington initially withheld diplomatic recognition of the junta, and on October 4, 1963, Kennedy ordered Secretary of Defense Robert McNamara to create contingency plans for a potential military intervention in the Dominican Republic. By November, however, Kennedy had decided that the United States needed to deal with the reality in the country rather than pursue lofty dreams. Thus Kennedy decided to recognize the junta, known as the governing Triumvirate, but he was assassinated before his order went through. The newly governing Johnson administration recognized the government on December 14, 1963, based on the agreement that it would hold national elections in 1965.

Revolution!

Reid Cabral's first year and a half as head of the country did not present any acute crises, which, after the reprisals following Trujillo's assassination and the disaster of the Bosch experiment, was not an unwelcome development as far as the Johnson administration was concerned. Then, on April 24, 1965, events took a sudden turn as a pro-Bosch armed revolt broke out in Santo Domingo. Almost overnight the capital's streets were full of residents, some armed and some not, and soldiers allied to various factions. The US embassy reported that two-thirds of the army stationed in Santo Domingo was in revolt and providing arms to civilians. Buoyed by thousands of civilians who had surrounded the presidential palace, the former Reid Cabral advisor and recently turned Constitutionalist (referencing the Bosch-associated Constitution of 1963) military commander Francisco Caamaño Deñó seized the palace, arrested Cabral, and affirmed his support for Bosch. The Constitutionalists—a set of diverse groups ranging from military officers, PRD members, democratic socialists, and orthodox communists to opportunists—proceeded to take control of the city without encountering resistance from the Loyalist forces, as the anti-Constitutionalist side was being called. It appeared that it was only a matter of time before Bosch's triumphant return to power. Soon, Radio Santo Domingo announced that the Constitutionalists should support the PRD leader José Molina Ureña, who had just declared himself "provisional constitutionalist president."

But the situation in Santo Domingo grew rapidly more convoluted. Communist groups such as the pro-Castro IJ4 and the Movimiento Popular Dominicano joined the Constitutionalist rebels, complicating Washington's ability to understand if the revolt was largely anti-Cabral, pro-Bosch, or communist in nature. The *New York Times* journalist Tad Szulc wrote that "machine guns, rifles and side arms were being issued to anyone who asked for them at army headquarters (now Constitutionalist-controlled) in Santo Domingo and yesterday all the military patrols in the capital were accompanied by armed civilians." More than ten thousand primitive gas bombs were believed to be in the possession of civilians. The Dominican Civil War, which would officially last for about four months, had broken out.

Intervention!

White House telephone recordings offer an incredible insight as to how, from April 24 onward, President Johnson reacted to the outbreak of hostilities and a potential Bosch return in Santo Domingo. In the first recorded conversation on the Dominican crisis, here is Johnson speaking to the hawkish senior State Department official Thomas Mann:

> JOHNSON: We're going to have to really set up that government down there and run it and stabilize it some way or other. This Bosch is no good. I was down there.
>
> MANN: And if we don't get a decent government in there, Mr. President, we get another Bosch. It's just going to be a sinkhole.

[handwritten margin note: set up gov proxies]

Johnson and his senior advisors, among whom was National Security Advisor McGeorge Bundy, were getting breathless intelligence reports from the CIA. On April 26 a report reached Bundy detailing how "evidence of participation in the movement to restore Bosch by Communists and other extreme leftists has continued to come to light. The reprisal threats among other indications point to increasing extremist domination of the movement. . . . Some of the military leaders [rebel leaders] now appear to realize they were duped by the Bosch supporters and extremists." The following day the CIA submitted an alarming report to Secretary of State Dean Rusk: "Should the [Loyalist] forces . . . supported by the major elements of the air force and elements of the navy over the next several hours or days be unable to defeat that revolution that started last Saturday, the Dominican Republic . . . will be so far on the way to becoming another Cuba that the tide may well not be able to be turned back, unless the US take prompt and strong action. Pro-Communist—if not Communist—people are emerging as members of the 'cabinet' of 'provisional president' Molina Ureña. Communists are gathering arms and reportedly have a real 'in' with at least one arsenal. They set up strong points within the city."

On April 28 Johnson ordered marines to evacuate US nationals from the island, which resulted in almost twelve hundred people being brought back. Just two days later the president received another dire intelligence report: "Early in the present insurrection it became apparent that the well-organized Dominican Communists and associated extremists were committing their full resources to the full effort. . . . [T]he well-armed mobs now resisting the hard-pressed loyalist forces are largely controlled by the Communists and other extremists. . . . While there is no evidence that the Castro regime is directly involved in the current insurrection, it is nevertheless clear that Cuban[-] trained Dominican extremists are taking an active part."

It's possible that the US intelligence agencies were fabricating and/or hyping their analysis to get the executive branch to act in a certain, decidedly more interventionist, way, but no evidence confirming this hypothesis has yet emerged. Indeed, even some of Johnson's more liberal advisors, such as Arthur Schlesinger Jr., were expressing deep concern at the unfolding situation. Schlesinger sent a note to Bundy on May 2 that reads in part: "The problem is to prevent a communist takeover in the DR while doing as little harm as possible to our general position in the hemisphere. . . . It is conceivable that we may have no choice but to accept hemispheric condemnation, damn the torpedoes and go ahead; but we clearly should not pursue a course so risky to our long-term objectives unless we had exhausted all other possibilities."

Johnson finally concluded that a second, more forceful intervention was warranted. On April 30 the 82nd Airborne Division landed at the San Isidro base outside the capital. Within a week there were twenty-three American troops in the country—half the number then deployed in Vietnam! To Johnson the litmus test for a successful operation was twofold: first, that the incipient civil war be quelled and, second, that Bosch and his leftist/communist instability not return. And this desired goal meant that, while trying to act as a peacemaking force, the US troops effectively sided with the Loyalists in the fighting in and around Santo Domingo. Here is how the joint chiefs of staff described the mission to the commanding officer: "Your announced mission is to save U.S. lives. Your unannounced mission is to prevent the Dominican Republic from going Communist. The President had stated that he will not allow another Cuba—you are to take all necessary measures to accomplish this mission. You will be given sufficient forces to do the job."

82nd Airborne Out, OAS (and the CIA) In

On April 29, 1965, the OAS passed a resolution on the Dominican crisis calling for an immediate cease-fire and the establishment of an international security zone in the capital. Even with the 16–0 vote (and four abstentions: Uruguay, Venezuela, Chile, and Mexico), there was a perception of the resolution effectively rubber-stamping US action, given that the marine evacuation had already occurred and the 82nd Airborne would land at San Isidro the next day. On May 6 the OAS created the Inter-American Peace Force (IAPF), but with only the minimum of fourteen votes. Complicating the Johnson administration's desire to present the mission as promoting democracy, most of the participating nations were under military regimes like Brazil's or strongman rule as in Paraguay and Nicaragua.

To cynical observers the IAPF was simply window dressing for the US move to restore conservative rule in the country, but over the next several months it managed to prevent the civil war from escalating and led both sides to begin negotiations. Behind the scenes, however, a fascinating side story began to emerge starting that May. National Security Advisor Bundy hatched a secret committee consisting of high-level officials like Deputy Secretary of Defense Cyrus Vance, the CIA's Richard Helms, and Thomas Mann. Within weeks Bundy had traveled to Puerto Rico to negotiate in secret with Silvestre Antonio Guzmán Fernández, a PRD member and Bosch ally. During the talks Bosch agreed to drop his insistence on the removal of US troops. Under the so-called Guzmán formula Bundy and Bosch agreed that Guzmán would be the compromise leader of a future government. Johnson's liberal advisors like Abe Fortas and Schlesinger supported the Guzmán option, but Mann and General Bruce Palmer, the deputy commander of the IAPF, felt that Bosch and Boschismo had to be prevented at all costs; the Guzmán formula was too big a risk. On May 15 a despondent President Johnson explained his decision to back the rejection of the plan: "Here's our problem. . . . My right wing . . . won't give me 40 cents if I'm not careful."

Despite the lack of international support, Juan Bosch threw his hat into the ring for the 1966 presidential election, where his main rival was none other than Joaquín Balaguer. Back in 1962 the leftist reformer Bosch had been widely popular, but his chaotic term in office had long since diminished his standing among the people. Given that polls in 1965 had Balaguer well ahead, Bosch would have likely lost the presidential vote had it been free and fair, but the Johnson administration left no room for chance, orchestrating a covert operation to help ensure Balaguer's victory. Gaining 57 percent of the vote share to Bosch's 39 percent, Balaguer won the decidedly imperfect election and proceeded to rule the country as an illiberal president over the next two decades.

Another Cuba?

A strong case can be made that the Johnson administration overreacted in the Dominican Republic. The oft-argued point is that the initial dispatch of US marines to protect US citizens was warranted but that the subsequent decision to send the 82nd Airborne into the heart of the fighting in Santo Domingo was when Washington went too far—too Big Stick. The difficulty with this reasoning is that the US actually successfully ended most of the fighting and after several months of gridlock initiated negotiations. In fact, Bosch's supporters even came around to the final US-brokered agreements more than their adversaries.

Part of the administration's failings in this crisis is how they, perhaps needlessly, overhyped the threats in play. An example is Johnson's address to the nation on May 2, which reads in part: "The revolutionary movement took a tragic turn. Communist leaders, many of them trained in Cuba, seeing a chance to increase their disorder, to gain a foothold, joined the revolution. They took increasing control. What began as a popular democratic revolution committed to democracy and social justice very shortly moved and was taken over and really seized and placed into the hands of Communist conspirators."

Domestic
*

Johnson's explanations did not always line up with what was being reported on the island, leading to a credibility gap perceived by many journalists. Tad Szulc, for one, began to openly question the extent of communist involvement in the revolt. On April 29 the US embassy handed out a list of fifty-three identified communists active on the Constitutionalist side, a contention Secretary Rusk reinforced on Capitol Hill. But then it became apparent that some of the names were double-listed, in jail, or no longer in the country. Johnson's credibility gap would later come to haunt him throughout the unfolding tragedy in Vietnam.

Many observers went deeper, directly linking the crisis of 1965 to the overthrow of Bosch in 1963. They posited the counterfactual idea that if the United States had worked harder to support Bosch's presidency, he would not have been overthrown, there would have been no pro-Bosch revolt and therefore no need for a US intervention. Or even when Bosch had been ousted, some wondered whether more US support for the Constitutionalists might have permitted a pacific return by Bosch, given how the ebullient Constitutionalist revolt would be stymied within days. William J. Fulbright, an Arkansas Democratic senator and chairman of the Foreign Relations Committee, asked Ambassador William T. Bennett Jr. at hearings later on in 1965 whether the United States had missed a golden opportunity to back the Constitutionalists.

Bennett's answer reveals that although US officials may have overhyped the communist threat, they certainly believed it was real. "I don't think so," Bennett replied. Why? Because by that point the communists had sufficiently infiltrated the Constitutionalist forces so that a Bosch return could have led to a communist takeover. Fulbright pressed further, asking Ambassador Bennett whether it was his opinion that a Constitutionalist victory would necessarily have led to a communist regime in the Dominican Republic. Bennett replied, "It is mine, and I think, almost every other observer on the scene, the Papal Nuncio, the British Embassy, most of the Latin American embassies, the Colombian, the Peruvian, the Guatemala, the Brazilian."

Fulbright was ultimately convinced by the assessment that there was significant communist involvement in the pro-Bosch revolt, but as is evidenced in later remarks to CIA director William F. Raborn, he wondered whether the US might have taken a less interventionist approach: "The question that interests me very much is not whether the communists were influential, which I think you have made clear, but whether they were dominant, and, more importantly, whether we tried to exert a countervailing moderate influence on the rebel leadership."

With bayonets fixed, US troops form a line for Dominicans awaiting foodstuffs
in the revolt-torn capital of Santo Domingo, Dominican Republic. May 27, 1965.
(AP Photo / Jack Thornell)

In the final analysis Johnson was caught in a bind: intervention would
make him unpopular in Latin America but doing nothing would make him
unpopular at home for appearing soft on tackling communism and, much
worse, potentially creating "another Cuba." In his own lament he said, "If I
send in the marines, I can't live in the hemisphere. If I don't, I can't live at
home." Ultimately, he decided that the danger of not acting was too great and
intervened. Bennett lectured Fulbright about the stakes at play in terms of
America's global credibility: "What would have been the reaction in Latin
America if we had not taken the action and the place had gone completely bad
and we had allowed another Cuba or incipient Cuba to develop there? I am
sure we would have been more heavily criticized than we have been."

The historian Piero Gleijeses has convincingly shown that Dominican
communists were largely marginal players in the pro-Bosch revolt and might
not have been able to command the revolt even without US involvement. Yet
this fact does not change the reality that Washington perceived the threat to be
serious, even if there was a significant amount of internal debate inside the
administration about its exact extent.

Some will continue to make the case that in late April 1965 Washington ended "five glorious days" of pro-Bosch Constitutionalist revolt in Santo Domingo. But any balanced analysis of the crisis must also ask what could have transpired if the United States had not intervened. It is not unreasonable to ponder that without US intervention there also could have been five hundred days of violent civil war or five, or fifty, years of communism. Johnson's predicament is perhaps best captured by Joseph Heller in his famous novel *Catch-22* about the strategic paradoxes of warfare: "Just because you're paranoid doesn't mean they aren't after you."

22 • A Very Brazilian Coup

"Military Intervention Already!! Brazil demands order and progress!!" Thus read several of the banners waved during public protests that overwhelmed Brazil's major cities beginning in 2014. Beaten down by a massive public corruption scandal, seemingly unchecked street violence, and economic malaise, Brazilians longed for clean governance and public safety. To many this translated into open nostalgia for the military regime that governed Brazil from 1964 to 1985. This environment also facilitated the 2019 presidential election of Jair Bolsonaro, a right-leaning populist who referred to the April 1, 1964, ouster of President João "Jango" Goulart as a "democratic revolution" as opposed to a military coup. Indeed, both the legacy of Brazil's military era as well as the nature of the coup itself remain highly contested—in spite of the ongoing declassification of US and Brazilian official documents. One fundamental question remains: What was the role of the US government in the 1964 coup?

When the Brazilian military presented President Goulart with the ultimatum to step down or be removed in April 1964, it was in many ways Latin America's best predicted coup. Jango was an accidental president, having taken the post unexpectedly when the elected president, Jânio Quadros, suddenly resigned just over two years prior. By 1964 the economy was saddled with 100 percent annual inflation and balance-of-payments difficulties exacerbated by growing international debt. Added to this was upper- and middle-class backlash against Goulart's recent radical decrees as well as overt criticism from the Catholic Church. Fearing that Goulart's land-expropriating, communist-sympathizing tendencies threatened the strength of the military as well as the fate of the country, military leaders had one by one abandoned him.

Unlike his presidential predecessor, Getúlio Vargas, who committed suicide in response to a not-dissimilar military conspiracy, Goulart silently slipped into Uruguay, leaving his post with virtually no violence. The outcome could not have been more favorable for President Lyndon Johnson's administration: a pro-US military officer, Castelo Branco, took office and pledged to repair the polarized politics in Brazil that led to his predecessor's ouster in the first place.

Many saw traces of US influence behind the seismic events, and in the ensuing decades the Goulart coup remained a commonly referenced example of US heavy-handedness and plotting in its backyard. There may be some justification to this charge, but it is important to take into consideration Washington's denial of any involvement as well as acknowledge the agency of the Brazilian military independent of US involvement. What is clear is that the US fear of communism was in play during this period: while US strategy for this problem might have changed since Guatemala and the Bay of Pigs, the game remained the same.

Kennedy Contains Communism

To go back a few years, before 1964, in the aftermath of the profoundly disturbing (to Washington, at least) Cuban Revolution in 1959, Kennedy was adamant that there could not be "another Cuba" in Latin America. After enduring the utterly humiliating debacle of the Bay of Pigs and Guatemala's gradual descent into strongman autocracy and revolution in the years following the US-hatched coup, Kennedy's team concluded that a better way to stem communism in Latin America was to avoid large-scale intervention and reckless military ventures. More effective, they thought, would be to deal instead with the root causes of inequity and injustice that led people in places like Cuba to turn to Marxist revolution in the first place. In the president's oft-quoted view, "Those who make peaceful revolution impossible will make violent revolution inevitable."

The hallmark of Kennedy's "peaceful revolution" strategy was the Alliance for Progress, a planned ten-year program of massive economic investment and assistance to promote sorely needed political, social, and economic reform in the region. In his inaugural address on January 20, 1961, Kennedy made a bold promise: "To our sister republics south of our border, we offer a special pledge—to convert our good words into good deeds—in a new alliance for progress—to assist free men and free governments in casting off the chains of poverty." Launched that same year, the alliance, in conjunction with the newly created Agency for International Development, sought to dedicate tens of billions of dollars to help Latin Americans implement better tax schemes, promote land-reform efforts, and give the majority poor and disenfranchised a stake in these reformist governments. Kennedy's men (they *were* all men) also put together a Task Force on Latin America led by Adolf Berle, the former assistant secretary of state and ambassador to Brazil during the Vargas years and a steadfast anticommunist. Its goals? Channel the revolutions in Latin America in the proper (read: democratic and capitalist) direction in coordination with the nascent Alliance for Progress.

Fearing that as goes Brazil, so goes the rest of Latin America, one of Kennedy's priorities upon taking office in January 1961 was to not "lose" Brazil to communism—an outcome that seemed increasingly likely given the revolutionary environment in Brazil post-1959. Kennedy's approach was twofold: Washington's provision of alliance-era aid meant millions of dollars of development aid to support Brazil's desperately poor northeast, while US military aid to Brazil also made a subtle yet meaningful change. Rather than providing support to protect from external enemies, as the US had done during World War II, its purpose now was to bolster the Brazilian government against the internal communist threat. As General William Enemark, a Defense Department director, testified in 1962, aid would bolster the efficacy of the armed forces, creating "well-disciplined and well-trained Latin-American armed forces, led by men of moderate views" who would provide internal stability and security.

However, in spite of the Kennedy administration's keen interest in the internal political developments of Brazil, Brazil's foreign policy, beginning with President Quadros in 1961, veered sharply away from pursuing any unwritten alliance with the United States. Brazil's new "independent" foreign policy was neither confrontational nor pro-Soviet by design; it instead asserted that the Cold War held no significance for Brazil. This meant Brazil would pragmatically increase its ties with Eastern Europe and the Third World, as it was called then, as those diplomatic relationships met Brazil's development needs. Specific measures included resuming diplomatic and commercial ties with Cuba and the Soviet Union, casting anticolonial votes in the United Nations, and developing closer ties with the nonaligned countries.

Relations between the US embassy in Rio de Janeiro and the Ministry of Foreign Affairs were cordial in the early 1960s, but Washington's interactions with President Quadros were strained throughout his short-lived presidency. He was aloof to US overtures of friendship and cooperation, dismissing an invitation to visit Washington after being elected in late 1960. The new direction of Brazil's foreign policy was unveiled later in his term when the nonaligned Quadros, in what was more about maneuvering against supposedly imperialist powers than about his own leftist beliefs, invited Tito of Yugoslavia to visit Brazil, received a goodwill mission from the Soviet Union, and awarded Che Guevara with Brazil's highest decoration for foreigners, the Cruzeiro do Sul. Nevertheless, after the Bay of Pigs, President Kennedy and Secretary of State Rusk still erred on the side of caution when it came to keeping Brazil on the right path, extending $100 million in new aid in May 1961.

Jango

Despite his alleged claim that he would leave the presidency only if dead or forcibly ejected, Quadros resigned on August 25, 1961, less than seven months after taking office. Citing the belligerency of an entrenched opposition, he believed that the military would step in and reinstitute him as the head, thereby strengthening his hand. It was a gross miscalculation. Two weeks of turmoil ensued in which much of the Brazilian military worked to stop Vice President João "Jango" Goulart from taking office, while others on the left supported his constitutional succession. US intelligence even reported at the time that three Brazilian marine regiments with navy destroyers were dispatched to southern Brazil in early September in a display of anti-Goulart force. Ultimately, a compromise was reached later in September in which the Brazilian Congress created a modified parliamentary system, with the respected statesman Tancredo Neves as prime minister and Goulart as president.

As noted, the Kennedy administration was initially open to cooperating with Goulart. In January 1962 Deputy Assistant Secretary Richard Goodwin wrote in a memo for Secretary of State Rusk that "the political situation in Brazil is extremely precarious. We have no choice but to work to strengthen this government since there appears no viable alternative." It was agreed to work with the Goulart administration and try to steer it toward the political center. Consequently, Goulart was invited to come to Washington, and he met Kennedy in April 1962; the visit was cordial and improved Goulart's image both in Brasilia and in Washington, DC. That same month the two formed the Northeast Agreement, an economic aid program that entailed the basis for

A remark by President Kennedy prompts a smile by his guest, President João
Goulart of Brazil, as they pose with advisors in his White House office after
lunching together in the executive mansion. In the background are *(left to right)*
Lincoln Gordon, US ambassador to Brazil; Roberto de Oliveira Campos, Brazil's
ambassador to the US; Foreign Minister Francisco Clementino San Tiago Dantas
of Brazil; and Secretary of State Dean Rusk. April 3, 1962. (Library of Congress
Prints and Photographs Division, Washington, DC)

the creation of the Alliance for Progress in Brazil and further elucidated the
US dedication to work with Goulart.

Greatly affecting the trajectory of US–Brazil relations, Lincoln Gordon became the US ambassador to Brazil in late October 1961, shortly after Goulart
became president. The ambassador ended up meeting personally with President Kennedy every few months in Washington. Gordon has been described
as having "super-ambassadorial power and influence" in both the United
States and Brazil. As an influential advisor on the Marshall Plan and a professor at Harvard University, Gordon was a respected intellectual, extremely
knowledgeable of Brazil, and, perhaps most important, had unprecedented
access to the US president.

The Tides Turn

election tactics #

The cautious acceptance of Goulart by the United States lasted approximately one year. After this honeymoon period the Brazilian's leftist tendencies were too pronounced to overlook, and Washington turned the thrust of its efforts to strengthen and encourage anticommunist forces outside the government. With Brazilian congressional and state elections coming up in October 1962 the CIA allegedly called upon private US companies to finance the Brazilian Institute of Democratic Action (IBAD, Instituto Brasileira de Ação Democrática), a public institution serving as a conduit of funds to electoral campaigns. Through two subsidiaries IBAD bought the allegiance of over a thousand congressional and state candidates. Pursuing the same goal, Alliance for Progress funds were also strategically redirected from the national capital of Brasília, landing instead in the hands of primarily anti-Goulart individual state governors. Boosting the standing of conservative gubernatorial candidates running against the Reds, estimates of financial aid ranged from Lincoln Gordon's $5 million to the former CIA spy Philip Agee's $20 million. Although IBAD's ties to external sources of funding were never proved, its offices closed in October 1963 by decree after evidence of illegal activities emerged.

Directly after the 1962 midterm elections Kennedy deepened Washington's involvement in the Goulart affair, sending a group of advisors to Brazil to report and advise on US policy. The message they sent back described a country on the brink of financial collapse, headed by an unpredictable leader who would have no qualms about turning to the Soviet bloc. Echoing these claims, Lincoln Gordon reported that there had been increased communist infiltration in Petrobrás, the national oil company, and that he was concerned about appointments made to Goulart's inner circle.

While Goulart did not surround himself with communist advisors along the lines of a Castro or Árbenz, he also refused to disavow those left-leaning cabinet members as requested by the United States. It was during this time that the Kennedy administration adopted its Islands of Sanity strategy under the conservative assistant secretary of state Thomas Mann. Rather than overall balance-of-payments support or other aid that would benefit the federal government more broadly, economic assistance would now support states directly. The aid policy was later defended by Ambassador William Rountree, who said that US aid was given to those areas where it would be most effective in terms of bringing benefits to Brazil: "If this meant concentration of aid programs at state levels or in particular areas," so be it. But cynics saw the policy as a way to undermine the Goulart administration through funding of anticommunist candidates. Washington had certainly made it no secret that it planned to circumvent the Goulart administration, even it if stopped short at actively undermining it.

Coup!

US officials and pundits alike believed that Goulart was either a communist or a communist sympathizer or that he was simply ignorant of the communist conspiracy occurring throughout the world. In congressional testimony in May 1964 Assistant Secretary of State Mann said, "We were aware in January [1963] by the time I got there—I do not know how much earlier—that the erosion toward Communism in Brazil was very rapid." This concern was reflected in the US press as well; according to a 1963 *Wall Street Journal* editorial, Goulart was a "desperately devious, totally ambitious figure whose aim is to seize permanent power and run a fascist state."

Goulart's actions in the spring of 1964 heightened US worry about the fate of Brazil and confirmed the fears of Goulart's critics. Responding to increasing political polarization, a rapidly declining economy, and weakened support, Goulart organized a massive rally in Rio de Janeiro on March 13, 1964. At this rally Goulart made a decisive shift to the left, announcing two major decrees. The first nationalized all private oil refineries; the second outlined the expropriation of supposedly underutilized lands of over twelve hundred acres located near federal highways and railways. Lands of at least seventy acres near federal dams or drainage projects were also subject to expropriation. Goulart further called on Congress to pass other basic reforms, including the legalization of the communist party, and he announced future plans for decrees on rent control and new legislation to allow illiterates to vote, a measure which would nearly double the electorate.

Goulart's shift exacerbated the polarization of Brazilian society, his critics interpreting his decrees as an abandonment of the democratic process. While he had certainly called for the expansion of the electorate, his sudden turn against the Brazilian Congress precipitated fears of a preemptive power grab. Shortly after the rally the Brazilian Congress deliberated impeaching Goulart for publicly advocating the "subversion of public order." Given the calls by Leonel Brizola, Goulart's brother-in-law, for a violent insurrection against Congress, and agitation by Brazil's principal labor union for radical change, the US embassy felt that some sort of popular uprising was imminent.

Domestic ✱

Washington's reading of Brazil's increasing precariousness wasn't inaccurate, but in truth Goulart was not entirely to blame, as economic disequilibria had plagued the country well before his taking of power. An arguably premature industrialization spearheaded by former administrations had accelerated the development of urban areas, but at the cost of rural Brazil, which consequentially began harboring socioeconomic discontent and even fury. Washington was especially cognizant of this unrest, given the bitter memory of how economic and social dislocation ushered in Castro's revolution.

In spite of a laundry list of economic problems that Goulart faced, including debt, inflation, and disappearing foreign-exchange reserves, in early 1964 the Johnson administration did not believe that a military coup was inevitable. In fact, a possibly destabilizing coup was not even deemed desirable, despite the fact that Washington's patience regarding Goulart was long exhausted. On March 19, 1964, Gordon wrote, "Like the Brazilian opposition, we hope the ship of state can stay afloat until the elections," which were scheduled to be held in October 1965.

However, less than ten days later US officials expressed genuine fear of a communist revolution in Brazil. On March 28, three days prior to the military coup that deposed Goulart, Gordon reassessed the situation and came to the very different conclusion that Brazil ran a very real risk of going over to the communist camp and that US support, both moral and material, of Brazilian resistance was paramount. For his part, Gordon was convinced that Goulart would, if left unchecked, create a communist regime. During Gordon's February 1966 testimony before the Senate Committee on Foreign Relations, Democratic senator Wayne Morse asked if Goulart sought to "set up a personal dictatorship of the El Benefactor type." "Oh yes," Gordon replied, "without any question whatsoever."

Washington was in crisis mode. President Johnson instructed Dean Rusk that "under no circumstances should Brazil be allowed to go Communist." In an operation dubbed *Brother Sam* the Joint Chiefs of Staff agreed to consign United States Navy tankers to Brazil to deliver petroleum; dispatch a naval task force consisting of an aircraft carrier, four destroyers, and two destroyer escorts; and assemble a shipment of 110 tons of ammunition, including tear gas for mob control. Johnson was personally involved in every decision, believing that the events in Brazil would affect the entire region. However, the naval task force never made it to the Brazilian coast, as its launch coincided with the start of the coup; it sailed for a mere day before Johnson ordered the fleet to return to port.

Prudently, Johnson wanted to ensure that anti-Goulart forces, which included the governors of Brazil's largest states, members of Congress, much of the middle class, and the traditional right, did not lose ground. Yet Johnson also had to consider the risk, and potential public relations disaster, of prematurely committing the United States to the anti-Goulart camp. Kennedy's acrid lesson at the Bay of Pigs was a poignant reminder to Johnson: do not get involved with any opposition movement in Brazil unless there is a critical mass willing to move against Goulart. As Under Secretary of State Ball asserted, "We don't want to get ourselves committed before we know how the thing is going to come out." Further, Johnson had no intention of committing overt support if the need didn't exist. When the Brazilian military's swift and decisive actions made it clear no US involvement was required, any US contingency plans disintegrated.

A key question which officials posed during these precoup days was whether momentum would continue on the anti-Goulart side without either overt or covert encouragement from the United States. When it became clear that the anti-Goulart momentum had solidified and that overt US support would only play into Goulart's hands by giving him an anti-Yankee banner, Johnson ordered the naval task force home. In the face of unified military pressure and wanting to avoid bloodshed, Goulart resigned on April 1, 1964. It was a rapid, nonviolent ouster.

All told, the Johnson administration was publicly pleased with Goulart's departure. The nearly bloodless coup was widely acclaimed as a victory for peace and democracy. Gordon declared that the new Brazilian government had rejoined the free world and predicted that "future historians may well record the Brazilian revolution as the single most decisive victory for freedom in the mid-20th century." President Johnson sent a congratulatory message to the acting president, Pascoal Mazzilli, on April 2 expressing warmest wishes and admiring "the resolute will of the Brazilian community to resolve these difficulties within a framework of constitutional democracy and without civil strife." The United States press echoed this characterization of the coup, calling it the "spectacular Brazilian revolution" and a "powerful shot in the arm for the cause of democratic moderation in Latin America."

The Question of American Involvement

Lincoln Gordon testified in 1966 that "the movement which overthrew President Goulart was a purely 100 percent—not 99.44—but 100 percent purely Brazilian movement. . . . Neither I nor other officials of the U.S. government

. . . in any way, shape, or manner was involved, aiding and abetting or participating." Gordon's assertion reflects the official US government line, namely,
that Goulart's removal was purely a Brazilian affair, caused by Goulart's inept
governance, implemented by the Brazilian military, and supported by a majority of the Brazilian people.

Undoubtedly Brazil was marked by a climate of polarization, fear, and uncertainty in March 1964, making the country ripe for political change, that
was not directly created by Washington. The disdain the Brazilian military had
for Goulart and its decision to overthrow him was also not directly created by
Washington. This wasn't a 1954 Árbenz situation that entailed direct US intervention. Local actors played the starring roles in Brazil's coup. Along these
lines, we also see a US involvement that consistently responded to events
rather than catalyzing them. Its final goal of regime change succeeded only
because it overlapped with the prerogatives of the Brazilian military.

That said, one cannot ignore the fact that Washington was prepared to materially support military intervention should the need arise, and it financially
supported Goulart's political opponents. One might also flip the question: If
the Johnson administration had actively supported Goulart and worked to prevent a coup, would the Brazilian military have acted with such confidence?
Ruth Leacock, for example, has argued that if Washington had shown more
support and patience, Goulart's policies could have succeeded.

The ties between the two militaries may also have contributed, directly or indirectly, to the ouster. In *O Golpe Começou em Washington* (The coup originated
in Washington) Edmar Morel accused the United States of actively cooperating
with the Brazilian military to establish a dictatorship. Brigadier General Clarke
McCurdy, who worked in Brazil in the mid-1960s, described how the US military occupied the entire top floor of the Brazilian Army Ministry and "exercised
a great deal of influence. . . . [R]eally the U.S. military presence was overwhelming." General Vernon Walters, Lincoln Gordon's military attaché in Brazil, had
served as liaison officer with the Brazilian Expeditionary Force in Italy during
World War II and, according to Ambassador John Tuthill, was on "intimate
terms with the Brazilian military." He was a close friend with then lieutenant
colonel Castelo Branco (they were roommates in Italy), and Branco reportedly
wired full details of the coup plan to Washington a week before it took place. So
Washington certainly knew of the pending coup and therefore granted the Brazilian military tacit approval and thereby implied support of its plans.

The shift toward military dictatorship in Brazil may also have been an unin-
tended consequence of US military training of Brazilian officers. In congres-

sional testimony in 1961 Brigadier General Bonner Fellers perhaps anticipated the more subtle dynamics behind the 1964 coup, describing how training in the United States changed the outlooks of young Latin American officers and created friction when they returned home: "Their governments appear inadequate, sluggish, and antiquated. They find U.S. dollar handouts have bred corruption in high places. They form a clique separate and apart from others. Convinced that they could run their country far better than their present Chief of State, they plot his overthrow. With weapons and training which we have provided, they have the means to take over the government by force. Thus, our military assistance programs are creating potential military dictatorships."

While not to deny the clear connections between the US and Brazilian militaries, it is important to remember that the military coup that ultimately deposed Goulart was certainly not planned or anticipated when Kennedy became president and was by no means a foregone or inevitable conclusion. The Kennedy administration was initially open to a Goulart presidency, sympathetic to his policies and hopeful that he could be a moderate influence on Brazil. Furthermore, the White House supported Brazil with developmental assistance and balance-of-payments support, even though these later became politically targeted.

In sum, it is impossible to understand the 1964 coup without discussing the power of US financial assistance, the influence of Lincoln Gordon, and the emboldening impact of US military support. Yet our narrative must also include the collapse of the Brazilian economy and Goulart's poorly planned and clumsily executed power grab as crucial factors driving the Brazilian military to intervene. And although Goulart would never again set foot in Brazil after the botched coup, his presidency did serve as an inflection point for democracy in Brazil: for the next twenty years the country would be ruled by military dictatorships.

23 • Killing Che

The duty of a revolutionary is to make revolution.
—Ernesto "Che" Guevara, 1962

Frenzy of Liberation

By the mid-1960s the revolutionary seed once planted by Castro and his twenty-five barbudos had blossomed into a flourishing communist regime. Cuba's revolution and its unique brand of anti-Americanism and *tercermundismo,* or third worldism, resonated throughout 1960s Latin America. The Dominican Republic, Venezuela, and Guatemala all experienced Cuba-inspired insurrections. Yet between nationalism, land reform, egalitarianism, and opposition to right-wing dictatorships, it wasn't difficult to explain why many Latin Americans were enamored of the Cuban Revolution. Factor in Moscow's hesitancy about exporting armed revolution lest it provoke Washington, and Havana quickly became the epicenter of communist thought in the Western Hemisphere and was fearless in its attempts to paint the region red.

The revolution's lead artist was Che Guevara. More than just a broodingly photogenic visionary, the Argentine developed the theoretical and practical framework behind the revolution, ensuring it would galvanize revolutions beyond Cuban borders. As outlined in his widely read and emulated 1961 how-to manual *Guerrilla Warfare,* his doctrine held that by creating a "focus" (*foco*) of discontent with the status quo, a core of quick-striking guerrillas could move a country's general population to demand and support revolution. While Guevara and his Cuban compatriots extended their tentacles out into the region, thousands of optimistic budding guerrillas ventured to Cuba for training, at least one thousand to fifteen hundred making the trek in 1962 alone. One Cuban official identified the central part of the island, which hosted many revolutionary training camps, as a "frenzy of liberation." A classified US intelligence report published in 1961 confirmed the observation, though with a decidedly different slant: "Castro's shadow looms large because social and economic conditions throughout Latin America invite opposition to ruling authority and encourage agitation for radical change." By 1962 Cuba monopolized the supply chain—from procurement to distribution—of physical and human communist capital in the Western Hemisphere, while for Castro, exporting the revolution had the added benefit of helping him secure his rule over Cuba. Washington, he claimed, "will not be able to hurt us if all of Latin America is in flames."

Domestic

The United States was not passive in the face of Havana's machinations. In addition to offering economic aid, Kennedy ordered US civilian and military officials to escalate the training and arming of Latin American police and military forces (a program that had begun during the Eisenhower administration) so that they could defend US allies from communist subversion. By 1963 the administration had increased military aid to Latin America by almost 50 percent over the levels of assistance given in the Eisenhower years.

In addition to military aid, Washington adhered special fastenings throughout the region to counterbalance Castro's influence. Military Assistance Advisory Groups (MAAGS) were stationed around the region, and starting in 1961 the Kennedy administration placed Special Forces Groups into vulnerable Latin American countries considered to be "hot," such as Guatemala and Colombia, to help with counterinsurgency work, including civil affairs, psychological operations, intelligence, and interrogation. Often these deployments of combat-seasoned Green Berets and embassy-based MAAGS were almost identical to the counterinsurgency models being tested at the same time in Vietnam.

As in the case of the Brazilian military and Goulart, Washington began training Latin American military officers at US institutions like the School of the Americas in the Panama Canal Zone. Between 1962 and 1970 upward of twenty-two thousand officers were instructed in organizational command, counterinsurgency tactics, covert and psychological operations, military intelligence, and interrogation techniques. US Secretary of Defense Robert McNamara announced that US-trained Latin American military leaders had an obligation to maintain internal security and to combat domestic subversion.

Ultimately, nearly all of the communist focos were defeated. Only the Marxist Sandinistas in Nicaragua managed to erect a Cuban-style revolutionary government, and even this sole, purportedly foco triumph was more a societal revolt against the country's dictator, Anastasio "Tachito" Somoza Debayle, another son in the ruling family. However, Washington didn't have it all its own way. In fact, governments in the region were sometimes able to push back against Washington's strong-arm approach. For instance, after it seized power in a coup in 1968, Peru's leftist military regime—an anomaly, as almost all military regimes were rightist—seized US boats reported to be fishing in Peruvian waters and evicted the US military mission. The old logic of US intervention did not apply either: according to the scholar Hal Brands, at the time, "Peru nationalized IPC [a subsidiary of Standard Oil] and the Marines were not sent there." The socialist president Salvador Allende of neighboring Chile was impressed with what the Peruvians had done, and, more important, that they had gotten away with it.

Che's Clandestine Offensive

Perhaps surprisingly, Che Guevara's first attempt at putting his foco strategy into practice was not in Latin America, but Africa. In late April 1965 Che and a band of Afro-Caribbean Cubans dismounted on the shores of Lake Tanganyika to aid the political heirs of the murdered Congolese nationalist Patrice Lumumba. Despite the high hopes surrounding this first, Cuban-exported foco their mission was doomed almost from the start. For one, the Africans did not take to a didactic outsider. Cuban lectures were ill-received, explaining Guevara's perception of Laurent Kabila's Congolese rebels as undisciplined and hopeless in their fight against the opposition and their contracted European mercenaries. In a post-Congo report to Fidel, Guevara lamented: "The soldiers are of peasant stock and completely raw, for whom the main attraction is to have a rifle and a uniform, sometimes even shoes and a certain authority in the area. Corrupted by inactivity and the habit of ordering peasants around, saturated with fetishistic notions about death and the enemy, devoid of any coherent political education, they consequently lack revolutionary awareness or any forward-looking perspective beyond the traditional horizon of their tribal territory. Lazy and undisciplined, they are without any spirit of combat or self-sacrifice."

This short-lived "African safari" ended disastrously. Che's relationship with his African hosts spiraled from initial mistrust into eventual, outright resentment. Che abandoned his African adventure and returned to Cuba in 1966 to refocus his energies on the region that had bred his revolutionary agenda: Latin America. Not one to sit idle, Che quickly dedicated himself to "breaking the chains" that impoverished Bolivia. Similar to the Congo case, however, Che's efforts were forced; in many aspects Bolivia didn't fit the archetypal model of a country ready for a foco-led revolution. Moreover, any desire for a leftist revolution had most likely already been exploited in the 1952 revolution, which had addressed common demands like land redistribution. Nonetheless, Che and his gang of guerrillas marched into Bolivia all the same, planning on igniting a revolt there before proceeding to do the same in Che's native Argentina.

Both Cubans and their Bolivian sympathizers trained intensively in a private camp before departing in November 1966. Che, the foco's dignitary, assumed the disguise of a clean-shaven and partially bald Uruguayan businessman and took a circuitous route to La Paz on false documents via Moscow, Prague, Madrid, Brazil, and Uruguay. While Che went to great lengths to covertly enter Bolivia, poor domestic preparations hamstrung the foco's operations. Lacking an equipped base camp in the Andean mountains, the *guerrilleros*, at this point an army of only a few dozen Cubans and Bolivians, and several Peruvians and other foreigners, were forced to carry their revolution east to the country's Gran Chaco region.

Relocating their launch point added to the campaign's unorthodoxy in terms of foco theory. In leaving the mountains, Che and his guerrillas abandoned the untold number of underpaid laborers whose work in the tin mines left them with a list of complaints—complaints that made them ripe to march on La Paz should a Cuban Moses appear. Instead, the guerrillas began their campaign in an underpopulated and inhospitable region. And when Che's insurgency did encounter Bolivians, the revolutionary fervor was underwhelming. Rather than building off of an outpouring of local support, as they had done in Cuba, the revolutionary hopefuls were alone, isolated both physically and ideologically.

Even when Che's group did find locals open to revolution, complicating issues existed. First, Che's guerrillas had received instruction in the Quechua language, but the region where the insurgency intended to launch operations spoke Guaraní. Consequently, the insurgents were barely able to communicate with the locals and unable to sway them toward the cause, resulting in a lack of material support and solidarity. The region's rural *campesinos* even labeled the insurgents as gringos because of their peculiar speech and thick beards.

Second, the sense of superiority of Che and his Cuban veterans won little favor with their supposed comrades in Bolivia. Che had met with the head of the Bolivian Communist Party before commencing the campaign, but the Argentine's insistence that his authority should supersede that of the local communist organizers caused a rift that would prove damning to the insurgency's mission. Local organizers would have provided critical resources and knowledge, as Celia Sánchez had done in Cuba, but without this support the roots of Che's efforts in Bolivia ran shallow. Last, the Bolivian recruits were raw, as Castro's had been when they landed in El Oriente. The difference between the two was that instead of banding together over their shared inexperience, as the barbudos had, Che's forces treated the Bolivians as inferior, creating dissention within the group.

Unrelenting, Che did manage to lead a successful expedition against the Bolivian government in spring 1967, albeit at a price. The topography was a greater adversary than the government, with thick jungle and roaring rivers making Cuba's Sierra Maestra look like a bucolic summer camp. Not having accurate maps, the *foquistas* squandered supplies and, more important, morale during their misguided expeditions. Even victories came at a cost: a fruitful ambush of an army patrol offered vital weapons and supplies yet gave away the rebels' position to spotter planes and helicopters. When the tide began to turn against them, the foquistas found they couldn't shake the bloodhound Bolivian military, no matter how deep into the jungle they fled. Their cover was soon blown, too, when the Bolivian strongman René Barrientos condemned the rebels as agents of "Castro communism." With the nation against them and the rebels growing increasingly dispirited under their crestfallen leader—Che's mournful behavior tempered the respect and admiration of his comrades—the Bolivian insurgency was in tatters. The guerrillas' ranks dwindled, as men were either captured or killed. In April Che summarized the bleak situation facing the group: "[Our] isolation appears to be complete, sickness has undermined the health of some comrades, forcing us to divide forces, which has greatly diminished our effectiveness. . . . The peasant base has not yet been developed although it appears through planned terror we can neutralize some of them; support will come later."

Che's approach to shaping his forces contrasted sharply with that of the Green Berets, who recognized and addressed the faults of the Bolivian counterinsurgency forces. In August a US Special Forces Mobile Training Team consisting of sixteen Green Berets under Major Ralph "Pappy" Shelton, the son of a Tennessee dirt farmer, came to help Barrientos in his hunt for Che.

In 1967 Shelton repurposed a former sugar plantation as a base outside of La Esperanza, roughly fifty miles north of Santa Cruz, and trained four hundred Bolivian conscripts who were tasked with taking down Che's battered foco. The Green Beret team also conducted civic action, as was the norm for US counterinsurgency efforts. Shelton's approach to winning the favor of locals through such activities as building schools in surrounding communities stood in stark contrast with Guevara's haughty approach.

Yet training their Bolivian counterparts would prove no easy task for the Green Beret team either, as the Bolivian armed forces had been almost entirely disbanded in the decade following the country's leftist revolution in 1952. A US Southern Command report in May 1967 revealed how far from fighting weight the Bolivians were in the eyes of US military planners: "The recent outbreak of guerrilla activity . . . has pointed up the serious deficiencies in the [Bolivian] armed forces organization, logistics, leadership, and intelligence capabilities and has raised the question of whether the military has the capability to counter even a small guerrilla movement." In June 1967 National Security Advisor Walt Rostow met with representatives from the CIA, State Department, and Defense Department to rehash the "whole guerrilla problem in Latin America." Rostow returned to President Johnson with a list of seven countries ordered by the "degree of urgency" for a US response. It was "the fragility of the political situation and the weakness of the armed forces," as opposed to "the size and effectiveness of the guerrilla movement," that won Bolivia the title of most urgent.

The Green Berets' tenacity and dedication paid off: they managed to create a Bolivian Ranger force ready to deploy by September 1967. For good measure, the CIA also scrambled its operatives to create another Bolivian unit. Among the agents recruited was a young Cuban American paramilitary operative named Félix Rodríguez, who had earned Washington's admiration by leading a communications unit of CIA-funded anti-Castro commandos out of Nicaragua since 1963. Rodríguez commanded more than three hundred members from Nicaragua, Costa Rica, and Miami, and the CIA equipped the unit with two 250-foot "mother ships," two 50-foot speed boats, and a C-47 transport plane, among other materiél. Rodríguez asserted that such equipment was necessary to checkmate Che in Bolivia: "[The CIA] feared [what might happen if] Che grabbed Bolivia. . . . With a secure Cuban base there, they could easily expand the revolution to important countries like Brazil [and] Argentina." Although the Bolivian army lacked Rodríguez's US-backed military capacity, it contributed to the counterinsurgency effort all the same, discovering caches of

weapons, medical supplies, and documents that contained lists of rebel sympathizers in Bolivia as well as deciphering radio messages from Havana.

Meanwhile, Che and his battered band of guerrillas set their sights on the remote town of La Higuera. Notably, during this final leg of Che's Bolivia campaign, the leader contradicted nearly all of the major rules of foco insurgency
strategy, such as avoiding roads and sticking to the cover of forests. The end was
not long in coming: in late September the US-trained 2nd Ranger Battalion deployed and, by early October, had surrounded Che's men at La Higuera and
taken the wounded Che prisoner. Rodríguez soon arrived by helicopter and docu-
mented the dilapidated state of the distinguished revolutionary: "He was a mess.
. . . Hair matted, clothes ragged and torn." Despite Rodríguez's alleged effort to
take him alive, on October 9 Che Guevara, thirty-nine years old, was executed by
gunshot by a bitter Bolivian army sergeant eager to avenge the casualties of his
fellow soldiers in the pursuit of a communist icon. The insurrection was over.

Aftermath

Two full days passed before Walt Rostow could send a memo to President
Johnson asserting that "this morning we are about 99% sure that 'Che' Guevara is dead." It is not clear why there was such a delay. In Rostow's opinion
Che's death had three immediate implications: "It marks the passing of another of the aggressive, romantic revolutionaries like [Indonesia's] Sukarno,
[Ghana's Kwame] Nkrumah, [Algeria's Ahmed] Ben Bella—and reinforces
this trend. . . . In the Latin American context, it will have a strong impact in
discouraging would-be guerrillas. . . . [And] it shows the soundness of our
'preventive medicine' assistance to countries facing incipient insurgency—it
was the Bolivian 2nd Ranger Battalion, trained by our Green Berets from June
[sic]—September of this year, that cornered and got him."

US officials celebrated the next day in an interagency meeting, declaring
Guevara's defeat in Bolivia a glaring blow to "Castro's theory and practice of
promoting guerrilla warfare in this hemisphere." By Washington's count, in
Latin America it was counterinsurgency one, foco zero. Overlooked by Washington, however, was the extent to which Che's defeat was the consequence of
the foquistas' own blunders rather than the brilliance of US counterinsurgency. Bolivia failed to meet many of the revolutionary prerequisites, as speci-
fied by Guevara himself, and the foco's own lack of familiarity with the country
was critically highlighted by the rural population's distaste for a revolution at
the hands of strongly accented foreigners.

Paradoxically, it seemed that Che had won more supporters on Washington's patio than in the US backyard. On October 21, 1967, twelve days after Guevara's death, an estimated fifty thousand Americans stood in silence at the Lincoln Memorial. Faces of Che dotted the crowd as demonstrators carried signs with his image. Even more perplexing were the cool reactions from Moscow and Beijing, who were not only disinterested in the communist icon's death but even critical of his final escapades. A poignant indication of how Cuban-style focos had fallen out of favor in non-Western communist realms, public Soviet channels poured scorn on his taste for "adventurism," while the Chinese press criticized the Argentine for allowing the gun to control the party and not vice versa.

All commentary aside, Bolivia remained Washington's shining example of America's counterinsurgency strategy: quickly trained Bolivians had been the antidote to Che's revolutionary plague. However, this new brand of US intervention was more controversial outside the Washington, DC, Beltway, to use the well-worn idiom. The death of Che has been seen in the literature as the end of Cuban adventurism, but in fact recent scholarship has shown that this was not the case.

Che after Che

In his engaging book *Che's Afterlife* the seasoned Latin America reporter Michael Casey makes clear that while Guevara's grisly "martyrdom" served as an abrupt end to his "little Bolivian insurgency," his legend has lived on; indeed, Che enjoys unrivaled status as the world's number-one revolutionary. The starting point for Casey's book is the Cuban photographer Alberto Korda's iconic image of Che taken in 1960, which now adorns T-shirts, keychains, and posters around the world. Casey asks a simple yet critical question: What does all this glorification of and passion for the late Guevara mean? The answer is not easy; for one, Che was an avowed anticapitalist whose legacy has come of age in a hypercapitalist global era. Casey concluded that the story of Che, one of history's "most contested" figures, was one of politicization, commercialization, and, yes, trivialization: "Che" had become as much a brand as the Nike "swoosh." Yet Che was also a towering historical figure and inspiration to subsequent revolutionaries in Latin America and around the world. More than a few Marxist guerrillas in Central America in the 1980s considered Che to be their guardian angel; his selfless New Man persona and reputation as a sage guerrilla strategist became part of the mythology of revolutionary and resistance movements in such places as Nepal, East Timor, Palestine, and Iran. Che's influence on subsequent guerrilla fighters manifested itself even more recently when, in 2008, Colombian commandos disguised themselves by wearing Che T-shirts in their successful attempt to fool hostage-holding Revolutionary Armed Forces of Colombia (FARC) guerrillas into thinking that the rescuers were in fact sympathetic revolutionaries. The FARC captors did not for a minute doubt the rescuers' "rebel bona fides."

24 • What Really Happened in Chile?

It's that son of a bitch Allende. We're going to smash him.
—Richard Nixon

Chilean democracy is a conquest by all of its people.
—Salvador Allende

Our tale about US involvement in the September 11, 1973, toppling of the Chilean president Salvador Allende begins in the early 1960s. Allende had been defeated in elections held in 1952 and 1958, but the upcoming presidential election of 1964 looked to be a close call, raising the possibility that the openly Marxist candidate would assume power. Such an outcome would not sit well with Washington and its Cold War posture, and the CIA duly spent $3 million to influence the outcome of the election in favor of the centrist Christian Democrat Eduardo Frei. (After losing three elections on the bounce, Allende jokingly claimed that his epitaph would read, "Here lies the next President of Chile.")

Despite losing to Frei, Allende was determined to run again in the September 4, 1970, election and was nominated by the communist party to run for president under the banner of the Popular Unity coalition. The development further stoked Washington's anxieties. In July 1968, six months before Richard Nixon took office, the CIA hatched a "modest covert program," placing anti-Marxist propaganda in the media to back nonleftist "individual electoral factions." By subtly helping build a congressional majority the CIA would be able to stymie the radical political agenda of a possible Allende presidency. As the CIA's official history put it, "The objective was to divide the left and create conditions for a non-Marxist candidate to win the elections. . . . The plan was

225

to alert the Chilean people to the dangers of a Marxist regime under Allende."
But the CIA's machinations did not check Allende's growing popularity. He
won a plurality of the vote (36 percent), just ahead of the rightist and former
president Jorge Alessandri (35 percent); the Christian Democratic candidate,
Radomiro Tomic (28 percent), came in third.

Off Track

Critics both inside and outside Chile held that, despite his legitimate electoral victory, Salvador Allende was not a conventional politician and that his
radical policies would push against the limits of Chile's storied constitutional
system. His elated supporters, though, held that Allende would not revolu-
tionize Chile but would effect needed change entirely democratically. Ultimately, however, no one knew what would happen to Chile after Allende
donned the presidential sash on November 3.

Nixon loathed the idea of Allende's impending inauguration. In mid-
September he met with National Security Advisor Henry Kissinger, CIA director Richard Helms, and other top foreign policy officials to consider what to do.
Kissinger offered his cold-blooded realpolitik assessment of the global stakes in
this bipolar global struggle between Washington and Moscow: "I don't see why
we need to stand by and watch a country go communist due to the irresponsi-
bility of its people. The issues are much too important for the Chilean voters to
be left to decide for themselves." Helms later recalled that Nixon pledged to
"save Chile" from Allende's destruction via a preventive coup, "even if the
chances [were] one in ten" of such a plot succeeding. Nixon also ordered the
CIA to "make the economy scream" in Chile "to prevent Allende from coming
to power or to unseat him." And it was not just Nixon and Kissinger inside the
US government who adopted a hard-line stance against the incoming Chilean
head of state. The US ambassador in Chile, Ed Korry, promised that "not a nut
or bolt shall reach Chile under Allende. Once Allende comes to power we shall
do all within our power to condemn Chile and all Chileans to utmost deprivation and poverty." The notion of a coup after Allende came to power was also
discussed, even if it cost $10 million to put into action.

That the US was so concerned about Chile under Allende was something
of a mystery. Kissinger himself had previously commented that the country
lacked strategic importance, derisively calling it "a dagger pointed at the heart
of Antarctica." But if Chile was strategically irrelevant, why did Nixon and
Kissinger respond so aggressively to Allende's electoral win? One suggestion

has been that what Kissinger feared most about Chile was that a Marxist government had come to power through the ballot box, which Kissinger thought would set a precedent and encourage other countries in the region to follow suit. The working thesis of the United States had always been that communist governments had to seize power violently. For their part, Marxist commentators saw the mighty dollar sign at work. In this take, Nixon and Kissinger, like the Dulles brothers and United Fruit back in Guatemala, were doing the bidding of US corporations like the mining giant Alcoa and telephone giant ITT, which were sure to be on the losing side once Allende started nationalizing key industries. In fact, the *New York Times* later reported that a mere month after Allende's election ITT had sent Nixon an eighteen-point strategy comprising an "economic squeeze" and "economic chaos" to stop Allende from "get[ting] through the crucial next six months," after which the military would "step in and restore order." Nixon did not act on the request.

Two plans eventually emerged from the deliberations in the White House. The State Department and the CIA drew up a scheme for Chile called Track I, a secret diplomatic effort to have the Chilean Congress refuse to endorse Allende's win and instead confirm the runner-up, Alessandri, as president. Nixon also ordered the CIA to initiate a second secret program, known as Track II, which coordinated with three rebel military groups, including the rightist paramilitary group Patria y Libertad, that were plotting preinauguration coups to keep Allende out of office. Track II was so confidential that not even the US ambassador in Santiago was briefed on it. Langley, the headquarters of the CIA, sent instructions to the CIA station in Santiago on October 16: "It is firm and continuing policy that Allende be overthrown by a coup. . . . We are to continue to generate maximum pressure toward this end, utilizing every appropriate resource. It is imperative that these actions be implemented clandestinely and securely so that USG and American hand be well hidden." The CIA did warn the executive branch that this was going to be a dicey effort: "You have asked us to provoke chaos in Chile. . . . We provide you with a formula for chaos which is unlikely to be bloodless. To dissimulate the U.S. involvement will be clearly impossible."

But US-hatched regime change, which had proved relatively easy to effect in Guatemala, ran into difficulty in Chile. The CIA quickly discovered that the idea of a military-led coup was out of the question due to the Chilean military's respect for constitutional democracy. Most emblematic of this constitutionalism was the deep opposition to a revolt of the Chilean army commander in chief, General René Schneider. As the conservative scholar Mark Falcoff put

it, "His view, simply stated, was that since the politicians had gotten the country into the mess in which it found itself, the politicians would have to find a
way out."

The CIA hastily tried to identify willing Chilean military personnel, like the
retired officer Roberto Viaux, who had links to Patria y Libertad, to remove
Schneider and clear the way for a military coup. But Kissinger reportedly wasn't
enamored of Viaux's plot, claiming in his memoirs that he had told Nixon he'd
"turned it off." Critics counter, however, that there is no record of Kissinger
making such remarks in the meeting's minutes. Meanwhile, the CIA kept
working with possible alternatives. According to declassified CIA documents,
on October 19 the agency delivered tens of thousands of dollars and guns to
one of the rebel groups (which one is not clear) to keep the covert plot against
Schneider "financially lubricated." The CIA also delivered three submachine
guns to a group led by General Camilo Valenzuela, who, after failing to convince General Schneider to join him in a coup attempt, wanted Schneider sent
out of the country. However, Valenzuela's men would never get the opportunity
to put the CIA-supplied weapons to use, as Viaux's group struck first.

On October 22 Patria y Libertad officers attempted to kidnap Schneider
while he was heading to work in the morning but wound up killing him. Only
hours after Schneider had been shot, Langley sent a congratulatory cable to
the Santiago office: "The station has done [an] excellent job of guiding [the]
Chileans to [the] point today where a military solution is at least an option for
them." The "military solution," in other words, was a putsch against Allende.
Showing how one hand of US policy worked while the other was blind, Ambassador Korry sent repeated cables to Foggy Bottom reporting that his embassy did not have any contact with Patria y Libertad, yet Korry was ignorant
of the fact that the military attachés under his command had orders to engage
this shady quasi-fascist group.

Almost everyone who has closely studied Track II has concluded that it was
an unmitigated failure in terms of Nixon's desire to forestall Allende's inauguration. The Schneider killing led to the appointment of his fellow constitutionalist General Carlos Prats on October 22. Prats also believed in the legitimacy
of Allende's election and opposed a military coup; his appointment ultimately
"discredited right-wing cabals both inside the army and out." Chileans lined up
behind Allende or at least the notion of him being the legitimate president-elect
even if they disagreed with him politically. There was no longer any appetite by
Chilean brass, no matter how radical, for a Track II–style preinauguration coup.

On October 24, 1970, two days after the assassination of Schneider, the Chilean assembly formally endorsed Allende as president-elect. While Allende's plurality may have been razor thin—such "minority" vote leaders, that is, lacking an absolute majority, had been features of the nation's democratic fabric for over a century—the Chilean assembly was maintaining the democratic norm. Less than two weeks after Schneider's assassination, Allende was sworn into power.

The Road to 9/11/73

The account of Nixon's failure to prevent Allende's inauguration is far less historically contested than the two subsequent years leading up to the September 1973 coup. After Allende's inauguration it appeared that Nixon had put aside his scheming and was willing to accommodate Allende. The CIA's Jack Devine, a former operative stationed in Santiago, affirms that "all coup plotting ended, and Nixon drastically altered his policy. The new goal was to support the political opposition and avoid giving Allende an excuse to exploit anti-American sentiment to increase his domestic popularity and international support." The CIA would not be stoking Track II–style orthodox coups but instead would be "making sure that Allende did not dismantle the institutions of democracy," like newspapers, political parties, and labor unions.

However, critics maintain that US policy makers "adjusted their strategy but not their ultimate goal," citing documents such as Kissinger's talking points from November 6, 1970, just days after Allende's swearing in. These addressed the notion of "actions we can take ourselves to intensify Allende's problems so that at a minimum he may fail or be forced to limit his aims, and at a maximum might create conditions in which a collapse or overthrow might be feasible." At that same meeting Assistant Secretary of State William D. Rogers added that "we want to do it right and bring [Allende] down." In this interpretation, Track II "never really ended," as the CIA operative Thomas Karamessines told Congress during a 1975 Senate investigation into US involvement in Chile. "What we were told to do was to continue our efforts," Karamessines said. "Stay alert, and to do what we could to contribute to the eventual achievement of the objectives and purposes of Track II."

Nixon and Kissinger supporters put forward a more moderate interpretation. At a National Security Council meeting on November 9 the Nixon team decided on a "correct but cool" diplomatic stance while still "maximiz[ing] pressures on the Allende government to prevent its consolidation and limit its ability to implement policies contrary to U.S. and hemispheric interests." To this end, the Nixon administration would reduce bilateral development funding, pressure US private interests in Chile to leave, and limit the investment of international lending bodies like the World Bank in Chile. To Nixon and Kissinger these were entirely appropriate measures to address an adversarial government in South America. Still, to legions of critics Washington was making Chile suffer in order to achieve regime change by alternative means, putting in place conditions that substantially increased the likelihood of Allende falling.

One problem in our assessment of the impact of US actions is that it is virtually impossible to determine the full extent of the cause and effect with regard to Allende's fate. For example, the CIA gave the anti-Allende newspaper *El Mercurio,* which critics painted as an "organ of the CIA," upward of $2 million in 1971–73. Yet CIA defenders counter that the covert funding simply kept the embattled daily afloat, given that Allende allegedly limited its access to newsprint. What's more, they contend, editors at *El Mercurio* actually had no interest in becoming a mouthpiece for CIA propaganda but instead valued its own deeply critical stance against Allende.

An October 1972 strike initiated by the country's truck drivers' union offers another example of the CIA's attempt to thwart the Allende regime. A skeptical take of this episode is that US operatives compensated the truckers so that they would strike and paralyze the long, thin country's economy, which relied overwhelmingly on road transportation. The CIA, however, contended that the truck drivers asked the US agency for cash but both the intelligence station in Santiago and the new ambassador, Nathaniel Davis, were against the notion.

Whether the money was paid or not remains a matter of debate. The 40 Committee, the high-level executive branch team responsible for the issue, did not approve direct aid but, in the words of one US official, funds "could have filtered [down]" to the striking truck drivers via local field operatives in receipt of CIA cash. Whatever the true story behind the assistance, the truck drivers embarked on a twenty-six-day strike protesting against what they perceived as the government's attempt to nationalize the transport industry. The strike was an economic disaster for the Allende administration, costing the economy some $200 million. When another truck strike commenced in August 1972, forcing around half of the country's lorries off the road, Allende's planning minister, Gonzalo Martner, was scathing: "This is a political strike aimed at overthrowing the Government, with the help of imperialism."

Although the scope and scale of US involvement remain somewhat ambiguous, it was clear that Allende faced deep political unrest. And in this period

Augusto Pinochet. (Sueddeutsche Zeitung Photo / Alamy Stock Photo)

leading up to the coup of 1973 the United States wasn't alone in trying to shape the playing field. Castro visited Chile and stayed for three months in 1972. He gave his Chilean ideological comrade an AK-47 assault rifle as a gift, inscribing it, "To Salvador, from his brother in arms, Fidel Castro." During that period, while offering tacit support for Allende, he continued to arm and assist the Movimiento de Izquierda Revolucionaria (MIR), a Cuban-style group that preached armed insurrection. In a 2014 *Foreign Affairs* piece, Devine recalled the polarized political climate inside Chile he found after being assigned to Santiago in 1970: "Rumors of a military coup against the socialist Chilean president, Salvador Allende, had been swirling for months. There had already been one attempt [in June 1973]. Allende's opponents were taking to the streets. Labor strikes and economic disarray made basic necessities difficult to find. Occasionally, bombs rocked the capital. The whole country seemed exhausted and tense."

On September 9 Devine sent a cable marked CRITIC, the highest priority, to Langley: "A coup attempt will be initiated on 11 September. . . . All three branches of the armed forces and the *carabiñeros* [national police] are involved in this action." Devine argues that this is "how the U.S. government learned of the coup in Chile."

The military revolt was led by the president's own top military commander, General Augusto Pinochet, who quickly took control. By midafternoon on September 11 the Allende-led resistance had been quelled. The president killed himself before he could be killed or captured, and Pinochet established a military junta. In Devine's analysis, "The Chilean military moved against Allende not because the United States wanted it to do so but because the country was in disarray. . . . The generals decided to take charge of the coup plotting to maintain discipline in Chile's military institutions and to preserve stability."

The longtime Allende coup researcher and fierce critic of US policy in Latin America Peter Kornbluh offered a fierce rebuttal (also in *Foreign Affairs*) of Devine's interpretation of events, but he does agree with Devine that Washington "did not directly participate in the coup." To Kornbluh, though, the far more crucial question is the extent to which Washington sought to bring down Allende by fomenting conditions "in which a collapse or overthrow may be feasible," and how much the CIA's programs "influenced the political environment and contributed to Allende's downfall." Kissinger's and Nixon's assessment of the US role is ambiguous yet suggestive. "In the Eisenhower period we would be heroes," Kissinger said in a September 16, 1973, telephone chat with his boss, referring to the operation by Eisenhower and the Dulles brothers that toppled Guatemala's Árbenz. Nixon added, "Our hand doesn't show on this one though." Kissinger clarified, "We didn't do it, I mean we helped them. [Word omitted] created the conditions as great as possible."

Kornbluh finds Kissinger's comment alone proof positive of "what really happened in Chile." Devine's counter was that a statement from Nixon or Kissinger about Chile "doesn't make it true." In this case it was "hardly uncommon" for politicians to "take excessive credit for developments they see as positive"—or vice versa. So with Allende gone, the logic goes, Nixon was eager to own this positive geopolitical move.

Interestingly, Devine did not disagree with Kornbluh's take on the CIA's role in fomenting coup conditions: "Against all odds, the Santiago station had helped create a climate for the coup without tainting the effort by becoming directly involved. In the heady days immediately following, we took pride in having helped thwart the development of Cuban-style socialism in Chile and having prevented the country's drift into the Soviet orbit."

Pinochet: Dictator

Kissinger was on to something when he lamented how he and Nixon would have gotten medals had their approach to Allende occurred back in the hysterical anticommunist days of the early 1950s. But Nixon's and Kissinger's gambit against Allende took place in the context of the catastrophic failure of the Vietnam War, when Americans tended to be more skeptical of the virtues and necessity of these sorts of aggressive, even illegal, operations. In addition, Kissinger appeared to have overlooked the fact that while Washington's ousting of Árbenz resulted in an immediate propaganda boost domestically, it also precipitated a regional backlash against US policies, which Nixon himself saw in terrifying color in Caracas in 1958. Short-term gain came with significant long-term consequences.

In the case of Chile these long-term consequences would be particularly harrowing. Like many Chileans, the CIA believed that Pinochet's new junta would rule temporarily before calling elections and thus return the country to democracy. Instead, Pinochet's dictatorship lasted for seventeen years and tortured and killed thousands of its citizens: twelve hundred in the first months following the coup and a total of around thirty-one hundred.

There are sharply divergent views about the nature of US support for Pinochet during this period. Kissinger appeared to emphatically back the autocratic ruler, telling General Pinochet in 1976, "We want to help you, not undermine you." William D. Rogers, the State Department's top deputy for Latin America, asserted that US policy was in fact aimed at reining in Pinochet's authoritarian tendencies. In a memo to Kissinger, Rogers wrote, "Like it or not, we are identified with the regime's origins and hence charged with some responsibility for its action. This accents our strong interest in getting the GOC [Government of Chile] to pursue acceptable human rights practices." Rogers thinks that critics overlook the "stern human rights warning" Kissinger personally gave to Pinochet during a visit to Santiago in June 1976. Rogers also cites that the diplomatic ties between Washington and Santiago (and Brazilian, Uruguayan, and Argentine military regimes as well) "went into a deep freeze," a situation that continued after Jimmy Carter took office in January 1977.

There is the burning counterfactual question as to how Allende's presidency would have turned out had Nixon not initiated Track II or fostered coup conditions. The scholar Kenneth Maxwell argues that "left to their own devices, the Chileans might just have found the good sense to resolve their own deep-seated problems. Allende might have fallen by his own weight, victim of his own incompetence, and not become a tragic martyr to a lost cause." But while apologists for the CIA's actions in Allende's Chile readily acknowledge that the agency's operations succeeded in "reducing support for Allende," they also emphasize that the "fierce opposition" to Allende came from within the country—particularly when the sitting president's "flawed economic policies" that initially stimulated the economy began to falter. These consequences hit not just the rich, and thus were innately anti-Allende, but also the middle and lower classes.

Analyzing this historical episode is further complicated by the fallout from the Watergate scandal: to many, Nixon's domestic duplicity would taint all his political dealings. Ultimately, the overthrow of Allende in 1973 can be thought of as a Cold War Rorschach test, where both sides tend to see what they want to see. That the US was involved, albeit indirectly, is uncontestable; how directly efficacious its fostering of "coup conditions" were in leading to the overthrow of the Allende administration is perhaps still open to debate.

25 • Guatemala's "Scorched Communists"

> If you [the Guatemalan people] are with us, we'll feed you; if not,
> we'll kill you.
> —Guatemalan army officer in Cunén, Guatemala, 1982

By the early 1960s Latin America was rife with guerrilla insurgencies, or focos, most funded and/or inspired by communist Cuba. US planners held that Guatemala was where the Marxist insurgents held the best chance of victory over the US-backed central government, which had been installed after the ouster of President Jacobo Árbenz in 1954. A US classified intelligence report in 1968 commented that "there are some indications that Fidel Castro is planning to increase his support of the Guatemalan insurgency, perhaps to the point of dispatching a small force of guerrillas now undergoing training in Cuba." Already riven by conflict, Guatemala was unstable, which made the country a prime candidate for revolution. "Short-term opportunities for the insurgents now seem the most promising," commented the same intelligence report, "because of the weaknesses of the government rather than the strength of the insurgents, who are few in numbers and divided by factional rivalry."

An anxious Pentagon sent Special Forces advisory and training teams numbering more than one thousand personnel in total to the conflict-plagued nation between 1966 and 1968. Some twenty-eight of these US soldiers died during missions, usually in small-scale firefights with the guerrillas. The US counterinsurgency presence did not result in the guerrillas' lasting defeat, and new or splinter rebel groups kept appearing. Over the next two decades a motley assortment of communists, trade unionists, students, and other leftists joined these guerrilla bands.

Guatemala Does It Alone

Despite an initial lack of success, US advisors eventually managed to shape Guatemala's military into a more effective and potent antiguerrilla force in the early 1970s. Strategy remained another matter entirely, however, as one junior US advisor and future US Army general officer later recalled: "We did not have a strategy. . . . We had little or no leverage on the Guatemalans. Our approach of our advisory effort was tactical rather than even operational or strategic. [Our message was that] the guerrillas are really bad and we'll potentially be good. That was about as strategic as we got."

US analysts were also growing increasingly alarmed about the Guatemalan military's harsh behavior. A CIA report in 1970 labeled the government led by Carlos Arana, which carried out the infamous Zacapa massacre in the late 1960s, "the most extreme and unyielding in the hemisphere." The US official Viron P. Vaky was concerned about the indiscriminate nature of the Guatemalan state's counterterror approach. In a confidential memorandum Vaky stated, "We cannot rationalize that fact away. The official [paramilitary] squads are guilty of atrocities. Interrogations are brutal, torture is used and bodies are mutilated." Vaky sensed deep moral and policy implications for Washington: "One can easily see there how counter-terror has blurred the question of Communist insurgency and is converting it into an issue of morality and justice. . . . We are associated with this tactic in the minds of many people, and whether it is right or wrong so to associate us is rapidly becoming irrelevant. . . . Have our values been so twisted by our adversary concept of politics in the hemisphere? Is it conceivable that we are so obsessed with insurgency that we are prepared to rationalize murder as an acceptable counter-insurgency weapon?"

The US-created "Frankenstein" military had, by the latter half of the 1970s, turned into a glaring embarrassment for the United States and its stance on protecting human rights, but there was little it could do. Washington was "half involved" in Guatemala: not deep enough to significantly influence the increasingly bloodthirsty counterinsurgency campaigns but enough that its international reputation might potentially be sullied by the long-standing association with this repressive regime.

For its part, the Guatemalan army vehemently disliked such criticism, and relations quickly deteriorated. The Carter administration's first global human rights report sanctioned Guatemala in 1977, but the regime of the strongman Fernando Romeo Lucas García rejected US military aid even before Carter could stop it. A Guatemalan cabinet minister told US officials that "Guatemalans had to protect their vital interests," even if this meant doing so without Uncle Sam.

The suspension of US military aid to Guatemala did not bring about a moderation of Guatemalan policy. Indeed, the late seventies and early eighties, the very years when US military aid was not flowing, witnessed some of the most severe "scorched earth" counterinsurgency campaigns, financed via fresh agreements with such governments as Spain, Chile, Argentina, Taiwan, and Israel, thus offering new sources of non-US aid and training. The Guatemalan military and conservative industrial sector seethed at Carter's perceived weakness on tackling communism. One industry executive, Roberto Alejos, asserted that "most of the elements in the State Department are probably pro-communist.... Either Mr. Carter is a totally incapable president or he is definitely a pro-communist element." The results of the US presidential elections of 1980, therefore, were much anticipated by Guatemala's hard-liners. Assuming that the new government in Washington would be a stalwart backer of their counterinsurgency war, conservatives like Alejos were among those celebrating "like New Year's Eve, with Mariachis, Marimbas, and firecrackers" when the Republican Ronald Reagan won a landslide victory in November.

By mid-1981 the Reagan administration was coming around to a policy whereby it would actively encourage the Lucas García regime to address human rights instead of simply imposing more sanctions, as was the criticism of the Carter administration's approach. More carrots than sticks, in diplomatic parlance. Here is the State Department official John Bushnell before two congressional committees in July 1981: "We are convinced that dialog is the only approach which can be effective in diminishing overreaction by government forces and toleration of illicit rightist activity." The changed US stance toward the regime can also be related to the fact that, despite Lucas García's repression, by the early 1980s the various guerrilla groups had grown bolder and more powerful. They now consisted of 6,000 persons under arms and a civilian support network of 276,000 dispersed over 16 of Guatemala's 22 departments.

There were also voices of caution. In a secret policy action memorandum from October 5, 1981, the US diplomat Robert L. Jacobs urged the Reagan administration against using "national security considerations" as a justification for renewing security assistance to Lucas García's regime:

> Whether President Lucas [García] is wrong or right in his conviction that repression will succeed in neutralizing the guerillas, their supporters and sympathizers, the U.S. posture ought [to] remain one of distancing

itself from the GOG [Government of Guatemala]. . . . The provisioning of such [suspended military] assistance would needlessly render us a complicit party in the repression.

If we are correct in our conviction that the repression will not succeed and will only exacerbate and compound the guerilla threat, then we ought to distance ourselves from the GOG until such time as it arrives at the realization and is prepared to address our human rights concerns in return for renewed U.S. political and military support.

Ríos Montt Seizes Power

In March 1982 General Efraín Ríos Montt, along with two other officers (whom he subsequently pushed aside), seized power in Guatemala in a bloody coup. Guatemala's new ruler posed a dilemma to US policy makers: despite his undemocratic ascension Ríos Montt seemed to be doing all the things the US had asked for. Immediately after the March 1982 coup he disbanded the infamous Detectives Corps of the National Police, initiated a smattering of human rights reforms, and garnered support from the Guatemalan population through anticorruption campaigns—including one that mandated government officials to wear pins that said, "I don't steal, don't lie, don't abuse"—and appointments of indigenous politicians to his regime.

Just a few months into his rule Ríos Montt touted a "rifles and beans" initiative that combined civic action programs, religion (Ríos Montt was an evangelical Christian), and antiguerrilla military units to win the hearts and minds of the crucial rural Maya population. In a July 1982 article Raymond Bonner, a *New York Times* correspondent, explained how the program was being realized in a rural hamlet in the mountainous and rebel-populated department of Quiché: "Church, state and army had gathered in this tranquil, isolated mountain village to deliver a message: a union of God, the army and the people can defeat 'the subversives.' " The moderate Christian Democratic movement, which had seen 130 of the party's leaders and activists assassinated in the previous two years under Lucas García's rule, also applauded Ríos Montt's actions.

Frederic Chapin, the top American envoy in Guatemala City, stated publicly that Ríos Montt's moves against corruption and the drop in extrajudicial abuses helped warrant the resumption of US assistance: "No question they're better. No question. The killings have stopped. This is light years ahead from what we had before. The Guatemalan government has come out of the darkness and into the light." This diplomatic warming came in the context of increasing communist influence in Central America: Nicaragua was now Marxist, and El Salvador was battling a Marxist insurgency far more potent than that of its Guatemalan counterpart. But it was not solely hawks like Reagan State Department appointee Elliott Abrams or even the career US diplomat Chapin who were inclined to give the new government the benefit of the doubt. Even outspoken critics of Reagan's Central America policies, such as the Democratic congressman Michael Barnes, echoed the sense of a new, less homicidal climate under Ríos Montt. "I think it's clear that there's been a change in Guatemala," Barnes asserted in January 1983. "The reports I've received are still mixed—some quite encouraging, some still quite pessimistic— but everyone concedes that the Government of Rios Montt seems to be operating in a way that's very different from that of Lucas García in trying to deal with the problems facing the country."

Nongovernmental actors also sensed an improved human rights climate. According to one Catholic Church source in the countryside, "Massacres are down in the sense that we have not heard in the past two months of those of the size that we had been hearing before that. . . . The basic rule in the *campo* [countryside] now is control—it doesn't seem to be killing anymore."

There was, however, another side to what was going on in Guatemala. Ríos Montt's reform push ran alongside a brutal approach to counterinsurgency. The guerrillas who occupied villages and towns throughout rural Guatemala would often flee before the army, now doubled in size to thirty thousand men, attacked, but Ríos Montt's cold-blooded strategy was "if you can't catch the fish, you must drain the sea." Hundreds of Mayan villages simply vanished; beheadings, garroting, immolation, and summary massacres were conducted throughout the alleged guerrilla strongholds; in 1982 Amnesty International estimated that ten thousand peasants were killed in just the first five months of Ríos Montt's rule.

To Ríos Montt, victory would come at any cost: "I must do what I must. . . . We here are fighting the Third World War." In late 1982 he famously denied accusations that his government was conducting a dirty war: "We have no scorched-earth policy; we have a policy of scorched communists."

"Bum Rap"

To what extent Reagan was cognizant of the situation in Guatemala has divided scholars ever since. Almost every text on US Cold War policy cites President Reagan's quip on December 4, 1982, during his trip to the region

Comalapa, Guatemala. Forensic anthropologists exhume the remains from
a mass grave at a former Guatemalan military base near Comalapa.
September 7, 2003. (Victor J. Blue)

that Ríos Montt was "a man of great personal integrity and commitment
[whose nation] is confronting a brutal challenge from guerrillas and supported
by others outside Guatemala." Later the same day, Reagan added that Ríos
Montt was "totally dedicated to democracy in Guatemala. . . . They made quite
a presentation and brought a lot of information and material to us. And
frankly, I'm inclined to think they've been getting a bum rap."

In the analysis of the scholar Kathryn Sikkink, Reagan's rhetorical endorsement was a "gratuitous, thoughtless gesture made for a man guilty of mass
murder of his population" that "gave a green light to repression." This could
very well be the case. At the same time, one cannot discount the fact that
maybe Ríos Montt pulled the wool over Reagan's eyes on the political and human rights reform front. Certainly he had been making efforts during Reagan's trip to paint the situation in Guatemala in a positive light, as evidenced
by a *New York Times* account from December 19, 1982, which stated that Ríos
Montt "sought to convince Mr. Reagan that the human rights situation here
had improved to the point that the country was now deserving of military aid."

Faced with Sikkink's charge, the Reagan administration would very likely
contend that, in contrast to abetting genocide, US military aid was intended to

make the Guatemalan government less abusive, not more. Here, our goal is not to defend or prosecute Reagan's words or his Guatemala policy but to understand the various factors in play behind exceptionally difficult, often life-and-death policy and moral decisions. In all historical cases, evidence and context matter. If, say, Ronald Reagan or Elliott Abrams pretended not to know about the abuses of Ríos Montt's regime to smooth the path for the resumption of US military aid, then they should answer to history; but one also has to consider that they may have been simply unaware of the full extent of Ríos Montt's brutality. In which case a relevant question would also be, why didn't they know? Truth in the matter is exceptionally difficult to discern. Some US officials, like Ambassador Chapin, were "pushing quite firmly behind the scenes on the human rights issue," an effort that made the US envoy "little appreciated" by the Ríos Montt regime. At the same time, internal US government agencies in-country were "investigating credible reports of numerous massacres involving the Guatemalan military." In retaliation for an earlier guerrilla ambush that killed a dozen soldiers, on December 6, 1982, two days after the Reagan–Ríos Montt press conference, Guatemalan special forces troops murdered more than two hundred villagers in what became known as the Dos Erres massacre. A trenchant counterfactual question might be, if Reagan had known about a Dos Erres–type massacre of civilians beforehand, would he have been so laudatory of Ríos Montt? Or if he did know of such heinous abuses, was the threat of communism so severe in Reagan's eyes that he would be prepared to overlook them?

Reagan's Renewed (and Restricted) Aid

In 1983 Abrams explained the logic of the Reagan administration's request to lift a five-year sanction on military materiél to Guatemala and provide the regime with millions of dollars in helicopter parts. "The amount of killing of innocent civilians is being reduced step by step," he told a television news program. "We think that kind of progress needs to be rewarded and encouraged."

It is debatable whether Abrams was being ingenuous or not, but one thing is certain: he was wrong. There was no progress—the killings continued—and a crucial question about the Reagan years emerged: To what extent did restored economic and military aid help fuel the ongoing repression? From the outset the Reagan administration was eager to get aid flowing again, but looming priorities in El Salvador and Nicaragua meant great care was needed to not antagonize Capitol Hill. And while certain types of aid would eventually be sent, Sikkink details how "during most of the Reagan administration and during the period of most intense repression in Guatemala, U.S. military aid was cut off and economic aid was at fairly low levels." The Carter-era restrictions remained largely in place, with all military and economic aid having to be signed off on by the Democrat-held Congress, although Reagan did get around some restrictions by, for example, classifying twenty-five Vietnam-era Bell helicopters as civilian. Some leftist observers have also contended that the Guatemalan security forces converted nonlethal aid into lethal weaponry, and thus these sorts of congressional proscriptions were a farce. This low level of US engagement, however, ultimately did little to stop the mounting atrocities. With "relative autonomy" Guatemalan security forces and Ríos Montt were able to maintain their scorching communist counterinsurgency campaign, relying on other state actors like Taiwan or Israel to fill the materiél gap.

"I Am Innocent"

On August 8, 1983, Ríos Montt was ousted in a military coup. By 1985 there was a new constitution, ushering in elections won by the Christian Democrat Vinicio Cerezo, the country's first civilian president in sixteen years. The military still held an outsized share of power, however, and although mass murders diminished, extrajudicial killings and other forms of abuse continued. To the dismay of many human rights activists and families of victims, Cerezo granted an amnesty to members of the army that gave them immunity from prosecution for historical human rights abuses. In total, approximately two hundred thousand people were killed in the protracted internal war from 1960 to 1996, overwhelmingly at the hands of state forces.

In 2013 a declining Ríos Montt was tried and convicted for being aware of but not stopping the widespread slaughter of civilians in the mountain hamlets in Quiché department. During the trial the former strongman was largely mute but did speak some words: "I am innocent. I never had the intent to destroy any national race, religion, or ethnic group." He contended that his "mission as head of state was to reclaim order, because Guatemala was in ruins," as opposed to actively managing the counterinsurgency war. Less than two weeks later, citing a technicality, Guatemala's constitutional court ruled against the conviction, and Ríos Montt's eighty-year prison sentence was rendered null.

Five years later, as he was being retried in absentia, Ríos Montt succumbed to a heart attack on April 1, 2018. The next day his obituary in the *New York*

Times painted the strongman's brutal legacy: "In the panoply of commanders who turned much of Central America into a killing field in the 1980s, General Ríos Montt was one of the most murderous."

A Question of Culpability

In March 1999 US president Bill Clinton visited Guatemala and issued an apology: "For the United States, it is important that I state clearly that support for military forces and intelligence units which engaged in violence and widespread repression was wrong." Notably, Clinton did not specify when the US support was provided, given how much controversy and condemnation has been associated with the Reagan years.

Was the United States fully or partially responsible for the Guatemalan genocide? For writers like the historian Stephen Rabe, Reagan's renewed aid and other forms of engagement are sufficient to back some categorical interpretations. "The Reagan administration assisted the slaughter of the Mayan people," wrote Rabe. The historian Greg Grandin's take is that the Reagan White House supported the genocide "materially and morally." However, while being clear-sighted about the damage of US influence, it is also important to weigh the agency and interests of those in Guatemala who perpetrated the violence. The searing question for scholars and students is to consider the evidence we draw upon for our conclusions, which may range from the damning to the more exculpatory.

26 • Nicaragua under the Sandinistas

On the morning of January 10, 1978, the political and media icon Pedro Joaquín Chamorro was gunned down by two assassins in Managua, Nicaragua, on his way to work. The country's dictator, Anastasio "Tachito" Somoza Debayle, son of "Tacho" Somoza García, who took power in 1937, contended that pro-Chamorro groups had perpetrated the murder in order to embarrass his government. An unconvinced, increasingly disgusted Nicaraguan population was having none of it. Many laid the blame at the feet of Tachito and his despised *somocista* National Guard; youth spontaneously rioted across the nation, throwing Molotov cocktails; and the crucial business class came on board, embracing the notion of a national strike to demand justice. The murder of Chamorro galvanized a splintered nation, ultimately sealed Somoza's demise, and ushered in a Marxist revolution hostile to Washington.

"Sandino Lives"

After Augusto Sandino's assassination in February 1934, the rebel's mythical and ideological influence remained strong in Nicaragua. His towering legacy created *sandinismo*, an eclectic ideological mix of nationalism, anti-imperialism, and principles of radical social change along Marxist lines. Middle-class Nicaraguan university students and other intellectuals gave these ideas political articulation when they established the Frente Sandinista de Liberación Nacional (FSLN) in 1961, more commonly referred to as the Sandinistas.

The Sandinistas were a relatively small rebel group, only a fraction the size of their fellow Marxist insurgency in Guatemala. Like many of the rebel groups then active in Central America, they received arms and training from

Havana. Their goal was to realize their cherished martyr's idealistic insurgency. By the mid-1960s US intelligence agents were confident the FSLN was "a Cuban-supported and Communist-infiltrated subversive group" but not a serious threat to the Somoza regime. This helps explain why fewer than fifty US military advisors were deployed to Nicaragua during the 1960s while over a thousand were active in Guatemala to stop it from "going red." Washington covered just under 15 percent of Managua's yearly defense spending, a significant but far from vital sum, although deeper ties linked the two militaries. The Somozas required all Nicaraguan Guard officers to spend twelve months at the US-run School of the Americas in the Panama Canal Zone for training and study. In the fifties and sixties this US institution hosted more Nicaraguan officers than those of any other nation in Latin America.

The US assessment initially appeared to be correct. In the late sixties and early seventies the Sandinistas' initial insurrection failed to gain traction against entrenched police and security forces. The group's leaders, Tomás Borge and Carlos Fonseca, had to send their scattered forces back to the mountains to regroup. The Guard relentlessly hunted down the poorly armed and organized middle-class rebels, who themselves were struggling to connect with the masses ostensibly at the core of the revolution. Wearied and forlorn after their setbacks, the Sandinistas were on the brink of extinction.

Then fate intervened—and not for the last time. A catastrophic earthquake hit Managua on December 23, 1972. That the Somozas and their cronies stole humanitarian aid while the mounds of rubble remained untouched only heightened the nation's ire and provided ample evidence that the Sandinistas' claim of Tachito's corruption and tyrannical governance was true. While the earthquake was not enough to tip the scales in favor of the rebels, hostility to the regime was rising. The grisly Chamorro assassination six years later built on this momentum, resulting in a boom in guerrilla recruitment. By May 1978 a broad coalition of anti-Somoza political parties, unions, and social organizations had founded the more moderate Broad Opposition Front (FAO). The creation of the FAO reinforced the increasingly undeniable fact that a critical mass of Nicaraguan society had turned against Somoza.

Carter Dumps Somoza, Revolution Sweeps Nicaragua

As Somoza's popularity inside and outside Nicaragua continued to plummet, one US congressional delegation came away terrified that the ruler was becoming the Idi Amin of Latin America, in reference to the bloodthirsty

Ugandan strongman of this period. Once a loyal S.O.B. to Washington, Somoza was now an embarrassing liability in light of Carter's progressive vision of the region. This put the Carter administration in a quandary, given that it had earlier expressed hope that "our days of unilateral intervention such as occurred in Vietnam, Cambodia, and the Dominican Republic are over."

Although Carter was sincere in his belief that the United States needed to resist the temptation to become too involved in Nicaragua's unfolding revolution, two perhaps contradictory realities remained unaddressed. The first was that, while US disengagement might have been morally and pragmatically persuasive, it would not have ensured a strategic success for US interests, namely, a stable, democratic Nicaragua. The second was that the new focus of the United States on human rights was itself a potent form of intervention. Further muddying this evaluation, US ambassador to Nicaragua Lawrence Pezzullo noted in a memo that the Sandinista-led revolution was "an authentic Nicaraguan phenomenon" and "a pluralistic movement, led by people with a wide range of backgrounds."

Ultimately, Carter concluded that supporting Somoza was no longer politically viable. He cut military aid and, within months, slapped sanctions on Managua, moves that expedited Somoza's downfall. In May 1979 the Sandinistas launched a final offensive, or the "hour of the overthrow," to borrow the language of its radio programming. Sandinista units attacked Guard outposts all over the country; a general strike began to take a severe toll on the economy. By now the Sandinistas were calling the city of León their provincial capital, and Managua was in the rebels' crosshairs. Additionally, some of the guerrilla attacks against the Guard were perpetrated by parties other than the Sandinistas, strengthening the impression that resistance to Somoza was broad and diverse. Indeed, it is highly unlikely that the Sandinistas could have seized power had a strong majority of Nicaraguans not actively opposed the regime, just as a broad consensus of Cubans had opposed Batista.

By July Somoza had fled the country. Now a new, five-person junta comprising both Sandinista and non-Sandinista opposition figures was in charge and benefited from almost universal international and domestic support. Carter's policy makers responded by trying to get more non-Sandinistas (read: more moderates) into the junta, but this task was complicated by Washington's crisis of credibility, given how long it had taken the Americans to abandon Somoza. In the post-Somoza climate, Washington still held enormous power vis-à-vis Nicaragua, but its ability to influence events in the Central American country had ebbed considerably, a situation that recurs time and time again in the history of US–Latin American relations. Within days of the July 1979 victory of the FSLN and the junta, senior US intelligence officials predicted that "the hard-core Marxists in the regime will quickly begin trying to neutralize the influence of the junta's more moderate members and seize control." And so it came to pass. The Sandinistas pushed out the more moderate members of the junta and consolidated their Cuba-inspired rule over Nicaragua, making themselves, one contemporary noted, "the real winners of the revolution."

Over the ensuing years, two brothers, Daniel and Humberto Ortega, became the public leaders of the Sandinista movement, much as Fidel Castro and his younger brother Raúl had done in Cuba. Sons of a Managua businessman who had served as one of Sandino's original guerrillas, the Ortegas had headed a relatively moderate Sandinista faction known as the Terceristas, which in 1978 had become the dominant revolutionary group both militarily and politically. Daniel consolidated his position as the head of the new revolutionary government while Humberto became the minister of defense.

Despite its continued enthusiastic support of post-Somoza Nicaragua in public settings, the Carter administration was becoming increasingly concerned about the threat of a communist advance via the Sandinistas. Among American policy makers and politicians the consensus was beginning to emerge behind the scenes that Managua was actively supporting the embryonic insurgency in El Salvador, the Farabundo Martí National Liberation Front (FMLN). In 1979 Carter was shown high-altitude photographs and other intelligence confirming that the Sandinistas were sending arms shipments to Marxist insurgents in El Salvador. Based on scores of more recently declassified documents, we now know that this assessment was correct. Sandinista commanders began discussions early on how to arm their Marxist *compañeros* in Guatemala and, most critically, El Salvador, to expedite a repetition of the stunning outcome in Nicaragua.

The Carter administration decided to use carrots over sticks to influence the Sandinistas, perhaps a wise choice considering its diminished credibility in the country. Washington extended development assistance to the tune of almost $25 million in 1979, sending emergency relief and recovery aid, primarily food and medical supplies. By January 1981, when the Carter team was leaving office, direct annual US assistance to Managua had reached $118 million. In early 1980, however, Carter also signed a classified intelligence finding that authorized the CIA to promote democratic elements in Nicaragua. This support took the form of money funneled to opposition parties to pay for expenses and propaganda. No money was provided for armed actions. Nonetheless, Carter's finding served to move the United States away from its hands-off approach to dealing with revolutionary change in Nicaragua. Once a staunch advocate of nonintervention, Jimmy Carter had become more hawkish toward the end of his term.

Reagan Arrives

The presidential elections of November 1980 brought in the Republican challenger, Ronald Reagan, an avowed foreign policy hawk who promised to combat communist expansion in the hemisphere. In early April 1981 the Reagan administration announced its indefinite cessation of aid to Nicaragua, but it also made an attempt to salvage the deteriorating bilateral relationship and strike a deal. That August the Reagan White House sent Assistant Secretary of State Thomas Enders to Managua for talks. Seeking to use "the threat of confrontation rather than confrontation itself," Enders engaged the Sandinista leaders in a frequently heated discussion of possible solutions. Enders warned that the United States would be inclined to involve itself militarily if the Sandinistas failed to halt the flow of arms to El Salvador, prompting one of Ortega's advisors to yell, "All right, come on in! We'll meet you man to man!" At the end of the meetings, Enders proposed the Reagan administration's bargain: in exchange for halting the export of arms to and insurrection in El Salvador and a reduction in Nicaragua's armed forces, the United States would provide Nicaragua with continued security arrangements and economic aid.

After a month of consideration Daniel Ortega firmly rejected the offer. In February 1982 Tomás Borge, now the head of the Sandinistas' intelligence service, contended that it was the government's moral duty to support its revolutionary comrades in Central America. "How can we keep our arms folded in the face of the crimes that are being committed in El Salvador and Guatemala?" he asked. "If we are accused of expressing solidarity, if we are forced to sit in the dock because of this, we say: We have shown our solidarity with all Latin American peoples in the past, we are doing so at present and will continue to do so in the future." Daniel Ortega went even further, arguing that his country was "interested in seeing the guerrillas in El Salvador and Guatemala triumph. . . . [It is] our shield—it makes our revolution safer."

Having spurned the US offer of security assistance, the Sandinistas began courting the global left. A visit to Moscow in November 1981 helped Humberto Ortega establish an intricate system of arms suppliers, including from Algeria, an early supporter of the Sandinistas, Bulgaria, and Vietnam as well as direct supplies from the Soviet Union, East Germany, North Korea, Czecho-slovakia, and Cuba. In March 1982 the CIA released aerial reconnaissance photographs that purported to show the location of Managua's new battalion of twenty-five Soviet-made T-55 tanks, two Soviet-made Mi-17 helicopters, and four airfields being updated to accommodate fighter aircraft.

The Contras Are Born

Fatefully, around the time Ronald Reagan was entering the White House in January 1981, a motley assortment of former *somocista* Guard personnel, ag-grieved Sandinistas, *campesinos* (peasants), and Miskito Indians banded to-gether to form what came to be known as the Contras. From a starting strength of two thousand the Contras grew to almost fifteen thousand at their height, and pervaded the region. One Contra faction based in Costa Rica, for example, was led by the now-disaffected ex–Sandinista hero Edén Pastora. Led by the "visible and appealing" former Jesuit priest and university president Edgar Chamorro, the so-called Fuerza Democrática Nicaragüense, seeking greater protection, was based mostly on the Honduran side of Nicaragua's northern border.

Reagan came to see the Contras as freedom fighters in the global struggle against communism, and they quickly came to represent the principal compo-nent of his policy in Sandinista-controlled Nicaragua. In December 1981 Reagan signed a new finding centered on the creation of a proxy force of Nicaraguan exiles. The CIA would play a low-profile role in supporting anti-Sandinista forces, opting to have Argentina's military conduct the training in the clandestine camps in Honduras. The arrangement suited all parties: not only did the ruling Argentine junta share the Contras' anticommunist ideol-ogy, but in training the militants Buenos Aires curried favor with the Reagan administration. The aim of the junta was to warm up the cooling in relations that followed Carter's criticisms of its human rights abuses. For their part, the CIA got to keep its hands clean.

In January 1982 President Reagan approved National Security Decision Di-rective 17 (NSDD 17), which included the stated intent "to assist in defeating the insurgency in El Salvador, and to oppose actions by Cuba, Nicaragua, or others to introduce . . . supplies for insurgents." The plan continued the Carter-era support of "democratic forces" in Nicaragua and also called for the military training of indigenous units and leaders both in and out of the country. Thomas Enders embraced NSDD 17, presenting the training of anti-Sandinista

Contra fighters in Yamales, Honduras, 1988. (AP Photo)

fighters to Reagan as "a lowball option, a small operation not intended to over-throw." Instead, Enders envisioned the support for anti-Sandinista forces as a "bargaining chip" to pressure the Sandinistas to return to the negotiating table to address their support of Salvadoran Marxist rebels.

The 1982 Falklands War between Argentina and Britain changed the plan: Argentina expected that the US would remain neutral, but when it emerged that the US was providing intelligence to the British forces, the Argentine military immediately closed its training camp for the Contras in Tegucigalpa. The CIA took charge of training and developed the Contras into a fighting force that could conduct far more frequent and more lethal operations against

Map of the Contra War, 1980s. (Andrew Rhodes, cartographer)

the Sandinista security forces and their civilian adherents. US-supplied equipment also greatly increased the insurgents' firepower: the Contras would fight with US-made M-16s, Belgian FAL automatic rifles, M-79 grenade launchers, mortars, and other state-of-the-art weaponry.

Having only just consolidated its revolution, the Sandinistas took the threat of the Contras seriously. By 1983 a rapid succession of Contra military strikes across the countryside sobered the Sandinista military brass. A senior Cuban general, Arnaldo Ochoa, took command of the counterinsurgency. Moscow immediately supplied fresh weapons and equipment, including ten Mi-8 helicopter transports, over three hundred new trucks, two dozen armored fighting vehicles and tanks, and scores of rocket launchers known as Stalin organs. US intelligence officials estimated that Soviet deliveries to Nicaragua doubled in 1983, from ten thousand tons of materiél to twenty thousand. Moscow also increased the number of advisors in-country from seventy to one hundred, and the Cuban presence grew from seventy-five hundred to nine thousand, of whom more than two thousand were military and internal security advisors. While during the Somoza era there had been no more than a few hundred secret police agents, under the Sandinistas the number of agents grew to more than three thousand. And, fatefully, the new counterinsurgency strategy required an increase in the already sizable army force of twenty-five thousand. In July 1983 the Sandinista army chief, Humberto Ortega, implemented a policy for universal military conscription, which proved abhorrent to legions of Nicaraguans in subsequent years.

"Siding with the Most Hated Group of Nicaraguans"

As news of the US covert funding of the Contras appeared in various press accounts in the early 1980s, the Reagan administration officials were forced into the difficult act of explaining a strategy that was not supposed to exist. As one senior official explained it, "We are not waging a secret war, or anything approaching that. What we are doing is trying to keep Managua off balance and apply pressure to stop providing military aid to the insurgents in El Salvador."

The California Democratic congressman George Miller was not persuaded, and in late 1982 he requested that Congress "go on record in getting control of those agencies who have convinced the White House to substitute covert action for policy, to substitute covert action for diplomacy, and take an action that without the express consent of this Congress is in fact illegal, unethical and against the best interests of this country." The Democratic Iowa congressman Tom Harkin was equally scathing, commenting in late 1982 that "news reports of late . . . clearly indicate that we are becoming ever more mired in the jungles and swamps of Latin America. . . . [T]he real mistake we are making is not only in doing something that is clearly illegal, but in siding with perhaps the most hated group of Nicaraguans that could exist outside of the borders of Nicaragua, and I talk about Somocistas."

This largely Democratic opposition yielded a highly ambivalent policy, reflected in the fact that US assistance to the Contras waxed and waned throughout the 1980s and was sometimes cut off entirely. In April 1982 the Democratic

representative and chairman of the House Intelligence Committee Edward
Boland added language to the secret annex to an intelligence authorization bill
declaring that congressional funding could not be spent "for the purpose of
overthrowing the government of Nicaragua or provoking an exchange between Nicaragua and Honduras." However, the Boland amendment focused
solely on intent, not actions, leaving tremendous flexibility for the Reagan
administration to push its secret program. A second Boland amendment was
duly passed in December 1983, further restricting Reagan's ability to assist
the Contras by limiting any aid "which would have the effect of supporting,
directly or indirectly, military or paramilitary operations in Nicaragua by any
nation, group, organization, movement, or individual." The chosen cap of $24
million functioned as a limit on the CIA's options in terms of assistance.

Despite the bickering over funding in Washington the CIA continued aiding
the Contras on the ground. In an early October 1983 operation a clandestine
CIA-sponsored raid on Corinto, a port city on the Pacific Coast, set ablaze the
fuel storage facility holding over three million gallons of petrol. Daniel Ortega's
government now had only a month's worth of oil remaining. The bold raid included Contras as well as so-called UCLAs (unilaterally controlled Latino assets, in the CIA's inelegant phrasing), hired by the agency to carry out secret
missions. In what reminded some of a small-scale Bay of Pigs, the Corinto
operation was the nearest the Reagan administration came to a direct hostile
action against the Sandinistas over the course of the Contra War, as it was
called in the United States. The CIA also had a hand in the mining of Nicaragua's harbors to deter merchant captains—a move unanimously condemned
by the International Court of Justice, with a US judge concurring—and delaying or halting oil tanker deliveries. The UN Security Council discussed the
issue for several days before Washington used its veto to forestall a censure.

The reaction back in Washington was similarly scathing. The vice chairman
of the Senate Select Committee on Intelligence, Senator Daniel Patrick Moynihan, resigned in protest, while the archconservative senator Barry Goldwater
sent a brusque letter to CIA director William Casey. "I'm pissed off. . . . I don't
like this," Goldwater wrote, "I don't like it one bit from the president or from
you. . . . This is an act violating international law. It is an act of war. For the life
of me, I don't see how we are going to explain it." In late 1984 the *Washington
Post* revealed that the CIA had produced a manual for the Contras that included instructions advocating the "selective use of violence" to "neutralize"
local Sandinista officials. For the legions of critics inside America, ranging
from human rights and religious organizations to congressional activists, the

Contras' barbarity and illegality became the new rallying cry of opposition to Reagan's Central America policies. By the end of 1985 the Nicaraguan Ministry of Health estimated that over thirty-six hundred civilians had been killed, over four thousand wounded, and about fifty-two hundred kidnapped during Contra raids. What was lost in the bitter debate was that the vast majority of the Contra aid was in fact coming not from Washington but from other governments, most notably Saudi Arabia. This practice was especially true after the passage of yet another Boland amendment in 1984 that prohibited all funding for the Contras and banned government agencies from "directly or indirectly supporting military operations in Nicaragua."

Despite the blowback Reagan doubled down on his public push for Contra aid, bolstered by his landslide victory over the Democrat Walter Mondale in the November 1984 election. For what was now being dubbed the Reagan Doctrine, the Contras were the moral and strategic poster child for what needed to be done in the Western Hemisphere. And while Congress was critical of the Reagan Doctrine, it was also still deeply concerned about the communist threat. In 1985 Congress approved two policies that had a profound impact on the situation in Nicaragua: the first was for humanitarian aid to be given directly to the Contras, thus dialing back the restrictions passed in previous years; the second was a trade embargo against Nicaragua, which made the country's desperate economic situation even worse. Put together, CIA sabotage efforts, the trade embargo, and the Sandinistas' incompetent fiscal and monetary effort turned Nicaragua into an economic basket case, undermining the ruling junta's crucial popular support. In 1982 just one-fifth of the national budget went to defense; by 1988 it was closer to 40 percent and rising. Ever more ideologically rigid, the Sandinistas were also reeling from sustained criticism of their handling of civil liberties and human rights leveled by the Roman Catholic Church, including from Pope John Paul II as well as the opposition newspaper *La Prensa*. Then came the greatest scandal to hit American politics since Watergate.

The Iran–Contra Scandal

On Sunday, October 5, 1986, a C-123K cargo plane took off from Ilopango, El Salvador, and flew into Nicaraguan airspace, just seven hundred meters off the ground to evade Sandinista radar. Deep in the jungle of Chontales department, José Fernando Canales and Byron Montiel, young soldiers just five months into their mandatory service in the Sandinista military, had set up a portable surface-air rocket, or "arrow," several days before. When they heard the engines of the unmarked cargo plane, Canales received the order to shoot. He aimed and fired, and within seconds the plane exploded in the air and fell to earth in pieces; only the tail section remained intact. When Sandinista troops reached the crash site they found 13,000 pounds of weaponry, including 50,000 AK-47 rifle cartridges, 60 collapsible AK-47s, a similar number of RPG-7 grenade launchers plus 150 pairs of jungle boots.

The C-123K carried three Americans and one Nicaraguan. The pilot, William Cooper, copilot Wallace Blaine Sawyer, and radio operator Freddy Vilches all died in the crash. Eugene Hasenfus, in charge of dropping the cargo, had seen the incoming rocket in time and jumped from the plane with a parachute given to him by his brother before leaving the United States. "Give up, gringo, or we'll blow you to hell!" reportedly shouted the twenty-year-old Sandinista conscript Rafael Antonio Acevedo when he found Hasenfus in an abandoned hut, eating a squash and lying in a hammock he had made from his parachute. The American was armed with a pistol and a pocketknife but immediately surrendered. Days later Nicaragua's defense minister, Humberto Ortega, decorated the Sandinista soldiers involved with gold medals.

During a broadcast from his trial in Nicaragua, Hasenfus claimed to be working for the CIA. The plot thickened when a "flying file cabinet" was discovered in the fuselage of the cargo plane. It contained logbooks with detailed descriptions of previous covert supply flights from airports in El Salvador and Honduras, including the type and quantity of weapons dropped in each flight. A month later the controversy deepened still further when reports revealed that funds for the Contras were being illegally obtained through the sale of arms to Iran in exchange for the release of US hostages in Lebanon. President Reagan initially insisted that he "did not—repeat, did not—trade weapons or anything else for hostages." Within weeks, though, Attorney General Edwin Meese announced that his investigation into the matter had uncovered evidence suggesting that between $12 million and $30 million of the arms sales to Iran had been "diverted" to the Contras. Several officials in the Reagan White House, including National Security Council aide and Marine Lieutenant Colonel Oliver North, were implicated.

The details soon emerged: attempting to get around the Boland amendment, North, sometime in 1986, began overcharging the Iranians for the arms and using the surplus to fund the Contra resupply operation that involved Hasenfus. (Interestingly, the former CIA official Félix Rodríguez, who had been at the Bay of Pigs and was present when Che Guevara was killed in

Bolivia, had also been assisting the Contra resupply effort.) North also relied on his colleague Richard Secord to transfer the funds and handle other logistical details. Secord and North netted over $16 million in profits from arms sales to Iran, though less than $4 million made its way to Contra coffers. To put that figure into context, Saudi Arabia contributed around $32 million in the same period.

The Iran–Contra scandal took its toll on the Reagan Doctrine. By the end of Reagan's second term in January 1989 even bona fide anticommunists like George Shultz wanted "to get the Nicaragua problem resolved if only because it had become too painfully divisive for the country." What helped this extraction along somewhat was the advent of a peace process in early 1987 led by the Costa Rican president Óscar Arias. The Arias plan called for immediate ceasefires in Nicaragua, El Salvador, and Guatemala, the suspension of all outside support for insurgencies, and plans for future elections. Within two months of the signing of the agreement, governments were to offer amnesty to guerrillas who had laid down their weapons and to start a dialogue.

While US officials were not thrilled by the plan's implications for its Contra funding, they soon realized the value it placed on democratic procedures, especially in light of (what it viewed as) the highly undemocratic Sandinista government. The Central American presidents met in Esquipulas, Guatemala, in early August 1987 and approved the Esquipulas II Accord, a slightly modified version of the Arias plan. The document did not call for an immediate ceasefire, but it eventually laid the broad foundations for each country to address its internal conflict. Multilateralism, not CIA machinations, was leading the day. Reagan advocates, however, would contend that it was only the sustained Contra military pressure that got the Sandinistas to the negotiating table in the first place. But even if that was the case, one has to consider the terrible human toll that resulted from the US backing of the Contras: ten thousand to forty-three thousand Nicaraguans dying during the course of the Contra War.

Regime Change—At the Ballot Box?

There was now great pressure on the Sandinistas to legitimize their rule. They were confident that they would win any popular vote handily, and they set presidential elections for early 1990. In September 1989 the new George H. W. Bush administration began efforts to provide funding for the elections. Officials insisted that the aid would be used for "non-partisan technical support of the elections process," but the funding went almost exclusively to the anti-Sandinista opposition known as the Nicaragua Opposition Union. This coalition party, which spanned the ideological spectrum from conservative to communist, fielded Violeta Chamorro as a presidential candidate, the widow of the assassinated journalist and anti-Somoza leader. Chamorro's credentials as a legitimate political figure were also burnished by her former role in the post-Somoza revolutionary government.

The National Endowment for Democracy (NED), a prodemocracy organization mandated by Congress in 1983 and funded by the US government, provided the Nicaraguan opposition to the Sandinistas with close to $2 million, although a considerable amount of this money did not arrive until very late in the campaign. Despite the US funding, the Sandinistas remained confident of a pronounced victory at the polls. In fact, as the election grew nearer the Sandinistas invited even more international observers to witness their expected electoral triumph. Amazingly, at the same time, the Sandinistas began escalating their supply shipments to the FMLN in El Salvador in preparation for an offensive in late 1989. A month later, in November, a small plane carrying arms from Nicaragua to the FMLN crashed in El Salvador. The shipment, recovered by Salvadoran security forces, included twenty-four Soviet-made SA-7 surface-to-air missiles, marking the first time the Sandinistas sent such heavy-grade weapons to their Salvadoran allies. The Sandinistas' delivery might have been a deliberate message to the Bush White House that they were still willing to cause problems for the United States in El Salvador if Washington resumed funding the Contras. Publicly, Humberto Ortega dismissed the "big fuss" that was being made because "some arrows have turned up in El Salvador."

There were an estimated seven hundred official observers of the elections on February 25, 1990. By the end of the day more than half of the almost forty-five hundred polling stations had been observed by teams from the UN, OAS, and Jimmy Carter's private democracy-watchdog organization, the Carter Center. More than two thousand unofficial observers and journalists were also in the country. That night the UN team's "quick count" of less than 10 percent of the vote showed Chamorro winning a decisive victory. Stunned, the Sandinista Directorate called a hasty meeting to decide its next moves. Within hours an official from the Supreme Electoral Council read the initial results aloud, further indicating a major upset. When the dust had settled and all the votes were counted Chamorro had taken 55 percent to Ortega's 41 percent. Indeed, Nicaraguans of all walks of life had given the Sandinistas a clear mandate: it was time to go. The Sandinista revolution was over, killed in the end by the ballot box.

Conservative US officials and politicians argued that the Sandinistas' ouster via elections was a vindication of the Reagan administration's hard-line policies, especially as the Contras kept pressure on an otherwise recalcitrant Managua. Liberals, on the other hand, contended that it was only the Bush administration's rejection of the hard-line Reagan approach that had allowed for this relatively pacific outcome. Other critics claimed that using, say, the NED to back the anti-Ortega actors was simply a thinly veiled version of regime change. One Cuban official in Nicaragua said, "You [Sandinistas] can't beat the gringos at their own game. . . . The opposition will have the best U.S. campaign advisers behind it. They will clobber you."

Ultimately, Washington succeeded in removing the Sandinistas from power, but at a heavy cost to its reputation, given the fallout of the Iran–Contra affair. The various struggles within Washington also contributed to an inconsistent approach. As the former Reagan official Robert Kagan reflected, the mix of intelligence oversight, late–Cold War dynamics, and historical involvement in Nicaragua made US–Nicaraguan relations during the Contra War a "disorderly mix of policies." Evaluating this disorderly mix is a difficult business, but a necessary one if we are to understand more fully hemispheric relations during this complex and bloody episode of the Cold War.

27 • Why Invade Grenada?

"It was right out of *Apocalypse Now*," recalled a US medical student in Grenada, describing the scene from his dormitory window as scores of military helicopters zipped across the early dawn horizon on October 25, 1983. Three days later President Ronald Reagan told the American public that he had approved the mission to ensure that several hundred American students—there were roughly one thousand US citizens on the island at the time—were not taken hostage as well as to liberate the Grenadian people from the clutches of a murderous, hard-line Marxist regime. And while the operation proved to be less of a cakewalk than expected, the Reagan administration largely succeeded in its goals: the visibly appreciative students were safely returned to the United States, the regime was ousted, and democratic elections followed soon after. Reagan's mission was also popular: over 90 percent of the Grenadian population supported it, while almost all of Grenada's island neighbors were resolutely behind the invasion too. Mission accomplished—or so it seemed.

Despite these apparent successes the invasion came under enormous scrutiny. In fact, the American action in Grenada appeared peculiar, even fishy, to legions of observers. The island was a tiny one at the end of the Windward Islands in the Caribbean Sea, far removed from the usual spheres of American activity in Latin America. Why did the superpower United States feel the need to invade such an insignificant country?

"There Is No Other Formula"

Our story of the Grenada invasion starts on March 13, 1979, when the Marxist political coalition the New Jewel Movement (NJM) ousted the island's longtime and increasingly hated ruler Eric Gairy. Gairy had ruled the country from the mid-1960s onward in an increasingly erratic and iron-fisted fashion, conferring on himself, in the spirit of the Dominican Republic's Trujillo, "some thirty honors, decorations, degrees, and titles." Gairy was also one of the world's bizarre political figures: he once asked the UN General Assembly to declare 1978 "the year of the UFO." By the early 1970s opposition to Gairy's rule began to mount. The NJM was a coalition of, among others, US Black Power acolytes, supporters of communist Cuba, and Lions' Club members.

The NJM's coup in March 1979 went off without a shot being fired—Gairy was in the United States—and a new government, the People's Revolutionary Government (PRG), was announced with the charismatic Maurice Bishop in charge. Cuba, East Germany, Bulgaria, and North Korea were all soon providing aid. Following the communist model in Cuba, Bishop's government launched free milk and lunch programs for elementary schools, eliminated secondary school fees, and built medical clinics across the island. Bishop did not hold elections after the coup, even though he would have certainly won them freely and fairly. The new Grenadian leader's communist credentials were such that when Fidel Castro visited Nicaragua in July 1980 he stated, "There is only one road to liberation: that of Cuba, that of Grenada, that of Nicaragua. There is no other formula."

Postcoup Cooperation

A few days after the 1979 coup Bishop met with US ambassador Frank Ortiz, who warned him that Jimmy Carter would not look kindly on his government if it developed closer ties with Cuba. Bishop offered a rejoinder a few days later when he declared in a national speech, "We are not in anybody's backyard." However, Ortiz also reported back to Foggy Bottom that Bishop was pleased with the Carter administration's "speedy recognition of the revolutionary leftist government" and that he seemed to want friendly relations with the United States, to keep the Peace Corps volunteers dispersed across the small island, and to honor the security of US citizens and property.

Still, the Carter administration was concerned about Grenada. Alarming intelligence reports were landing on the desks of State Department and NSC policy makers, who were particularly on edge after the August 1979 discovery of a Soviet combat brigade of some two thousand to three thousand troops stationed in Cuba. The brigade had in fact been stationed on the island since 1962. On April 14, only a month after the anti-Gairy coup, the White House aide Robert Pastor wrote a memo to his boss, National Security Advisor Zbigniew Brzezinski, titled, "New Direction in Grenada: The Cubans Arrive."

Pastor wasn't wrong. Starting in 1979 Cuba became Grenada's main supplier of military hardware and training. In late 1981 the PRG and the Cuban government signed a protocol of military collaboration that established a twenty-seven-man Cuban military mission in Grenada, a group given the task of training the newly formed People's Revolutionary Army. Havana subsequently supplied thousands of rifles, machine guns, and rocket launchers up until the US invasion in October 1983. Grenada also signed military assistance agreements with the Soviet Union and North Korea, paving the way for weapons shipments from both countries. According to then prime minister of Barbados, Tom Adams, Grenada was "one of the perhaps dozen most militarized states in the world in terms of population under arms."

Reagan Rhetoric

As was the case in Nicaragua, the Reagan administration that took office in January 1981 was not thrilled with Grenada's postcoup tilt to communism. Echoing how the Nixon–Kissinger nexus dealt with Salvador Allende, Secretary of State Alexander Haig, a hard-liner, directed his subordinates to work so that Grenada did not receive "one penny" from any international financial institution. Yet these efforts were met with mixed results, as other countries were often unwilling to go along with Washington's punitive policy. Escalating the rhetorical war, Reagan, in February 1982, told representatives of the OAS that Grenada was in the "tightening grip of the totalitarian left," and a few months later he told Caribbean leaders in Barbados that Grenada had the "Soviet and Cuban trademark." On March 10, 1983, Reagan addressed the nation on the potential threat:

> Grenada, that tiny little island—with Cuba at the west end of the Caribbean, Grenada at the east end—that tiny little island is building now, or having built for it, on its soil and shores, a naval base, a superior air base, storage bases and facilities for the storage of munitions, barracks, and training ground for the military.
> I'm sure all of that is simply to encourage the export of nutmeg.
> People who make these arguments haven't taken a good look at a map lately or followed the extraordinary buildup of Soviet and Cuban military power in the region or read the Soviet's discussions about why the region is important to them and how they intend to use it.

It isn't nutmeg that is at stake in the Caribbean and Central America.
It is the United States' national security.

Reagan was "deeply interested in the airport issue" and was briefed on it "all the time." During his March 23, 1983, address to the nation, Reagan showed aerial reconnaissance photographs of Grenada and explained that "the Cubans with Soviet financing and backing are in the process of building an airfield with a 10,000-foot runway. Grenada doesn't even have an air force. Whom is it intended for?" By October 1983 Cuban assistance for the airport had reached an estimated $60 million.

The intended use of the runway remained a controversial question years after the 1983 invasion, which is a good reminder of how ideological frameworks (and in some cases, blinders) can create a spectrum of different interpretations of the same events. Reagan's critics argued that the runway was the key to Grenada's economic well-being, especially tourism, and cited reports that American medical students lived within a mile of the strip and used it as a jogging track. Reagan's team countered with its own allegedly compelling and accurate evidence, such as the claim that no hotels were being built for said tourism. Reagan and his advisors believed that the airport was intended for military purposes.

To keep up the pressure on a regime that it perceived as being firmly in Cuba's camp, the United States, between 1981 and 1983, held its largest naval operations since World War II. Called Ocean Venture, the operations involved 120,000 troops, 250 warships, and 1,000 aircraft. Part of the exercise was labeled "Amber and the Amberdines," a thinly veiled reference to Grenada and the Grenadines. The saber-rattling exercise took place on the Puerto Rican island of Vieques and simulated an invasion and occupation of a "small island." By early 1983 Grenada was undoubtedly a concern to the Reagan administration, but it would take a series of events in the fall of that year—most critically, on the single day of October 23—to lead to the decision to launch a full-scale invasion.

Bishop Murdered, Reagan Decides

By and large it was an anemic economy, not US pressure, that by the middle of 1982 was causing deep divisions within the NJM's leadership. Within a year the situation had become incredibly intense, which led to more fractures within the party. In early October 1982 the desperate Central Committee proceeded to place Bishop under house arrest, a move that sparked widespread protests in St. George's in favor of Bishop. A week later, on October 19, a day which became known as Bloody Wednesday, the pro-Bishop protests swelled to over ten thousand people, who gathered in St. George's central square chanting, "We want Maurice." Nevertheless, that same day the hardcore party member and plotter Bernard Coard ordered Bishop to be executed, along with seven of his close supporters, including his mistress Jacqueline Creft. All were shot by firing squad in front of a mural of Che Guevara. The day after Bishop's assassination, the commander of the armed forces, Hudson Austin, announced the establishment of a sixteen-person junta called the Revolutionary Military Council (RMG), although Coard remained the power behind the scenes. The pro-Cuba, ideologically pure RMG quickly imposed a twenty-four-hour shoot-to-kill curfew.

The coup against Bishop sent shock waves through the Caribbean, creating widespread regional support for swift action to deal with Grenada's chaos, although not necessarily an outright US invasion. On October 21 a State Department cable reported that Prime Minister Edward Seaga of Jamaica had proposed a naval blockade as an alternative to an invasion. The report also indicated that Seaga had expressed deep concern over the Soviet/Cuban menace in Grenada and that he believed the "successful consolidation of Cuban control in Grenada would promptly destabilize St. Vincent and perhaps other adjacent islands."

Within twenty-four hours the White House received another cable, this one from Ambassador Milan Bish in Bridgetown, indicating that Tom Adams and Eugenia Charles, the leaders of Barbados and Dominica, respectively, had said that within the regional bloc called the Organization of Eastern Caribbean States (OECS) there were "no reservations whatsoever" about a military invasion. Bish continued that the OECS had formally resolved to form a "multinational Caribbean force" to "depose the outlaw regime" in Grenada by "any means."

The Pentagon remained hesitant about a full-scale invasion, believing that the mission was still ill-defined (rescue of US citizens or regime change?) and that Grenada was of little importance. At one point in the planning of a response to the crisis one of the members of the Joint Chiefs told senior State Department officials that, with respect to a full-scale invasion, "you guys are out of your minds."

Then, on Sunday, October 23, President Reagan was roused from bed at 2:37 a.m. with news from Lebanon: a terrorist attack against the Marine barracks in Beirut had killed 241 US service members, including 220 Marines.

Reagan spent most of the day discussing the Beirut tragedy with officials. Only later in the day did their conversation turned to Grenada. With the deaths of hundreds of Marines on his mind and the potential for US hostage taking in Grenada, Reagan appeared tired and dispirited and is believed to have lamented, "I'm no better than Jimmy Carter." Secretary of State George Shultz urged the president to "strike while the iron is hot." Reagan uttered only one word when he approved the largest US military operation since Vietnam: "Go." Preparation for a full-scale invasion had been underway for only four days, and Reagan signed the directive only thirty-six hours before the main assault force was to go in, but from this point on the Pentagon was fully committed.

Operation Urgent Fury

Then and today critics have argued that the Reagan administration cynically concocted the Grenada invasion in order to distract the American public from the tragedy in Beirut. However, the invasion plan had been in the works before the Beirut bombings. In fact, when warned by his advisors that the timing of the Grenada invasion might bring about that very criticism, Reagan said privately, "If this [invasion] was right yesterday, it's right today and we shouldn't let the act of a couple of terrorists dissuade us from going ahead."

Late on Monday night Reagan invited Speaker of the House Thomas "Tip" O'Neill (DMA), Senate Majority Leader Howard Baker (RTN), House Majority Leader James Wright (DTX), and Senate Minority Leader Robert Byrd (DWV) to the White House, where he briefed them on the still-secret imminent invasion. Reagan then called Prime Minister Margaret Thatcher in Great Britain to inform her of the impending invasion. Thatcher was surprised by the late notification and told Reagan in the "strongest language" to call off the operation. She reminded Reagan that Grenada was still part of the British Commonwealth and that the United States "had no business interfering in its affairs." Unmoved by the curt words of his special ally in London, Reagan stuck to his decision. Administration officials were also taken back by Thatcher's vituperative response, as Washington had supported the British effort during the Falkland Islands crisis a year earlier.

Code-named Urgent Fury, the invasion entailed a Marine amphibious unit assault at daybreak on October 25 at the older Pearls airport and nearby locations. These forces were then supposed to secure the northern half of the island. Army Rangers from the 75th Ranger Regiment were to simultaneously parachute onto the incomplete Point Salines airfield, which would allow an

Air Force C-141 troop transport to land, carrying a brigade from the 82nd Airborne Division, the same division that landed outside Santo Domingo in 1965. These troops would then rescue the medical students at the nearby True Blue medical campus and move on St. George's. Navy SEALs and other elite forces were to be inserted to capture General Hudson Austin and rescue Paul Scoon as well as capture the main radio station and free political prisoners from Richmond Prison.

All told, approximately 8,000 American soldiers and 353 troops from Caribbean forces participated in the operation. The Grenadian forces were estimated to be 1,200 men strong, with an additional 2,000 to 5,000 militia and 300 to 400 armed police. The Cuban presence was set at 30 to 50 advisors and 650 construction workers. While a small force, the extent of Cuban resistance turned out to be a tactical surprise. Indeed, the biggest intelligence failure was in underestimating the number of Cuban personnel on the island, who put up a spirited fight. While Chairman of the Joint Chiefs of Staff John W. Vessey bragged that "we blew them away," he also admitted that "we got a lot more resistance than we expected."

The military operation took three days. By October 31 all Marines were back aboard their ships, and the 82nd Airborne and OECS troops were conducting cleanup operations. All told, 599 American citizens and 121 foreign nationals were evacuated. An estimated 100 to 200 Grenadians, 50 to 100 Cubans, and 18 Americans (11 soldiers, 3 marines, and 4 Navy SEALs) were killed; 116 US troops were wounded. In what became the source of some embarrassment for the Pentagon, the US military awarded 8,633 medals out of the 7,000 US military participants in the invasion, compared to the 679 medals that the British military awarded in the Falklands War a year earlier, which had involved 28,000 participants.

There was some looting on the island in the days immediately following the fighting, but it quickly dissipated. Electricity was restored within a week, and soon after US combat troops were relieved and replaced by troops from the Caribbean Peacekeeping Force. After the quagmire of Vietnam, Americans were not accustomed to a local population that had just been invaded by the US military displaying joy and appreciation. But Grenada couldn't have been farther from Vietnam in terms of domestic sentiment. A CBS News poll found that 91 percent of Grenadians were "glad the United States troops came to Grenada," and 81 percent said that US troops were "courteous and considerate." Another 67 percent said they thought Cuba wanted to take control of the government, and 65 percent said they believed the airport was being readied for Cuban and Soviet military purposes. In fact, many Grenadians took issue with the term "invasion," preferring "rescue operation."

But despite Grenada's glowing report card of the US performance, speculation about ulterior motives still surrounded the event. Immediately after the mission, skeptics wondered why it took two Ranger battalions, a brigade of the 82nd Airborne, a marine amphibious unit, an aircraft carrier, and air force transports to defeat some seven hundred Cubans and a Grenadian army that barely provided any resistance. Moreover, all the medical students were not accounted for until three days after the invasion.

Gunboat Democracy?

The afternoon of the invasion Secretary of State Shultz explained at a press conference that President Reagan had launched an intervention in Grenada for two reasons: "First was his concern for the welfare of American citizens living on Grenada. . . . Second, the President received an urgent request from . . . the Organization of Eastern Caribbean States."

In the subsequent weeks, however, critics began to question the administration's justifications. The most cutting criticism was that the lives of the American medical students were not in any real danger from the chaotic political and security situation following Bishop's execution and that, at the very least, they could have been evacuated. In truth, an evacuation was one of the first options considered by US officials. They even considered using a nearby Cunard cruise liner. But evacuation was ultimately discarded, as officials believed they could not rely on the regime, or the Cubans for that matter, to grant safe passage.

Critics also picked holes in the idea of this being a multilateral intervention. Prime Minister Charles of Dominica quickly emerged as an articulate, strong-willed advocate of the invasion. Her tough words and television appearances standing next to Reagan reinforced the administration's claim that the OECS had freely requested US assistance. But that did not prevent the *Boston Globe* from crying foul. In an editorial the newspaper asserted that "pretending that this unilateral move was a 'joint maneuver' insults the intelligence of Americans. Pretending that the United States has suddenly developed a lively interest in the democracy that it has ignored in the rest of Latin America insults the rest of the world." Even harsher attacks on the administration came from congressional Democrats. For example, on October 25 Senator Patrick Moynihan claimed that the US government did not have the right to promote democracy "at the point of a bayonet" and that the invasion was "an act of war" that the Reagan administration "does not have the right" to undertake. Representative Theodore S. Weiss (D-N.Y.) introduced a resolution calling for Reagan's impeachment for "the high crime or misdemeanor of ordering the invasion of Grenada."

Reagan's adversaries also jumped on the fact that the president failed to mention anything about Cuban or Soviet involvement on the island in his first press briefing. Therefore, Reagan's subsequent citation of the leftist bogymen must have been cover up for the fact that the danger to the US students had been overstated. While Reagan did not initially mention Cuba, however, he had made a great deal about Cuba's involvement in Grenada on prior occasions, such as his March 1983 national television address. Over the course of the next several days the administration's public reasons for the invasion fell into the same vein, shifting toward Grenada's geopolitical significance, specifically the threat that the island would turn into another Cuba. On October 27 President Reagan made a thirty-minute address to the nation that focused on the Beirut bombing and Grenada invasion. "Grenada, we were told, was a friendly island paradise for tourism. Well, it wasn't. It was a Soviet–Cuban colony, being readied as a major military bastion to export terror and undermine democracy. We got there just in time."

While critics screamed hyperbole and strong-arm tactics, a large majority of the US public responded overwhelmingly positively to Reagan's explanation of the invasion. An ABC News poll found that 64 percent of Americans had favored the invasion before Reagan's October 27 speech and that 86 percent favored it afterward. Seventy-four percent of Americans agreed with the statement "I feel good about Grenada because it showed that America can use its power to protect our own interests." Inquiries at marine recruiting stations surged to two to three times their normal rate. (One hopeful volunteer was a seventy-one-year-old woman.) Conservatives held up the Grenada case as a symbol of US resolve and a much overdue response to Soviet–Cuban expansion in the region. A *Wall Street Journal* editorialist wrote, "The lesson is that it's once again known that the U.S. is willing to use its military as an instrument of policy. . . . The world will not assume otherwise, and will be better for it."

Although the information was not available to the public, intelligence reports in the postinvasion weeks and months reinforced Reagan's theory that the Soviets and Cubans had greater intentions for Grenada. Deputy Secretary of State Kenneth Dam wrote to Reagan that "the overall picture presented by the evidence is that by October 1983 the USSR and Cuba had made real progress toward turning Grenada into a center for further subversion for the region." Dam concluded that "Cuban control" had started in earnest in April 1983 and that the Cubans had shipped in arms and advisors by "a number of surreptitious means."

Morning in Grenada

Regime change had been achieved: new elections were held in 1984, and the political moderate Herbert Blaize was elected prime minister. On December 4, 1986, a Grenadian jury convicted eighteen members of the regime for the crimes of October 1983; fourteen Grenadians, including Hudson Austin and Bernard Coard, were tried and convicted.

For the US, Grenada became a shining example of a successful, relatively quick operation against the iniquities of a dangerous regime and the insidious communist threat. The 1984 platform at the Republican National Convention stated that "Grenada is small and its people few; but we believe the principle established there—that freedom is worth defending—is of monumental importance. It challenges the Brezhnev doctrine [a post-1968 Soviet-dominated Eastern Bloc collective security strategy]. It is an example to the world." Vice President Bush told the delegates that "because President Reagan stood firm in defense of freedom [in Grenada], America has regained respect throughout the world."

On February 20, 1986, Reagan told an audience of around ninety thousand Grenadians, roughly the entire population, in St. George's, "I will never be sorry that I made the decision to help you." Urgent Fury ended up costing $134.4 million, or $224,000 per rescued student, while the columnist George Will wrote, "U.S. soldiers' boot prints on Grenada's soil will do more than the MX [a tactical nuclear missile] to make American power credible."

On the first anniversary of the invasion, Shultz said, "Our response should go beyond passive defense to consider means of active prevention, preemption, and retaliation." But Reagan for one was content to count his winnings in Grenada: after Vietnam, he knew that regime change through military invasion in Cuba or even Nicaragua was not an option. But the Reagan administration had undoubtedly achieved an extraordinary "bang for its buck" in Grenada. The operation simultaneously demonstrated America's willingness to use force to back up its policies, rally Americans around the flag, address a perceived national security threat, and overthrow a repressive regime hated by an overwhelming share of locals and replace it with a democratic one, all with broad regional support to boot.

It certainly did not hurt that Grenada was "close, convenient, and small," whereas Vietnam was "far, inconvenient, and jungly," and that the US public

Freed US medical students from the St. Georges Medical University during the US invasion of Grenada, code-named Operation Urgent Fury. Commenced on October 25, 1983, the Grenada operation was the first major military action by the United States since the end of the Vietnam War. (DOD Photo–Alamy Stock Photo)

received the news of the invasion as a successful fait accompli. With its population of around one hundred thousand and size of 142 square kilometers, Grenada was not very representative of the sacrifice and effort normally needed to roll back communist regimes and install democracy around the globe. A joke that circulated at the time went something like, "Why didn't Reagan invade Rhode Island instead?" Answer: "Too big!"

Although Grenada is a small island, for one simple reason the invasion there has an outsize place in US Cold War history. Perhaps astonishingly, given the levels of political tension that had been reached during the previous four decades, Grenada underwent the first real US military invasion during the Cold War. (Santo Domingo in 1965 is more properly understood as an intervention.) On that basis alone Grenada is an essential event for our broader understanding of this era.

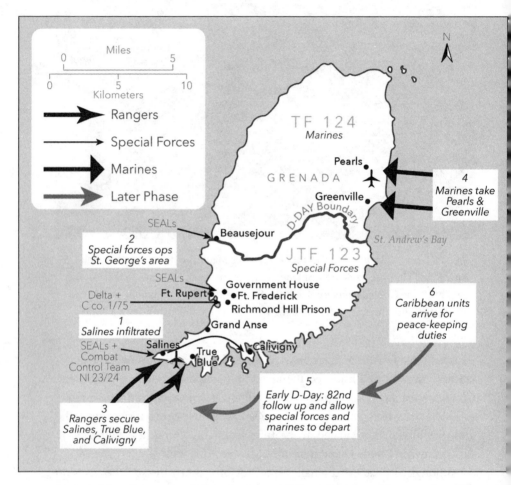

Map of the US invasion of Grenada, Operation Urgent Fury, October 24–28, 1983.
While the self-declared rescue mission was a political success for President Ronald
Reagan, critics wondered why Washington felt the need to unleash its potent military
on the tiny Caribbean island. (University of Wisconsin–Madison Cartography Lab.
Christopher Archuleta, cartographer)

28 • The Salvador Option

On March 24, 1980, Archbishop Óscar Romero was celebrating Mass at the small chapel of the Divine Providence Hospital in San Salvador. Romero had risen to prominence in El Salvador as one of the most outspoken exponents of liberation theology, a socialist-inspired movement that emerged in Latin America in the 1960s and 1970s. Under the new theology the church had taken a strong line against human rights abuses and sided with the poor and marginalized. In his Lenten homily the day before the archbishop had appealed directly to Salvadoran soldiers: "No soldier is obliged to obey an order counter to the law of God. . . . We want the government to seriously consider that reforms mean nothing when they come bathed in so much blood. . . . I beseech you, I beg you, I order you, in the name of God, to stop the repression!"

As the priest performed the service, a professional assassin took aim and fired a single .22-caliber bullet from a red Volkswagen. The bullet ruptured the archbishop's aorta, and he bled to death. Romero's last words were reported to be, "May God have mercy on the assassins."

American officials told journalists that Romero's assassination represented one of the worst blows to stability experienced in El Salvador. US secretary of state Cyrus Vance stated, "We are deeply shocked by this deplorable criminal act," calling Romero "a man who embodies the basic principles of compassion and concern for all the citizens of El Salvador." Two years earlier twenty-three members of the US Congress had written in support of Romero's nomination for the Nobel Peace Prize: "An individual of unsurpassed courage and integrity, Romero has not allowed government prosecutors to frighten him into silence or submission. He has remained a forthright and compelling advocate of human rights, nonviolence and social progress—setting a standard in defense of human liberty which can be applied not only in Latin America but throughout the world."

On Palm Sunday tens of thousands of Salvadorans filled the streets on their way to the archbishop's funeral at the National Cathedral, but the procession turned chaotic when unidentified gunmen opened fire on the mourners, killing and wounding dozens. The government and security forces claimed it was the protestors who instigated the violence in order to provoke a backlash. These claims fell on deaf ears when images emerged of unarmed demonstrators and mourners being gunned down on the steps of the National Cathedral. The catastrophic event reinforced the impression of the international community that the Salvadoran government was repressing its people.

Romero's brutal murder galvanized many on the left in El Salvador, leading them to conclude that the archbishop's message could be realized, somewhat paradoxically, only through the barrel of a gun. It also revealed the gulf that had formed between the church and El Salvador's oligarchs, who had long run the country. One businessman stated, "How could the army tolerate a man in his position telling the soldiers not to obey orders; lay down their guns, rather than shoot?" For many, the Romero assassination marked the beginning of El Salvador's "irredeemable horror" that was the civil war.

Deep Roots

Understanding how and why El Salvador reached such a crisis entails looking at the country's history. Since its independence from Spain in 1821, El Salvador had been dominated by an oligarchy, Fourteen Families, who owned most of the land and managed the vastly profitable coffee industry, which constituted over half the government's revenue between 1880 and 1914. Most histories contend that the priorities of this coffee industry dictated a shift in the mission of the embryonic armed forces from defense of the national territory to the maintenance of internal order, El Salvador's stability resting on an alliance between the oligarchy and the military.

The system was extremely iniquitous and the source of deep unrest among ordinary Salvadorans. In the 1920 a young Salvadoran intellectual from a wealthy family named Agustín Farabundo Martí Rodríguez worked tirelessly to organize Salvadoran workers, often wearing a red star as his lapel pin. His name was adopted decades later by the civil war guerrillas. In January 1932 Farabundo Martí led a revolt, in part fomented by communist party militants.

Peasants armed with machetes and rusty shotguns began to attack munici-palities of the country's Depression-plagued coffee-growing region, but the rebellion did not gain much traction in San Salvador as communist leaders had been rounded up during the first hours of the uprising.

The government response to the uprising was brutal: an estimated twenty thousand to thirty thousand Salvadorans were killed in about a week. Some scholars believe that the legacy of what came to be known as La Matanza (The slaughter) was unrivaled over the next half century. One scholar wrote, "In-deed the whole [subsequent] political labyrinth of El Salvador can be explained only in reference to the traumatic experience of the uprising and the Matanza."

Both the oligarchy and the military, shaken by the events of 1932, estab-lished rural paramilitary groups, the most notorious of which was known as the National Democratic Organization (Organización Democrática Naciona-lista, ORDEN), created in 1962. Known by the Spanish acronym for "order," ORDEN relied on retired military officers and roughly sixty thousand recruited conservative peasants. With these paramilitary groups snuffing out the leftist threat at the ground level, the power of the oligarchs and the rule of the mili-tary were seemingly assured. The oligarchs continued to enjoy their wealth and power, and the Salvadoran armed forces (FAES) effectively controlled the country for the next half century, until 1979, spearheaded by the repressive General Carlos Humberto Romero (no relation to the archbishop).

Rise of the Guerrillas and the Death Squads

The 1970s saw the rise of several guerrilla groups as government and para-military repression and repeated electoral fraud radicalized many leftists. Deeply influenced by the 1932 massacre, the Popular Forces of Liberation (Fuerzas Populares de Liberación, "Farabundo Martí," FPL), the main guerrilla force, carried out selective bombings and kidnappings and increasingly the executions of important rightist politicians and businessmen. In the summer of 1977, for example, within a span of weeks the FPL executed the military regime's eighty-seven-year-old foreign minister and ex–military president Col-onel Osmín Aguirre, the two senior military commanders in Chalatenango, and Carlos Alfaro Castillo, a large landowner and university rector.

Another notable guerrilla force was the People's Revolutionary Army (Ejér-cito Revolucionario del Pueblo, ERP), comprising radicalized converts from the disillusioned ranks of the centrist Christian Democrats. In 1975 Joaquín Villalobos (nom de guerre Comandante Atilio) assumed leadership of the

ERP. The son of a middle-class family who had studied economics before joining the guerrillas, the young and brilliant Villalobos opted for a Cuba-style
foco strategy hatched from the isolated and underpopulated mountain province of Morazán to promote a rapid revolution through popular insurrection.

The oligarchs were naturally the prime target of the guerrillas. On February
11, 1971, Ernesto Regalado Dueñas, a young, progressive businessman, was
kidnapped by a leftist revolutionary organization calling itself El Grupo. Regalado's body was found a week later with two .45mm-caliber bullet shots to
his head. Regalado had apparently been killed before the multimillion-dollar
ransom was collected, although some claimed it had been paid.

Many conservative Salvadorans considered February 11, 1971, the day Regalado was kidnapped, as the effective beginning of El Salvador's civil war.
The manner of Regalado's killing also helped convince the country's hard-line
businessmen to support retaliatory operations by so-called death squads that
grew into the "planned massacre" of thousands of guerrillas, their supporters,
and the multitudes of Salvadorans who were somewhere in between. Death
squad activity became so common and lethal that one foreign correspondent
concluded, "For an outsider, even one conditioned over a decade to the standard savageries of Asian wars and African rebellions, El Salvador is a nightmare beyond comprehension."

But the rise of the death squads also marked the beginning of a schism in
the oligarchy–military axis that had ruled the country for so long. As the war
years passed, some FAES officers increasingly saw the oligarchy withdraw
their wealth and families from the country while the military was left to deal
with the guerrillas. Crucially, the military was also beginning to realize that it
did not need the oligarchy to remain in power.

The Nicaraguan Effect

The stunning July 1979 Sandinista victory in neighboring Nicaragua, de-
posing President Anastasio Somoza Debayle, had an enormous impact in El
Salvador. Slogans appeared in city streets pronouncing, "Somoza today,
Romero tomorrow." In fact, the Carter administration had been worried about
the domino effect Somoza's fall would have on neighboring El Salvador even
before the Nicaraguan dictator was ousted. On June 25, 1979, nearly a month
before the Marxist Sandinistas took power, Defense Secretary Harold Brown
sent Carter a memorandum titled "Limiting the Consequences of a Sandinista
Victory." Brown warned that "a Sandinista victory will strengthen the leftist

insurgents and increase the likelihood of left–right confrontations in the neighboring countries." To Brown, General Romero, while not appealing, was still one of the very few Salvadoran military leaders who would be receptive to American suggestions for "internal political liberalization."

But forces had already been set in motion that would lead to General Romero's ouster. In May 1979 a small number of Salvadoran officers began to meet secretly and soberly concluded that the Marxist–Leninist guerrillas and their supporting organizations could overthrow the Romero regime by the end of the year. They decided to act before this "nightmare became a reality." On October 12, 1979, the Salvadoran air force staged a coup against General Romero, promising to install a new government to restore order. Aware of a disillusioned Carter administration and realizing that he had little support among the military ranks, General Romero went into exile in Guatemala without a shot being fired.

Within days of the October coup a five-man first junta was formed and within weeks announced a radical new program that included nationalization of banks, land reform, and greater state control of the export crop sector, including coffee. The junta abolished ORDEN due to its gross human rights abuses, enacted a general amnesty for exiles and political prisoners, and pledged to support free elections. The junta soon appointed a new cabinet that included opposition representatives and independents. José Napoleón Duarte, a Christian Democrat who had been defeated in the 1972 presidential election, became the country's first civilian president in forty-nine years.

Most guerrilla leaders were not sold on the new regime. The ERP rejected the new government and called for an insurrection while setting up barricades in San Salvador's suburbs. The FPL described the ERP's call for insurrection as suicidal but also rejected the new progressive junta as an "American-hatched conspiracy." There was some truth to the charge: Duarte's ascension had depended on the US government and the support of the Salvadoran military. As Duarte himself noted, "The only reason I am in this position is because I have the support of the army."

Carter Walks a Fine Line

As well as providing an example of what a successful leftist coup looked like, the Sandinistas soon became directly involved in El Salvador. Within days of seizing power in Managua in 1979, the Sandinista leader Tomás Borge hosted the first of a series of meetings with the FPL to discuss support for the revolution in El Salvador. That same year Havana was brokering talks among the fractious Salvadoran insurgent groups: the FPL and ERP were intense rivals. Castro apparently made Cuban military and political support conditional on a united Salvadoran guerrilla front, which led to the creation in October 1980 of the Farabundo Martí National Liberation Front (El Frente Farabundo Martí para la Liberación Nacional, FMLN).

By the end of 1980, in addition to their six thousand to eight thousand guerrilla fighters, the united FMLN claimed over one million sympathizers, including one hundred thousand militia members. The latter provided food, storage, refuge, intelligence, and rearguard support to military operations. The FMLN also benefited from being plugged into the global communist weapons network: over time Vietnam, Ethiopia, Czechoslovakia, Cuba, and Nicaragua would all provide weapons to the FMLN.

Washington was faced with a conundrum: sit back and see what happened, risking a communist takeover, or ramp up its intervention. US officials had begun providing military assistance to El Salvador in the 1930s, but the amounts were not especially significant. In 1970, for example, the US military mission totaled seventeen personnel. The US government delivered less than $17 million from 1946 to 1979, an amount that put El Salvador at the bottom of the Central American countries in terms of US assistance. Romero's regime had defiantly rejected US military aid, but his ouster offered Washington an opening to reengage the Salvadoran military and potentially influence the outcome on the ground. Two weeks after the coup US officials announced that Washington would give the new government significant military aid as well as moderate amounts of nonlethal riot control and military gear as an inducement to get the junta to implement further reforms; but there would be no American combat troops on the ground.

Not everyone was convinced that the US could avoid being pulled further in, however. Secretary of State Vance, for example, feared that greater aid and more training would lead to higher levels of US involvement, creating a "quagmire effect" similar to what had happened in Vietnam. The situation on the ground remained volatile, and widespread protests continued against the military's use of force. In February 1980 Archbishop Romero denounced the "unscrupulous military" and pleaded for the Christian Democrats to stop using the junta as "cover for repression." That same month Romero sent a letter to Carter demanding that the United States cease military, economic, and diplomatic intervention in El Salvador, as even nonlethal military aid was "being used to repress my people." Vance wrote to Archbishop Romero on March 12, only weeks before the archbishop was assassinated, to defend the US line: "We believe that the reform program of the Revolutionary Junta offers the best prospects for peaceful change to a more just society. The United States will not interfere in the internal affairs of El Salvador. Nevertheless, we are seriously concerned by the threat of civil war . . . which might endanger the security and welfare of all the Central American region."

But the junta was not a fixed political entity. The first reformist junta collapsed in January 1980, followed by the second three months later, with the military covertly consolidating its influence with each iteration. US policy appeared likewise in flux as it attempted to respond to the rapidly changing situation in El Salvador. On December 2 the bodies of four female American church workers were discovered along a rural road near the village of Santiago Nonualco, fifteen miles northeast of the airport. All of the women had been beaten, raped, and shot in the head. Less than twenty-four hours after the discovery of the crime, the indignant Carter administration announced that it was suspending all economic and military aid to El Salvador. On December 13, however, the administration announced a resumption of economic aid, and three days later approved a new $20 million international loan for economic development. The justification was that the third junta, which seized power in December, merited the assistance. Carter officials added that military aid would not be restored until the FAES took greater steps to improve the human rights situation.

This stance likewise came under fire, literally, when, on January 10, 1981, the freshly coalesced FMLN launched a massive military offensive called the Final Offensive that rattled the outgoing Carter White House officials. More than twenty-five poorly trained guerrillas and a few hundred Cubans initiated scores of attacks against the FAES positions. In the cities, buses were burned; in the countryside, rebels stopped buses and exhorted passengers to join the revolution. The FMLN occupied eighty-two cities and villages, including four department capitals. Expecting a repeat of Nicaragua, the rebels assumed that the offensive would spark a full-scale popular insurrection, which, according to a US State Department report, would lead to a "total breakdown of the government and immediate victory." This never came to pass "because the overwhelming majority of the Salvadoran population ignored the guerrillas' appeals." Shocked by their stalled insurrection, FMLN leaders quickly claimed that it was not in fact a final offensive but a more general operation.

On January 14, 1981, the Carter administration went back to funneling several million dollars in military assistance, including M-16 rifles and ammunition, grenade launchers, and Huey helicopters. In addition, a team of military advisors was sent into El Salvador. A few days later the White House announced $10 million in emergency aid and the deployment of three more advisor teams, citing the need to "support the Salvadoran government in its struggle against left-wing terrorism supported covertly . . . by Cuba and other Communist nations."

Overall, the Carter administration reluctantly concluded that the fledgling junta was worth supporting, at least compared to a possibly more rightist and abusive military rule or the looming possibility of Marxist insurrection. Some observers, however, believed that Washington's myopic embrace of the Salvadoran junta had catastrophic consequences. A vocal critic was Robert White, Carter's ambassador to El Salvador, who supported the Salvadoran junta's objectives against the guerrillas but later contended that the introduction of military advisors "emphasized a military solution and strengthened precisely the wrong group." The historian John Coatsworth concluded that the Carter administration's successful efforts to avoid the collapse of the military and secure the installation of a "reliably pro-U.S. civilian [junta] . . . pushed El Salvador into full-scale civil war." The *New York Times* editorial page was equally scathing: "Of the legacies of the Carter Administration, surely the sloppiest is its policy in El Salvador. The decision, in its last days, to resume the shipment of combat weapons to a besieged and divided junta made a hash of whatever political objectives Washington once had there."

Reagan = Carter Plus?

Tiny El Salvador represented one of the largest foreign policy challenges when Reagan entered the White House in January 1981 bearing a hawkish anticommunist agenda. In March the new president made it clear that he saw the Salvadoran conflict as part of a much larger national security issue: "It isn't just El Salvador. What we are doing is going to the aid of a government . . . to halt the infiltration into the Americas by terrorists . . . who aren't just aiming at El Salvador but . . . who are aiming at the whole of Central and possibly later South America, and, I'm sure, eventually, North America."

Making good on his rhetoric, Reagan agreed to send $25 million in new military aid, a sum almost twice the amount sent to El Salvador from 1946 to 1979 and more than any other Latin American country received in 1981. Of these funds $20 million were to be sent immediately without congressional approval, using the same special emergency power Carter had used in office. A country the size of Massachusetts was now receiving the largest aid budget of any Latin American country. The incoming ambassador to El Salvador,

Deane Hinton, summed up the Reagan strategy: "Save the economy, stop the violence, have the elections and ride into the sunset."

Despite the very different rhetorical approaches of the Carter and Reagan administrations, there was perhaps more continuity to US policy than at first appeared. Reaganite hard-liners had routinely criticized Carter's Salvador policies on human rights and land reform as destabilizing and wreaking havoc, and they saw winning the war as their priority. Yet despite the political divisions with the outgoing administration, some State Department officials responded to the initial decisions being made in the White House—more economic and military aid but no boots on the ground—by privately calling the Salvador policy "Carter plus."

Whatever the rhetorical slant, the political danger of increased US involvement with the Salvadoran military soon became clear. On December 11, 1981, units of the US Special Forces–trained Atlacatl Battalion executed hundreds of men, women, and children in the village of El Mozote. According to survivors, as soldiers slit the throats of children they shouted, "You are guerrillas and this is justice. This is justice." Atlacatl conducted similar operations in nearby villages over the course of four days. All told, the FAES killed more than eight hundred civilians in what came to be known to the world as the El Mozote massacre. More than four hundred of the victims were children under the age of eighteen, and some were only a few months or days old. A subsequent ballistics investigation examined over 250 cartridge cases recovered from the El Mozote execution site. Of these samples, 184 had discernible headstamps, identifying the ammunition as having been manufactured for the United States government at Lake City, Missouri.

Likely influenced by the initial skeptical reporting from the embassy in San Salvador, senior Reagan administration officials held the line that a massacre did not take place. Echoing the confidential cable sent from the US embassy in San Salvador, the State Department's senior Latin American official, Thomas Enders, stated publicly, "There is no evidence to confirm that government forces systematically massacred civilians in the operations zone, or that the number of civilians even remotely approached the 733 or 926 victims cited in the press." Assistant Secretary of State for Human Rights Elliott Abrams told a Senate committee that the reports of mass killings at El Mozote "were not credible" and that "it appears to be an incident that is at least being significantly misused, at the very best, by the guerrillas."

But it soon became clear that the US denials were erroneous: a devastating massacre had indeed occurred. The episode was a public relations disaster for

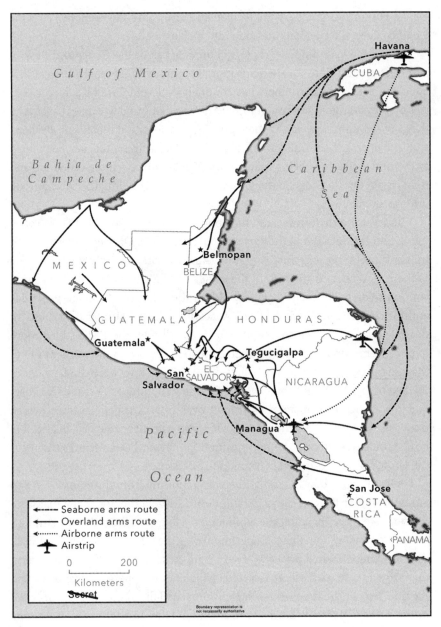

Map based on a declassified 1982 US intelligence document indicating clandestine arms shipments to El Salvador's Marxist guerrilla group, the FMLN. (University of Wisconsin–Madison Cartography Lab. Christopher Archuleta, cartographer)

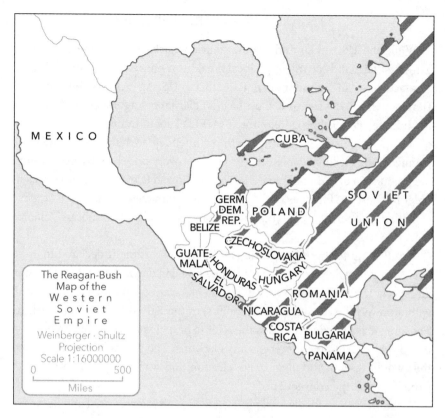

This map from circa the 1980s lampooned US conservatives' view of the Soviet threat in Central America. (University of Wisconsin–Madison Cartography Lab. Christopher Archuleta, cartographer)

the United States, some alleging that American involvement in the country made the US in part responsible for the massacre. And the bad news out of El Salvador just kept coming. For example, on September 23, 1983, the Salvadoran air force indiscriminately bombed the small town of Tenancingo, killing fifty civilians, a grisly episode that deeply frustrated US military trainers. Of critical concern to the robust and still bitter debate in Washington over US policy, El Salvador continued to be a "disaster zone" for human rights, although the numbers of reported disappearances and massacres had ebbed from the high toll of a few years earlier. A *Newsweek* poll in March 1982 found that 74 percent of the American public familiar with the conflict in El Salvador believed that it could turn into the Vietnam of the 1980s. Of these respondents, 89 percent said that the United States should not provide troops.

El Salvador Goes to the Ballot Box

While the US military efforts dramatically backfired in some cases, Reagan's first term did see major political breakthroughs in El Salvador. US agencies active in El Salvador, like the official US Agency for International Development (USAID) and the quasi-official labor organization American Institute for Free Labor Development (AIFLD), spent hundreds of thousands of dollars to bolster government efforts intended to help ensure that the planned 1982 elections were orderly. On the covert side the CIA helped fund the production of campaign materials and radio and television commercials in order to boost the fortunes of the centrist Christian Democrats at the expense of both the guerrillas and the right-wing Nationalist Republican Alliance (ARENA) party.

Heading up to the 1982 elections the junta government declared that the FMLN could participate in the vote if they first laid down their arms. This was an especially bold demand given that 1982 had started out much like 1981 had: with a powerful guerrilla offensive that sent the Salvadoran military reeling. The guerrillas quickly dismissed the offer to participate in the vote, reiterating that power sharing must precede any elections. The guerrillas also promised they would disrupt the illegitimate election and warned Salvadorans not to partake or risk the consequences.

When the voting finally took place on March 28 international and domestic electoral observers were stunned by what they witnessed. Defying the guerrilla calls to stay away, over 1.5 million Salvadorans went to the polls, roughly 80 percent of the electorate. Despite their chilling predictions, the FMLN did not disrupt the voting process. In a postelection news conference, an observer delegation comprising congressmen, church officials, and election experts declared that they believed the elections had been free and fair. An ecstatic Ambassador Dean Hinton cabled back to Washington that "the results of this election have exceeded our most optimistic expectations. . . . Thousands of Salvadorans walked overnight through guerrilla strongholds, waited hours in line to vote, and are now walking back home through the same strongholds."

The ballots tallied, the Christian Democrats had garnered 35 percent of the vote, assuring them of twenty-four of the sixty deputies in the assembly. The rightist ARENA did surprisingly well, though, taking second place with 26 percent. The US put pressure on the military to block the appointment of ARENA leader Roberto D'Aubuisson—one of the masterminds of the death squads and linked to the assassination of Archbishop Romero—as provisional president, as the election procedures indicated. Álvaro Magaña, a businessman, was appointed instead. On April 27, 1983, Reagan announced before a joint session of Congress his intent to secure a doubling of annual military aid, which amounted to over $136 million.

In 1984 El Salvador once again braced for national elections, this time a historic presidential race between Duarte and D'Aubuisson. Coming on the heels of the stunning vote in 1982, the 1984 vote was eliciting much greater confidence that it would be successful. Yet, as in 1982, US officials were deeply concerned that ARENA might win again, and this time winning meant D'Aubuisson taking the presidency. That represented an unacceptable outcome for Carter/Reagan engagement, which wanted to back moderates and democrats over rightist ideologues.

Using a 1981 presidential authorization, the CIA pumped in an estimated $1 million to $3 million in covert assistance to cover Duarte's media and campaign materials, while Washington disbursed over $1 million in assistance through the various AIFLD-backed labor unions campaigning on Duarte's behalf. The State Department covered the $10 million costs of the election itself, and the embassy went to great lengths to encourage influential Salvadorans to promote a favorable democratic outcome. Duarte also received external funds from Christian Democrat parties in Venezuela and West Germany.

Much as in the 1982 vote the FMLN condemned the elections as a sham intended to legitimize the corrupt regime. Villalobos explained the FMLN's logic: "We are certain that we have the people's support, and this is obvious to everyone. We have no need to prove it on paper. No voting at the polls can be more eloquent or convincing than the facts of war." In towns throughout the country the FMLN painted this slogan on walls: "Dialogue Yes, Elections No." Guillermo Ungo, an ex-junta member who had joined forces with the FMLN, wrote in the New York Times on March 22, 1984, that "the decision to hold this election was made in Washington, by Washington, and for Washington."

Nevertheless, almost 1.4 million Salvadorans, nearly 78 percent of eligible voters, went to the polls in the first round on March 25, but glitches with the new, untried electoral registry system necessitated a rerun on May 6 using the old method. Duarte won with 54 percent of the vote compared to D'Aubuisson's 29 percent, and he consolidated his success in the 1985 Constituent Assembly elections. His Christian Democratic Party gained thirty-four of the sixty assembly seats and swept most of the country's municipal offices. Unlike the 1982 vote, this time Duarte's centrists did not require Yankee intervention to achieve a victory.

The Cost of War

The transition to democracy had come at a high price: according to US government evidence, by 1985, after five years of "insurgent war and transition toward democracy," an astounding forty thousand Salvadorans were estimated to have been killed in the wanton violence. A CIA report stated that death squad activity had declined to "only a fraction of the [activity in the] peak years" of 1980 and 1981. But the 1984 rate would roughly be cut in half by 1987. One million people, close to one-fifth of the Salvadoran population, fled the country over the course of the war, a majority of whom went to the United States as undocumented immigrants.

The economic toll was also devastating. The guerrillas were very effective at destroying what little infrastructure or industry existed in the country. Cotton, coffee, and sugar harvests and, by extension, exports, for example, were reduced by a third to a half during the conflict, an effort helped by an international solidarity campaign to boycott Salvadoran coffee. During the mid-1980s El Salvador's already sclerotic economy was functioning at roughly 50 percent of capacity; more than half the adult population was unemployed. By the end of the war both the decrease in exports and the damage to infrastructure had cost the battered nation over $2.2 billion. US aid attempted to rescue the situation: between 1980 and 1989 economic assistance totaled $2.6 billion. With the military aid factored in, El Salvador during the 1980s received more US aid per capita than any country save Israel.

By 1989, after nearly a decade of war, it seemed that little progress had been made in improving El Salvador's judiciary and rolling back the pervasive climate of impunity that in effect protected the military from charges of human rights abuses. US ambassador William Walker stated that year that "If there is any area where this country [El Salvador] has made zero progress, that's the area of judicial reform and the administration of justice. There ain't no justice here." Some US officials, however, did believe that the Salvadoran justice system had made some notable gains during the 1980s. In May 1984 a jury convicted and sentenced to the maximum thirty years all five of the National Guard troops implicated in the killings of the American church women. It was "the first time a jury had convicted any member of the armed forces for a slaying with political overtones."

The end of war still seemed a distant prospect, however. A Marxist revolution may have been averted, but the conflict appeared to be locked in a bloody stalemate. In 1988 the *Los Angeles Times* journalist Morris Blachman said that "the war is going badly," yet the Reagan administration "has insistently argued that U.S. policy is succeeding in El Salvador." A number of factors would soon change the political calculus and make peace a viable prospect. President George H. W. Bush entered the White House in 1989 with a Central America policy that emphasized pragmatism and compromise over conflict and principle. As recalled by Bush's secretary of state, James Baker, from the very first days of taking office in January 1989 the Bush administration "looked for opportunities to signal our support for a negotiated settlement, particularly one related to elections and democracy" in El Salvador. Moreover, the fall of the Berlin Wall in November 1989 and the precipitous implosion of Soviet-backed communism meant that in El Salvador the new president did not have to confront the existential threats of Marxist takeovers that so perplexed the Carter and Reagan administrations. Cuba began suffering its own withdrawals after losing badly needed economic subsidies from the Soviets, an estimated $4 to $6 billion annually. The Sandinistas' largely unexpected electoral defeat in 1990 removed the FMLN's closest ally from power in Managua. Having been reliant on external funding and solidarity for years, the FMLN was now on its own. Perhaps anticipating the imminent decline of communism, in November 1989 the guerrillas made one last attempt to spark a revolution.

The Second Final Offensive, 1989

Reflecting months of planning in consultation with Havana and relying on logistical support from the Sandinistas, the FMLN's second final offensive—dubbed *Al Tope y Punto* (all at once to the maximum)—began on the morning of November 11 when urban commandos launched mortar attacks against National Guard installations and FAES general staff headquarters in the capital. That night thousands of insurgents launched simultaneous attacks on FAES positions throughout the country. They struck at the presidential palace and President Alfredo Cristiani's private residence in order to assassinate the Salvadoran president, who happened to be outside the capital at the time. Within three days of the initial attack, however, the sheer numerical troop advantage of the FAES and their relentless air forays against the guerrilla-held positions began to take their toll on the insurgents. But it took until early December for the FAES to succeed in pushing the majority of the rebel forces out of the capital.

The insurgent offensive witnessed in the heaviest fighting of the war reinforced to both sides the need to bring the war to an end. The situation appeared particularly hopeless to the FMLN: despite being well trained and funded by Cuba and the Soviet bloc, the Marxist guerrillas had once again failed to win the hearts and minds of either the rural or the urban population. And despite the massacres, the US-backed reforms of the military and five elections in a decade had contributed to legitimizing the government. "We had to face the reality that we could not win," said Gerson Martínez, an FMLN commander.

Not long after the guerrilla offensive concluded, President Cristiani and the FMLN leadership separately asked UN secretary-general Javier Pérez de Cuellar to increase his organization's support for the fledgling negotiations that many assumed were left for dead in the offensive's bloody aftermath. And sure enough, in April 1991 came the first breakthrough when the two sides agreed on constitutional reform, a development that helped convince Washington that the FMLN was serious about negotiations. Talks in New York continued for several months in the fall of 1991 until they reached their culmination in late December. New Year's Eve was Pérez de Cuellar's last day as secretary-general, and the two parties officially signed the New York Act four minutes before midnight on December 31, 1991, agreeing on "all technical and military aspects relating to the separation of the warring parties and the cessation of the armed conflict." On January 16, 1992, representatives from the Salvadoran government and the FMLN participated in a formal peace ceremony at the Castle of Chapultepec in Mexico City, where they signed the Chapultepec Accords, which contained the same terms as the New York Act. The combatants ended fighting the day after the ceremony, and the formal cease-fire began on February 1. The FMLN was officially demobilized as a fighting force on December 15, 1992, eleven months after the peace pact was signed in Mexico. The war was over.

The Salvador Option

Given the remarkable resolution of the Salvadoran civil war, it is easy to understand how many concluded that El Salvador appeared to be a clear victory for the US counterinsurgency strategy. A light US military presence trained indigenous forces to do the actual fighting while simultaneously legitimizing the local client government through economic reforms and democracy. The Pentagon even gave it a name: the Salvador Option. But to what degree can the outcome in El Salvador be attributed to US intervention?

To its backers the US campaign to save El Salvador represented a dramatic success in the protracted Cold War, especially when compared with the disaster of Vietnam. But many critics of the Salvador Option told a much less honorable tale, one filled with some of the worst stories of Cold War atrocity and abuse that in total claimed the lives of seventy-five thousand people. Instead of pushing for a negotiated settlement between the warring factions in 1981, Washington had embraced a military solution that made the violence and suffering worse. Via often nefarious and deceptive means US officials took what was a domestic and popular insurgency fighting a repressive Washington-backed government and painted it as a Moscow- and Havana-manufactured communist insurgency. Some people, including US officials, were also not convinced by Washington's justifications for its involvement. In a *New York Times* interview the former ambassador Robert White asked, "How can a country the size of Massachusetts—where you can see the entire country from 9,000 feet from a helicopter—how can a homegrown revolution in that country threaten the security of the United States?"

Perhaps most damningly, some wondered if the US had played any meaningful role at all. An April 2005 editorial in the left-of-center *New Republic* explained how, "contrary to conservative conventional wisdom," US policy in El Salvador was "ultimately ineffectual" other than "contributing to the death of tens of thousands of civilians." According to this school of thought, what accounted for the ultimate outcome was the winding down of the Cold War and the mutual understanding of the Salvadoran military and the Marxist guerrillas that neither side could win outright.

Against these criticisms, it can be argued that Washington's decision to engage El Salvador meant that while the Salvadoran military never came anywhere close to being a model professional military, US involvement helped to dampen its most reflexive and deeply held authoritarian tendencies. And while the US did reject the guerrillas' attempts to start negotiations, the format of the UN-brokered negotiations that led to the war's dramatic resolution entailed the guerrillas giving up their long-standing demand for power sharing and instead competing for political power through elections—exactly what Washington had insisted on from the beginning as a precondition for a settlement. US backing most likely made some things worse and some better—and this mixed bag precedes the question of whether those negative costs contributed to any lasting, positive outcomes. Set against the recent history of the protracted and bloody wars in Afghanistan and Iraq, figuring out the truth of this seemingly paradigmatic case of the light-footprint approach is all the more relevant.

29 • Getting Rid of Pinochet

On September 21, 1976, an especially sultry morning in Washington, Orlando Letelier, the forty-four-year-old former Chilean ambassador to the United States under Salvador Allende's government, was driving to work at the Institute for Policy Studies, a left-leaning policy think tank. Riding with Letelier was his twenty-five-year-old work colleague Ronni Moffitt and her husband, Michael. As he sped down Massachusetts Avenue a remote-controlled explosive hidden underneath the car detonated. The burning vehicle skidded to a stop near the Romanian embassy. In a commemorative piece marking the fortieth anniversary of the attack the *Washington Post* painted a graphic picture of the carnage: "There was blood and debris everywhere and a human foot in the roadway. A fatally wounded man lay on the pavement; his legs were missing from above the knees."

The man was Letelier, an economist who was sent to multiple detention camps after the 1973 coup and was the most influential Chilean exile living in the United States. He would live only a few more minutes, shouting, "Assassins, fascists!" before he died. Ronni Moffitt drowned in her own blood from a shrapnel cut to her throat. Miraculously, Michael was uninjured. In the *Post*'s account, Letelier and Moffitt were victims of a "brazen, perhaps unprecedented" state-sponsored terrorist plot on American soil to assassinate Letelier. The rub, though, was that the perpetrator was one of the US's principal anticommunist allies in Latin America: Augusto Pinochet of Chile.

Carter Cracks Down, Reagan Reconciles

Scholars and policy makers continue to bitterly dispute the moral and strategic significance of the US role in the overthrow of Chilean democracy in the early 1970s, which paved the way for Augusto Pinochet to become a dictator.

To many this was an unambiguous instance of the United States sacrificing its
putative commitment to democracy and human rights at the altar of realpolitik anticommunist exigencies. However, far less ink has been spent analyzing
the US effort to end Pinochet's iron-fisted rule two decades later.

In fact, the US and Pinochet had been uneasy allies almost from the beginning of the dictator's rule, as the United States was divided on the wisdom of
toppling Allende. In his second televised debate on October 6, 1976, with the
Republican incumbent, Gerald Ford, the Democratic candidate, Jimmy Carter,
lamented the destruction of Chilean democracy and decried the strong support
of the United States for Pinochet. Carter's language was a rebuke of the Nixon–
Kissinger approach to Chile, which had continued with Kissinger as Ford's secretary of state. Soon after the victorious Carter entered the White House in
January 1977 his administration cut military aid to military regimes in El Salva-
dor, Argentina, and Brazil. Many assume that Carter also cut aid to Chile, but
Capitol Hill in fact denied arms to Pinochet's regime before Carter took office.
As part of an expansive revamping of foreign military aid programs, in June
1976 Congress approved language that embargoed US weapons being sent to
Chile. Following Senate approval, the Minnesota Democratic senator and drafter
of the legislation, Hubert H. Humphrey, declared a new era in ensuring that
US-made arms no longer went to rogue regimes. His colleague Senator Ted
Kennedy of Massachusetts was equally upbeat. "Now is the time to close the
loopholes and end all arms traffic to Chile where the ruling military junta is using the weapons to repress the Chilean people," he said. Kennedy added that the
Ford administration had been "extending largesse to the junta for two and a half
years" and that Congress had to act since the Ford White House had not.

With the matériel component addressed by Congress, the incoming Carter
administration added economic sanctions and supported the appointment of a
special rapporteur for Chile at the UN Commission for Human Rights. The US
representative Brady Tyson, a Methodist minister and aide to UN ambassador
Andrew Young, expressed "our profoundest regrets" for the US role in toppling
Allende and abetting Pinochet's bloody reign. Time and again the Carter team
used public and private sticks to embarrass Pinochet over his heinous conduct,
hoping to get him to liberalize. To top things off, the White House engaged
with the South American nation's political opposition, ensuring that the Chilean despot was thoroughly infuriated.

Then the tinderbox that the Carter–Pinochet saga had become caught
fire. All hell broke loose in early 1978 following the Chilean Supreme Court's
decision to reject Washington's request to extradite three Chilean secret police
officers, including the spy chief, Manuel Contreras. The three men had been

indicted by a US grand jury in the Letelier–Moffitt plot. Following a prolonged investigation the FBI concluded that the Pinochet regime's secret police agency (DINA) had coordinated with Argentina and Paraguay, Chile's counterparts in rightist military rule, as part of the infamous Operation Condor. This "covert reign of terror" involved a coordinated web of rightist military intelligence agencies that "tracked, abducted, and assassinated" tens of thousands of suspected leftist activists, politicians, intellectuals, and other putative subversives throughout the region. In murdering Orlando Letelier, Operation Condor had brought its war against leftist insurgents to US soil.

There was internal executive branch disagreement over how to respond to the Chilean court's ruling against extradition. The Justice Department and a few offices at the State Department urged for swift countermeasures. State's Bureau of Inter-American Affairs, however, wanted a gentler approach because it believed there were few effective diplomatic tools ready and that their use would cause complications in US–Latin American relations. But liberal members of Congress like Edward Kennedy, Frank Church of Idaho, and Iowa representative Tom Harkin helped persuade Secretary of State Vance to back the harsher line. In the end the Carter administration denounced the court's decision as deplorable and labeled the released intelligence agents terrorists. It also recalled Ambassador George Landau, cut the embassy staff by 25 percent, and served notice that the entire US military mission in Chile was also leaving. On cue vocal congressmen like Kennedy and Church pushed for even harsher economic and military sanctions if Pinochet did not rescind the ruling.

However, despite the genuine pressure via sanctions and jawboning the administration and its allies on Capitol Hill failed to get Pinochet any closer to political reform or departure. In fact, while he made some pro forma gestures on political liberties in this period, the Chilean strongman was more entrenched than ever. What's more, he had gone eyeball-to-eyeball with Washington and lived to tell the tale. In this case, he was not unlike the generals in El Salvador, Brazil, and Argentina, who had also rejected Carter's sermons on human rights and democracy.

Reagan Changes Tack (Twice)

Reagan's approach would be very different from Carter's. It is not inaccurate to assume, as many experts do, that the incoming Reagan administration in 1981 "closely embrace[d]" Pinochet since he was a "pro-market and anti-Communist ally worthy of support and understanding." In this telling the new commander in chief was swayed by his policy advisor, Jeane Kirkpatrick, who, in a much-discussed essay in the November 1979 issue of *Commentary*, argued that there were key differences between the authoritarian and totalitarian regimes of the developing world. The former were generally more amenable to US interests and able to eventually transition to democracy. The implicit rebuke of Carterism was that a more conciliatory stance vis-à-vis authoritarian regimes (read: the Pinochets of the world) would pay greater dividends.

It was also the case that the ascendant US conservative foreign policy community, above and beyond the Reagan administration, believed Pinochet had prevented communism under Allende's watch. Pinochet's late 1970s experiment with hyper-free-market economic policies further ingratiated him with Reagan conservatives. This despite the Chilean regime's brutal form of governance and the fact that Pinochet appeared determined to use his dubious 1980 constitution as the mechanism to maintain himself in power for the next two decades, if not for life.

Around the time Reagan's second term began in early 1985 a host of global events upended the White House's approach to dealing with repressive, usually pro-US regimes like those in the Philippines, South Korea, Brazil, and Uruguay, all of which would make democratic transitions within a few years that were either welcomed or facilitated by Washington. Perhaps most significant was Mikhail Gorbachev's 1985 appointment as the general secretary of the Communist Party in the Soviet Union. Gorbachev's liberalizing instincts resulted in an unexpected but fruitful diplomacy with his US interlocutors, first Ronald Reagan and then George H. W. Bush. Increasingly, Kirkpatrick's notion of tolerating rightist dictators was simply unsavory in this increasingly democratic global picture, even if the end of the Cold War was not yet in sight.

Pinochet was a test case for just how far the softening of US policy would go, though in the end his autocratic governance limited the policy options for Reagan's team. The Chilean ruler's obstinacy in dealing with the most conservative elements of the democratic opposition made him increasingly unpopular in the Reagan White House. By the end of 1986, after much deliberation and disagreement, the Reagan administration came around to a policy of trying to get Pinochet out of power and replace him with a moderate, but still decidedly noncommunist, civilian government. As Secretary of State Shultz discussed in his memoir, however, Reagan was not completely committed to the new policy shift, still seeing the dictator as a "friend of the U.S. and a bulwark against communism."

Eventually, Shultz's State Department helped the president see the self-serving logic and hollowness behind Pinochet's contention that his regime

was the only thing keeping Chile from chaos. Assistant Secretary of State Elliott Abrams was steadfast in his advocacy of a more forceful line against
Pinochet. His proposed policy would be two-track: on one hand, nudging Pinochet with a "mix of quiet diplomacy, public criticism and largely symbolic
economic pressures," while on the other working with moderate opposition
organizations. Some were not optimistic about the plan's chances for speedy
success. The choice between Pinochet and the democratic opposition was, as
one US official put it, akin to a "choice between a dead horse and a snail." But
there was now the sense that inaction was not possible: leaving Pinochet in
place would only exacerbate the communist threat felt to be brewing inside
the country. "We feel that Pinochet's actions play into the hands of the extremists by creating a clandestine opposition" controlled by communists. Note that
the Chilean Communist Party was anything but a spent force, especially in the
poor slums around Santiago and other industrial cities. Lucky for the Schultz–
Abrams strategy, in August 1985 the Chilean political opposition factions
signed a pact committing members—a motley bunch ranging from former
Allende ministers to centrist Christian Democrats to *pinochetistas* who had
fallen out with the regime—to the prodemocracy components of the 1980
constitution.

Still, there were inconsistencies in the US message to Pinochet. In one
embarrassing episode, the head of the Inter-American Defense Board, US
General Robert Schweitzer, who was in Chile in 1985, "presented Pinochet
with a sword and gave a speech clearly indicating his support for . . . [Pinochet]
. . . in Chile's current internal disputes." A furious Abrams wrote his Pentagon counterpart, Richard Armitage, to convey how the strategy was "walking
a tightrope by trying to maintain normal relations with the [Chilean] government while pressing it to hold elections and permit establishment of a civilian,
democratic government."

To manage matters on the ground, Shultz sent one of the Foreign Service's
most distinguished diplomats, Harry Barnes, to be the new ambassador in
Santiago, where he arrived in November 1985. Reagan and Abrams were fully
aware that Pinochet understood the gravitas of Barnes's appointment: the US
was taking the situation in Chile very seriously. A meeting Barnes had with
leaders of the Socialist Party sent "shockwaves throughout the Pinochet government." Pro-Pinochet activists started dark rumors that if Barnes "left Chile,
it would be in a six-foot box."

The US was not alone in sensing that the winds of change were blowing.
Fidel Castro believed that the anti-Pinochet activism had peaked, making it an

ideal moment to provide arms to the pro-Havana guerrillas inside Chile, the Frente Patriótico Manuel Rodríguez. Fidel reckoned that the time for a joint, widespread guerrilla–street protest operation was ripe given the level of anti-Pinochet social agitation. General John R. Galvin, who commanded the US Southern Command in the Panama Canal Zone, allegedly notified the Chilean military of a massive arms shipment destined for the communist rebels. Regardless of whether a verbal warning occurred, the Chilean military, from August through September 1986, intercepted "thousands of pounds of rocket launchers, automatic rifles, grenades and ammunition" in ten caches along the country's northern Atacama Desert coastline. Some of the arms were used in a failed attempt to assassinate Pinochet on September 7 of the same year, although many opponents of the Pinochet dictatorship dismissed the Cuban weapon delivery as a regime ploy to justify more repression.

The Reagan administration feared that this radical left's agenda—and the more generalized and swelling antiregime sentiment—might propel the nation into a full-blown civil war, a consideration that led it to contemplate offering political asylum to the Chilean dictator. One declassified document described how the offer would provide "an honorable departure for President [Pinochet], who would be received as a guest of our [US] government."

Despite the cordial invitation, the Reagan administration was simultaneously deciding whether it should respond to new classified revelations that Pinochet had directly ordered Letelier's assassination. In September 1987 Secretary Shultz was informed by the CIA director William Webster that his spy agency had convincing evidence that Pinochet had "personally ordered his intelligence chief to carry out the murders." In addition, the CIA reckoned, Pinochet subsequently "decided to stonewall on the case to hide his involvement and, ultimately, to protect his hold on the presidency." These stunning revelations convinced Shultz, who was already inclined to ramp up the pressure on the Chilean despot, to make the case directly to Reagan. "The CIA has never before drawn and presented its conclusion that such strong evidence exists of [Pinochet's] leadership role in this act of terrorism," the secretary of state wrote his boss. "It is not clear whether we can or would want to consider indicting Pinochet," assessed Shultz. "Nevertheless, this is a blatant example of a chief of state's direct involvement in an act of state terrorism, one that is particularly disturbing both because it occurred in our capital and since his government is generally considered to be friendly." As Shultz saw it, Reagan had to punish the author of anti-American terror: "What we now know about Pinochet's role in these assassinations is of the greatest seriousness and adds further impetus to the need to work toward complete democratization of Chile."

Just Say NO!

Chile's 1980 constitution outlined that a single-candidate presidential referendum would take place in 1988, in which a junta-nominated candidate (Pinochet predictably nominated himself) would go before voters in a simple yes or no decision for a fresh eight-year term. If the candidate was rejected in the October 5 nationwide vote, then presidential elections would be conducted within a short amount of time. The vote was quite simple: "No" for elections, "Yes" for a continuation of military rule.

The Reagan administration saw an opportunity to effect democratic change via the quasi-autonomous NED. Before 1988 Congress did not designate where and how NED funds were spent; in 1988, though, as noted above, Congress stepped in to direct the NED to work with anti-Pinochet political opposition before the 1988 plebiscite in Chile. Regime change by other means, screamed critics. The NED had been active in Chile since 1986, when it started providing money and training to a labor union linked to the centrist Christian Democratic Party, whose anticommunist instincts were appealing.

With only months to go before the referendum proregime newspapers like *El Mercurio* blasted the NED's subversive involvement in Chile's internal matters, claiming that the program was not a "neutral and impartial option to promote democracy." Pinochet's ambassador in Washington, for his part, wrote a letter to the US Congress questioning why the NED was getting involved in democracy promotion when that was the very nature of the plebiscite itself. The irony is that these regime apologists were entirely correct that the NED was a partisan actor in this agitated drama. It ended up giving $600,000 to the opposition National Command of the No (NCN), an umbrella organization of sixteen political parties, including the socialists, which prompted its leader, Heraldo Muñoz, to label the Washington–Chilean opposition relationship "open collaboration" to defeat Pinochet.

A month before the plebiscite, both the No and Yes camps were allotted fifteen minutes of gratis media exposure each day. In conjunction with the voter registration push, the No side employed a deft media campaign—a catchy musical tune, "La alegría ya viene" (Joy is coming), and a rainbow symbol—which was in part hatched by New York executives. The strategy served as a critical component of the campaign, convincing Chileans that a rejection of Pinochet would lead to a new, better era. The junta, by contrast, emphasized a darker message: the long food lines, labor strikes, and overall chaos from the Allende years to show citizens what the country would return to without Pinochet's rule.

With the vote looming, US diplomats feared foul play if the election went against the regime. Having replaced Barnes in December 1988, US ambassador Charles Gillespie reflected, "We knew that Pinochet was planning something." The US embassy's sharp message was, "If they implemented a plan to jigger the results of the plebiscite . . . we were going to blow the whistle." Pinochet's initially optimistic mood "plummeted with each passing hour" as the results came in. He became aware soon after the polls closed that the vote did not look good, which led to a delay in announcing the results. Then Defense Minister Fernando Matthei told media outlets, "It seems to me that the No have really won," making it virtually impossible for Pinochet to declare an emergency and null the plebiscite, as was his inclination. Matthei knew that such an intervention would make the regime even more of a pariah, especially vis-à-vis Washington. To the US diplomat Robert Gelbard, Matthei's announcement made him the "hero of the referendum." It later emerged that the chiefs of the Chilean air force, navy, and Carabineros had, after realizing that "No" had won, visited Pinochet on the night of the plebiscite. They informed him that they would not support any attempt on his part to annul the vote and that the army would be alone if he insisted on retaining power.

It will almost certainly never be fully known what impact US official funding via the NED and other sources had for the No campaign. More critical, perhaps, when one assesses Washington's mark on the referendum, was Reagan's broader shift to regime change via diplomatic carrots and sticks as opposed to guns. But it is also undeniable that key factors in the referendum's unlikely victory were fully Chilean in nature. Washington was a supporting side act.

As planned, presidential elections went off without a hitch on December 14, 1989, the Christian Democrat Patricio Alwyn winning. As part of his transition from power, Pinochet maintained his post as commander in chief of the Chilean army until March 1998, at which point he became a senator-for-life, as per the 1980 constitution. On a trip to London in October 1998 Pinochet was arrested after being indicted on human rights abuses by a Spanish magistrate, Baltasar Garzón. British authorities held Pinochet for a year and a half before releasing him on the grounds of impaired health in March 2000, when he then stood trial back in Chile. Upon his death on December 10, 2006, hundreds of criminal charges against him were pending "for numerous human rights violations and embezzlement during and after his rule." In 1993 the

DINA chief Miguel Contreras received a seven-year prison sentence for his involvement in the Letelier–Moffitt murders.

Coda

Barack Obama's secretary of state, John F. Kerry, visited Chile in early October 2015 and delivered an unusual package to the nation's president, Michelle Bachelet, herself a victim of *pincochetista* torture. The package held a computer disk which declassified some 282 US government documents related to Pinochet's involvement in the Letelier–Moffitt killings. In 2016 Kerry made another attempt at "declassification diplomacy" during a stop-off in Buenos Aires, where he gave President Mauricio Macri a "first batch" disk filled with documents related to Argentina's antisubversive "dirty war" in 1976–82.

This novel approach to hemispheric ties was first started under President Bill Clinton when he ordered declassifications related to US involvement in El Salvador and Chile. The outcome? To the researcher Peter Kornbluh, "allies are grateful and historians are delighted," and the United States is able to "advance the cause of human rights" and even "redress the dark history of Washington's support for repression abroad." What is fascinating about the declassifications, in the Pinochet case at least, is that some of Washington's most sensitive secrets revolved around using a successful mix of sanctions, democratic support, and popular sentiment to get rid of a rightist S.O.B. in Chile—a definite step forward from the Coke bottles and arms shipments of old.

PART IV

POST–COLD WAR, 1989–

POWER AND AGENCY IN A POST-HEGEMONIC HEMISPHERE

The fall of the Berlin Wall in 1989 ushered in a new age of multilateralism following the half century of East–West struggle. One key question for observers was whether the end of the Soviet Union would prompt Washington to either increase or decrease its presence in the Americas. Many feared that Washington would simply find a new bogyman (for example, drugs) that would nominally justify its continuing hegemony and militarization. More sympathetic commentators perceived the postcommunist era as a chance for a "Wilsonian surge" involving a more enlightened and genuine focus on democracy, human rights, and development. A third possibility was that Washington would simply ignore the region, now that it no longer mattered in the pitiless geopolitical calculus of the Cold War era.

The truth is that the United States did all three. In the period immediately after the Cold War it escalated its "war on drugs" (which increasingly filled the policy vacuum left by communism), targeting the key coca-growing locales of Bolivia, Peru, and Colombia, known as going "supply side," and, later, Mexico. But it also displayed a commitment to uphold the principles of democracy, at least in some cases. And it should not be forgotten that the first three decades of the post–Cold War era indeed saw a decline, albeit uneven, in the willingness of the United States to exert control in the region. This occurred in part because more pressing issues, including the wars in Afghanistan and Iraq, forced Latin America down the policy making food chain. But there was also the indisputable reality that the region itself was now more confident acting on its own. After decades of rule by military dictatorships, the countries of Latin America became part of the "third wave" of democratization washing across the globe in the 1980s and 1990s. Coupled with the rise of international capital flows, many Latin American countries also benefited from the advantages (and risks) that economic liberalization brought them.

Yet in the ensuing years and decades the region grappled with newly arisen impediments. Democratic practices, such as open elections, struggled to take root, as did longer-term democratic institutions, such as independent judiciaries. The long-fought-for macroeconomic stability, achieved after bouts of hyperinflation in the so-called lost decade of the 1980s, did not translate into lasting cross-class social gains. Some even looked back fondly on the old mano dura regimes, and at times Latin Americans used their newfound electoral power to elect democratic populists like Hugo Chávez in Venezuela, Alberto Fujimori in Peru, and Jair Bolsonaro in Brazil, who, even if broadly popular, often governed in autocratic ways.

Too Hot! Too Cold!

In the wake of the September 11, 2001, terrorist attacks President George W. Bush pursued an imperious, unilateral strategy in Latin America, pushing hard to get regional governments to endorse the US invasion of Iraq and ensure US soldiers' exemption from the jurisdiction of the International Criminal Court (ICC). This approach backfired. Many governments, including traditional US partners such as Chile and Mexico, dug in their heels and did not cooperate with Bush's ICC immunity scheme. In his second term (2005–9) Bush attempted a more conciliatory approach, cultivating, for instance, a genuine amity with the leftist president Luiz Inácio Lula da Silva in Brazil. But it was too little, too late, and Chávez and other radicals profited domestically from Bush's reputation as a bully.

After Barack Obama took office in 2009, however, it became much harder for Latin leaders to exploit the US-bashing catapult for domestic support. In April 2009, at the Summit of the Americas in Trinidad, Obama emphasized mutual respect and outlined a vision of equal partnerships and joint responsibility. His deferential yet serious style quickly put the most conspiratorial anti-US critics, including Chávez, Evo Morales in Bolivia, and Daniel Ortega in Nicaragua, on their back foot.

Still, leftist critics were quick to blast Obama for his seemingly conventional Big Stick policies when it came to dealing with the Honduran president and Chávez ally, Mel Zelaya, who was ousted in a 2009 coup. Obama was faulted as well for the negotiated but never implemented defense pact with Colombia that outlined the deployment of US troops in the South American country. To these skeptics, Obama's policies were simply a case of the wolf in sheep's clothing: US hegemony veiled by sublime orations.

The chorus from the right end of the ideological spectrum was that Obama's diplomatic overtures only legitimized despicable regimes like that of Chávez and his successor Nicolás Maduro and communist Cuba, which Obama visited in 2016. This was a stark contrast from Obama's successor Donald Trump, whose much more aggressive anti-immigration agenda was epitomized by his infamous wall and characterized by his demonization of Central American migrants. Under Trump, it appeared that the US was retreating behind its geopolitical moat (read: the Rio Grande), unwilling to get involved in Latin American affairs except in matters of trade.

All told, it could be said that the post–Cold War, postideological period sees the United States as well as the region struggling to hit that Goldilocks state in which Washington is neither meddling in nor neglecting the region. In recent years the question of Washington's involvement with the region has grown more acute in light of the rise of China as a major world power and especially China's decision to cultivate clout in the region. Beijing's foreign policy vision, implemented through its Belt and Road Initiative, sees China at the heart of a global network of infrastructure, trade, and financing. And Latin America, a region rich in resources and in need of investment and better connectivity, firmly fits the bill. Many Latin American countries embraced their new benefactor for supplying needed direct investment, and China quickly became the region's most important trade partner, gobbling up Latin America's commodities.

There are further indications that, after a long hiatus, the US may be taking a more active interest in Latin American affairs, even casting shadows of its Cold War approach. With Venezuela in turmoil under the corrupt regime of Maduro, in 2019 Trump's secretary of state, Mike Pompeo, said that "military action is possible [in Venezuela]. If that's what's required, that's what the United States will do." How the US balances the presence of China in its backyard and the destabilizing effect of regional crises with its own national security and economic interests will form the next, as yet unwritten, chapter of our history.

30 • Invading Panama

> You can't buy Noriega, only rent him.
> —Secretary of State George Shultz, circa mid-1980s

On December 20, 1989, twenty-four thousand US troops made a hostile entry into Panama to overthrow the country's military dictatorship and apprehend its leader, Manuel Antonio Noriega. At the time, the invasion represented the largest US military operation since the Vietnam War, and it came just a month after the fall of the Berlin Wall. Officials in the Reagan and Bush administrations had been receiving reports documenting hundreds of incidents of violence committed by Noriega's forces against US citizens in Panama, and by late 1989 US policy makers perceived that Noriega's regime posed an imminent threat to American installations and citizens.

As in the case of the medical students in Grenada, a potential hostage crisis was a real concern but not the full story. Drugs also played a central role: with the United States consumed by a cocaine and crack cocaine epidemic, President George H. W. Bush opted to flex his muscles and deal with the increasingly antagonistic, although questionably threatening, narco strongman Noriega. Reagan's domestic and international triumph with the Grenada invasion undoubtedly made such a maximalist approach more attractive, and like Grenada after 1983 Panama emerged from the invasion far more democratic than before, but as always the path by which the United States arrived at the decision to invade was convoluted, and questions continue to linger about whether invading was the best available option.

Our Man in Panama

Beginning in the late 1960s Manuel Noriega positioned himself as an indispensable resource to the US intelligence community. In 1967 he took classes
at the School of the Americas in the Canal Zone, quickly ingratiating himself
to US officials with his seemingly unparalleled intelligence-gathering capabilities. By the early 1970s Noriega was in command of G-2, the Panamanian
National Guard's intelligence service.

Contrary to the impressions of some observers, however, Washington did
not support Noriega in order to create an American puppet in Panama City.
The reason was in fact more trivial: Washington simply needed sufficiently
accurate and reliable intelligence on budding Marxist guerrilla movements,
communist Cuba, and the burgeoning scourge of drug trafficking. And
Noriega delivered, though his loyalty was far from clear. He served the gringos, but he also worked for the Cubans and the Colombian drug cartels. In
1980 the former Costa Rican president José Figueres was visiting Fidel Castro
when Figueres commented that Castro had the best intelligence in the region.
Castro responded, "No, Noriega is the best-informed man. He knows everything the left and right are doing." US policy makers labeled Noriega "rent-a-
colonel," and it was said that in the drug underworld he was called the
"Caribbean Prostitute."

Over the next decade Washington paid Noriega hundreds of thousands of
dollars to report on the seedy Central American intelligence world. He had
become such a cherished resource to the US intelligence community that by
1976, when Ambler Moss arrived as the US ambassador in Panama City, he
was informed that Noriega was the liaison for the CIA, FBI, Customs Service,
and a few military intelligence agencies. During these years Noriega worked
with the highest-level US policy makers, including the CIA director William
Casey and the National Security Council director Oliver North. In December
1976 Noriega even met with then CIA director George H. W. Bush at an event
at the Panamanian embassy in Washington. A 1978 piece of correspondence
from Peter Bensinger, President Carter's Drug Enforcement Administration
(DEA) director, demonstrates how highly US officials had come to think of
him. "[The DEA] very much appreciates all of your support and cooperation
which you have extended to our agency during the last year," Bensinger wrote,
wishing Noriega "very best regards for a happy and successful new year." The
DEA sent Noriega letters of encouragement known as "attaboy" letters, up
until just a few years before the invasion.

In August 1981 Panama's de facto dictator Omar Torrijos died in a plane crash that has still not been fully explained. Within a few years Noriega and two other officers ousted Rubén Darío Paredes del Río, who had eventually succeeded Torrijos as commander of the National Guard. Noriega soon had total control over the guard, which rebranded itself as the Panamanian Defense Forces (PDF). For the next five years Noriega dominated all aspects of Panamanian life. Having no need to appoint himself president, Noriega instead allowed political figures to fill the post, lending a veneer of democratic legitimacy to his rule.

About the same time Noriega was cementing his rule, Colombian cocaine traffickers were ramping up their presence in Panama. After taking heat from the Colombian government for killing the Colombian justice minister Rodrigo Lara Bonilla in 1984, the drug lord Pablo Escobar's Medellín organization left en masse for Panama, a relocation of over one hundred persons: "accountants, bodyguards, lawyers, and families." The Medellín Cartel's ties with Noriega ran deep: over the previous few years the cartel had being paying him hundreds of thousands of dollars every time a cocaine-laden plane used an airstrip in Panama. When the Medellín trafficker Jorge Ochoa was arrested a few months later, he and his family were traveling with Panamanian diplomatic passports. The cartel bosses who most needed security and secrecy rented US officers' homes at Fort Amador, which had reverted to Noriega under terms of the Panama Canal Treaties. A few even lived in penthouse suites atop the tony Caesar Park Marriott Hotel.

Escobar's decision to relocate was made easier by the fact that Noriega owed him a favor. In 1983 Escobar and Noriega had agreed that the Colombian would construct a huge cocaine lab in the El Sapo mountains of Panama, in the inhospitable Darién region adjacent to Colombia. But then Noriega, in true duplicitous form, informed the DEA and, mustering the PDF, raided the lab. Some twenty-one cartel members wound up in jail. A furious Escobar threatened to murder Noriega if he didn't make amends, and Noriega took the threat seriously.

Washington Wakes Up

In mid-June 1986, as Noriega received an award from an official US hemispheric defense policy think tank, the *New York Times* ran a long piece chronicling his shady dealings. It suggested that Noriega was behind the grisly 1985 killing of Hugo Spadafora, a fierce critic of Noriega, and implicated the commander in drug trafficking. For so long an asset to US national security, Noriega quickly became an embarrassing liability for Reagan, making the president appear muddled on the big issue of drugs and drug trafficking. The Reagan administration began considering its options for getting rid of Noriega. As a first step, in 1987 Reagan imposed economic and military sanctions on Panama. Congress was also becoming increasingly concerned about how instability would affect the planned turnover of the Panama Canal to Panamanian hands in 1999. The Massachusetts liberal freshman John Kerry and conservative North Carolina Republican Jesse Helms used Senate hearings to ring the alarm bell on Noriega's criminal misdeeds. As an aide to Helms stated in July 1986, "We want to turn the canal over to a viable, stable democracy, not a bunch of corrupt drug runners."

On February 5, 1988, the crisis over what to do about Noriega received fresh impetus when two separate grand juries in Florida announced indictments against him, contending that he had helped the Medellín Cartel traffic two tons of cocaine through Panama in return for a payment of $4.5 million. According to one of the prosecutors, "In plain language, he utilized his position to sell the country of Panama to drug traffickers." But, critically, the United States did not have an extradition treaty with Panama, which meant there was no ready legal mechanism to get Noriega to Florida. Still, Reagan signed an executive order slapping further economic sanctions against the Noriega regime, sanctions that would subsequently be extended by the incoming Bush administration. The sanctions were not entirely leakproof, however, as many US corporations were easily finding ways to maintain their business with the Noriega regime. Panama's gross domestic product did fall by 17 percent in 1988 and 8 percent in 1989, prompting Reagan's national security advisor, Colin Powell, to announce that the sanctions were having a "telling effect." But while the sanctions certainly hampered Panama's economy, Noriega was buoyed by seemingly limitless drug revenues. Critically, he was able to continue paying his fifteen thousand PDF members, the key factor in his political survival. Immune from extradition, Noriega responded to the indictments with his usual scorn, calling them "a joke and an absurd political movement."

In what was widely seen as a poorly coordinated policy gambit, on May 11, 1988, the Reagan White House stated that the indictments against Noriega would be dropped if the strongman retired from power. Illustrating how acute America's preoccupation with drugs had become, Capitol Hill was almost uniformly opposed to the idea, seeing as it would amount to a unilateral surrender on the hot-button topic. Accordingly, on May 17, the Senate passed a nonbinding amendment stating that no US negotiations with Noriega should "involve the dropping of the drug-related indictments against him." Senator Robert Dole (R-KS) criticized Reagan's offer to Noriega, stating that the White House was sending the wrong signal on drugs: "We have said that under certain circumstances we'll negotiate with leniency for those who are responsible, directly or indirectly, for the addiction and death of our children." Senator Pete Wilson (R-CA) opined that negotiating with Noriega was akin to "[cutting] a deal with the devil." By the end of May the White House quietly withdrew the offer. But Vice President Bush, in a tight election campaign against the Massachusetts Democrat Michael Dukakis, was vulnerable on the drugs and thugs in Panama issue, and Dukakis bashed Bush for his supposed longtime connection to Noriega: "How about telling us who in this administration was dealing with Noriega. Who was paying Noriega? Who was ignoring the fact that we knew he was dealing in drugs and making millions and we're still doing business with him?"

With Noriega still firmly in control and sanctions not producing the desired effect, a split emerged within the administration during the summer and fall of 1988 about how to proceed. The State Department believed that a more muscular approach was needed and that Washington should start considering a plan for a military intervention, namely, a commando-style raid, to nab Noriega. The Pentagon, on the other hand, was more cautious, as the generals worried that a military operation could easily lead to a hostage situation. According to one White House official who participated in the discussions, "The diplomats wanted a muscular military policy. The soldiers, who would have to do the fighting, wanted negotiations with Noriega."

Things Fall Apart

By mid-1988 the United States was involved in a low-intensity conflict with Noriega's forces. From February 1988 to May 1989 more than six hundred incidents involving harassment of US civilians and troops were reported, including several instances in which US servicemen were detained and beaten. US policy makers were becoming concerned about the potential for a Tehran-style hostage situation. Exacerbating concerns, the CIA had supported numerous attempts to oust Noriega to no avail.

In 1989 the newly inaugurated president, George H. W. Bush, faced a difficult situation. Among his first acts as president was the approval of several covert operations against the Panamanian strongman. He also supported Congress's move to transfer $10 million through NED to opposition groups and candidates who were planning to run against Noriega's handpicked candidate in the May 1989 presidential elections.

That election unfolded amid rampant fraud, protests, and violent attacks by PDF so-called Dignity Battalions against opposition candidates and their supporters. They culminated in Noriega's annulling of the election and the installing of his crony Francisco Rodríguez as president. Echoing his fellow Republican Teddy Roosevelt from the other end of the century, Bush responded by declaring that the United States "will not recognize or accommodate a regime that holds power through force and violence at the expense of the Panamanian people's right to be free." Ambassador Arthur Davis was immediately recalled, and Bush ordered an additional two thousand troops to Panama, a move that was only reluctantly agreed to by the Joint Chiefs chairman William Crowe. Bush then announced a seven-point plan intended to remove Noriega through a combination of pressure and incentives. The points included greater regional diplomacy with the OAS, more diplomatic and economic sanctions, and preventive measures such as encouraging US companies to send dependents back to the United States. Save military intervention, Washington was pulling out all the stops.

Throughout 1989 the Policy Coordinating Group of the National Security Council met regularly to discuss Panama policy. There was a growing sentiment that more forceful action was needed. While some top officials still preferred no operation at all, a full-scale invasion was gaining traction. Pressure mounted that October, after a military coup failed and Noriega narrowly escaped with help from the elite PDF force Battalion 2000. The three months following the revolt were by far the most intense in US–Panama relations since the public feud with Noriega began two years earlier. In early November Bush approved an additional $3 million to fund covert operations in Panama, though he blocked the CIA from attempting to assassinate Noriega. Noriega responded to the coup by cracking down on domestic opposition. Political opponents were jailed, tortured, and killed. American and PDF troops frequently traded shots inside the Canal Zone.

Then, in a surprise move on December 15, Noriega removed Rodríguez as president and installed himself as the "Maximum Leader of National Liberation." Noriega then declared before the Panamanian legislature that Panama was in a state of war with the United States. Wielding a machete, he opened his speech with a "word of praise and thanks to the just and merciful God of the universe, as Jehovah, as Allah, as Yahweh, as Buddha, as the universal conscience of the soul." He claimed that US military forces had "launched psychological attacks and have carried out a plan to poison minds by inventing all sorts of lies and trying by every means to win the minds of the weakest. We have resisted, and now we must decide to advance in our land to strengthen our internal front to improve our resistance and advance toward an offensive of creativity and development in the generational project of the new republic. . . . Render unto Caesar what is Caesar's, to God what is God's, and to the Panamanians what is Panama's."

The Invasion of Panama

On December 17, 1989, a day after Noriega's forces had shot and killed an unarmed US soldier in the Panamanian capital, President Bush called a meeting with his senior advisors to decide among three military options. Bush apparently ended the meeting with the words, "This guy is not going to lay off. . . . It will only get worse. Ok, let's do it." Two days later a full-scale invasion, Operation Just Cause, was ready to go.

Just Cause had several objectives: protect US lives and installations; capture Noriega and eliminate the PDF; replace Noriega's regime with the democratic government of the likely winning democratic candidate from that May's jilted presidential election, Guillermo Endara; and rebuild the Panamanian military.

The invasion began in the early morning of December 20, with Special Forces attacks and bombing runs on key PDF installations. By daylight ten thousand American troops had joined the others already in the combat zone. The Americans secured the US embassy and overran the PDF headquarters on the first day. All told, 23 American soldiers were killed and 323 wounded; around 300 PDF troops were killed. Though two days of chaos and widespread looting in the capital followed, the relative ease of the military operation enabled Joint Chiefs chairman Colin Powell to focus on the political side, installing Endara and eliminating the PDF. On December 22, the 96th Civil Affairs Battalion landed in Panama with the task of establishing a police force, distributing emergency food, and supervising Panamanian contractors cleaning up the city. It was also charged with the sensitive task of spurring "grassroots" efforts into action to sell the Endara government to the Panamanian public. On December 22 Endara formally abolished the PDF and announced the creation of an organization called the Panamanian Public Forces.

At this point, however, the American command faced one particularly acute embarrassment: US forces had still not located Noriega. The fugitive had learned of the invasion while spending the night with a prostitute at a hotel near Panama City and fled. Over the next five days more than forty Special Forces operations across the country were conducted to apprehend Noriega. All of them failed, even after the Bush administration placed a $1 million bounty on Noriega's head.

Then, on Christmas Eve, officials at the Vatican embassy in Panama City sent a car to meet Noriega at a secret location and bring him back to the embassy. The deposed strongman appeared to have decided that an attempt at political asylum was his last hope to escape a prison cell in the United States. Noriega entered the embassy dressed in running shorts and a T-shirt and carrying two AK-47 rifles. When Defense Secretary Dick Cheney was informed that Noriega had just surfaced at the Vatican embassy, he apparently told Powell to not "let that guy out of the compound." The State Department immediately contacted the Vatican in Rome and requested that it not grant political asylum to Noriega. But US officials were unable to broker a deal with Vatican officials to secure Noriega's peaceful transfer to US hands.

Over the next week a surreal scene unfolded outside the compound. The US commander on the ground, General Max Thurman, ordered rock music— songs such as "I Fought the Law (and the Law Won)" and "Voodoo Child"—to be blasted at the embassy around the clock. Panamanians congregated to shout slogans against Noriega—"Death to Hitler" or "Justice for the Tyrant"—and to hand flowers to Americans keeping watch. After spending more than a week in the embassy, Noriega was finally convinced by Papal Nuncio Monsignor José Sebastián Laboa that his only option was to give himself up. On January 3 Noriega, dressed in his military uniform and carrying a Bible, emerged from the embassy. US troops immediately apprehended him and put him on a plane to the US. Significantly, it was not military but US DEA agents who escorted the strongman to Miami.

On the flight Noriega is reported to have given his autograph to several of the US agents. But that same night Noriega's critics were relieved to have their infamous dictator shipped out, with thousands of celebrating Panamanians packing the six-lane Calle Cincuenta in Panama City. Just days before the invasion this extradition might not have been a viable move, owing to the 1878 Posse Comitatus Act, a law that forbade US military personnel from conducting police work in either the US or abroad. However, a few days before the attack the administration had released a "clarification" that allowed the military to arrest persons overseas who were wanted under a US warrant. As it turned out, this small jurisprudential edit would become a core part of US counternarcotics strategy in Latin America over the coming decades.

Invasion or Liberation?

Bush's reputation as a weak foreign policy president vanished overnight. Some eight out of ten Americans supported the invasion, and his approval rating stood at a whopping 76 percent, one of the highest for a president since the Vietnam War. The Panamanian people were even more enthusiastic, with 92 percent supporting the invasion. During his visit to Panama in late January 1990 Vice President Dan Quayle was greeted by shouts of "Viva Quayle" and signs reading "Gringos Don't Go Home. Clean Panama First." Bernard Aronson, Bush's top envoy for the Western Hemisphere, quipped that in post-Noriega Panama "you could feel a sense of liberation in the air." The newly installed President Endara, who had been beaten nearly to death by Noriega goons during the marred May 1989 elections, told a US television anchor to think of the operation as "more a liberation than an invasion. After seeing the paramilitary organizations working and the more than 80,000 arms that Noriega distributed among his cronies and thugs, I am convinced now that U.S. action was necessary for establishing freedom and democracy in Panama. Without U.S. help, we couldn't have done it ourselves. This is the opinion of a very, very high percentage of the Panamanian people. We are thankful to the United States."

Despite the strong support within the United States and in Panama, the invasion came under withering criticism, largely from the political left at home and globally. The UN General Assembly condemned the invasion in a 75–20 vote, with 40 abstentions, forcing the United States, Great Britain, and France to use their vetoes to block a resolution. An OAS resolution "deeply regretted" the invasion and called for an "immediate withdrawal" of foreign troops. Writing two years after the invasion, the former Costa Rican president and Nobel Peace Prize winner Óscar Arias wrote that the invasion brought back memories of the Big Stick policy and that the United States "must learn that the use of force is never a good substitute for the strength of reason. . . . They must realize that war and intervention produce no winners, and that constructive and lasting relations cannot be based upon mistrust and resentment."

On Capitol Hill, Senator Ted Kennedy (D-MA) argued that the United States "roam[s] the hemisphere, bringing dictators to justice or installing new governments by force or other means. Surely, it's a contradiction in terms and a violation of America's best ideals to impose democracy by the barrel of a gun in Panama or any nation."

Similarly, the *New York Times* editorial board concluded in January 1990 that "except for the death, destruction, and diversion it brought, 'Operation

Just Cause' was as phony as its name." It added that if Bush had "kept his cool" and acted more like the reformist Soviet premier Mikhail Gorbachev "vis-à-vis his former satellites in Eastern Europe—General Noriega would sooner or later have been overthrown by his own people." The notion that the Panamanian people would have eventually removed Noriega gained increasing credence among critics of the invasion. Michael Massing wrote in the *New York Review of Books* that "a policy of disengagement might enable General Noriega to hang on to power longer than would otherwise be the case. But such a strategy, by leaving Panama's political future to the Panamanians themselves, would provide a much more solid foundation for the development of democracy. And, not least, it would leave intact the principle of non-intervention."

The US investigative television program *60 Minutes* ran a segment on the Pentagon's supposed cover-up of civilian deaths. The military brass stated that four thousand civilians had been killed, but other groups put the number at eight thousand. The documentary *Panama Deception,* which won the Academy Award for best documentary, reported that thousands of civilians were killed, far more than the official US count. Some Panamanian residents claimed that the US troops used weapons with lasers that made its victims disappear.

An exhaustive 1992 report by the Investigations Subcommittee of the House Armed Services Committee concluded that a very large proportion of the "civilian dead" were in fact members of the pro-Noriega Dignity Battalions, which helped explain the fact that only 13 percent of the dead civilians were women and children. Working with numbers provided by various independent human rights organizations, the report estimated that the total civilian dead, including Dignity Battalion members, was around three hundred, and a reasonable estimate of the numbers of "innocent bystanders" killed during Just Cause was "almost certainly less than 100." In hindsight we see that the Pentagon provided the most accurate statistics for civilian deaths during the invasion. In fact, it overreported them.

End Game

The Bush administration wanted the invasion to be considered a victory in the war on drugs. William J. Bennett, Bush's drug czar, told reporters that Panama "has been used as a sanctuary, a vacation spot, a banking center for traffickers, a place to go when the heat is turned up. I believe Panama is unlikely to be used in that capacity in the future." However, the subsequent three decades have revealed that the impact of the invasion on the drug supply reach-

President George H. W. Bush on a telephone call regarding the invasion of Panama, December 20, 1989. Standing with him in the Oval Office Study are (*left to right*) National Security Advisor Brent Scowcroft and Chief of Staff John Sununu. (Everett Collection Inc. / Alamy Stock Photo)

ing the US was negligible; the devastating blow to the international drug-trafficking business that Noriega's removal was expected to deliver never came.

On Thursday, January 4, 1990, Noriega appeared before a federal judge in Miami and was charged with narcotics racketeering. On July 10, 1992, he was given a forty-year prison sentence but was released for good behavior after seventeen. The former tyrant was extradited to France in 2010, where he was convicted on drug charges and sentenced to seven years. But then, in late 2011, he was extradited back to Panama—and into custody. Released in early 2017 owing to a diagnosis of a brain tumor, Noriega was placed under house arrest and, at the age of eighty-three, died on May 29, 2017.

There are valid criticisms of the Bush administration's invasion of Panama. Was the Bush team out of line in using overwhelming military force to remove a "two-bit thug"? Would a massive invasion have been necessary if Washington had not spent millions of dollars supporting Noriega's dubious

US marshals' mugshot of the apprehended Manuel Noriega. Florida,
circa January 4, 1990.

Alternatives?,

intelligence network for over two decades? Even if there was indeed as great a
threat to US assets as the Bush team perceived, the administration could have
ordered a massive show of military force inside the Canal Zone to let Noriega
know that the United States would not be intimidated; it could have maintained or strengthened the economic sanctions it levied in early 1988; it could
have attempted a commando-style raid to snatch Noriega; or it could have
done nothing.

While such counterfactuals are intriguing, it is impossible to say how they
would have panned out. Two aspects of the actual invasion, however, are par-

ticularly noteworthy and lead to a broader understanding of the evolving US posture toward Latin America in the dying days of the Cold War. First, the United States did not exploit its dominant role in the country to reshape matters according to its own interest, as it had done before. The US did not attempt to change the Torrijos–Carter Treaties signed in 1977 and handed the canal over to Panama on December 31, 1999, as stipulated. The second is that tackling the scourge of drugs, real or otherwise, had replaced the Cold War focus of the US on communism as the leading driver (or excuse, in the view of critics) of its relationship with Latin America.

31 · The Washington Consensus Goes South

In the midst of the Cold War it was easy to overlook any sort of US economic policy toward Latin America. Washington's ongoing anticommunist security efforts certainly dwarfed any concerted emphasis on economics, such as trade integration. What is more, the period between the 1950s and late 1980s was a time when Latin American governments looked inward, in accordance with the prevailing economic (and Marxist) orthodoxies of the day. During these years Latin America often avoided dealing with the United States in the economic realm; instead, they placed restrictions on imports in order to spark domestic industries, an economic philosophy known as import-substitution industrialization (ISI). With the glaring exception of Chile following Pinochet's takeover in 1973, ISI dominated Latin American economic policy during the Cold War.

The prevailing economic strategies of the era argued that the region's position on the "periphery" in the Global South, as opposed to the core of the Western industrialized North, ensured that Latin America would grow poorer while its northern neighbors became richer. Latin economies, therefore, could not afford to let their fortunes be decided by some invisible hand; rather, governments needed to steer the economic ship through exchange rate management, import tariffs and quotas, and investment in state-owned industries. But while ISI saw initial success and some sustainable gains, notably in the larger economies such as Brazil, the path was not ultimately fruitful for most economies. Mired by regionwide overborrowing, inflation, and massive unemployment, the ISI of the 1950s–1970s paved the way for the supposed lost decade of the 1980s. The region's economic malaise drove a robust debt-reduction initiative promoted by the administration of George H. W. Bush (1989–93), effectively marking a new beginning in Washington's economic policies in the Western Hemisphere as it expanded into the vacuum left by the spectacular fall of the Soviet Union.

Part of the Bush administration's motivation for getting involved in the region's economic matters was financial: bankrupt countries were unable to pay back loans owed mainly to US banks. The Bush team also realized the tremendous social cost this debt crisis was having on the newly hatched democratic governments in the region. Known as the Brady Plan, this policy initiative was innovative in its explicit acceptance of the argument that what Latin America needed in the late 1980s was debt relief, not just fresh loans. All told, the Bush administration provided almost $50 billion in collateral support as part of the debt-reduction strategy, a campaign widely considered to be successful in bringing relief to the beleaguered region.

Washington Consensus: A New Dawn?

If the 1980s was the lost decade, the 1990s was the decade of the so-called Washington Consensus, which still is widely understood as promoting the neoliberal, free-market policies that characterize Western capitalism. The actual definition of the Washington Consensus has, however, been much disputed: the term was coined originally in 1989 as a way of describing a series of economic reforms that were already taking place in Latin America, including a commitment to reduce budget deficits, broaden the tax base, and privatize state enterprises. It was not intended, as was frequently believed to be the case, to be a recommendation or US-led imposition of a set of free-market policies on its southern neighbors.

Indeed, as the 1994 Miami-hosted Summit of the Americas general agreement over free trade initiatives indicated, at times it was Latin American leaders who were pushing Washington on free trade agreements or the privatization of state-owned enterprises. Many of these "technocratic democratic" leaders had been educated in US universities and were unapologetic proponents of free-market economics. The presidents Carlos Salinas de Gortari of Mexico, Carlos Menem of Argentina, Fernando Henrique Cardoso of Brazil, and Alberto Fujimori of Peru all aggressively implemented the broad tenets of the Washington Consensus.

In some ways the US often played more of a secondary or indirect role in promoting free-market policies during the 1990s. Instead, the IMF, World Bank, and Inter-American Development Bank often took responsibility for directly, though not exclusively, promoting market friendly reforms. The IMF's involvement began in earnest during the 1980s, when it became one of the few creditors willing to loan money to the region after Mexico's stunning debt default in 1982. The inevitable quid pro quo for the fresh loans required Latin American borrowers to implement severe "structural adjustment" programs intended to bring their often-unsustainable fiscal deficits into balance. This form of bitter medicine was highly controversial. Critics accused the IMF of forcing the Latin American governments to cut critical social spending programs—during a recession no less—in order to balance their budgets; supporters countered that the IMF was only responding to a crisis, not creating it, and that "conditionality" was critical in order to prevent future crises. Some observers argued that while the IMF appeared to be independent, it was effectively controlled by the White House and Western financial interests.

Although the Washington Consensus had its critics, the early 1990s was undoubtedly a time of faith in the power of free-market economics in the US and Latin America. One of the landmark achievements in bilateral relations during this time was the North American Free Trade Agreement (NAFTA).

NAFTA: Location! Location! Location!

NAFTA marked a radical departure from traditional policy in Mexico, which for more than a century had been highly suspicious of any sustained integration with the Colossus of the North. The idea of a US–Mexico trade pact had first been conceptualized in the 1980s, but it took the efforts of the aggressively protrade president Salinas to turn the idea into a reality. The technocratic, US-educated Salinas had concluded that his country's economic future lay not in economic isolation but in deep integration with the massive US market. Mexico, he reasoned, needed to use the "comparative advantage" of its privileged geographic position next to the US in order to launch it into the age of globalization. Salinas duly proposed the idea of a Mexico–US free trade agreement in the spring of 1990. Even though it had already negotiated a trade pact with Washington, Canada soon joined the talks, making the trilateral NAFTA. The Bush administration negotiated the agreement, which was signed just before Bush left office, leaving the daunting task of guiding NAFTA through Congress to his Democratic successor, Bill Clinton.

During much of the 1992 election campaign it was unclear whether Clinton intended to support NAFTA, especially given that labor unions, a key electoral base, vociferously opposed the pact. But he clarified his position in a noted speech in October 1992, saying, "In the end, whether NAFTA is a good thing for America is not a question of foreign policy. It is a question of domestic policy." Accordingly, he promised to support side agreements on labor and environmental standards. After assuming the presidency, Clinton decided to make NAFTA one of his biggest priorities. This move surprised observers, who felt that the new (more liberal!) Democratic president would attempt to ignore the treaty. Yet, as a "new Democrat" in this post–Cold War era of globalization, Clinton boldly pursued the agreement, knowing full well that the major obstacle to approving this trade accord lay not with the opposition Republicans but with his own party. The blue–green coalition of labor and environmentalists opposed the agreement because it believed NAFTA would export jobs southward and harm the environment in both countries, in spite of labor and environment side agreements. Clinton invited former presidents Bush, Ford, and Carter to the White House for the signing of the side agreements to show that NAFTA was not a narrow political or partisan concern but rather a treaty in the nation's best interest.

Perhaps the biggest breakthrough for the Clinton White House occurred when Vice President Al Gore and the former 1992 presidential candidate Ross Perot debated the merits of NAFTA on the *Larry King Live* television show. Millions of Americans tuned in to watch this verbal exchange between the two politicians. Arguing that NAFTA would hurt the US economy, Perot famously made his point metaphorically by predicting a "giant sucking sound" of US jobs heading for Mexico. But Gore out-debated him, promoting the administration's claim that the trade deal would be a plus for the US economy, especially in terms of job creation. The treaty ultimately was most contentious in the Democrat-controlled House of Representatives, where it passed by 234–200 in November 1993. Clinton received the backing of 132 Republicans on the vote, but just 101 members of his own party showed their support. The subsequent vote in the Senate was not as contested; the treaty passed by a vote of 61–38.

NAFTA achieved the remarkable feat of bringing 360 million people together in a legislated free trade zone that spanned from "the Yukon to the Yucatan." While critics howled that the trade pact was going to be catastrophic for the US, it did serve to bring the US even closer to Mexico, its historically "distant neighbor," in what some considered a seminal step toward a more equitable and conscientious partnership. But the treaty's difficult birth had deep implications: the free trade impulse in the US that began with NAFTA slowed dramatically after its ratification. In many ways the agreement represented the high-water mark for the liberalized trade policies of the United States toward Latin America during the 1990s.

Storm Clouds: Mexico, 1994

In the immediate post–Cold War period Wall Street and the US government touted Mexico's market economic policies as a model for the developing world. Indeed, to many international bankers Mexico appeared to be on the verge of an economic breakthrough, the landmark NAFTA pact being only the latest signal that Mexico's economy had come of age. What is more, Mexico's legions of savvy, Ivy League–trained, English-speaking technocrats reassured international investors and US government officials that the Mexican economy was a sound investment and that the government had finally left behind its economic bad habits, such as excessive state ownership of industry. A liberalized capital account facilitated a frenzy of foreign investment, Mexico receiving a fifth of all capital flows heading toward emerging markets.

Yet 1994 was the year of living dangerously for the Mexican people and government, and the country's shaky finances were only the beginning of the problem. On January 1 the ski-mask-wearing Zapatistas declared the beginning of their far-left insurrection and dramatically descended on provincial towns in the southern state of Chiapas. The images of impoverished "Indians" rising up to protest against injustice and neoliberalism (including NAFTA, which came into effect that same day) instantly became an embarrassment for President Salinas. As Mexico descended into a flurry of political scandals and assassinations, financial analysts began to question the country's putative entrance into the elite club of industrialized economies. As Mexico's "country risk," a valuation of financial risk that includes political factors, crept upward, both domestic and international investors began, mostly quietly, to sell Mexico.

At this time Mexico was committed to a fixed exchange rate of about three pesos to the US dollar. Given Mexico's long history of exchange rate volatility, the fixed exchange rate was intended to provide both the Mexican public and foreign investors more certainty about the currency's long-term stability. Capital outflows began to put pressure on the exchange rate, but Salinas's governing party, the PRI, had little desire to see the peso devalued, as that would spark a surge in inflation and dollar-denominated debt, given that presidential elections were scheduled for July 1, 1994.

By December 1994, though, the devaluation of the peso had become all but inevitable. The Bank of Mexico, Mexico's central bank, had bled billions of dollars of foreign reserves in its efforts to prop up the currency, leaving it with a paltry $5 billion. Yet to be seen, however, was which presidential administration would see this devaluation occur. Historically, the PRI had tended to devalue the peso right as a president was leaving office, thereby allowing the incoming president to blame the economic mismanagement and resulting ills on his predecessor. But this time around the outgoing president, Salinas, had his eye on becoming the head of the newly created World Trade Organization (WTO) and thus held up the façade in part to facilitate a smooth transition. Freshly inaugurated on December 1, the new president, Ernesto Zedillo, was left holding the "hot tamale" when just days into his term Mexican authorities devalued the peso by 13 percent. Yet furious selling of pesos continued unabated, depreciating the peso by roughly 30 percent in a single week as the Bank of Mexico stood by helplessly.

Clinton's Bailout

Following Mexico's dramatic devaluation of its currency, attention quickly turned to what role, if any, Washington would play in responding to the unfolding financial meltdown. Given that only a year earlier a seemingly confident and dynamic Mexico had entered into NAFTA, top Clinton administration officials were concerned about the broader economic ramifications—often referred to as economic contagion—that could pull down the economy of the US and other countries in the region.

After diagnosing Mexico's financial predicament as more a question of liquidity than solvency (liquidity is the ability to pay current liabilities with current assets; solvency is whether you have the money at all), the Clinton administration concluded that Mexico required a massive and immediate loan (read: bailout) from the international community. In the administration's estimation, the loan would fill up Mexico's foreign reserves so that it could avoid default, restore confidence, and reschedule its future debt on more favorable terms.

Yet while Clinton administration officials focused on preventing their neighbor's domestic financial crisis from ballooning into a regional financial catastrophe, sentiment on Capitol Hill was less enthusiastic. The Republican Party had achieved a historic midterm win in November 1994, gaining control of both houses of Congress. And since Republicans had campaigned on a smaller government platform, the notion of a multibillion-dollar aid package for Mexico garnered little support.

Interestingly enough, while the Republican rank and file in Congress was opposed to a bailout, the party's leadership supported the White House's plan to ensure that Mexico received the loans. Following the advice of Republican leaders such as Senator Robert Dole of Kansas, the Clinton team decided to tap the little-known Exchange Stabilization Fund (ESF). Established in 1934 to help stabilize the dollar's value, the ESF funds were available to the executive branch without congressional approval. Next, Clinton leveraged roughly $20 billion from the ESF, with contributions from other international donors. Given the US voting power on the board, the IMF quickly offered almost $18 billion for the speedily assembled program, which totaled just under $53 billion. Knowing that critics were likely to claim that the bailout was just throwing good money after bad, the Clinton administration ensured that the package included substantial conditionality, which linked the disbursements to Mexico's adherence to IMF-prescribed economic reforms. In addition, the Mexican government agreed to tie its formidable oil revenues to the loans.

While the bailout may have contributed to so-called moral hazard issues in subsequent years and decades, in hindsight there is a near consensus that the rescue was an extremely effective policy decision, providing a financial life preserver to a country nearing economic Armageddon. With this aid, Mexico rescheduled its debt in order to address the liquidity crunch; only two years later it repaid the entire loan, ahead of schedule and with billions of dollars in interest. Even more important, the Mexican economy rebounded from the crisis with a string of years of robust economic growth and relatively low inflation. Although an initial contagion known as the "tequila effect" spread throughout Latin America, the financial fallout from Mexico's crisis was very likely contained to a greater degree than if there had been no rescue package.

Much to its deep frustration and surprise, the Clinton administration's response to a subsequent and seemingly quite similar currency crisis in Brazil in 1998 had far less success. The Clinton–IMF bailout for Brazil totaled $41.5 billion, but a key difference with the Mexico situation was that Brazil was to get the influx of cash *before* devaluation, while Mexico got it afterward. The logic here was that the preemptive infusion of cash reserves would prop up the *real* and therefore deter investors and speculators, who were betting on devaluation, from continuing to make a run on the currency. In the end, however, the Clinton-led bailout for Brazil not only failed to forestall devaluation but actually financed capital flight as investors cashed out of the *real*. Criticism from both left and right ensued. Liberals once again saw the IMF's and US

Treasury's financial imperialism in action, while conservatives saw the program as a bailout for irresponsible policies.

How to Solve a Problem Like Argentina?

Between 1991 and 1997 Argentina ranked at the top of Latin American economies, with an average growth rate of just over 6 percent. Following the punishing hyperinflation and generalized economic crisis of the 1980s, many Argentines were ecstatic at their country's newfound and seemingly endless economic boom. More than any other figure, the "superstar" economy minister, Domingo Cavallo, embodied Argentina's confidence and dynamism, though critics would also add hubris to his character traits.

Among his many talents, Cavallo was a master at selling to the rest of the world, especially Wall Street investors, Argentina as a stable and lucrative emerging market. Cavallo's reputation was linked to what was at that point the novel, apparently brilliant "convertibility" exchange rate system which linked the peso to the US dollar at one to one. As Cavallo explained, because this currency board system prohibited the printing of money to cover debts, convertibility ensured that Argentine officials would not be able to revert to their old ways of profligate spending. What Cavallo usually neglected to mention was that, while convertibility took monetary policy out of the hands of the Central Bank, it did nothing to prevent the Argentine government from *borrowing* money to meet its obligations. Because Argentina's borrowing continued to soar during the boom years of the 1990s, convertibility became a time bomb waiting to go off. The stable exchange rate and robust economic growth suggested that Argentina was thriving, while beneath the surface the gradually accumulating debt made the magnitude of the inevitable crash even greater.

In hindsight, the massive overborrowing should have sounded alarms both in Argentina and abroad, yet during the boom years few analysts predicted Argentina's dramatic implosion. In fact, Argentina was one of the model emerging markets in which stability combined with high yields to ensure dramatic profits for investors. In addition, the strong bilateral relations between Bill Clinton and his Argentine counterpart, Carlos Menem, reinforced the belief that a Washington Consensus–driven convergence between US and Latin American interests and policies was taking place, with Argentina spearheading the charge.

By the late 1990s the dramatic financial crisis in Asia, combined with currency devaluations in Brazil and Russia, shook the international financial system to its foundations. Triggered by a precipitous decline in Asian demand, the global prices for Argentina's commodity exports fell by 20 percent in 1998. This was of critical concern, given that the commodity exports were a key source of desperately needed foreign exchange that enabled Argentina to meet its growing foreign debt obligations. To make matters worse, the US dollar continued to appreciate during this time, which in a fixed system meant that the peso appreciated as well, causing Argentina's exports to become relatively more expensive—particularly in comparison to its main trading partner, Brazil, whose export market was benefiting from a weaker currency.

By 2000 Argentina's financial situation was grave. The country's now inescapably high debt levels gave investors an extra incentive to move their money out of the country. Fearing devaluation at a time when many believed the international economy could not suffer another one, the Clinton administration supported a robust IMF package for Argentina. Known as *blindaje* (or "armor," for the protection it would give the Argentine economy), the IMF package set aside more than $20 billion, while in return Buenos Aires agreed to a series of policies intended to rein in debt, increase government revenues, and cut government spending. In one more example of controversial IMF-imposed conditionality, Argentina agreed to rigorous austerity measures in return for the loans intended to preserve convertibility. The package bought some badly needed time.

George W. Bush Holds Back

In 2001 the incoming Bush administration expressed little desire to support continued IMF bailouts. High-level officials like Under Secretary of the Treasury for International Affairs John Taylor had no appetite for more welfare for deadbeat countries. In fact, while he was still an economics professor at Stanford University, Taylor had once advocated abolishing the IMF. Moreover, Treasury Secretary Paul O'Neill told Congress early in his tenure that the IMF "had been too often associated with failure." These sorts of comments, O'Neill's in particular, were replayed widely in Argentina and were interpreted by many as a sign of US indifference toward Argentina's economic ills. The situation felt grimly ironic given that Argentina had embraced the Washington Consensus more than any other Latin American country.

The problem was that Argentina's economic situation had not improved, and it was clear that the government would not be able to meet IMF targets. In spite of another IMF injection of resources in August 2001, in December of that year it cut off the tap, and the Argentine government was forced to implement capital controls to halt the flight of deposits from the banking system. Dubbed the *corralito* (little corral), it drastically restricted Argentines' access to their bank accounts, sparking political, social, and economic chaos in the country. Cavallo and President De la Rúa resigned amid the unrest, and a month later the acting president defaulted on Argentina's debt and ended the convertability system.

Overnight, Argentines' peso savings were decimated. Once fully interchangcable with the US dollar, peso assets were now worth a fraction of their previous value. By 2002 a quarter of the working population was unemployed and an astonishing half of the population was living under the poverty line. Wealthy Argentines auctioned off their Degas or Gauguin masterpieces. One middle-aged woman walked into a bank, doused herself with rubbing alcohol, and ignited herself. Buenos Aires teemed with *cartoneros* (recyclers) poring through trash in order to find food or something of value. An overwhelming majority of Argentines believed that both the IMF and Washington were largely responsible for the crisis.

In Argentina's presidential elections in 2003 the nationalist and leftist candidate Néstor Kirchner beat his predecessor Carlos Menem, who dropped out of the race upon realizing that he was certain to lose. With Kirchner in office, any notion of friendly relations with Washington and the Bush administration was out of the question. Instead, Kirchner publicly and routinely denounced the IMF. According to Kirchner, his government would refuse to make debt payments "at the price of hunger and exclusion of Argentines," and he proceeded to move forward with the largest sovereign default in world history. Freed by massive write-offs of its debt instruments, the Argentine economy proceeded to recover, assisted by commodity exports. Indeed, Kirchner went head-to-head in debt negotiations with the IMF and Washington and won.

A Fading Vision

During the late 1990s and early twenty-first century, the consensus that drove the aggressive free-market reforms began to crumble. Many citizens of Latin America, after looking around at the still-pervasive poverty and equality, blamed the Washington Consensus; earlier victories such as that in Mexico looked like long-gone flukes. From Mexico to Argentina many of these voters voiced their frustration with the failures of neoliberalism by throwing their political weight behind newly energized left-wing political candidates. New platforms promised a more leftist set of policies that would not sacrifice citizens' welfare for the profits of Wall Street, the US Treasury, or the IMF.

For its part the US had incurred high costs in attempting to bring and subsequently prop up the free-market practices which formed the engine of its capitalist strength. Billions of dollars had been sent south—for little ready return, in some eyes. After the glow had faded, NAFTA proved highly contentious, with Donald Trump making it a target in his 2016 election campaign. It was, he described, "the worst trade deal ever made," and he pledged to renegotiate it if elected (and subsequently did).

That free-market practices and the engagement of the region's brittle economies with the world's finance and trade markets resulted in a series of economic implosions is undeniable. But in this regard there are perhaps two salient questions. The first is whether the policies of the United States, IMF, and other international organizations had a positive long-term impact in bringing Latin American economies into the global marketplace, albeit with tough restructuring reforms that were a shock to many. Or whether the Washington Consensus was, as many critics perceived it to be, a heartless form of capitalism imposed by Washington, the IMF, and the World Bank that sought profits at the expense of Latin America's workers and environment.

In assessing this issue it is important to remember that the United States did not act according to a monolithic set of principles throughout this period but rather changed course from administration to administration. The George H. W. Bush White House was deeply involved in debt reduction in the late 1980s and early 1990s, and the Clinton administration expended sizable political capital to bail Mexico out of the peso crisis in 1994. But the administration of George W. Bush refused to get involved in what it considered a crisis of Argentina's own making in late 2001.

The second question involves looking back to the late 1980s and early 1990s: with communism consigned to the historical trashcan and the West seemingly triumphant, capitalism seemed the only game left in town. It appeared that the world had entered a new era of capitalism-based globalization. In economic terms there was a gap in the ideological market in Latin America, and the West was keen to prove that its model could work. Once unmoored by the collapse of communism, what other route could Latin America have taken? Continue with ISI? The rewards of the West seemed great in the immediate post–Cold War climate, but as Latin America found out, the risks were not insignificant.

FTAA: The Failed Dream of Hemispheric Unity

The inaugural Summit of the Americas, held in Miami in December 1994, was a landmark moment for US–Latin America relations. It was the first time that all of the leaders present had been democratically elected, which resulted in an unprecedented convergence of direction, in the shape of a commitment among the region's governments to push for a hemispheric-wide free trade accord. The Free Trade Area of the Americas (FTAA) was intended to be the forum through which the regional economic integration process would take place. Unlike subregional trade agreements such as NAFTA, the FTAA was anticipated to be all-inclusive—it would obligate its members, thirty-four Western Hemisphere countries, save Cuba, to abide by one agreement. To the Clinton administration the FTAA represented its vision of economic integration in its backyard in the post–Cold War era. The George W. Bush administration supported it as well, although it also proceeded to sign bilateral and/or subregional pacts with Chile, most of Central America, Panama, Peru, and Colombia.

FTAA negotiations did not begin in earnest until 1998, at the second Summit of the Americas meeting in Santiago, Chile. Progress on the pact proved extremely difficult, a reality that was compounded by the actions of Clinton and Bush officials. Part of the impasse was attributable to the actions of two hemispheric heavyweights, Brazil and the US, and their drastically different ideas about how the FTAA should function. In particular, Brazil was eager to see the US liberalize its domestic agriculture sector by cutting farm subsidies. Key Brazilian agricultural goods, such as orange juice, faced stiff competition in the US because of these subsidies, which allowed US growers to sell their crops and related products at artificially low prices.

During the November 2005 Summit of the Americas in Mar del Plata, Argentina, it appeared that the Bush administration had little idea of how it wanted to move forward with hemispheric trade accords. Even though the FTAA had been the hallmark of the numerous US-championed Summit-related ministerial negotiations, it was not clear even at the last hour if trade would be included on the agenda at Mar del Plata. The FTAA was ultimately placed on the agenda, but only after President Hugo Chávez's Venezuelan delegation proposed that the FTAA process be ended. Protestors cheered Chávez at a parallel "people's summit," where the Venezuelan leader told the audience, "Mar del Plata is the tomb of ALCA [the Spanish acronym for the FTAA]. . . . We brought shovels to bury it." By contrast, Bush, responding to an interviewer's question about how he might interact with his Venezuelan counterpart, attempted to remain diplomatic: "I will, of course, be polite."

In the end FTAA negotiations failed to meet the 2005 deadline, sealing its fate. The perhaps unrealistic consensus and hemispheric convergence surrounding the birth of the FTAA in 1994 no longer held in 2006, having been replaced by greater contestation of the (neoliberal) premises embodied in the FTAA. Times had changed, and the dream of hemispheric economic integration had foundered on the unyielding rocks of state interest.

32 • Haitian Tragedy
Act One: George H. W. Bush

After nearly two hundred years of strife and repression Haiti experienced a fleeting moment of democracy between 1990 and 1991 in the shape of the nation's first legitimate elections since independence in 1904. Approximately 68 percent of voters picked Jean-Bertrand Aristide, a former Roman Catholic priest and prominent member of the prodemocracy uprising that had ended Jean-Claude Duvalier's murderous rule, to be their next president. An international team of observers, including the UN, deemed the election to be "open, fair and peaceful." Aristide was sworn in as president on February 7, 1991, but was ousted in a military coup less than a year later.

Yet Another S.O.B.

A brief turn to history is necessary to make sense of the context surrounding Aristide's rise and swift fall. Haiti did not prosper after the nearly twenty-year US military occupation came to an end in 1934. A deep social and economic divide remained between Haiti's tiny group of wealthy mulatto elites and its poor, black majority, causing considerable social tension. In 1957 François Duvalier, a provincial black physician, rose through the tumult to become the Haitian president, winning a considerable, though disputed, plurality in that year's elections. "Papa Doc" Duvalier, as he came to be known, soon emerged as a driving force of terror and tyranny in Haiti. His paramilitary militia, the Tonton Macoutes, brutalized political opponents. But in the climate of anxiety generated by the Cuban Revolution in 1959, by the mid-1960s US policy makers had come to regard Papa Doc as a necessary, if unsavory, regional ally against the threat of communism.

Jean-Betrand Aristide during
his first mandate. Port au
Prince, 1991. (Julio Etchart /
Alamy Stock Photo)

Duvalier remained in power until his death in 1971, when his son Jean-Claude assumed the presidency. Apart from instituting a series of superficial reforms, "Baby Doc" Duvalier upheld his father's tradition of tyranny and lavish personal spending amid unspeakable poverty. Nonetheless, Washington's Cold War mindset led it to pump aid into the country, although tensions rose when Jimmy Carter's strong human rights agenda took over the White House. The Reagan administration that followed was initially inclined to appreciate Baby Doc's anticommunist stance, but a popular and violent reaction against Duvalier's attempt to make himself President for Life in February 1986 forced Reagan to change track. As Baby Doc fled the island nation for exile in France, it became obvious that the Reagan administration's sustained support of the Duvalier regime had undermined its goals for democracy in the region. The Duvaliers' policy of systematic repression, long endured by Haiti's poor, had created a climate of instability that threatened to allow communism to take root.

Bent on "saving" Haiti at this critical junction, Reagan sent a delegation led by Lieutenant General Henry Namphy to aid the interim National Council of

Government (CNG) in developing democratic institutions, including a new constitution. At first, a lasting peace seemed within reach, but neither Reagan nor the CNG had fully anticipated the impact of Duvalierism's legacy on Haiti's society and politics. As one observer explained, "The government in Haiti under the Duvaliers' regime became a patrimonial system that functioned on a patronage and spoils basis. The government recruited *Tonton Macoutes* to maintain political control and resorted to extortion to meet financial needs. Those who were not part of the Duvaliers' clique were left to fend for themselves. Under Jean-Claude Duvalier, corruption was honed to perfection, and the greed of the elites was more evident."

In fattening cronies and impoverishing the masses, Duvalierism had widened the already immense gap between the wealthy and the poor in Haiti, the consequences of which became evident in 1987 when democratic elections were interrupted by a massacre of dozens of voters. Ex-Duvalierist military officials led the attacks against political opponents, urged on by prominent Haitians who had thrived under Duvalier. The situation initiated a four-year period of instability and violence in which a pattern of democratic elections alternated with violent countercoups, until finally the stage was set for the 1990 vote.

The Aristide Enigma

The 1990 election saw a significant shift in US policy toward Haiti. After decades of supporting the tyrannical Duvaliers and the rapid-fire succession of autocrats who had ruled in their wake, the Bush administration came out in strong support of Haiti's democratic endeavor. With the fall of the Soviet Union, times had definitely changed. No longer preoccupied with the threat of communism, the United States appeared to actually believe in its rhetorical stance of promoting democracy in the region by helping fund the country's first real democratic election.

Yet critics questioned the use of US funds amounting to millions of dollars, particularly in regard to the Bush administration's support of the candidate Marc Bazin. It was another instance of that age-old paradox: how could the United States claim to support democracy while using its sizable economic influence to secure an electoral outcome in line with its own interests? Others wondered if the Bush administration would accept Aristide at all, given that many conservatives in Washington feared that an Aristide presidency would incite further unrest, given his fervent promises to purge the Haitian government of Duvalierists and redistribute the wealth of the country' s elite to its six million impoverished black citizens.

As the results were being tallied the Bush administration remained coy about the polarizing but also domestically beloved Aristide. When questioned about the anti-imperialist candidate, US ambassador Alvin Adams Jr. rejoined that "our interest is in the process, not the outcome" of the vote, although in reality Washington very much preferred Marc Bazin and his Movement for the Installation of Democracy. Ultimately, though, the administration stuck to its stated position when the election results were announced, openly endorsing Aristide as the clear winner.

It did not take long, however, for Bush policy makers to realize that their hunch about Aristide's thuggishness was on target. Rumors and intelligence reports circulated that he was directly or indirectly inciting his supporters to "necklace" their political foes, a heinous act that involved putting burning automobile tires over their torsos. Wanting to diffuse the swelling tension around the White House now that Aristide was president-elect, Bernard Aronson, Bush's assistant secretary of state for inter-American affairs, pledged that the United States would "extend political and financial support" to the incoming Aristide government. But first Aristide had to make it to power: he had not yet assumed office when, in January 1991, the former Duvalier minister Roger Lafontant attempted to stage a coup against the provisional president. Proclaiming, "I'll never deny that I'm a Duvalierist," Lafontant was met by tens of thousands of pro-Aristide protestors demanding that the Haitian army quell his putsch.

That the army swiftly tackled Lafontant's coup attempt appeared to reflect a couple of constructive shifts in Haiti: first, that the army's hitherto dubious fidelity to Aristide was on firmer ground than expected; and, second, that Duvalierism's once viselike grip in Haiti was finally a thing of the past. Washington quickly denounced the coup attempt, and Aristide's swearing in proceeded normally. Within months US worries about Aristide's tendencies began to ebb, during which time the priest, eager for a fresh start with Washington and other key foreign countries as well as global bodies like the UN, ramped down his anticapitalist, anti-Western discourse. His new rhetoric adopted a more placatory tone toward foreigners—and, by extension, toward foreign donors, who would be invaluable in helping build up the impoverished Caribbean island's economy and society.

One manifestation of Aristide's new outlook was the unlikely relationship between the Haitian head of state and US Ambassador Adams. The latter was effusive in his praise of Aristide, asserting that "he has gotten off to a very credible start. The process is well begun." Conversely, Aristide, at a UN conference in late September 1991, was bullish on stability going forward: "Democracy has won out for good," he said. "The roots are growing stronger and stronger."

Yet it was a false dawn. While Aristide's reputation with Bush officials was steadily, and somewhat surprisingly, rising, Aristide faced the implacable opposition of the Haitian elite and armed forces. To them, his soft-Marxist platform of industrial nationalization, land reform, and redistribution of wealth was an existential threat. At the end of this same pivotal month of September 1991, anti-Aristide uprisings that had originated at an army base and police station the previous night broke out into far more menacing revolts in the capital, Port-au-Prince. Mutinying troops seized the presidential palace, captured Aristide, and held him at army headquarters until Venezuelan, French, and US officials could negotiate to save his life. Ambassador Adams escorted Aristide to the airport, while the Bush administration immediately blasted the coup d'état—led by Aristide's erstwhile military chief, General Raoul Cedras—and demanded an immediate halt to violence and Aristide's restoration. At Foggy Bottom US diplomats suspended all military and economic aid until the Cedras military junta relinquished power.

Regional Convergence

The Cedras coup unexpectedly aligned Washington with the region, given that everyone wanted the same thing, namely, Aristide's return. In June 1991 the OAS had passed the landmark Santiago Resolution, which had formalized the member nations' obligation to back democracy in the Americas. The Santiago Resolution required a special OAS convocation to determine a multilateral policy in the event of an unconstitutional overthrow. On October 8, 1991, the OAS Permanent Council convened and, after multiple unproductive deliberations with the Cedras regime, declared an embargo against Haiti and froze assets. To many observers and certainly to the Bush White House this was a crucial moment for inter-American solidarity in the newly emerging post–Cold War global order.

Had the embargo worked as intended, a reassuring case of prodemocracy unity across the region might have taken form. Yet despite his seemingly good intentions Bush was met with withering criticism that the embargo was only harming desperately indigent Haitians. As the economic situation further deteriorated and Cedras appeared as entrenched as ever, some began asking about the possibility of using US military force to "restore democracy." But while a few administration officials mentioned the potential for such action to the press, it never appeared to receive serious consideration at the highest levels of executive branch deliberations. Officials seemed confident that the bite of sanctions would be enough to run Cedras out of the country and into some sort of lavish exile in a third-party country.

Driven by the domestic chaos and economic strife, thousands of Haitians embarked on rickety rafts to reach American soil and plead for asylum there. Bush's response was to double down on the Reagan administration's approach of rescuing Haitian nationals on the open ocean and sending them to the US naval base at Guantánamo Bay in Cuba to have their refugee status determined. But in spite of extra manpower dispatched to Guantánamo, it quickly became evident that the Coast Guard and the camp's facilities were unable to process the thousands of asylum seekers. Bush's approach was also criticized by many human rights groups and members of Congress, such as Representative Charles Rangel (D-NY), who called the policy "racist and discriminatory." These critics contended that the administration was keeping Haitians out because they were black and poor, an especially unfair policy considering its automatic acceptance of political refugees from nearby Cuba.

As refugees kept coming Bush again shifted course: in May 1992 he declared that all intercepted Haitians would immediately be returned to Haiti. By this time more than thirty-seven thousand Haitians had attempted to flee their country. Washington returned nearly two-thirds of them under the new policy, while those remaining were housed in an improvised refugee camp at Guantánamo. The boat people crisis sparked public demonstrations: in September protestors, including the former tennis star Arthur Ashe, staged a rally outside the White House, urging the president to at least grant temporary asylum to the refugees.

While the exodus represented a humanitarian crisis, Bush knew that allowing thousands of Haitian refugees into the United States would not be a popular or economically viable solution to Haiti's democracy deficit. He also hoped that by sending the boat people back he would increase the pressure on the despised Cedras junta. But despite both the embargo and refugee policy aimed at pushing the despot out, Cedras did not budge. Bush's pro-Aristide, regime-change strategy appeared to have failed entirely. Yet Bush would not have to face Haiti's woes much longer. His electoral defeat in November paved the way for a new Democratic president to tackle the crisis: Bill Clinton.

33 • Haitian Tragedy

Act Two: Bill Clinton

Upon taking office in January 1993 President Bill Clinton was immediately confronted with the Haitian dilemma. After sixteen months in power, the Cedras junta was showing no inclination that it would step down, and there was yet another surge of desperate Haitians taking to the seas. As a presidential candidate, Clinton had supported the embargo, but he had also bashed Bush's putative "cruel policy" of repatriating the refugees. And in a stance applauded by liberal Democrats he committed to reversing the practice when he became commander in chief.

Only days into his presidency, though, upon learning that some one hundred thousand Haitians were about to attempt the crossing, Clinton broke his pledge. A week before his inauguration, President-elect Clinton declared that the Bush policy would stay in place for the foreseeable time. "I think this is a policy for the moment," he said, but then added, "I still believe that people who leave their country, come into ours, are entitled to some refugee hearing before being summarily turned back."

Clinton was counting on the fact that the issue of repatriation would become moot once Haiti gained some semblance of stability. In order to shore up domestic support for this embryonic Haiti policy and to quell the punditocracy already critiquing the apparent lack of coherence in his foreign policy, Clinton reiterated his desire to reinstate the deposed Haitian president. "We want to step up dramatically the pace of negotiations to restore President Aristide," he said, stating that the "United States is committed strongly to a much more aggressive effort to . . . over the long run, work with the people of Haiti to restore conditions of economic prosperity." In early June Clinton announced stiffer sanctions against Haiti, including a freeze on all the US assets of those who had done business with the junta and an ultimately successful push for a worldwide, UN-imposed embargo against the country. The Clinton administration balanced these punitive policies with the carrot of diplomatic immunity for Haiti's illegal rulers if they agreed to leave power pacifically. Aristide did not appear interested in any solution that would allow military traitors to govern with him once he was back in office. At long last Cedras indicated that he was prepared to address the ending of the junta and Father Aristide's return.

In early July 1993 Clinton triumphantly announced that, under UN, OAS, and US auspices, Aristide and members of the junta had reached what was being called the Governors Island Accords, after the New York City location for the talks. The outlines of the agreement entailed, inter alia, Cedras's resignation, amnesty for the junta, military modernization and a new police force, and an end to the international sanctions once Aristide was back in office. Just a few weeks prior the UN had slapped a ban on oil deals with Port-au-Prince. Most notably it set a date, October 30, 1993, for Aristide's return.

While some supporters on the left called the agreement a foreign policy success, critics cautioned against premature victory celebrations. Worryingly, a resurfacing Tonton Macoutes faction murdered a prominent Aristide activist on September 12, 1993, after dragging out him of a church service. Yet both sides appeared to be adhering to the mandates, which led the UN to lift sanctions in August. Now all that was left was for Cedras and his thugs to stand down. Could it indeed be an instance where both the Bush and Clinton administrations had worked in a multilateral spirit to check tyranny and bolster "small 'd' democracy" in its backyard?

Harlan County–ed

On October 3, 1993, eighteen US soldiers were killed by an insurgent ambush on the streets of the Somali capital, Mogadishu. One naked body was dragged through the city's dust-choked streets. Along with millions of Americans watching on television President Bill Clinton was despondent about the situation in Somalia; Haiti could not have been further from the young president's mind. Just a week later, though, Haiti returned front and center to Clinton's foreign policy.

Notwithstanding all the evidence suggesting that Cedras would respect the agreement he had struck with Aristide, the Clinton administration dispatched the USS *Harlan County*, carrying two hundred US and Canadian military police and engineers on board, to help facilitate Aristide's new government. On

October 11 the ship prepared to dock at Port-au-Prince when a mob of pro-regime protestors approached, wielding guns and axes and whooping anti-American chants. For an entire day US troops on board were subject to the mob's cries of "Somalia! Somalia!," an ominous warning for what awaited the American forces if they came ashore. Fearing another politically toxic Mogadi-shu, the Clinton administration cancelled the mission within twenty-four hours and ordered the vessel home. Anxious that their own personnel might also find themselves in danger, the UN and OAS ordered all human rights observers to leave the island nation. In response to the *Harlan County* inci-dent, on October 13 the UN Security Council passed a resolution establishing a naval blockade of the island to reimpose the oil and arms embargo.

The retreat was blasted by domestic and foreign observers, who contended that it would only embolden the Cedras regime. This appeared to be the case: on October 14, 1993, Guy Malary, Aristide's newly appointed justice minister, was shot dead in Port-au-Prince. The UN Security Council demanded that member states double down on the blockade, but the momentum was now with the Cedras regime, which critically defied the October 30 deadline for Aristide's return.

Eyeball to Eyeball

Clinton felt boxed in, given the dire situation in Haiti—pro-Aristide activ-ists were having their faces chopped off with machetes—and the domestic furor over his policy toward the island, including his controversial position on the repatriation of refugees fleeing the terror. Congress was beginning to question the effectiveness of multilateral sanctions in Haiti, which appeared to be making the masses even worse off instead of punishing Cedras and his cronies as intended. In a February 9, 1994, statement to the House Subcom-mittee on Western Affairs, Representative John L. Mica (R-FL) cited data indi-cating that the UN sanctions were "doubling infant mortality" and that "little of the aid being sent to Haiti to help the poor is getting through."

At this point Clinton's preference was for a dual approach: prepare for a mili-tary invasion to oust Cedras and reinstate Aristide but also hope that rattling the saber would expedite the junta's decision to get out before the 82nd Airborne would have to be sent in à la Santo Domingo 1965, Grenada 1983, and Panama 1989. Yet as the weeks and months passed with no movement from Cedras, Clinton too acknowledged his government's failings in Haiti, publicly stating in April 1994 that, "we ought to change our policy; it hasn't worked."

Then, in April 1994, came a key development. The African American activist Randall Robinson of the nongovernmental organization TransAfrica went on a twenty-seven-day-long hunger strike. He was reenacting a publicity move that the dancer Katherine Dunham had made to protest Haiti policy when George H. W. Bush was still in office. Robinson lost thirteen pounds in the process but succeeded in getting the Clinton team to agree to interview Haitians on the ocean to determine if they warranted political asylum. President George H. W. Bush's vice president, Dan Quayle, criticized the move, telling ABC News, "This is foreign policy by a hunger strike, and that is not the way to conduct foreign policy."

Clearly fed up, President Clinton concluded it was time to test Cedras's dire warning against interference: "I am the pin in Haiti's hand grenade—if pulled an explosion will occur." In July the Pentagon began training exercises off the coast of the Bahamas. Observers claimed that the practice operations resembled what might happen in the case of an invasion of a "small Caribbean island." The prospect of military action seemed further confirmed when the UN ratified Resolution 940, which called on member nations to form a US-led multinational force and "use all means necessary to restore Aristide." All the signs now pointed toward an imminent US-led invasion with considerable regional and international support.

The Clinton administration worked aggressively in the summer of 1994 to win a UN Security Council Resolution authorizing the removal of the Cedras junta. Security Council votes also called for Aristide's reinstatement and a half-year mandate for a UN Mission in Haiti (UNMIH) that would keep order following the operation. The UN moves also paved the way to enlist personnel from other Caribbean countries to join in the postinvasion police force.

By September the US military had completed its planning for the secretly called Operation Uphold Democracy, to be launched on September 19, 1994, by twenty-five thousand personnel. The assembled force also included members of Caribbean states who joined under UN authority. Clinton informed the nation that the invasion would be limited and specific: oust the junta and halt the violence. These combat troops, he claimed, would be replaced by a UN peacekeeping force that would help establish a stable government in Haiti to pave the way for Aristide's return.

Clinton indicated that the invasion would proceed as scheduled but nonetheless sent a team led by former president Jimmy Carter, Democratic senator Sam Nunn, and former chairman of the Joint Chiefs of Staff Colin Powell to Haiti on September 17. Over a tense forty-eight hours through September 18

Clinton's team gave Cedras two options: he could either leave without a fight or lead his troops against what Powell insisted would be a powerful US-led force. Only after learning that sixty-one aircraft carrying paratroopers from the 82nd Airborne had already departed their air base for Haiti did Cedras agree to hand the presidency back to Aristide and leave the country by October 15. The paratroopers were recalled a little over an hour later when the accord was agreed upon.

Once the hostile invasion force was aborted, the first of fifteen thousand troops arrived the next day to "impose order and smooth the way" for the ex-president's comeback. Cedras kept his word and resigned on October 10, and a triumphant Aristide returned home five days later. All told, this hastily made agreement varied little from the Governors Island agreement, although as Secretary of State Warren Christopher "noted dryly" at a press conference, instead of trusting Cedras there would now be thousands of US troops guaranteeing that the junta did not renege on the deal. As Secretary of Defense William Perry put it, "Our protection will be in our arms, not in trust."

The Hard Part

Clinton worked to uphold the stated goals of the mission, vowing to withdraw all US combat troops that had landed with the multinational force by the end of February 1996. But in order to ensure that Haiti was stable enough for the soldiers to leave, US policy makers needed to tackle the crucial task of training Haiti's police forces, still rife with corrupted elements of the Cedras regime.

A year after the first boots hit the ground, just two thousand combat troops remained, and the force had dropped to around four hundred by March 1996. That month UN mission troops, with mainly humanitarian mandates, took over from the multinational force even though significant numbers of US personnel were part of the new command.

Despite the relative peace following the invasion, neither Haiti's political nor security front looked any better. In the parliamentary elections of June 1995 Aristide's Lavalas Party received an overwhelming majority of the vote. Robert Pastor, a former Carter administration official and an electoral observer from the Carter Center, called the elections "the most technically disastrous" of any he had ever seen. In many areas eligible citizens were kept from voting, and many ballots were soiled or burned. Aside from Lavalas, an all-party coalition rejected the results. Clinton officials pushed for another election round, but the subsequent presidential election in December 1995 was also marred by improprieties, although not the outright fraud seen before. For legions of Haitians the winner, René Préval, was a handpicked successor of Aristide, who could not run again due to the constitutional ban on consecutive terms. An agronomist by training, Préval won an incredible 88 percent of the vote, beating fourteen other candidates. However, as only 15 percent of eligible voters went to the polls, Democracy 101 was proving exceptionally difficult in Haiti. The Clinton administration's claims that the elections were impressive was not an easy sell.

Handholding

After the elections the Clinton administration continued to take a keen interest in Haiti, dispatching the newly appointed secretary of state, Madeleine Albright, to facilitate compromise between Préval and opposition legislators at crucial moments. Within the administration, a senior official under Clinton reflected, "There was no question in anybody's mind that the Clinton administration was absolutely committed to restoring democracy in Haiti."

Inside the Beltway, though, opinion remained split, especially in Congress, as to how the United States should continue to operate in Haiti. After learning of the reports of fraud and ballot tainting in Haiti's 1995 parliamentary election, several Republican members of Congress, many of whom had never trusted the left-wing Aristide, demanded that Clinton withhold aid to the new government. Clinton was unconvinced by their arguments, and Washington, eager to restore democracy and get the hell out of Haiti, pumped in over $500 million in foreign aid in the latter half of the decade. But money, goods, and humanitarian workers alone simply were not enough to address the multitude and severity of Haiti's crises. In the absence of a working parliament, the country could not pass even a budget resolution to coordinate aid-funded expenditures. Préval's dilatoriness in executing key financial reforms caused many multinational lenders and investors to cancel financial packages for Haiti.

Many critics argued that Clinton's haste to extract American troops had prevented the establishment of a stable environment necessary for fair, nonviolent political processes to take place. Others claimed that it was impossible to expect democracy to take root so quickly in a country where it had never existed in the first place. Over the subsequent years Haiti destabilized as its police forces became increasingly corrupt, organized crime syndicates with narcotics connections developed, and human rights violations, including extrajudicial killings, swelled. Opponents of Préval attacked government officials, and violence escalated among rival political parties.

In January 1999 Préval dissolved the Haitian parliament after a political impasse involving his administration materialized. Clinton responded by working with other countries and international bodies to freeze a sizable chunk of economic aid. In stark contrast to the failure of the international economic sanctions lodged against the Cedras regime in 1994, this renewed multilateral diplomatic effort seemed to work. After Clinton offered Préval the carrot of several million dollars to fund new elections in May 2000 the Haitian leader agreed to fresh voting. However, in this new round many international observers reported irregularities, and Aristide's party swept almost all the open seats in parliament.

As the December deadline for presidential elections loomed, and with Préval unable to run again because of the ban on consecutive presidential terms, it soon became clear who would succeed Préval. The ex-president Aristide, once the poster child of democracy and social justice but now a menace to these very ideals—or at least that's what Washington thought—came to the forefront again. Announcing his candidacy months before the election, Aristide won handily with a reported 91.5 percent of the vote, even though turnout was once again well below 25 percent. Most Haitians knew Aristide would win long before the vote. It was clear that building democracy from scratch in Haiti was a monumental task, more prone to backstepping than to sustained progress.

34 • Haitian Tragedy

Act Three: George W. Bush

In January 2001 the Republican George W. Bush was inaugurated president after a contested election against his Democratic opponent, the sitting vice president Al Gore. Only a few weeks after the US election, Jean-Bertrand Aristide—in the phrasing of a British news article, "the slum parish priest once hailed as the democratic savior"—won Haiti's equivalent vote, although his opposition had boycotted the election because they believed the electoral council was biased toward the former pastor. During the initial years that followed, George W. Bush took a back seat in what had become a decade of Haitian affairs, leaving other countries and international organizations like the UN and OAS to do the heavy nation-building and diplomatic lifting. Bush, however, was focused enough on the issue to maintain the freeze on aid to the Caribbean country after Port-au-Prince neglected to address the marred parliamentary elections of 2000. This ostensibly was a stern warning to the Haitian government that its violations of democracy would be met with disapproval.

By 2003 Bush policy makers, now eager to demonstrate that they had not abandoned multilateralism vis-à-vis Haiti, put $2.5 million into the OAS's diplomatic efforts to facilitate reconciliation among Aristide, Haiti's precarious legislature, and the country's myriad political factions. This didn't change the fact, though, that the Bush team was decidedly more reluctant than its predecessors to promote policies that either directly or indirectly bolstered Aristide, who once had looked to so many like a harbinger of democracy. Bush's executive branch officials had worked for Republican members of Congress during the 1990s and were less than keen on the Haitian leader. More specifically, it was an open secret that many individuals in the Bush administration, including the State Department official Otto Reich, were deeply wary of the Haitian leftist head of state and were ready for him to be gone.

Aristide endured more opprobrium later that year when he ordered the arrest of dozens of people implicated in a raid on Haitian police stations and then held them in custody without a warrant. Not to mention the track record he had accrued leading up to the Bush administration's approval of aid. In December 2001 Aristide faced yet another coup attempt when several armed people attacked the National Palace in Port-au-Prince. In response, pro-Aristide mobs took to the streets, vehemently denying that their beloved leader had masterminded the coup as a means to quell civic dissension. Whether Aristide had orchestrated the coup or not, the mobs certainly helped bolster his position by setting fire to the offices of the opposition parties.

Conservatives inside the Beltway saw these developments as categorical evidence of Aristide's increasingly erratic and illegal conduct. They pointed to a heated public address in which he declared a "zero tolerance" crime policy and said that now it was "not necessary to bring criminals to court." Critics asserted that the president's legions of devoted followers were being summoned to armed vigilantism and pointed to the worrying evidence of the nascent Chimères, a gang of thugs that Aristide and his supporters reportedly hired from the slums like Cité Soleil to do their bidding.

Bush policy makers held that providing significant aid to the corrupt Aristide regime would only worsen the deplorable conditions in Haiti. On the other hand, many US liberal politicians and activists criticized the withholding of aid. They claimed that the White House's unwillingness to back the IMF's release of $200 million in funds as well as its cuts in humanitarian relief to Haiti since Clinton's tenure had exacerbated the political and social tumult as much as Aristide's undeniably divisive rhetoric. The liberal critic James Dobbins, who had served as Clinton's special representative to Haiti from 1994 to 1996, suggested that the Bush team had actually thrown its lot behind the anti-Aristide political forces: "This administration continued to provide counsel and moral support to the opposition but . . . provided no assistance to the Haitian government." Bush's repatriation of refugees and authorization to arrest the hundreds of Haitians who arrived on Florida's shores in 2001 was, for these critics, yet more evidence of the administration's unyielding stance at the expense of the nation's destitute citizens.

Another Aristide Exile, Another Military Intervention

In January 2004 the celebrations surrounding the bicentennial of Haiti's independence took place against a backdrop of violent riots and protests in the capital. Police officers and armed gang members reportedly hired by Aristide attacked demonstrators, prompting the United States to condemn the government and push hard for new elections. Increasingly, Haiti began to turn against Aristide. On January 31 several thousand citizens staged a march in the Haitian capital demanding his resignation. The violence worsened as rebels began seizing control of Haiti's cities just weeks later.

In addition to backing multilateral mediation efforts Bush continued pushing for compromise in Haiti. Both Assistant Secretary of State Roger Noriega and Secretary of State Colin Powell attempted speaking directly to Aristide in order to clarify that a solution would not necessarily entail his early departure from office. However, Aristide's opponents would settle for nothing less. Violence increased, and several US marines were deployed to protect the US embassy in late February. Powell, Noriega, and officials from other nations kept pushing compromise, urging Aristide to negotiate directly with the armed rebels who had begun closing in on Port-au-Prince. But with Aristide vehemently refusing to back down, the rebels said there was no chance of a deal.

When the rebels reached the capital, all hell broke loose. With Haiti in pandemonium, US officials began to adopt a new approach, publicly questioning Aristide's fitness to govern and asking him to reexamine his position. Whether in response to American insistence, the chaos outside the National Palace walls, or both, Aristide fled his country on February 29, 2004, heading into exile first in the Central African Republic and then in South Africa.

The US role in the coup was immediately seen as deeply controversial. Charles Rangel (D-NY) criticized the Bush administration for making it "abundantly clear that Aristide would do best by leaving the country," thereby giving the rebels implicit backing for the coup and undermining the rhetorical stance of the United States respecting the rule of law. "We are," Rangel continued, "just as much a part of this coup d'etat as the rebels, as the looters, or anyone else." Aristide agreed. Blaming the Bush administration for Haiti's continued crises, he alleged that US marines had kidnapped him and forced him into exile that February night. Allegations began to fly that the Bush administration had taken an active, if covert, role in engineering Aristide's overthrow, working through democracy-promotion organizations like the International Republican Institute (IRI) to back anti-Aristide groups. US ambassador Brian Dean Curran subsequently stated that Stanley Lucas, the top IRI representative in Haiti, had mandated Aristide's opposition to not cooperate with the Lavalas Party in an effort to cripple the government—an allegation Lucas denied. Nevertheless, to detractors, especially those on the left, these types of actions were definitive evidence that the Bush administration backed only a certain form of democracy, one that fit the administration's neoconservative ideologies and interests. In any case, according to Curran, the charges alone made US policies and goals in Haiti "infinitely more difficult."

Attempts to Stabilize

The same day Aristide left Haiti the UN Security Council adopted a resolution authorizing the deployment of a multinational interim force for three months to create a secure and stable environment in the country. The Bush administration had refused Aristide's requests to send troops earlier that year but now contributed troops to be deployed with the intention of securing Haiti for its transition to an interim government led by Supreme Court Justice Boniface Alexandre.

However, despite American ambassador James Foley's March 2004 pledge that the United States "would not walk away from Haiti before the job was completed," US forces were withdrawn after three months to make way for a new UN peacekeeping force, known by its French acronym, MINUSTAH. Bush committed a paltry $116 million for the first fourteen months of the MINUSTAH, less than 15 percent of the entire budget. Washington's deep involvement in Iraq made a sustained commitment to Haiti problematic, but it was also true that Clinton's generally unsuccessful "soft occupation" of Haiti a decade earlier, which had cost the United States more than $2 billion, was still fresh in the minds of many Washington officials. This precedent added to the tough job policy makers and Bush would have if they tried to justify sending more permanent forces to a country where the United States had few political or economic interests.

MINUSTAH took over in June 2004, arriving just after severe floods in the southern part of the country caused considerable fatalities and property damage. Initially authorized for six months, it numbered eight thousand troops, including a contingent from China, which for some right-wing politicians in Washington was an alarming development worthy of invoking the Monroe Doctrine. Washington now had fewer than a dozen of its own soldiers in-country and had contributed none to the new UN mission, which by September 2004 was still two-thirds short of the number of promised troops.

Provided these insufficiencies, it is perhaps unsurprising that UN forces failed to transform the situation on the ground, and insecurity remained rife in the months following the coup. Observers began to speak of guerrilla warfare taking place between Aristide's supporters and his myriad opposition forces. The UN-led disarmament program didn't gain traction, mainly due to the fact that the UN failed to offer incentives for rebels to hand over their weapons. Making matters worse, the Haitian police force of several thousand proved far too few to stem the savagery; in fact, undermanned Haitian police patrols were reportedly terrorizing the slums of Port-au-Prince. Some officers were executing people believed to be affiliated with the former president. The interim government and Prime Minister Gérard Latortue were criticized for allowing and even condoning such heinous acts.

Préval Prevails Again

Democracy appeared to be a distant goal, but elections were nevertheless scheduled for December 2005. The UN extended the peacekeeping force's mandate until 2006 in order to guarantee that elections took place. The lead-up to the vote, however, witnessed fresh waves of violence and a rash of kidnappings. Pro-Aristide vigilante outfits killed a handful of UN soldiers, and Haiti's under-equipped and understaffed police force were comprehensively outgunned. Several logistical problems, such as the sluggish pace of voter registration, led to the postponement of the elections four times, but finally, on February 2006, Haitian voters went to the polls, electing René Préval to once again be their next president.

The result was not uncontroversial: Haitian electoral officials had nullified 850,000 blank ballots from the count in order to avoid a runoff and to ensure that Préval won more than a 50 percent vote majority. The irregularities galvanized heated protests by numerous other candidates. However, the new president stepped in, asking his supporters to remain calm and to leave violence out of their celebrations. And this time, mostly, they did.

The White House proclaimed the elections a success and wholeheartedly endorsed Préval. Undoubtedly relieved at Préval's willingness to establish a coalition government and to distance himself from Aristide, the United States, as put by Secretary of State Condoleezza Rice, "wants this government to succeed."

The months following Préval's inauguration were a period of unusual political harmony. Préval made gains in promoting the political incorporation of disparate parties by opening parliamentary slots to opposition members. He also qualified Haiti for debt relief under the IMF's Heavily Indebted Poor Countries initiative. Additionally, the IMF, World Bank, Inter-American Development Bank, and the European Union pledged new economic development funding.

USAID signed an understanding with Préval in September 2006 to the tune of just under $500 million over three years.

Scorecard

Haiti's difficulties, however, would not come to a close with the ascension of Préval. Perhaps nothing demonstrates the complexity of the challenge better than the fact that MINUSTAH's mandate, which had originally been for a six-month period, eventually ran from 2004 to 2017. It is difficult to determine the extent to which the Bush administration's indifference contributed to Haiti's tumult. A greater commitment on the ground may have yielded only results similar to those of the UN mission, leaving the political foundations of the country still uncertain. Indeed, unlike Afghanistan and Iraq, the US, it can be argued, was clear-eyed about what it could actually achieve in terms of nation-building in Haiti, and it relied predominantly on multilateral approaches to promote democracy as opposed to unilateral regime change.

The post-2004 history of US involvement with Haiti offers a more nuanced reading of US engagement with its backyard: while the United States has not been the lead international actor, it has not been absent either, and its assistance has been varied in scope, approach, and efficacy. For example, President Obama's secretary of state, Hillary Clinton, oversaw $4.4 billion that Congress designated for Haiti in the aftermath of the catastrophic magnitude 7.0 earthquake of January 12, 2010, that killed at least one hundred thousand people. Recurring natural disasters and continuing political instability have meant these efforts have had questionable benefits.

In taking stock of the long, varied dynamics between the two countries, one sees that the bilateral relationship of the United States with Haiti is among the most complicated in the region. Haiti has experienced military interventions and occupations (1915, 1994, 2004), involvement to both instill then remove Aristide from power, billions of dollars in aid, and even criticisms of neglect during the post-Aristide nation-building years. The case of Haiti confirms the commonly held notion that policy attention is dedicated to Latin America only in times of crisis, resulting in a sense of all or nothing engagement.

35 • Supply Side

Part One: Peru

Although Richard Nixon is well known for declaring "an all-out war on global drugs" in 1973, his motive was overwhelmingly domestic. He had labeled drugs "public enemy number one" in 1971. It was tackling the supply of drugs into the US, however, that led Nixon to develop a subsidiary component of his antidrug program that addressed "source countries" such as Mexico, which produced marijuana and heroin. While there were several agencies working on the drug issue before 1973, Nixon upped the ante with the establishment of the DEA in 1973, a move that consolidated the often-competing efforts of the multiple existing agencies into one federal operation with an annual budget of $75 million and fifteen thousand agents. Approximately a half century later the budget had soared to $2.7 billion, and there were some five thousand agents spread across sixty-three countries.

It would be interesting to know what Nixon imagined "victory" in this drug war might look like. He might have said that a far smaller share of Americans would be dealing and using dangerous drugs like marijuana, heroin, and cocaine; and he would likely be appalled by the huge rise in drug use in subsequent decades. Despite the billions of dollars spent on prevention, treatment, law enforcement, and interdiction, almost 23 million Americans (and 120 million to 225 million globally) between the ages of twelve and sixty-five were illicit drug users by 2015, including 2.5 million youth. Roughly three-quarters of these Americans were using marijuana, but for most of those taking other illicit drugs pot had been their gateway to harder substances.

Despite Nixon's initial foreign interdiction efforts in Mexico, it was only post-1986, when Reagan signed National Security Decision Directive 221, that Washington's supply-side strategy took off in Latin America. The strategy

ranged from smashing cocaine laboratories to extraditing kingpins and tracking money-laundering flows. The renewed political impetus for the drug war
formed in response to the so-called crack cocaine epidemic that began in the
early 1980s and threatened to overrun schools, ruin neighborhoods, and destroy families. First Lady Nancy Reagan launched the Just Say No! campaign in
the mid-1980s, while President George H. W. Bush, echoing Nixon, labeled
drugs as "the gravest threat facing our nation today."

Americans overwhelmingly concurred. One report in February 1990 found
that two-thirds of Americans agreed with the notion that using illegal drugs
solely for intoxication was morally wrong. A similar number were ready to relinquish "some freedoms" to fight the drug epidemic. Writing in the *New York
Times* in 1989, Mark H. Moore, a Harvard professor of criminal justice, set out
a hard-line approach that was indicative of the stance advocated by many: "The
United States is in the early to middle stages of a potentially widespread cocaine epidemic. If the line is held now, we can prevent new users and increasing casualties. So this is exactly not the time to be considering a liberalization
of our laws on cocaine. We need a firm stand by society against cocaine use to
extend and reinforce the messages that are being learned through painful personal experience and testimony."

The Bush official William Bennett, the nation's unofficial "drug czar," was
put in charge of the White House Office of National Drug Control Policy. He
assured anxious Americans that the national rate of drug usage would drop by
10 percent before 1991 and 50 percent by 1999. While drug use rates had in
fact been dropping in the 1980s, they increased dramatically during and beyond Bennett's watch, almost doubling over the next twenty years. Further,
between 1990 and 2007 the street price of cocaine and heroin, which Bennett
sought to drive up in order to deter new users, plunged by up to 80 percent.
The falling prices were not due to reduced enforcement: the DEA's budget
tripled during the same period.

Going Supply Side

The cocaine and crack cocaine epidemic sweeping the US made urgent the
question of how to tackle the supply side. In the 1980s a powerful analogy for
the war on drugs held that if you wanted to get rid of the bees, you needed to
kill them at the hive, not once they scattered. In the case of drugs, the hives
were the poppy, coca, and cannabis fields of Peru, Bolivia, Colombia, and Mexico. Colombia was the source of over 80 percent of the cocaine pouring into

the United States. As major sources of raw coca production, Peru and Bolivia were also critical in the drug supply chain.

In June 1989 Bennett explicitly endorsed the idea of using US military force to take down the Colombian kingpins, most critically Pablo Escobar, headquartered in the provincial city of Medellín. "We should do to the drug barons," Bennett declared, "what our forces in the Persian Gulf did to Iran's navy." Bush himself pushed his military to be part of the strategy, although the Pentagon, chastened by the experience of the Vietnam War, was initially reluctant to get involved in what seemed to be an unwinnable war with an amorphous enemy and undefined goals.

Matters came into sharp focus on August 18, 1989, when the Colombian presidential candidate Luis Carlos Galán, a vociferous campaigner against the Medellín Cartel, was gunned down by cartel hitmen at a campaign event. On August 21 Bush agreed to National Security Directive 18, allocating over $250 million in military, intelligence, and police assistance to fight drugs in the Andean region over the next five years. Soon thereafter Bush doubled down with a $2.2 billion, five-year Andean Initiative intended to produce a "major reduction in the supply of cocaine."

The strategy represented a massive escalation of the militarized supply-side strategy initiated by Reagan. The first two of three pillars entailed a new use of brute force: eradicating coca crops and decapitating the cartels (read: taking out the leadership, also known as the kingpin strategy), which were turning coca leaf into cocaine and smuggling it into the United States. The third pillar took a softer, so-called alternative development approach: the United States would fund programs to help farmers transition from coca to licit crops such as cacao, citrus, or hearts of palm.

In February 1990 Bush visited Colombia and declared, "We have committed ourselves to the first common, comprehensive international drug control strategy." Some experts, however, remained skeptical about the approach, particularly the idea of eradicating the coca crop fields in the Andean region, given that coca could be grown almost anywhere. "Nibbling around the edges of the leaf market is terribly inefficient," said Paul Boeker, a University of California scholar, in 1991. Despite the criticism, not all of Bush's three pillars were questioned. In 1993 Colombian police gunned down the cocaine baron Escobar as he fled from a safe house in Medellín. After his death Escobar became something of an antihero legend in the burgeoning history of the US-led war on drugs, although Mexican kingpins like Joaquín "El Chapo" (Shorty) Guzmán of the brutal Sinaloa Cartel soon garnered an equally mythological standing.

Air Bridge to Nowhere

Until the early 1990s the vast majority of the coca plants grown in Peru and Bolivia were turned into a primary paste and trafficked into Colombia via small planes, a method that became known as using the air bridge. The paste would be processed into cocaine and exported once again, this time to North American and European markets.

The air bridges in the northern Andes became a focus of US counternarcotics strategy in the 1990s. Like that of the equally vaunted kingpin strategy, which held that taking out the drug boss and his "intellectual capital" would critically weaken the whole drug-trafficking organization, the logic of shutting down the air bridge and breaking the production chain was compelling. In 1995 President Clinton signed off on the creation of a CIA-led Air Bridge Denial Program, which resulted in Peruvian air force pilots utilizing CIA intelligence to shoot down dozens of planes believed to have been running drugs. US officials touted the air bridge as a patent success story, but then things went dramatically awry.

On April 20, 2001, Peruvian jets shot down a single-engine Cessna that they had assessed as being an illicit flight. The Cessna had been tracked by CIA surveillance aircraft flown by American contractors, who passed along intelligence to the Peruvian air force, but the intelligence was wrong: it was a civilian flight. Kevin Donaldson, the pilot, suffered grave wounds but still conducted an emergency crash landing. However, the American missionary Veronica Bowers and her infant daughter Charity were killed. Her husband, Jim Bowers, and their six-year-old son Cory were not hurt. A CIA investigation into the event laid blame for the politically sensitive tragedy at the feet of the Peruvian air force. The air force had, the report claimed, "misidentified the plane as involved in drug trafficking and engaged the aircraft over the objections of CIA personnel." At the same time, the report did acknowledge "problems with the program" and noted that more than a dozen CIA officers had received "administrative punishment." The program was suspended and then reopened in 2003 on the Colombian side of the bridge.

While the Bowers tragedy highlighted the fundamental weakness of the intelligence chain in the program, the program's relocation pointed to another, even more unexpected outcome. It had largely succeeded in stopping coca production in Peru, but when the cost of shipping from Peru became too high Colombian traffickers simply started planting coca inside Colombia, particularly in the sparsely populated *llanos* (plains) and Amazon regions to the east. In the parlance of the war on drugs, this was an example of what insiders called the balloon effect: interdict something in one place and watch it pop up somewhere else instead. The relocation of production resulted in a financial bonanza for both the rightist paramilitaries and Marxist guerrillas like the FARC operating in Colombia, who taxed coca plantings and cocaine manufacturing: an example of what is known as policy blowback, whereby a policy leads to unexpected and unwelcome consequences.

Our Man in Lima

On May 11, 1996, local Lima authorities discovered 174 kilograms of cocaine hidden in the fuselage of a Peruvian air force Douglas DC-8 jet. The plane, scheduled to fly to Russia, had been commissioned only weeks earlier by none other than the Peruvian president, Alberto Fujimori. Fujimori, insistent on his innocence, was determined to solve the crime and attempted to convince Peruvians on local television that he would stop at nothing in his search for the truth—"even if generals fall."

A state official involved in drugs was nothing new in Peru; in the years leading up to 1996, 240 Peruvian police officials and 40 military members had been linked to drug trafficking. And so it is unsurprising that the military's own internal investigation went nowhere. Javier Zavaleta, a security analyst, claimed in a Spanish-language daily that Peru's military intelligence eagerly pressured military brass to uncover which officials were scheduled for the now-infamous flight to Russia, but the shipment's sender and recipient remain a mystery to this day.

The breakthrough on the military's involvement came via an unexpected source. Mere months after the military's DC-8 scandal, the notorious drug traffickers Demetrio Chávez "El Vaticano" Peñaherrera and Abelardo Cachique gave government officials a list of three specific generals within their own trafficking network. To effectively gain immunity El Vaticano went further, testifying that he had bribed Peruvian military officials on numerous occasions. And then, stunningly, the existence of a full-woven network came to light when Peñaherrera confessed that he had bribed the de facto chief of the National Intelligence Service (SIN), Vladimiro Montesinos.

Vladimiro Lenin Ilich Montesinos Torres, born in 1946 in the southern provincial city of Arequipa, was the son of devout communists (hence his unmistakable nomenclature). Montesinos gravitated toward militaristic ideals early in his life, graduating as a cadet in 1965, before turning twenty, from the

US Army's School of the Americas in Panama. He graduated from a military school near Lima the following year and by the 1970s had achieved a middle-ranking officer position. It surprised many, therefore, when Montesinos was sentenced to twelve months in prison in 1977, guilty of informing US intelligence sources about a growing Peruvian market for Soviet weapons. After his release in mid-1978 Montesinos started anew in Lima as a private drug attorney with high-level Colombian traffickers among his infamous clients.

These cocaine traffickers and drug peddlers soon paled in comparison to the relationships Montesinos later developed, such as his representation of future Peruvian president Alberto Fujimori in a real estate fraud case. Montesinos capitalized on the opportunity to latch onto Fujimori. He gained entrance to an elite political circle when the unknown Fujimori decided to run in Peru's 1990 presidential campaign, thus bringing Montesinos along. Montesinos took on a more ambiguous role when it was rumored that he had amended Fujimori's birth certificate to prove that he had been born in Peru, not Japan, thereby making him eligible for election. At the polls Fujimori caused a major upset, defeating the world-renowned Peruvian novelist Mario Vargas Llosa. He appointed Montesinos as the head of the SIN soon after, empowering the former attorney with hefty responsibilities, such as overseeing Peru's antidrug cooperation with the US embassy, Washington's conduit for sponsoring the SIN's antidrug unit.

Montesinos quickly made an impact. Although many accused the SIN of carrying out extrajudicial killings and disappearances under his watch, the former military official was instrumental to Peru's victory over the Maoist guerrilla group, the Shining Path. Operating with impunity, Montesinos was further emboldened by Fujimori's April 1992 "auto-coup," in which Fujimori shuttered Congress, suspended the constitution, and invested himself with full authority over matters of state. Montesinos reopened correspondence with the CIA, offering intelligence which "proved to be true, and his reliability was confirmed." Throughout the 1990s the CIA "repeatedly argued successfully" in interagency dialogues (read: the executive branch's policy deliberation process involving multiple government agencies and interests) that Montesinos was a crucial interlocutor with Fujimori's government, overlooking the accusations of the spy head's 1992 extrajudicial murders. One anonymous US official reasoned in an interview with Karen DeYoung of the *Washington Post* that there was a "deliberate decision balancing the nature and severity of the . . . abuse against the potential intelligence value of continuing the relationship." In this case, he contended, the balance favored continuance.

With the Shining Path defeated by the mid-1990s, the Washington–Lima relationship circled back to focus on drugs. By the end of the twentieth century Peru and Bolivia held the infamous title of world's largest exporters of coca leaves and derivatives. Montesinos was, in the words of DeYoung, "seen by many U.S. officials, even outside the CIA, as indispensable to U.S. counter-narcotics efforts." He was "Peru's designated chief of counternarcotics and the only game in town," but he didn't come cheap, costing the CIA at least $10 million by 2000, in addition to "high-tech surveillance" gear gifted to the SIN for drug efforts.

As this tacit relationship grew, however, the doctor, as Montesinos was known in CIA circles, discreetly wove a "vast web" of illicit operations, including graft, gunrunning, and drug trafficking. Unbeknownst to the CIA, Montesinos's clandestine activities earned him $250 million, deposited in Swiss, US, and Cayman Islands banks, where Montesinos may have also deposited CIA cash. As one US official explained, "It was an agency to agency [CIA to SIN] relationship with Montesinos as the intermediary. . . . Montesinos had the money under his control." But despite their suspicions, there was little the US could do if it wanted to maintain an antidrug presence in Peru. Montesinos was "key to Washington's drug war in the Andes." Another official told an investigative journalist that "if we moved against [Montesinos], Fujimori would cut us off and tell us to go home."

By the late twentieth century Montesinos was using the SIN to corral political opponents and the media. His methods, whether bribery, intimidation, or a combination of the two, established hegemony over not only the SIN but also the media, military, and courts. Yet by 1997 concern over Montesinos's questionable track record reached a tipping point: a State Department human rights report cited Montesinos for his previously suspected crimes. Over the next two years the Senate Appropriations Committee "repeatedly expressed concern about U.S. support for the Peruvian National Intelligence Service" and requested a consultation be made "prior to any decision to provide assistance to the SIN."

Ten Thousand AK-47s, Courtesy of Vladimiro

In 1998 Montesinos conducted a piece of business that was outlandish even for him, disguising operatives as military officers in order to procure fifty thousand Soviet-era AK-47 assault rifles from Jordan. The arms landed in the hands of Peruvian authorities in 1999 thanks to the broker, Sarkis Soghanalian, a "rotund arms trafficker and occasional U.S. intelligence informant" who was known to have supplied weapons to dictators like Saddam Hussein in Iraq.

Not all of the fifty thousand weapons reached the authorities: the trafficking mogul air-dropped over ten thousand of the AK-47s into the hands of FARC guerrillas in southern Colombia. When news about the drop got out, press reports battered Montesinos and Fujimori for their involvement, sparking firm rebuttals from the two, and ultimately an announcement by Montesinos on August 21, 2000, that the SIN had apprehended the gunrunners who had delivered the weapons to the guerrillas. But Soghanalian, among those accused in the crime ring, retorted: "The weapons I sold went to the Peruvian government. . . . None went to the Colombian side. If any illegality occurred, it was on the side of the Peruvians." Eventually, the truth emerged, perhaps from the mouths of military officers antagonized by Montesinos's pervasive control, that Montesinos had in fact orchestrated the sale of weapons to the FARC.

Los Vladi-videos

Montesinos dug his hole deeper later that year when he attempted to help Fujimori run (illegally) for a third presidential term. Even then, the Clinton administration's public condemnation of Montesinos met CIA resistance, and the internal dispute grew even more heated in September 2001 when a leaked video showed the SIN chief bribing an opposition congressman to join Fujimori's coalition. The anti-Montesinos movement expanded further when Fujimori dramatically tried to distance himself from the now-tainted Montesinos and repair the damage. Fujimori called for new elections, withdrew his candidacy, and instead swung the thrust of his efforts to dismantling Montesinos's intelligence network. In the months following hundreds of "Vladi-videos" circulated, revealing Montesinos's and his associates' common practice of bribing upper-echelon Peruvian politicians and media magnates. In addition, more evidence came to light confirming Montesinos's instrumental role in the FARC AK-47 deal.

At this point Peruvian politics devolved into pandemonium. Montesinos resigned and soon filed for political asylum in Panama, while Fujimori resigned from office in November 2001. Despite the millions Washington had paid for his services, the former SIN chief was apprehended in Caracas on June 23, 2001, with the help of US officials. A plethora of Peruvian military officers, among others once caught in Montesinos's web, testified at the trial in Peru. One arrested arms dealer accused Montesinos of recruiting him to hatch the AK-47 deal, adding that the gunrunners were "tortured to prevent them from implicating the spy chief." At the conclusion of the trial, which ran for nearly three years, Montesinos was sentenced to twenty years in September 2006 for masterminding the Jordan–FARC arms deal.

The *Post*'s Karen DeYoung perhaps best summarized the US–Montesinos saga in 2000, highlighting the inconsistencies in US foreign policy given the competing agencies and shifting priorities: "The story of Montesinos's relationship with Washington—at least from the American side—is a familiar tale of conflicting U.S. priorities in Latin America. Montesinos is the most recent in a long line of intelligence assets, including Chilean intelligence chief Manuel Contreras and Panamanian strongman Manuel Noriega, who ended up behind a changing policy curve."

36 • Supply Side
Part Two: Bolivia

Soaring global demand for cocaine in the early 1980s fueled an almost in-stantaneous spike in coca cultivation in Peru, Colombia, and Bolivia. Bolivia's remote jungle region of Chapare proved to be an ideal growing locale, and production rose exponentially. According to a November 1987 CIA report the Chapare region, which had twenty-six thousand hectares under cultivation, ac-counted for 75 percent of coca leaf production in Bolivia. Coca sales brought huge profits to those involved in its cultivation, particularly against the back-drop of Bolivia's economic recession, and the money from coca formed a sub-stantial part of Bolivia's national income. The prospect of these windfalls created a Bolivian "coca gold rush" as desperately poor and predominantly in-digenous Bolivians relocated from the highlands to the Chapare region to get their share of the booming new economy. Coca cultivation became the occupa-tion of an estimated 7 to 13 percent of Bolivia's workforce, and the *cocaleros* (coca farmers), inspired by the multigenerational success of Andean miners, erected labor federations. Alongside the boom in coca supply came an in-creased sophistication in manufacturing the final product. One local from the region reminisced that "back in the 1980s in the Chapare, you would walk into a market and see what you thought were piles of flour. But it was cocaine. It was all perfectly legal. Ah, the good old days."

As American cities became ravaged by the so-called cocaine and crack co-caine epidemic, Washington decided to tackle the leaf problem (literally) by going supply side. As well as putting pressure on successive Bolivian govern-ments to enact stricter antidrug reforms, Washington launched joint pro-grams such as the semiclandestine Operation Blast Furnace in July–October 1986, which promoted alternative-crop development, implemented voluntary and forced coca eradication drives, and mandated the outlawing of processed cocaine. A senior US counternarcotics official in La Paz explained Washington's rationale behind the carrot-and-stick approach: "The whole idea is to get people to switch to, say, hearts of palm. But these crops can never compete with coca because the narcos will always pay top dollar for it. Folks only switch when there is the threat of losing their entire coca crop."

Crop eradication affected the farmers growing coca destined to be processed into cocaine as well as those growing the plant for legal purposes. Accordingly, in 1988 the Bolivian government ratified Law 1008, the Coca and Controlled Substance Law, which permitted coca intended for traditional use to be grown on twelve thousand hectares of the Yungas region, where the crop had a centuries-long cultural history. Traditionally, coca leaves were chewed or brewed as a tea to help with altitude sickness, increase strength, and stave off feelings of hunger. Coca intended for illicit derivatives was banned, and Law 1008 articulated brutal punishments for the consumption and possession of controlled substances, that is, cocaine. By making one rule for the Yungas region and another for Chapare, the law clearly discriminated against the Chapare cocaleros and sparked deep resentment among the wave of coca farmers who suddenly found themselves engaged in an illegal trade.

Coca continued to be grown in Chapare, however, much to the ire of the Americans. In 1997, after nearly a decade of Washington's incessant demands for the eradication of coca, the Bolivian government agreed to accelerate its efforts in Chapare via the Operation Dignity Plan, which aimed to eradicate coca in the region by 2002. If successful, the zero-coca strategy would deprive the Chapare region of $700 million in annual income. Cocaleros in the region staged a series of major strikes, fighting to save the industry upon which their livelihoods depended. The strikes often devolved into violence and resulted in the death of legions of cocaleros as well as several police officers. One key figure during this time was Evo Morales, an Aymara heritage coca farmer from Chapare, a leader of a cocalero union leader, and, from 1997, a member of Congress. Morales was known for his anti-Americanism. Conflict continued until in 2004 President Carlos Mesa approved thirty-two hundred hectares for traditional cultivation in Chapare. Sensing that all available alternatives would be much worse, the US government did not publicly oppose the compromise.

Ultimately, although the zero-coca strategy in late-twentieth-century Chapare came at the cost of many casualties, it did manage to reduce production of the polarizing crop. Commercial coca production was almost entirely absent from the region by the early 2000s, save for the thirty-two hundred "compromise"

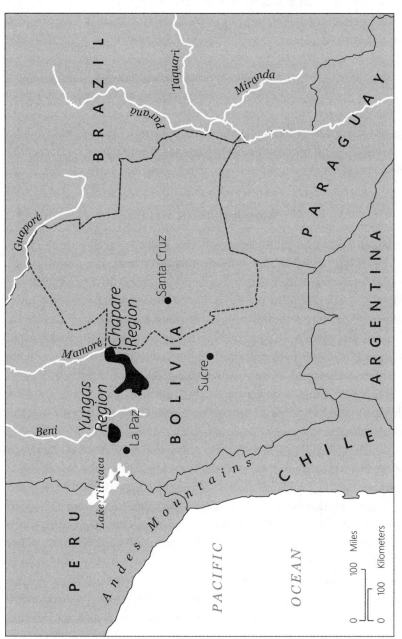

Map of Bolivia showing the Yungas and Chapare coca-growing regions. (University of Wisconsin-Madison Cartography Lab. Christopher Archuleta, cartographer)

hectares and the twelve thousand legal hectares in the Yungas. The early 2000s also saw a return on the hundreds of millions of dollars the US had invested in alternative development. The value of permissible agriculture in Chapare, practically nonexistent in the late 1990s, amounted to approximately $25 million in 2002.

Encouraged by Washington's long-anticipated returns, USAID funds quickly poured into projects of critical infrastructure and technical assistance to globalize the products of Chapare famers. Instead of cocaine, it was bananas that carried the Chapare seal in Europe. Ramiro Orias, a human rights lawyer renowned for his expertise in La Paz's social development, commented, "It took almost twenty years, but there [were] tremendous successes."

Mr. Morales Makes His Bid

Although coca cultivation had rapidly dropped, the social turmoil engendered by Washington's supply-side agenda persisted. The country went through five presidents between 2001 and 2005, and popular revolts that bordered on civil war ousted two of them. The Mexican journalist Alma Guillermoprieto characterized the disruption: "Dozens of people were killed; and even in areas not involved in the conflict, roads were blocked for weeks on end and commerce was virtually paralyzed."

Evo Morales capitalized on the frustration and indignance felt toward the conservative, pro-Washington government by marginalized and now-unemployed cocaleros. He also broadened his appeal by adopting a socialist agenda. In taking this route, Morales was responding to and in some sense driving the trajectory of the domestic turmoil. In Guillermoprieto's assessment, he pitted the "impoverished *altiplano*," the seat of Morales's indigenous base, against the "tropical east," the resource-rich region where "most of the country's self-described white people live." In 2000 Morales won huge popular support after siding with antigovernment protests during the so-called water war that erupted in the provincial city of Cochabamba over the privatization of the city's water infrastructure and a subsequent hike in water rates.

Washington was not unaware of Morales's rise. With the 2002 Bolivian presidential elections looming, US ambassador Manuel Rocha, hoping to persuade Bolivians to elect a malleable candidate, stated that a Bolivian president who was soft on drugs could spark a jarring reduction in the sizable counternarcotics assistance of the United States. The remark backfired, coming across as a diplomatic threat against Morales. Although Morales ultimately failed to secure the 2002 presidency, Rocha's intervention benefited Morales, who later quipped that the ambassador was his best campaign manager. On a larger scale, Rocha's behavior fell in line with the uncanny talent of Washington's representatives to inadvertently push Bolivia further into the anti-America camp headed by communist Cuba.

Morales ran in the 2005 elections on a dogmatic anti-American and anti–drug war platform, and this time he was victorious. Like Fidel Castro in 1959 and Hugo Chávez in 1999, he wasted no time in pursuing his "socialist revolution," nationalizing the country's immense natural gas reserves and renegotiating contracts with foreign energy companies, some of which were US-based, on more profitable terms. These unmistakable rejections of Washington's minimal-state, capitalist prescription for Latin American countries—the so-called Washington Consensus—made the new chief of state one of the hemisphere's most controversial figures.

nationalization

Morales made it clear he would no longer march in lockstep with Washington's supply-side campaign when he announced an end to forced coca eradication. Under the slogan "*Coca Sí, Cocaína No*," Morales held that Bolivians could mass-cultivate coca for licit products while curtailing narcotics trafficking. Morales was thereby reasserting the cultural role coca had historically held in Bolivia.

However, the rest of the world did not view the cultural use of coca leaves as being wholly benign. As early as 1949 a broad international campaign against chewing coca leaves first brought the conflicting perspectives to light when Howard B. Fonda, the chief of the incipient UN Commission of Inquiry on the Coca Leaf, explained the commission's reasoning for banning the practice: "We believe that the daily, inveterate use of coca leaves by chewing . . . not only is thoroughly noxious and therefore detrimental, but also is the cause of racial degeneration in many centres of population, and of the decadence that visibly shows in numerous Indians. . . . Our studies will confirm the certainty of our assertions and we hope we can present a rational plan of action . . . to attain the absolute and sure abolition of this pernicious habit."

The Bolivian military government was convinced in 1964 to sign the UN Single Convention on Narcotic Drugs (1961), imposing a twenty-five-year UN timeline to wean indigenous communities off the cultural practice of chewing coca leaves. But given the deep history and cultural associations of the practice, it was little surprise that in 1989, at the plan's end, the issue remained "under dispute."

To Washington's distress, soon after assuming the presidency Morales backed the preexisting limit of one *cato* (one-sixth of a hectare) per coca grower but left uncapped the number of coca growers in the Chapare. As expected, the one-cato policy initiated a flow of new, hopeful cocaleros into the Chapare. Coca production increased by roughly 10 percent the following year, as US officials feared that Morales's agenda would wash away progress in crop eradication.

In February 2017 Morales's government codified greater cultivation of the crop. Through the General Coca Law, Morales revisited the aggregate land stock allocated for coca for the first time since Law 1008 of 1988, and the result was a near-doubling of permissible coca hectares from twelve thousand to twenty-two thousand. Morales reasoned that the growing demand for traditional-use coca—about a third of Bolivians chewed coca leaves, according to a 1913 study by the Latin American Public Opinion Project—would lead to an embarrassing shortage in the crop that was the emblem of both Bolivian heritage and defiance of gringo imperialism. The codification of the General Coca Law thus bolstered morale as much as bank accounts, symbolizing an unwavering stance against US policies for coca eradication and drug control. In effect, the law accentuated Morales's antidrug war identity, the defining characteristic of his presidency.

Many, however, questioned the legitimacy of the Bolivian government's claim that none of the Chapare coca crop was being funneled into the illicit cocaine market, especially in light of a 2013 EU-funded study by the OAS's Interamerican Commission for Drug Abuse Control. The report asserted that only 14,705 hectares were needed to meet Bolivia's traditional-use demand, leaving a healthy surplus of hectares under the General Coca Law. Morales replied that the solution to the coca surplus wasn't to reduce the supply but to create alternative licit avenues for the product in the Bolivian economy. This undisguised lobbying for coca cultivation, pawned off as *industrialización,* explored converting coca into toothpaste, hemorrhoid cream, flour, and even wine. The Bolivian government even considered sending 500,000 tons of coca leaf to China for medicinal uses.

The various plans yielded few results. Many of the new coca products simply couldn't compete with existing products. One US official remarked that "coca flour costs three times as much as normal flour and it tastes like shit." A Bolivian academic questioned Morales's taste for coca: "Why can't Evo understand that people like to drink wine made from grapes, not coca?" The difficulties of industrialización stemmed from more than the crop's distinctive herbal taste: all consumption of the surplus crop had to be internal, given the existence of a UN treaty forbidding signatory countries from importing coca derivatives. Thus sending coca tea to China was out of the question. Although

Morales lobbied for coca to be removed from the UN list, only Venezuela supported him. To critics, financing new licit coca markets in the region would only facilitate crop flows to cocaine producers. To the antidrug campaigners, it was always *"coca sí, cocaína sí."*

Morales Goes Solo

Morales's coca-centric rhetoric consistently distressed the US, with Washington officials and several members of Congress perceiving the evolution of a Bolivian "narco democracy." By the fall of 2006 the Western Hemisphere Bureau in the State Department was on the verge of decertifying Bolivia's drug-control efforts, an act that would have sizable consequences, not least to US economic assistance. Proselytizers of decertification condemned Washington's failure to sanction Morales as "rewarding bad behavior." Anti-decertification campaigners, who emphasized patience and engagement with the Bolivian government, had an admittedly more difficult argument to make given Morales's frequent outbursts against American imperialism. Yet others took a more pragmatic approach, bypassing Morales and citing instead the increasingly small amount of Bolivian cocaine that reached the United States as rationale for the Bush administration to ignore the Bolivian president's histrionic rhetoric. Bolivian cocaine, after all, was primarily destined for Brazil, Argentina, and Europe. Both George W. Bush and Obama wound up decertifying Bolivia.

Although the debate was intense, it could not disguise the fact that decertification was in some sense a moot point. Morales's government, emboldened by Venezuela, Cuba, and even China, was no longer dependent on US aid, and the US no longer had the leverage it once did to keep Bolivia onside in the US-led drug war. One fretful American diplomat questioned, "What's to prevent Evo from saying, 'Forget it. Take your toys and go home'?"

Such fears were well founded: the DEA and the US ambassador Philip Goldberg were expelled in 2008 and USAID followed in 2013. Later that year Congress and the Obama administration finished what Morales had begun, winding down the last of the State Department's already diminished counternarcotics funding and programs in Bolivia. Washington would instead prioritize cooperative countries like Peru and Colombia as the recipients of precious antidrug dollars.

By then, the US response to Bolivia seemed almost irrelevant in comparison to Bolivia's increasingly confident stance on the world stage over drugs. In 2011 Morales announced Bolivia's withdrawal from the UN Single Convention on

Billboard showing (*left to right*) Hugo Chávez, Fidel Castro, and Evo Morales in La Paz, Bolivia. March 8, 2007. (Mark Pearson / Alamy Stock Photo)

Narcotic Drugs and simultaneously requested readmittance should the UN revoke the convention's language that criminalized coca. Morales argued that the convention contravened Bolivia's 2009 constitutional ratification of the state's commitment to "protect native and ancestral coca as cultural patrimony" and definitively stated that coca "in its natural state . . . is not a narcotic."

A widespread international row immediately unfolded. Bolivia's new status would be reviewed only if more than one-third of the close to two hundred signatory countries opposed Morales's decision. Washington and London as well as Rome, Stockholm, Amsterdam, and Moscow allegedly lobbied other signatory nations to stymie Morales's move. Ultimately, Morales's gambit was successful: Bolivia rejoined the Single Convention in 2013, with an accommodating exclusion of traditional coca chewing from the accord. One activist at the Transform Drug Policy Foundation remarked, "The Bolivian move is inspirational and ground-breaking. It shows that any country that has had enough of the war on drugs can change the terms of its engagement with the UN conventions."

After Morales's perceived victory with the UN Single Convention, the "Bolivian model" became an appealing alternative for drug-war pundits. The president proudly remarked, "We in Bolivia, without U.S. military bases and without the DEA, even without the shared responsibility of drug-consuming countries, have demonstrated that it is possible to confront drug trafficking with the participation of the people." In a September 2016 column by the *New York Times,* the editorial board praised Morales's gentler approach, constructed as it was on consultation with coca growers, as an alternative to Washington's historical prohibitionist and heavily militarized war on drugs.

Change on the Ground?

Despite falling hectare cultivation statistics, research on the ground indicates that many people in Bolivia believe that narcotrafficking continued to flourish under Morales. Some Bolivians alleged that La Paz's urban expansion was the concrete result of the drug kingpins' money-laundering operations. Despite the occasional raid, the Bolivian government was understood to be tolerating the narcos, provided they maintained a low profile and minimized violence. Reports detailed the construction of airstrips in the remote jungles and the low plains, indicating that the Bolivian coca industry was alive, thriving, and protecting its seedy relationship with foreign users. Uncle Sam, however, was no longer laser-focused on the supply side in Bolivia but was rather deeply anxious about Mexico's gangland drug trafficking much closer to home.

Coup Classic?

On election day, October 20, 2019, Morales once again was on the ballot for president. Back in 2016 citizens had narrowly rejected their sitting president's bid for an unprecedented *fourth* term in office. The following year his self-selected Supreme Court issued a seemingly comical ruling that Morales had a "human right" to be a candidate however many times, prompting the swelling constitutional critics to claim a power grab. Their slogan: "Bolivia Said No." The October election which saw Morales pitted against the opposition candidate Carlos Mesa, a centrist former president, among others, was thus already under a shroud of suspicion and rancor.

Morales's goal was to avoid a runoff that he would almost certainly have lost, meaning he needed to beat Mesa in the first round by over 10 percent. Media reports first indicated on the evening of the election that a second round was in the cards. Then, quizzically, the reporting ceased for an entire day, resuming with the news that Evo had won by a margin just over the vital 10 percent threshold. Opposition figures cried foul, including many who once supported Morales but now saw nothing more than a power grab. An October 30 OAS report affirmed, although its statistical methods were later challenged, that "intentional manipulation and serious irregularities" made it "impossible to validate" the results.

With anti-Morales protests and violence continuing for close to three weeks after the dubious vote, Evo resigned and fled to exile in Mexico, claiming that a "civic coup" had been hatched against him. Other prominent voices, like the British Labour Party leader Jeremy Corbyn, also claimed a nefarious coup and one more instance of the reactionary right getting its way in Latin America. President Trump, by contrast, countered that the protests and Morales's subsequent resignation were a win for democracy: "The United States applauds the Bolivian people for demanding freedom and the Bolivian military for abiding by its oath to protect not just a single person, but Bolivia's constitution."

37 · Supply Side

Part Three: Plan Colombia

By the summer of 1999 the situation in Colombia appeared to have reached a nadir. Three American activists had been killed by the FARC; there had been a spike in coca cultivation; and there had been no progress in the putative peace negotiations between President Andrés Pastrana's administration and the FARC, which had been fighting the Colombian state since 1964. As if that weren't enough, the country was plagued by paramilitary groups, gangs, and leftist insurgents who collectively controlled large swathes of territory. In 1999 there were approximately two thousand terrorist attacks and three thousand kidnappings in Colombia, and the country's murder rate reached sixty per one hundred thousand residents, far higher than in drug-gang-riddled Mexico in 2011, which saw a rate of twenty-four per one hundred thousand. That same year the FARC's ranks had swollen to over eighteen thousand soldiers, adolescents, and women, and drug revenues had surged into the billions. Much as President Bush had concluded at the height of Escobar's power in the 1980s, the Bill Clinton administration (1993–2001) judged Colombia's instability to be a serious risk to US national security.

With Republicans in Congress clamoring that more should be done to stabilize Colombia, in August 2000 Plan Colombia was unveiled, with a whopping $1.1 billion start-up budget for two years. President Pastrana issued the initial public announcement, allowing the Clinton administration to act as if it were merely addressing the request of a reliable hemispheric ally. Pastrana even went so far as to present Plan Colombia as his own program: $7.5 billion—$4 billion supplied by the Colombian government, $3.5 billion to be provided by the international community—to revive the Colombian economy, promote social development, eradicate illicit crops, and jump-start the stalled peace talks.

(Note that a Spanish-language version of the plan did not even exist until months after the first English copy had been drafted).

The initial military component consisted principally of a combination of Huey and Black Hawk helicopters designated for antidrug operations. The proposal also called for the creation of two more Colombian counternarcotics battalions, which were to be deployed in Putumayo, where drug cultivation had increased in recent years. To hasten congressional approval, the Clinton administration emphasized the time-critical nature of the package.

In what had the hallmarks of an all-too-common way for Washington to address a foreign policy crisis, the deliberations on Capitol Hill and at the Clinton White House were less about the actual issues in Colombia and more about pork barrel politics, as politicians tried to secure government spending for their local districts. While much was made of the unprecedented sum of money supposedly allocated for Colombia, the reality was that most of the funds were destined for domestic defense contractors to construct and deliver the materiél. One squabble broke out over whether a helicopter order would go to the defense contractor behemoth Bell-Textron, headquartered in Texas, or Sikorsky, based in Connecticut. Even Senator Christopher Dodd of Connecticut, a longtime Latin America policy dove who had been a fierce critic of Reagan's militarized Central America strategy, got into the act, making sure the package included one hundred Sikorsky Black Hawks and exactly zero Bell-Textron Hueys. All of this maneuvering led one cheeky policy onlooker to retort, "This was supposed to be Plan Colombia, not Plan Connecticut." But this was just Beltway Politics 101.

The Soft Side

Plan Colombia produced quick results, albeit not anything as dramatic as rescuing Colombia from collapse. Its immediate impact was a steep increase in the amount of military hardware used to fight the drug war, from high-tech helicopters to night-vision goggles. One of the initial dismissals of Plan Colombia was that it was a counterinsurgency policy camouflaged as an antidrug policy, but the Clinton administration addressed this head on, leaving no ambiguity as to whether or not the US was stepping into the nearly half-century conflict between the Colombian government and the FARC. As Assistant Secretary of Defense for Special Operations Brian Sheridan testified in September 2000, "The targets are the narco-traffickers, those individuals and organizations that are involved in the cultivation of coca or opium poppy and the subsequent production and transportation of cocaine and heroin to the U.S. Only those armed elements that forcibly inhibit or confront counterdrug operations will be engaged, be they narcotraffickers, insurgent organizations, or illegal self-defense forces. I know that some are concerned that we are being drawn into a quagmire. Let me assure you, we are not."

A clever move by the White House, this resolve placed any opponents of Plan Colombia in the awkward domestic political position of appearing to be dovish on the drug war. At the same time, Clinton soothed more liberal members of Congress who feared Plan Colombia was too militarized by significantly expanding soft-side, that is, social and economic, assistance like judicial reform and alternative development (read: don't grow coca but something licit like bananas!). The legislation also provided $51 million for a broad range of human rights issues, including programs to protect human rights workers and bolster existing human rights units within the Colombian military. Moreover, the language proposed by the Senate required the State Department to certify the military's performance on human rights before the aid could be delivered, although the Senate's final bill was loosened to include a presidential waiver option, on national-security grounds.

But even if Plan Colombia did include substantive soft-side programs, they were never the focus. The popular impression was that Plan Colombia entailed Washington's footing the bill for Colombia's defense spending, although even at its height US assistance represented only 6 percent of Colombia's annual military budget. And as Colombia developed and institutionalized the capacity of its military and police forces, Plan Colombia money, eventually totaling over $8 billion, shifted toward economic development assistance. Indeed, one of the ironies of the US-hatched antidrug plan to save Colombia was that most Colombians thought the money would have been better spent going directly after the illegal armed groups.

9/11 Game Changer

USAID and others backing the importance of the development aspect of Plan Colombia emphasized that this was not a counterinsurgency initiative. Plan Colombia funds were not intended for the fight against the FARC. But the reality on the ground was that the Marxist guerrillas were "financed by the world's cocaine habit" and thus were inextricably tied to this illicit drug business. Counterinsurgency and counternarcotics were two sides of the same coin in Colombia. After the September 11, 2001, terrorist attacks, however, the counterinsurgency versus counternarcotics debate became moot. George W. Bush, in office only since early 2001, allowed Plan Colombia aid and training to be used for counterterrorism as well as drug war operations. Improving and training police forces as well as soldiers were now on the table.

Freed from the narrow, so-called narcotized restrictions of the original plan, US personnel engaged in much more expansive training of the Colombian military, which would eventually grow to more than four hundred thousand soldiers during the first decade of Plan Colombia. With security forces, materiél, and lethal capability all on the rise, Colombian military convoys began opening up key highways held by the FARC by placing an armed soldier every kilometer or so. Enhanced air mobility allowed the security forces to chase FARC rebels across high mountain ranges and thick jungle. The message to Colombians was clear and unequivocal: the Colombian state will protect you; you will no longer be a prisoner in your own country. In 1999 almost two hundred of the country's one-thousand-plus municipalities had mayors who would not go to their offices for fear of leftist or rightist threats. By 2013 each municipality had a police force and a mayor who showed up for work.

The importance of the Colombian security forces as a competent US partner, however, should not overshadow the vital role of the Colombian political class. Colombian elites, predominantly of European descent and 37 percent of the population, had been detached from the country's general misery long before the FARC ever existed. This aloofness, in fact, probably explains in large part why the FARC arose in the first place. The highly urbanized elite decided that enough was enough only when the insurgency began to touch its members directly. Their new resolve manifested itself in the 2002 election of the hawkish president Álvaro Uribe. Uribe made a remarkable promise to the Colombian people: if they placed their trust in him, his government would establish security in all areas of the country. The boldness of Uribe's promise is even more striking in light of the fact that the Colombian state had effectively never governed wide swaths of national territory, especially in parts of the country far from large cities such as Bogotá and Medellín. Uribe's insight—"security first and everything else later"—was considered politically incorrect abroad on account of its polarizing mano dura component, but it resonated with a Colombian populace that was fatigued from years of violence. Almost immediately after being elected Uribe imposed a war tax on wealthy citizens that was projected to raise more than $4 billion over the next four years, a sum roughly three times the size of total US assistance for Plan Colombia to that point.

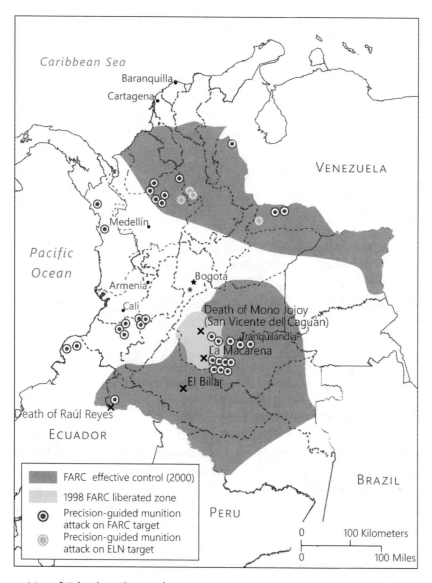

Map of Colombia. The Revolutionary Armed Forces of Colombia (FARC) was
Latin America's largest and strongest Marxist insurgency. At the height of its
power in the early 2000s the Leninist narco-guerrilla force had a presence in
more than a third of the national territory. (University of Wisconsin–Madison
Cartography Lab. Christopher Archuleta, cartographer)

Not surprisingly, Uribe's hard-line approach was controversial. Critics believed that it simply used violence to fight violence. Yet Uribe's iron-fist approach can be understood only in the context of what had transpired in Colombia during the administration of President Andrés Pastrana over the previous four years. In 1998 Pastrana unilaterally granted the FARC a liberated zone the size of El Salvador as a diplomatic carrot to incentivize it to negotiate peace. Pastrana was far from the only person inside or outside Colombia who felt that an olive branch would entice the FARC to lay down its arms and integrate into Colombia's democratic system. Many believed the FARC had maximized its military reach and therefore its negotiating leverage and would therefore be eager to cut a deal. But instead of sitting down for peace talks the FARC used the zone to grow coca, traffic cocaine, host Irish Republican Army (IRA) bomb-making specialists, and train and arm its swelling ranks. Buoyed by a huge narco war chest that financed the purchase of highly sophisticated weaponry and foreign mercenary advisors, the FARC went "downtown" for the first time in 2003, placing bombs in large cities, including Bogotá. The FARC declared that anyone who ran for or held elected office was under a sentence of death. Perhaps most shockingly, on the day of Uribe's inauguration, August 7, 2002, they brazenly fired mortar shells on the presidential palace and an adjacent urban slum, killing fourteen civilians, including three children. It was no surprise that by 2002 few Colombians believed that the FARC would negotiate a settlement, so Uribe's "war first, peace later" stance made sense to a political majority.

Uribe's hard-line approach delivered. The FARC's ideological leadership began to suffer during the presidencies of Uribe and his successor, Juan Manuel Santos. The military began using precision-guided missiles in March 2008 to target FARC commanders in what US advisors dubbed the bombs-on-foreheads approach. This approach was first used in a controversial Colombian military attack on a FARC jungle camp just over the border in Ecuador: the raid violated Ecuador's sovereignty, but it killed Raúl Reyes, the FARC's second-in-command. The Colombian military recovered FARC laptop computers, which were full of incriminating information, including, most sensationally, the group's clandestine relationship with President Hugo Chávez of Venezuela.

The FARC sustained more blows in the weeks following the Ecuador raid when its original leader, Manuel "Sureshot" Marulanda, died, reportedly of a heart attack. Thereafter, in July 2008, the Colombian military conducted one of the most successful hostage rescue operations in history when, without firing a shot, it freed the former Colombian presidential candidate Ingrid Betancourt, three American counternarcotics contractors, and several other Colombians.

Using commandos disguised as humanitarian workers, the military's Operation Check deprived the FARC of its highest-profile hostages.

But while Plan Colombia had succeeded in making the Colombian military more professional and effective, the military still suffered from an institutional legacy of insufficient respect for the rule of law and civilian oversight. In 2008 members of the security forces lured eleven youths from a poor town near Bogotá to a location hundreds of miles away, dressed them in guerrilla clothing, and murdered them. Known as the "false positives" case, the officers attempted to cite these deaths as FARC kills (the positives) to boost their stats. There were hundreds of these suspected false positive cases. That the security situation could nevertheless be reasonably described as much improved goes to show how bad things were before the turnaround, both in terms of security in the country and the high prevalence of human rights abuses by the military before Plan Colombia was launched.

The Brink of Peace?

In a January 2016 piece the *Economist* magazine contended that while finding a US foreign policy that was a clear success was quite rare, a possible candidate was Plan Colombia. The newly inaugurated president, Barack Obama, most likely agreed. In February 2016 Obama hosted his Colombian counterpart, Juan Manuel Santos (2010–18), in the East Wing of the White House as well as ex-presidents George W. Bush and Bill Clinton and the Colombians Andrés Pastrana and Álvaro Uribe to celebrate Colombia's "remarkable transformation." "A country that was on the brink of collapse is now on the brink of peace," said Obama. The equally effusive Santos lauded Washington's "friendly hand—from both sides of the aisle," which had been crucial in getting Colombia on its feet. Santos went out of his way to address what he believed was a misperception that Plan Colombia was "an exclusively military or security initiative": "It's true that Plan Colombia helped us to have the most powerful armed forces, the most effective armed forces that Colombia has ever had in its history, and they, today, are out there training armed forces of other countries in the region. But the reason for its success was that it was a comprehensive strategy—a strategy that also bet on social programs, on justice, on rural development, and on strengthening our democratic institutions."

There were certainly statistics to back up the rosy spin that Obama and Santos were putting on the multibillion-dollar aid program. Between 2005 and 2013, the very heart of the Plan Colombia years, kidnappings dropped by

95 percent to about two hundred per year. Murders were down by half, tracking at a rate last seen in 1984. The country's democratic government passed legislation in 2011 that, for the first time, allowed citizens to be recognized as victims of the state or other armed actors. The government also recognized the existence of an internal armed conflict, something once considered taboo.

Colombians were slowly but decisively adapting to life in a normal country. They now took domestic vacations, traveling from rural towns to provincial cities without the fear of, say, *pescas milagrosas* (miracle fishings), whereby FARC guerrillas would use roadblocks to fish for wealthy citizens worth kidnapping. Bolstered by a dynamic economy, part of the ongoing peace dividend, between 2002 and 2014, six million Colombians were lifted out of poverty, and for the first time in the country's history Colombia had a larger middle class than lower class.

However, while the country in many respects enjoyed a much more stable situation, human rights violations, absence of the rule of law, and economic deprivation remained a way of life for many Colombians who still cited security as their chief concern. At the time of the fifteenth-anniversary celebration, leftist critics like the nongovernmental organization Witness for Peace had some tough questions for Plan Colombia triumphalists: "Can military success be equated with true peace? Or does true peace rather require investment in social and economic programs, to build a sustainable peace founded in social justice?" Some Colombians, Witness for Peace said, told a different story of Plan Colombia, painting a picture in which "U.S. military intervention has increased human rights violations, especially among vulnerable populations including Afro-Colombians, indigenous communities, small-scale farmers, women, trade unionists, and human rights defenders."

A Model to Emulate?

While it is tempting to seek larger lessons from Colombia's experience with counterinsurgency and nation-building, the temptation should be indulged with great care. Colombia's gains were unusual in the timeless, murky realm of counterinsurgency, and the reasons for these gains are not easy to understand. Plan Colombia played a key role in the successes of the past decade, yet it achieved success not in the narrow, narcocentric focus of its original mandate but only when it spilled over into other areas. Colombia needed militarization and pacification efforts to quell threats to its existence as a democracy—and even to its existence as a state. From there, it needed development aid to encourage and support an elite open to formulating a more in-clusive definition of Colombian society.

No one could have foreseen this complex sequence of events in the late 1990s, but Plan Colombia met these needs as they arose, morphing and adapting to the situation. It is perhaps a case study of a US policy that managed to be both idealistic and pragmatic in equal measure, in it for the long haul but with a clear idea of the goals to be achieved. The contrast with the intensely difficult experience of the United States in Iraq and Afghanistan at the same time demonstrates how difficult it is to implement lessons learned from one geopolitical context to another.

Still, it would be a mistake to conclude that Plan Colombia achieved all this by itself. Its immediate impact was a marked increase in the amount of Colombian military hardware used to fight the drug war, but all that hardware meant that the Colombian armed forces had to dramatically increase training. That training proved to be far more important than the equipment: Colombia's security forces demonstrated that they were capable of becoming the endogenous national actors that are central to almost all successful counterinsurgencies. As the country absorbed and institutionalized the capabilities of these forces—and as the fixed military outlays had been spent—Plan Colombia money from the US, which by 2016 amounted to approximately $10 billion, went more toward economic development assistance. The real lesson here is that unless the US government has a willing and capable local counterpart, no amount of money or equipment will make a difference in an insurgency.

If one were to judge US counternarcotics efforts in Colombia by their effect on the war on drugs in Latin America, the conclusion would have to be that they fell far short. Whenever the policy succeeded in suppressing drug activity in Colombia, it merely migrated to other countries—not least Mexico, Peru, Bolivia, and Central America. As the *Economist* correspondent Michael Reid summarized, "Two decades and several billion dollars later," drug warriors could "point to a series of tactical victories, in particular places and times," but the flow of coke to America was "never seriously interrupted." Yet while Plan Colombia may have failed as the antinarcotic operation as originally construed, it arguably succeeded in the unexpected, secondary sphere of counterinsurgency and nation-building. Almost by accident the US ended up safeguarding the principles of democracy and society in its backyard.

A inadvertent benefits [handwritten marginal note]

38 · The (Almost) Coup in Caracas

> This town is full of coup rumors, something that was not the
> case of a few weeks ago.
> —US State Department cable reporting on events in Caracas,
> November 7, 2001

On Thursday, April 11, 2002, the incoming US ambassador to Venezuela, Charles Shapiro, attended a lunch in his honor with several members of Venezuela's economic aristocracy at the estate of the media giant Gustavo Cisneros. The political situation in Caracas, the capital, had been uncertain for months, but there had been no concrete moves to topple the populist, polarizing left-wing president, Hugo Chávez. Suddenly, in the middle of lunch, there arose the discordant ringing of mobile phones conveying unconfirmed news of an apparent shooting of civilians at a massive nonviolent anti-Chávez march in the city. Within hours key industry and media elites were backing a military revolt against the president, and it soon became clear that a coup attempt was underway.

After being informed of the events, Ambassador Shapiro announced to the assembled gathering that the United States would not countenance an illegal ouster of Chávez. But Shapiro's pledge rang hollow when the George W. Bush administration quickly endorsed the coup attempt. Bush's move backfired badly: Chávez was ousted, but only for two days. Thereafter the president was helped back into power by the swift actions of elements of his security forces. The Bush team's reaction to the coup became as newsworthy as the coup itself and made a lasting dent in US–Venezuela relations, which had been stable, if sometimes strained, during the Clinton administration. The very different

*Bush
Backfire*

approaches taken by these two administrations to the unexpected resurgence of communism (or what Chávez deemed "21st-century socialism") in their backyard highlights that however much the US tried to distance itself from Cold War calculations, the anti-imperialist leftist threat remained a potent factor in US strategic thinking at the dawn of the twenty-first century.

Chávez and Washington, before the Coup

In the immediate post-Cold War years US policy makers were not concerned about Venezuela. The country appeared to be relatively stable politically and was a reliable source of oil. But Chávez's rise to power changed this perception dramatically. A former army paratrooper and leader of a failed coup attempt in 1992, Chávez assumed office in 1999 and came out swinging: an early February 1999 US cable reporting on Chávez's inaugural address commented that he "left little doubt that anyone who opposed him should be ready to fight." The State Department assessment also noted his "flashes of populism" and "the authoritarian threat which lurked behind his tough policy statements." Chávez immediately launched into what he called a Bolivarian Revolution, implicitly associating himself with Venezuela's iconic early-nineteenth-century independence leader, Simón Bolívar. He drafted a radically different Bolivarian constitution, expanding presidential powers and renaming the country the Bolivarian Republic of Venezuela. The electorate approved the constitution that same year. Such changes characterized the first few years of Chávez's presidency, as he worked aggressively and mostly democratically to change the rules of the game. Chavez's Venezuela was to reflect his leftist Bolivarian vision of greater state control over political and economic institutions.

While never thrilled with Chávez's bluster, the Latin American officials in the Clinton administration as well as the US government's intelligence community tended to see Chávez's fiery rhetoric between 1999 and early 2001 as just that: rhetoric. For his part, Chávez initially balanced revolutionary socialism and anti-Americanism with more conciliatory instincts. Echoing Fidel Castro's meeting with a dazzled *Washington Post* editorial board, he rang the closing bell at the New York Stock Exchange and tossed out the first pitch at a New York Yankees game. Despite his hyperbolized rhetoric and swollen ego, he appeared quite reluctant to fully carry out his promised radical agenda. "Watch what Chávez does, not what he says," became the motto of Clinton's team.

Amid all of Chávez's fanfare and Washington's war-room talks, declassified documents can shed much-needed light on the nuance of the Clinton–Chávez link and why Clinton was prepared to tolerate Chávez's anti-Americanism. In a December 23, 1998, State Department cable, Chávez, fresh from winning the presidential vote, is said to have asked the Colombian head of state Andrés Pastrana for insights on how to develop a productive relationship with the United States. Pastrana's response: candor and consultation. A month later a State Department "scene setter" memo preparing Clinton for his meeting with Chávez indicated that the newly installed Venezuelan president's programs for democratic and constitutional reforms could be paradigms for the region. Then US ambassador to Venezuela and longtime Western Hemisphere hand John Maisto wrote, "He [Chávez] has told us that Venezuela's relationship with the U.S. is of transcendental importance and that he wants to do everything he can to improve that relationship," before affirming on behalf of the Clinton administration: "We want to do the same." Another top career Foreign Service Officer with deep experience in the region, Peter Romero, told a collection of US private sector chiefs in Venezuela that if Chávez achieved "50 percent of what he says he wants to do, that is good."

But as in the case of Castro this era of good feelings gradually gave way to one of mutual suspicion. The change in the Clinton administration's perception of Chávez was driven by the ramifications of his left-wing, new constitution; his unwillingness to permit US antidrug aircraft missions over Venezuelan airspace; and, perhaps most significantly, his close relationship with communist Cuba. Under the terms of an agreement signed with Cuba in 2000, dubbed oil for services, Venezuela supplied the island nation with close to one hundred thousand barrels of oil per day. The estimated value of this gift to Cuba was between $6 billion and $8 billion over a fifteen-year period. The Cuban government reexported the surplus oil after it had met its domestic demands, providing Havana with badly needed foreign exchange. In return, Cuba sent between thirty thousand and fifty thousand technical specialists to Venezuela. Although this force was primarily composed of medical doctors, other professionals were lent also, including teachers and coaches as well as security, intelligence, and military advisors. Of particular note, given their familiarity with Russian technology and equipment, the Cuban military advisors were a critical component in the Venezuelan government's efforts to overhaul its military, including ideological indoctrination.

Chávez was growing increasingly active in pushing his political, social, and economic agenda, which was almost literally fueled by a dramatic increase in the Venezuelan government's oil revenues: in 1999 the government was earning roughly $8 billion annually from oil when the world price fetched around

$25/barrel; but with the price of oil trading around $50 barrel these revenues rose to around $85 billion in 2006, almost a tenfold increase. Ironically, it was the insatiable demand for oil in the United States that kept prices high, and despite the sharp downturn in the bilateral relationship between Caracas and Washington following the failed April 2002 coup, the United States continued to purchase the overwhelming majority of Venezuela's oil. In this instance, economic interdependence between the two countries appeared to overshadow stark ideological differences between the two governments. Awash with petrodollars, Chávez worked tirelessly to increase (read: buy) his influence both regionally and globally. Leftist figures and political parties and organizations around the world became recipients of Chávez's oil-driven largesse, the Venezuelan allocating an estimated $16 billion to $25 billion on foreign aid between 1999 and 2006.

Anatomy of a Coup

While the Clinton team avoided conflict with Chávez by allowing him to denounce the United States while merely keeping an eye on his relatively conventional oil policies, the 2001 Bush administration would see the precarious relationship deteriorate. Personal antipathy featured heavily: one top diplomat for the Western Hemisphere under Bush, Otto Reich, was a former ambassador to Caracas and held a deep personal dislike for the leftist, pro-Castro Chávez. Thus when officials like Reich saw the same intelligence reports as their predecessors, they often reached wildly different conclusions as to what the reports represented and what the response should be. On the Venezuelan end, Chávez was no longer a fussing political leader with words louder than actions; emboldened by petrodollars, he actually began carrying out his promises.

Chávez was facing greater hostility at home, however, in response to a series of decrees allowing a greater government role in private industry; business and some labor groups had become concerned with the degree of power concentration in the executive branch. In December 2001 a surprisingly diverse political opposition—composed primarily of Venezuelan labor union leaders, oil workers, and business magnates—viewed Chávez's economic policies as increasingly draconian and attempted to use protest as a way to change them. What began as a one-day strike gained traction in early 2002 when demonstrations grew to involve hundreds of thousands of protestors. Chávez's once-soaring public approval ratings sagged to around 30 percent. Nonetheless, this ardent third of the population, many of them self-described *chavistas*, continued to support Chávez, their fierce loyalty explained by their belief that he was the one president who had their long-neglected interests at heart.

Early in April 2002, during his weekly television show, *Aló Presidente,* Chávez did himself no favors in announcing the removal of a group of senior managers at Petróleos de Venezuela, S.A. (PDVSA), the state-controlled oil company. This flagrant show of power fueled public indignation over Chávez's politicization of the entity. The announcement sparked a new oil workers' strike that crippled oil exports. Massive protests in Caracas followed, demonstrating the now-nonnegligible level of public discontent and high threat of violence. As the strike reached its full expression, the Venezuelan media covered what many reporters labeled a people power movement, referring to the peaceful protests against the Philippine strongman Ferdinand Marcos in the mid-1980s. As a horde of protestors shook the streets of Caracas on Thursday, April 11, pro-Chávez snipers, global media outlets were speculating, fired down on the demonstrators, killing at least eleven.

At this point the once-discreet current of military discontent with Chávez became publicly recognizable. Some reports indicated that Chávez had not only given order to the snipers but also requested that the Venezuelan military use its tanks in order to crush the protest. The high-level military officers' refusal to carry out his orders to send in tanks was an early indication that Chávez was in trouble; not long after, a group of ten high-ranking officers refused to recognize Chávez's authority as president. Then, the army commander Efraín Vásquez Velasco announced publicly that Chávez had resigned even though Chávez had not resigned outright but rather agreed to "abandon his functions," a move that should have transferred power to the National Assembly. The coup plotters, nonetheless, took advantage of the confusion and hastily swore in a new presi- dent the next day, Pedro Carmona, the head of the business group Fedecamaras. Carmona announced the creation of a provisional government, supposedly sealing the fate of Chávez, who was whisked away from the presidential palace to a series of military installations over the next day and a half. During the ceremony members of the country's business and economic organizations toasted Chávez's removal with eighteen-year-old Scotch.

The coup's backing by a broad, united front of anti-Chávez business and labor leaders was short-lived, however, because Carmona revealed his naked appetite for power by suspending the National Assembly and constitutional court. His actions startled many within the anti-Chávez movement and fed into concerns regarding Carmona's interest in the demands of nonbusiness, anti-Chávez groups, such as petroleum labor unions. In addition, procoup

PDVSA managers ordered a halt to Chávez-brokered oil shipments to Cuba, citing the fact that Havana had not maintained its part of the accord. Just as quick as it had originated, it appeared to supporters that the nature of the coup had changed.

Unwilling to be silenced by Chávez, dissenters again exercised their right to criticize the heads of power. One long-standing Chávez critic, the Venezuelan journalist Teodoro Petkoff, began to sound the alarm that the more broad-based coup had been hijacked by rightist factions and twisted the reality of Chávez's exit: "This is a classic coup. . . . There is no letter of resignation for Chávez. We do not see it anywhere." Carmona further damaged his now-tenuous standing by appointing several navy officers to key positions within his new cabinet, including the minister of defense. The larger, much more influential Venezuelan army resented being upstaged by the smaller navy, and Carmona subsequently lost support from upper-ranking military officers. Compounding Carmona's problem was the fact that most middle-level officers, who tended to be more directly influential with rank-and-file troops, had remained loyal to Chávez, along with powerful army cohorts such as the presidential guard. Needless to say, an anticoup agenda quickly began to coalesce within the Venezuelan army.

By contrast, the Venezuelan media, driven by a fierce ideological opposition to Chávez's Bolivarian Revolution, which they believed was turning the country into another Cuba, abandoned any semblance of balanced reporting and instead provided a highly biased account of the events over this long weekend. The media refused to report the fact that Carmona's support was slipping and failed to cover the pro-Chávez protests in the capital. At Carmona's swearing in, one media magnate was reported to have told the new president that "we can't guarantee you the loyalty of the army, but we can promise you the support of the media."

By Saturday morning, however, less than thirty-six hours after Chávez's supposed resignation, a countercoup was underway. Indignant with the biased coverage, pro-Chávez protestors began attacking media outlets. Meanwhile, various Latin American governments were making it known that they did not support the coup. As the tectonic plates of politics shifted again, Ambassador Shapiro weighed in during a breakfast with Carmona, advising him to reconsider his decision to close the National Assembly given that it was flagrantly unconstitutional. Capitalizing on the moment, the still-imprisoned Chávez ordered that a photocopied letter written by him be distributed throughout the capital. A sympathetic corporal assigned to guard Chávez hid the note in the trash and then faxed it to pro-Chávez forces. In the letter Chávez contested the generals' assertion by stating, "I, Hugo Chávez . . . have not re-linquished the power legitimately given to me by the people." The circulation of the note reinforced the view that, though he was ousted initially for his pur-portedly undemocratic orders to fire on the protestors, Chávez—not the coup leader—was the one adhering to the constitutional principles. By Saturday evening, under pressure from protestors and the US government, a desperate Carmona announced that the National Assembly had been reinstated. Car-mona's last-ditch effort failed when the assembly immediately met and swore in Chávez's former deputy president, Diosdado Cabello, as president. Cabello announced that he would hold the post until Chávez returned and extin-guished the coup. At ten o'clock Carmona resigned. Almost five hours later, released from an island military facility, Chávez returned to the presidential palace triumphant and accompanied by the presidential guard. By sunrise Sunday morning tens of thousands of chavistas had taken to the streets of Caracas to celebrate the return of their *comandante,* looting hundreds of stores along their way.

Bush's Gaffe

Washington's decision to recognize the fledgling coup was driven by anti-Chávez sentiment, but there was an also an attempt at ideological justification: to protect democracy. The coup plotters were adamant that Chávez had "re-signed," which would have made his departure constitutional. Washington appears to have seized on this point. The White House spokesman Ari Fleischer told the media that "the [Chávez] government has suppressed what was a peaceful demonstration of the people, which led quickly to a combusti-ble situation in which Chávez resigned." The White House also labeled Chávez's ouster "a victory for democracy."

 In this the US may have been trying to adhere to the letter, if not the spirit, of the OAS's Inter-American Democratic Charter (IADC), approved on Sep-tember 11, 2001, which Washington had originally strongly supported and which Chávez opposed. The IADC's language was unequivocal: "The peoples of the Americas have a right to democracy, and their governments have an obligation to promote and defend it." Even more significant was the charter's binding sanction of collective action when member states believe democratic norms are being violated, including "an unconstitutional alteration of the con-stitutional regime." To the US, Chavez's resignation meant that the alteration had indeed been constitutional.

But it quickly became clear that the region did not see things in the same way. On Friday, April 12, when Carmona still appeared to be firmly in control, Assistant Secretary of State Otto Reich summoned several Latin American ambassadors to his Foggy Bottom office to discuss the evolving situation. The Brazilian ambassador apparently stated to Reich that the Brazilian government could not condone this break in democratic rule in Venezuela. According to some of the participating ambassadors, Reich told them that Chávez's removal was not a rupture of democratic rule and that the provisional government of Venezuela needed the support of its Latin American neighbors. The OAS, however, begged to differ, invoking Article 20 of the IADC and convening a meeting of the OAS Permanent Council on April 13, in which it adopted a resolution that "condemned the alteration of the constitutional order" in Venezuela. Interestingly, as the parameters of the debate emerged, both sides used the same charter and same language for justifying opposite stances.

At the same time, there were indications that certain US officials were also questioning the ouster's legality. One State Department report cited "the essential elements of democracy, which have been weakened in recent months, must be fully restored." On April 12 Ambassador Shapiro, in a joint statement with the Spanish government, called for "democratic normalization" and "the consolidation of a stable democratic framework."

By Saturday, as reports from Caracas clearly indicated that the new regime was in trouble, Carmona's swift fall from grace exposed the Bush administration's awkward position on the now-losing side. The White House tried to change tack by signing an OAS resolution rejecting the coup, but this was hardly convincing given that the coup had already effectively failed. Bush's officials scrambled to make statements distancing the administration from the coup. Secretary of State Powell commented that a violent overthrow of a Latin American government was against US interests and values. After Chávez had returned, National Security Advisor Condoleezza Rice backed away from supporting Chávez's removal but also claimed that Chávez had brought the entire episode upon himself: "I hope Hugo Chávez takes the message that his people sent him: That his own policies are not working for the Venezuelan people, that he has dealt with them in a high-handed fashion."

But the damage had been done. The Bush team's response to the coup reinforced a common criticism of the US government's view of democracy in Latin America: when push came to shove, the United States cared about democracy in the region only when it involved a leader who fell in line with US interests.

US Involvement?

Given the alacrity with which the Bush administration approved the coup, some have suggested that the US was complicit in the undertaking. No available evidence suggests that the US government, or the Bush administration in particular, were directly behind the planning or implementation of the coup against Chávez. But US officials had been meeting with anti-Chávez plotters the year prior to the coup, attempting a fine-line strategy of tacitly encouraging efforts to remove Chávez, albeit only through constitutional means. Accounts of the fine details of the US approach differ, however. According to one US official, "Our message was very clear: there are constitutional processes. We did not even wink at anyone." Another official's take was a little less absolute: "We were not discouraging people. . . . We were sending informal, subtle signals that we don't like this guy. We didn't say, 'No, don't you dare,' and we weren't advocates saying, 'Here's some arms, we'll help you overthrow this guy.' We were not doing that."

From what we can glean from the declassified materials (and at the time of writing there was much still under wraps), in 2001 and early 2002 the CIA was in this instance reporting about but not participating in the plotting. Tellingly, on April 6, 2002, the CIA produced classified materials indicating that "efforts to organize a coup" against Chávez were afoot, with an execution date as soon as that month. The same CIA report deduced that the plot would target Chávez and his top political and military officials. On August 8 the CIA flatly stated that "disgruntled officers are planning a coup." And in the days before the coup US officials went out of their way to preclude any potential entanglement, issuing "repeated warnings that the United States will not support any extraconstitutional moves to oust Chávez." In fact, in the weeks and months following the coup US officials privately confirmed that over the previous year they had provided Chávez with cautions. "I did say to him, there are all these rumors of coup plotting, which we were very concerned about, and he almost dismissed them," an unnamed diplomat stated in 2004. "He was dismissive of that, as if it were no big thing."

In the last analysis the April 2002 coup in Caracas was not a classic Cold War–style, CIA-hatched plot, as in Guatemala in 1954 or, more indirectly, in Chile in the early 1970s. On the contrary, the coup against Chávez was Venezuelan-crafted and Venezuelan-perpetrated. The CIA knew the key actors and had spoken with them, but when the situation began to heat up it kept the US out of the picture. It remains indisputable that the Bush administration was eager to see Chávez removed from office and that it initially condoned an un-democratic transfer of power in Latin America. But a subsequent ninety-five-page report by the State Department's inspector general did not find fault with the Bush administration's response to the coup. Yet critics would con-tend that an executive branch agency doing the evaluation would be anything but unbiased.

Postcoup Relations

Embarrassed by the coup episode, the Bush administration took a relatively low-profile approach toward Chávez in the following years. The Clinton era's stance of setting aside the rhetoric and focusing on Chávez's actions became the Bush administration's de facto postcoup policy. But over these postcoup years there were still sparks, often initiated by Chávez. In an especially pro-vocative diplomatic gesture at the height of his petro-fueled bravado, Chávez held aloft a copy of Noam Chomsky's book *Hegemony or Survival: America's Quest for Global Dominance* during his September 2006 speech to the UN General Assembly. He said to the audience that "the devil [George W. Bush] came here yesterday. It still smells of sulfur today. . . . He came here talking as if he were the owner of the world." But for anyone following Chávez's actions up until that time, his comments about Bush were nothing new. Some of Chávez's more contemptuous nicknames for the US president were "donkey," "drunkard," and "coward." While it usually tried to ignore the bombastic Ven-ezuelan, the Bush administration periodically made public its own views re-garding Chávez. Over her tenure as secretary of state, Rice called Chávez a "negative force" in the hemisphere, criticized his ties to Cuba, and claimed that he was pursuing a "Latin American brand of populism that has taken countries down the drain."

While in the Cold War such behavior by a communist leader may well have brought about an intervention or even an invasion, times had changed. In the more democratic post–Cold War realm, the international and regional climate around democracy and the rule of law had shifted—for the region and also for the lone superpower. The plotters might have had Bush's blessing, but once they failed, Bush did not intervene to prevent Chávez from returning to power, despite the hostility several members of his team felt toward the communist firebrand. As the plotters' veneer of democracy quickly tarnished, the White House's convoluted logic justifying Chávez's overthrow was indisputably null and void. But the legacy of Bush's fleeting moment of support is crucial in our

Hugo Chávez, flanked by Argentine president Néstor Kirchner (*left*) and Brazilian president Luiz Inácio Lula da Silva, or Lula, at the opening ceremony of the G-15 summit in Caracas. February 27, 2004. (Camilo González)

reading of the event amid the greater theater of US–Latin American relations. The US–Venezuelan relationship, for one, was battered; as the former Clinton White House foreign policy aide Arturo Valenzuela put it, "I think it's a very negative development for the principle of constitutional government in Latin America. I think it's going to come back and haunt all of us." But perhaps most saliently, we should read into the gap between what the ambassador believed the US would do in the wake of the coup—support Chávez—and what the president did—support the plotters. Without clarity or a unified vision about its backyard, Uncle Sam flopped rather than stomped into the twenty-first century.

39 • El Narco Mexicano
Land of the Traffickers

Pablo Escobar is like a Boy Scout compared to the Mexicans.
—US Army veteran

In the 1970s and 1980s Pablo Escobar's Medellín Cartel ruled the cocaine business, exporting the drug from Colombia to Florida via the Caribbean islands, from where it was distributed north to American cities. In the late twentieth century, however, Washington began cracking down more aggressively on trafficking in the Caribbean, forcing the Colombians to look for a new route. Enter Mexico. Given that Mexican gangs had been smuggling home-grown marijuana and heroin into the US since the 1960s, the country already harbored the criminal infrastructure necessary to maintain coca's northward flow. One DEA agent remarked that the Colombians in effect told the Mexican bosses, "We are going to provide cocaine and you are going to deliver it from somewhere in Mexico to somewhere in the United States, and you are going to turn it [the money] back over to us, to our cartel emissaries."

Soon enough, cocaine dollars poured into Mexico by the billions, with Mexican smugglers charging Colombian suppliers for the movement of cargo. It didn't take long, however, for Mexican traffickers to realize where the real money lay. As the writer Patrick Radden Keefe put it, they soon wanted "[to] stop serving as logistical middlemen and invest in their own drugs instead." The Mexicans saw the enormous profits being made by the Colombians: a kilogram of cocaine was worth $25,000 in the US but cost only $2,000 to produce. Instead of making one or two million dollars a shipment by trafficking Colombian cocaine, Mexican cartels could make twenty or even forty million dollars at a time pushing their own product. As if Washington's clampdown on the Caribbean hadn't helped Mexico enough (think the balloon effect), the US antidrug focus began shifting to extraditing Colombian traffickers.

As a result, Mexican gangs were soon managing 90 percent of the cocaine entering the United States. Benefiting from cocaine's late-twentieth-century spike of $100 per gram, the gangs were generating an estimated $70 billion a year, a figure which didn't include the profits from marijuana and methamphetamine. The latter could be produced with ease in Mexico, where there was ready access to chemical precursors not easily available in the US. In 2013 Mexico's illicit laboratories were manufacturing 80 percent of the crystal meth sold in the United States. Yet business didn't stop there. Armed with American guns smuggled across the border, which in the 2010s accounted for nearly 70 percent of the firearms found at Mexican crime scenes, the Mexican cartels also pursued human trafficking, the exploitation of immigrants, kidnapping, murder, money laundering, and general corruption to solidify their power. Cartels grew to operate with effective impunity, assassinating politicians and investigative journalists, holding civil society hostage with fear, and ultimately undermining the country's government and judiciary. Having gleaned more than arbitrage from their Colombian forerunners, the Mexican cartels quickly turned to the slums of provincial cities for recruitment of assassins, known as *sicarios* (hit men). Similarly, the Mexican cartels imitated the Colombian practice of drive-by ambushes but traded the motorcycles and pistols of the Colombians for SUVs and AK-47s. It wasn't uncommon for some fifty-plus rounds to be discovered lodged into an ambush victim and another three hundred spent shells on the ground nearby.

Calderón's "War on Drugs"

In 2006 President Felipe Calderón of Mexico declared his mission was to eradicate cartel violence in what became known as his war on drugs. Shaped by the US-led strategy in Colombia from two decades prior, Calderón's approach was to apply a mano dura, deploying seven thousand Mexican military troops to Acapulco, thirty-three hundred to Tijuana, and similar numbers to other regions mired in crisis, like Tamaulipas. Going after cartel bosses, the so-called kingpin strategy, was a central part of Calderón's plan. All told, as the operation wound down about two-thirds of the roughly three dozen major kingpins were either killed, captured, or extradited to the US.

The wisdom of Calderón's strategy was hotly debated, but it was inarguable that it sparked a huge wave of violence. Paralleling the Medellín Cartel's war against the Colombian state in the early 1990s, the Mexican cartels inaugurated a campaign of terror. By late 2006 the country echoed with harrowing stories of violence and assassination. María Sagredo Villareal, a sixty-nine-year-old man in Ciudad Juárez, the blue-collar neighbor of El Paso, exemplified the horror faced by some Mexicans almost daily. Tired of finding dead bodies discarded outside his home, Sagredo called out the killers and erected a sign reading, "PROHIB-ITED: LITTERING AND DUMPING CORPSES." Bodies continued to appear until October 2008, when Sagredo himself was shot in front of his door. In the months following Sagredo's daughter Cinthia was also shot and deposited beneath the sign. The brutality came full circle when Sagredo's other daughter and her friend went to attend Cinthia's funeral and were also shot dead.

The case of the Sagredo family was far from an isolated incident. Between late 2006 and early 2010 Mexico suffered from more than thirty thousand drug-related murders. While the majority of statistics reported narco-on-narco massacres involving Mexico's biggest players, Los Zetas and the Sinaloa Cartel, civilians were increasingly caught in the crossfire. Particularly affected were journalists, over seventy of whom were murdered between 2000 and 2016, and another fifteen were disappeared between 2010 and 2016.

The intragang battle between Los Zetas and the Sinaloa Cartel gradually bled into half a dozen states as territorial standoffs evolved into the broader question of which gang claimed dominance over the drug market. Each gang was estimated to have roughly ten thousand gunmen, with Los Zetas leading the way in exploiting slums for fresh recruits. Both sides, however, were making their presence known through crude videos and beheaded corpses. La Familia Michoacana, a Michoacán State gang working with the Zetas, infamously rolled five human heads onto a dance floor. Zeta fighters once left a note on some of their rivals' corpses: "[Sinaloa kingpins] . . . send more *pendejos* [pubic hairs, a popular Mexican slur] like this for us to kill." John Gibler, a reporter on the drug wars, summarized the savage logic of these *narcomensajes:* "All that is left is your body destroyed in a vacant lot, hanging from a highway overpass, or locked in the trunk of a car. Your name is severed, cut off, and discarded. The history that remains attached to your body is that of your particular death, bullet holes, burns, slashes, contusions, limbs removed. . . . [T]hey will turn your body from that of a person into that of a message."

This cold-blooded one-upmanship in savagery and brutality explained part of the war's staggering toll. Dozens of identified decapitations were reported over the course of Calderón's first year as president, with hundreds more in the years to come. Overall, more than fifty-five thousand people were murdered between 2008 and 2016, and the number of disappearances likely fell somewhere between the official figure of six thousand and unofficial estimates as high as twenty thousand.

As the Mexican government struggled to contain the violence, self-defense militias, or *autodefensas*, began to form in the ungoverned vacuums created by the state's evaporation. In desperation, the government attempted to incorporate these civilian bands into the state apparatus, yet as their numbers swelled, the autodefensas quickly became dominated by violent elements: the expanded militias were less selective of their victims and more susceptible to cartel corruption. In fact, even though the autodefensas were created mainly as a response to the cartel-led violence, they ultimately furthered the bloodshed rather than ameliorated it.

Plan Mexico?

Concerned by the rising insecurity in its southern neighbor, Washington began deepening its involvement in Mexico in 2008 to the tune of $400 million a year. Washington's funding package, known as the Mérida Initiative (or Plan Mexico), was intended to halt the erosion of Mexico's national security. Initiated by President Bush and executed under President Obama, the Mérida Initiative drew on Plan Colombia, emphasizing judicial reform and lending military equipment and intelligence support. US Army Special Forces began training their Mexican army counterparts. Simultaneously, an exchange program kicked off between the US and Mexican Marine Corps to implement urban warfare tactics employed in Iraq and Afghanistan. All told, during the George W. Bush and Obama administrations Mérida provided $2.3 billion for antidrug enforcement, an effort comparable to the successful—at least from Washington's outlook—multibillion-dollar Plan Colombia.

Inevitably, the plan engendered criticism. As one writer noted, the border seemed to impede much of the Mérida cash: US taxpayers' money often stayed domestic, funding private US contractor corporations for surveillance "software, computers, ion scanners, gamma-ray scanners, satellite communication networks, and other goods and services" (a critique that echoed the helicopter debates of Plan Colombia). Some of the largest budget recipients included Textron, Inc., just over $100 million for eight Bell helicopters for troop transportation and mission support; and Sikorsky Aircraft Corporation, $100 million for three Black Hawks plus $10 million to cover the delivery of three single-engine aircraft "for surveillance of drug trafficking areas and for a wide range of surveillance missions."

Still, there was broad consensus that Mexico was in a dire situation. Pundits on both sides of the border worried that Mexico was slipping toward becoming a narco state. Others claimed the real risk was not state collapse or recognizable gang control but instead that Mexico would become something like Russia, "a state heavily influenced by mafias." As was the case in Colombia, Mexico's cartel wars were tied to the country's incomplete transition to democracy, exploiting the uncertain situation that arose in 2000 when seven decades of the PRI's authoritarian rule came to an end. By the time the Mérida Initiative took effect, Mexican cartels had replaced the country's retreating democratic institutions, assuming a state's traditional role by stabilizing the peso via the use of illicit greenbacks to purchase the falling domestic currency, providing thousands of jobs, and having a presence in the numerous regions in Mexico desperate to alleviate poverty. As illicit profits came to permeate nearly every industry—hotels, cattle ranches, racehorses, music labels, football teams, film studios—the gangs assumed many local and regional administrative functions. In the eyes of many Mexicans the various cartels coalesced into one gross conglomerate, El Narco, which through its many facets earned tens of billions annually.

Making the distinction between the two sides of this struggle even more blurred, US antidrug officials were by no means impervious to the drug trade's allure. Cartels offered US agents north of the border two choices: ignore the northbound drugs or join in and make some money. Bribed agents waved tons of drugs across the border as well as thousands of unauthorized immigrants. In May 2015 the Department of Homeland Security communiqué categorized corrupt Border Patrol agents as a national security threat. Writing in the *New York Times*, Keefe noted that between 2004 and 2012 there had been 138 indictments or convictions of Immigrations and Customs Enforcement agents for corruption. "In their hurry to fortify the US–Mexico boundary with uniformed personnel," wrote Keefe, "officials may have made allowances on background checks and screenings. In some instances, job offers have been extended to the immediate relatives of known traffickers." By 2018 the rate of corruption was estimated at roughly 1 to 5 percent of the Customs and Border Protection's (CBP) sixty-thousand-strong legion.

The Anti-Border Corruption Act of 2010 spoke to Congress's efforts to vet officials more carefully, mandating polygraph testing for new employees, but this questioning did little to solve the corruption already on the inside. President

Drug tunnel, Tijuana, Mexico, October 30, 2013. US authorities shut down a secret underground tunnel equipped with electricity, ventilation, and a rail system for smuggling drugs between Tijuana and a San Diego industrial park. At the rented warehouse where the passageway ended on the US side, border control and drug enforcement agents seized more than 7,700 kilograms of marijuana and 147 kilograms of cocaine from the tunnel, arresting three men. (Jorge Duenes / Reuters Pictures)

Obama's drug czar and then CBP commissioner Gil Kerlikowske explained, "Polygraphs have made it so we don't hire people with significant problems. The bigger problem is what happens to people who are already on board." A 2017 *Atlantic* story reported that the system wasn't entirely futile, however, because two-thirds of CBP applicants failed the polygraph.

Issues with the CBP extended beyond corruption, as the force's size, cost, and purpose came into increasing question. Between 2001 and 2017 the price tag for customs and border enforcement rang in at $100 billion, surpassing the total budgets of the FBI, Secret Service, US Marshals, Alcohol, Tobacco, and Firearms, DEA, and New York City Police Department combined. In a *Politico* article, "The Green Monster," Garrett Graff highlighted that this outrageous budget funded not only sixty thousand agents but "a fleet of some 250 planes, helicopters and unmanned aerial vehicles like the Predator drones the military sent to Iraq and Afghanistan, making CBP both the largest law enforcement air force in the world and equivalent roughly to the size of Brazil's entire combat air force."

Kingpin-ed?

The US–Mexican kingpin strategy soon led to some serious policy blowback, revealing that some US officials had failed to learn from the lessons of recent history. In making the case for the Mérida Initiative, the George W. Bush administration spoke of dismantling the cartels into smaller organizations— "breaking down boulders into pebbles"—forgetting that this approach had ultimately made it *harder* to plug the Andean drug flow when the DEA applied the kingpin strategy in Colombia in the 1990s. Much like Colombia after the Washington-driven Medellín and Cali takedowns, the Calderón era (2006–12) so-called decapitations simply atomized the bigger cartels into smaller outfits. By 2008 Calderón had already abandoned the idea that the antidrug crusade "might one day eliminate the drug trade altogether." Jorge Tello, an advisor to Calderón on the matter, created a colorful analogy: "It's like a rat-control problem. The rats are always down there in the sewers, you can't really get rid of them. But what you don't want are rats on people's front doors."

With the old cartel power structures disintegrating, the increasing number of smaller gangs turned to violence as they vied for control of the drug market: the homicide rate nearly tripled. Some of the new gangs, such as the Jalisco New Generation Cartel, even outstripped the old cartels in their use of extreme violence. Calderón's successor, the centrist Enrique Peña Nieto of the PRI, took office in 2012 amid public frustration over rising levels of violence. Peña Nieto continued the militarization strategy of his predecessor, increasing the use of Special Forces in operations against the cartels, but he combined it with a suite of social and economic reforms detailed in the Pact for Mexico, endorsed by all the major political parties. Violence decreased in the first years of Peña Nieto's term but rose to then-record-high levels in 2015, the homicide rate reaching 27 per 100,000, and topped that in 2018. Tellingly, neither Calderón nor Peña Nieto sufficiently addressed the corruption present at all levels of government, federal, state, and local, on which organized crime thrives.

Yet while fractured cartels gave way to heightened violence, drugs continued to flow across the border seemingly unabated. Between 2013 and 2016, according to a DEA report, Mexican opium poppy cultivation tripled, while in 2017 US Customs interdicted more than fifty-four thousand pounds of crystal meth crossing into the United States from Mexico, a threefold increase compared to 2012. And as the cartels began to cultivate the domestic market for drugs, the devastating toll of addiction began to ravage Mexican society as well. As Joshua Partlow reported in the *Washington Post,* "The opioid epidemic that has caused so much pain in the United States is also savaging Mexico, contributing to a break-down of order in rural areas." Violence reached epidemic proportions. Díaz Navarro, a retired schoolteacher and courageous social activist monitoring the violence, described his community of Chilapa in central Guerrero as being "bathed in blood." In the first six months of 2017 alone 150 people were slain. "We don't know who is involved with whom," he said, "but the criminals kill anyone for whatever reason." The embattled Guerrero governor, Héctor Astudillo, even floated the notion of legalizing poppy cultivation "as a way of lessening the gangland rivalries."

AMLO's Approach

When Andrés Manuel López Obrador, more commonly known as AMLO, became Mexico's president in December 2018 his supporters hoped for a new era characterized by less violence and stronger rule of law. The former mayor of Mexico City, López Obrador won 53 percent of the vote, the largest share of the electorate of any presidential candidate since 1982. He took this as a mandate to implement his campaign pledge to enact a new approach to fighting Mexico's criminal cartels. López Obrador's central idea was to shift from the militarized policies of his predecessors to one he called *abrazos, no balazos,* or "hugs, not gunshots." He argued that peace could be achieved only by addressing poverty and improving education in order to break the cycle assumed to drive the cartels' recruitment process.

Despite the new approach the massacres of civilians continued. In October 2019 the shortcomings of Mexican public security were put squarely in the spotlight when the National Guard botched the arrest of Ovidio "El Ratón" Guzmán López, a leader of the Sinaloa Cartel and the son of the notorious Joaquín "El Chapo" Guzmán. The National Guard was meant to locate, arrest, and extradite the younger Guzmán to the US on charges of trafficking cocaine. After he was located in Culiacán, in the northern state of Sinaloa, officers raided Guzmán López's hideout and arrested him. Outside the compound hundreds of Guzmán López's forces began burning vehicles to block escape routes and instigated a shoot-out that killed at least a dozen people, including at least one civilian and one National Guardsman, along with members of the cartel. To avoid further escalation of the crisis, the authorities released Guzmán López and left Culiacán empty-handed. In a subsequent press conference AMLO defended the decision to release Guzmán López as the correct one, arguing that engaging in a prolonged shoot-out in the streets of Culiacán risked losing lives unnecessarily. To many, however, it appeared that the federal government had voluntarily surrendered both a wanted criminal and control of an important state capital to a criminal organization, symbolizing the absence of the rule of law in Mexico and potentially providing a worrying precedent that gangs could use violence to effectively control the security forces.

López Obrador's approach was further undermined in November 2019 with the grisly slaying in northeastern Sonora of three adults and six children, including three infants. The victims were US–Mexican citizens who belonged to the prominent fundamentalist Mormon LeBarón clan, a group that had fled to Mexico in the late nineteenth century to escape US prohibitions on polygamy. In an ambush, gunmen targeted three SUVs driven in a convoy by LeBarón women, thinking they belonged to gang members. The attack left one vehicle riddled with bullet holes and burned mostly to ashes, according to the family's social media postings. Seven other passengers, all children, some of whom were gravely wounded, narrowly escaped death by hiding out in the brush alongside the highway.

The day after the LeBarón massacre, President Donald Trump and AMLO discussed shared efforts to combat the growing violence, according to the White House. Trump also tweeted his readiness to "wage WAR on the drug cartels and wipe them off the face of the earth." AMLO rejoined that, while the offer was appreciated, US intervention was unnecessary, stating, "You cannot put out fire with fire" and reiterating that the root causes of crime needed to be addressed. The response among some on Capitol Hill was fiercely belligerent. Senator Ben Sasse, a Republican from Nebraska and a member of the Intelligence Committee, urged AMLO to join Washington in a "full-scale offensive against these butchers." He added that "Mexico's president hasn't taken the threat seriously and innocent lives have been lost again." The "hard truth," he asserted, was that Mexico was "dangerously close to being a failed state." Another Republican senator, Josh Hawley of Missouri, pushed for sanctions on Mexican authorities unwilling to combat the drug gangs. The *Wall Street Journal* argued that a "U.S. military operation can't be ruled out."

These US senators overlooked the fact that the LeBarón murders did not appear to be linked to AMLO's new strategy. Furthermore, Mexico was not close to being a failed state. While there could be a scenario in which the maximalist response suggested by the *Journal* could be justified, it would have run the risk of precipitating a bilateral crisis. In addition, nonmilitarized US approaches to checking the power of drug cartels had been somewhat effective. Sentencing reform and cannabis legalization, for example, had helped to curb demand for Mexican marijuana. It was also notable that while Trump was calling for war, his administration had in fact scaled back Mérida funding. According to the Congressional Research Service, the White House's budget request for rule-of-law efforts in Mexico for the 2019 fiscal year was only $78.9 million, a 48 percent reduction from the estimated appropriation of $152.6 million from fiscal year 2018.

The general tenor of Trump's Mexican policy, despite his rhetoric, was to shift the burden of tackling the gangs on to Mexico while he focused on bilateral issues he perceived to be of more immediate benefit to the US. Among these were the renegotiation of NAFTA and the strong-arming of Mexico into controlling undocumented immigration on the US southern border. Indeed, in April 2019 Trump used an economic Big Stick to threaten Mexico over the drug issue: "We're going to give them a one-year warning, and if the drugs don't stop, or largely stop, we're going to put tariffs. And if that doesn't stop the drugs, we close the border."

Like Tony Soprano

The capture of El Chapo Guzmán in 2014 came amid a wave of high-level takedowns of key cartel leaders, including the head of Los Zetas, Miguel Ángel Treviño Morales, known by his alias, Z-40. On June 25, 2015, US officials sent a formal extradition request to Mexican justice officials for the Sinaloa Cartel boss, who had escaped prison once before in 2001 by hiding in a laundry basket. But the Mexican government disdained the idea of extradition, preferring instead to keep El Chapo in chains on its own turf as a demonstration of national sovereignty. Six months earlier the previous attorney general, Jesús Murillo Karam, had made this point emphatically: "El Chapo must stay here to complete his sentence, and then I will extradite him. So about 300 or 400 years later—it will be a while."

Such displays of national confidence were literally undermined when, in July 2015, El Chapo broke free from his Mexican prison in plain view of the video camera in his cell. He fled through a series of sophisticated tunnels that led from the floor of his cell bathroom to a spot his henchmen had purchased seventeen months earlier, a mile away from the prison. The journalist Azam Ahmed wrote in the *New York Times* that Guzmán's second escape "cast a lurid spotlight on the incompetence and corruption that has [sic] long dogged the Mexican state, driving many to view the government on a par with criminals."

Not until early 2016 did Mexican marines in the coastal city of Los Mochis, in the northern part of Sinaloa, finally catch up with their quarry. Before dawn on January 8 seventeen Mexican Special Forces marines raided the safe house where Guzmán was hiding, killing five of his bodyguards but missing the *capo* (kingpin) yet again. They found him just hours later driving a stolen car out of town. Here is Keefe's humorous take on Guzmán's appearance after his arrest: "As he was duck-walked before the cameras, bedraggled in a grubby tank top, he looked not so much like Chapo Guzmán as like a man wearing one of those rubber Chapo Guzmán masks that were popular on both sides of the border last Halloween, his pale and hairless shoulders out of proportion with the big, familiar, square-jawed face and the improbably black mustache."

In January 2017 Guzmán was extradited to the United States to stand trial in Brooklyn. The mesmerizing trial unfolded like a Mexican *telenovela,* as text messages from Guzmán's many mistresses were used in evidence. As described by the *Washington Post,* they provided an inside glimpse into the "inner workings of the Sinaloa drug cartel, complete with tales of gruesome murders, diamond-crusted pistols, caches of cocaine smuggled in cans of peppers and, at the center of it all, a defendant who twice escaped from prison." The jury found him guilty on ten criminal counts, and in July 2019 Guzmán was sentenced to spend the rest of his life in a US maximum security penitentiary. (In 2017 the United States had assured Mexico City it would not pursue the death penalty as part of the extradition.) US District Judge Brian Cogan explained why leniency was not warranted: "The overwhelming evil is so severe." Reading written comments through an interpreter, Guzmán claimed "there was no justice" in the trial and condemned the "psychological, emotional, mental torture, 24 hours a day."

Coda: Backlash against the War on Drugs

There seemed to be a consensus in the Americas in the 1990s and 2000s on the overall validity of the drug war, despite its many problems and lack of clear success. However, in 2009 three prominent former Latin American presidents—including César Gaviria of Colombia, who was in office at the height of Escobar's savage war on the Colombian state and political class—stated publicly that it was time to "break the taboo" on the long sacrosanct drug war. In November 2011 an open letter entitled "The Global War on Drugs Has Failed" was published. Organized by the UK-based Beckley Foundation and signed by diverse current and former heads of state, including Colombian president Juan Manuel Santos,

Guatemalan president Otto Pérez Molina, former US president Jimmy Carter, former Mexican president Vicente Fox, and former Colombian president César Gaviria, the letter claimed that "the global war on drugs has failed. . . . The drug-free world so confidently predicted by supporters of the war on drugs is further than ever from attainment. The policies of prohibition create more harms than they prevent. We must seriously consider shifting resources away from criminalising tens of millions of otherwise law-abiding citizens, and move towards an approach based on health, harm-reduction, cost-effectiveness and respect for human rights. Evidence consistently shows that these health-based approaches deliver better results than criminalisation."

The mood in Latin America regarding the US-led war on drugs appeared to be changing quickly. Shortly after his arrival at the April 2012 Summit of the Americas, held at Cartagena, Colombia, President Barack Obama received an unexpected earful from some of his Latin American counterparts, who denounced the overly militarized and criminalized drug war strategies as creating havoc in their often-fragile democracies. The summit host and erstwhile reliable US drug war ally Juan Manuel Santos told an American journalist, "There's probably no person who has fought the drug cartels and drug trafficking as I have. But at the same time, we must be very frank: after 40 years of pedaling and pedaling very hard, sometimes you look to your left, you look to your right, and you are almost in the same position. So you have to ask yourself: Are we doing the correct thing?"

Cast on the defensive, Obama did acknowledge that the drug war was "a legitimate topic for debate" and that it was "entirely legitimate to have a conversation about whether the laws in place are ones that are doing more harm than good in certain places." As the summit concluded, the participating hemispheric heads of state commissioned the OAS to conduct a report detailing various alternative scenarios to the status quo approach.

Published to little fanfare a year later, in 2013, the findings of the report were decidedly modest. Apart from the banal contention that past and present approaches had not worked, the most stirring language in the report was that the single most important goal in the drug war was to tackle the violence associated with this illicit trade by "reducing the power of criminal organizations" while bolstering the "strength and effectiveness of democratic institutions and the capabilities of security, judicial, and law enforcement personnel." Did we not know this already?

Ironically, and frustratingly for President Obama, the OAS report sanctioned more status quo compared to Obama's domestic drug stance, which included implicit endorsement of state-level legalization of recreational can-nabis. Perhaps this attitude of keeping things the way they are was due to the fact that, Uruguay's marijuana liberalization notwithstanding, Latin American publics were decidedly against any shift toward legalization. The OAS report found no significant support in any hemispheric country for decriminalization or legalization.

One has to wonder, then, whether President Santos's purportedly coura-geous stance in Cartagena was just another act in Latin America's lively po-litical theater. One American diplomat in Bogotá stated privately and half-jokingly that Santos's dovish rhetoric on drugs was an attempt to secure the position of UN secretary-general after he left office. Santos's professional motives aside, North American prolegalization groups that expected the OAS report to condemn the US interdiction approach in the region were likely dis-appointed. For the time being there seemed to be no regional consensus re-garding a viable alternative to the war on drugs.

40 • Washington–Havana Whiplash

In 2016 Barack Obama became the first US president to visit Cuba in almost a century, explaining to the world that he had come "to bury the last remnant of the Cold War in the Americas." Obama believed that his opening to Cuba would be one of his most important foreign policy legacies given that relations between the two countries had been effectively frozen since the imposition of the 1960 US trade embargo. His claim was not without justification. As he made clear in an interview before his trip, Obama was confident that his visit would have an impact and persuade holdouts in both Washington and Havana to at last lift the embargo: "My strong prediction is that sometime in the next president's administration, whether they are a Democrat or a Republican, the embargo in fact will be removed, because it makes sense for us to be able to sell into Cuba, to do business with Cubans, to show our business practices and how we treat workers and how we approach issues of human rights."

Eager to demonstrate that his engagement with the decidedly undemocratic Havana regime did not mean the jettisoning of human rights, Obama met with civil society activists and with Cardinal Jaime Ortega, the archbishop of Havana. Ortega, at the behest of Pope Francis, had helped broker the secret deal between the two governments in 2014 to begin normalizing relations. Yet the idea that Obama's charisma and bold policy rapprochement would bring swift social reform was quickly brought into question by reports that Cuban security forces had made dozens of arrests hours before the visit. One of them took place during the weekly march of the visibly dissident outfit Ladies in White, whose leader, Berta Soler, was scheduled to meet with Obama. Another dissident, Elizardo Sánchez of the Cuban Commission of Human Rights and National Reconciliation, told the *New York Times* that over five hundred activists had been detained in March, a decided uptick. As Sánchez explained, "It's the climate of intimidation the government is creating for Obama's visit. Right now what you see is preventive repression, so it does not occur to anyone to say anything to Obama while he is here." Or as another regime opponent in the eastern provincial city of Santiago de Cuba characterized the unfolding crackdown, "It's the third law of Newton: the greater the actions for democracy, the greater the repressive reaction by the regime."

Even the benign event of Obama's presence as Major League Baseball's Tampa Bay Rays took the diamond against the Cuban national team could not escape politics and intrigue: tickets for the invitation-only ball game were distributed mostly to regime loyalists. In the press conference that followed, Obama maneuvered an obviously unhappy Castro into taking questions from reporters, including awkward questions about political prisoners. Obama was betting that his brief rapprochement would help trigger the seismic tremors that might one day weaken or even topple this communist regime. He stupefied his communist hosts when, in a televised address while sitting next to Raúl, he repeated the US nation's creed whereby "every person should be equal under the law . . . citizens should feel free to speak their mind without fear . . . and to criticize their government, and to protest peacefully."

Cuban Thaw?

Predating the so-called Cuban thaw, a stunning Obama–Raúl Castro declaration took place on December 17, 2014, the result of eighteen months of painstaking high-level negotiations facilitated by Canada and the Vatican. The Cubans released two political prisoners: the USAID contractor Alan Gross, who was serving a fifteen-year prison sentence, and the Cuban national Rolando Sarraf Trujillo, who was convicted of spying for the United States. In return, Washington freed three notorious Cuban operatives who had been incarcerated in the United States since 1998. The two sides also agreed to upgrade each other's "interest sections" into full embassies, and Obama would ease travel, remittance, and banking restrictions as well as remove Cuba from its list of state sponsors of terrorists. "We will end an outdated approach that for decades has failed to advance our interests, and instead we will begin to normalize relations between our two countries," he declared in a White House address. He vowed that the agreement would "begin a new chapter among the nations of the Americas" and move beyond a "rigid policy that is rooted in events that took place before most of us were born." The economic

reaction was swift. One example of the global economy's activation on the island is Airbnb, which began enrolling scores of Cubans hoping to rent out
their houses to the expected deluge of yanqui tourists.

To put Obama's Cuba gambit in perspective, his immediate ten predecessors,
Republican and Democratic alike, had not departed from a policy of isolation. If
the embargo-era Big Stick had not worked in the previous decades of futility,
could one really fault Obama for trying some diplomatic carrots, especially now
that the Cold War had been over for almost three decades? If Eisenhower and
Reagan believed in the power of people-to-people interactions during the existential global Cold War, why would the US fear to attempt to do the same with a
small Caribbean island? Over half of Cuban Americans backed the normalization while more than three-quarters under fifty years of age supported it.

To Senator Marco Rubio (R-FL), however, the Cuban Marxist dictatorship
was a foreign policy white whale that had to be slayed rather than engaged, no
matter the cost. The son of Cuban immigrants, Rubio was scathing as the bilateral thaw was announced in December 2014: "This entire policy shift announced today is based on an illusion, on a lie, the lie and the illusion that
more commerce and access to money and goods will translate to political freedom for the Cuban people. . . . All this is going to do is give the Castro regime,
which controls every aspect of Cuban life, the opportunity to manipulate these
changes to perpetuate itself in power."

While running for president in 2016, Rubio told the *Washington Post* about the
shadow of his loving grandfather, *papá,* "a Ronald Reagan–loving, cigar-smoking
shoemaker" with a deep American patriotism. "He was a huge influence on me.
He felt that more countries would become like Cuba if America wasn't the strongest country in the world. So that was instilled in me from an early age." Rubio
revealed in his memoir that as a boy he had once "boasted I would someday lead
an army of exiles to overthrow Fidel Castro and become president of a free Cuba."

This background explains Rubio's unyielding stance vis-à-vis the Cuban
thaw. According to Rubio, the Cuban regime is a dictatorship, insulated from
the whims of popular opinion, and thus the "hope that a flood of American
tourists will one day lead to a democratic opening . . . will not [work] because
it never has anywhere in the world—and it will not now." Obama was foolishly
indulging tyranny and granting "international legitimacy" to a rogue regime,
argued Rubio, citing US economic and diplomatic engagement with autocratic China as an instance in which such an approach had failed to make any
democratic headway. His alternative was to cut ties and tighten sanctions until
Havana showed demonstrable progress on human rights and democracy.

A sign in Old Havana featuring Cuban president Raúl Castro and US
president Barack Obama welcomes Obama to Cuba. Obama's historic visit
was the first by a sitting US president in ninety years. March 20, 2016.
(Paul Hennessy / Alamy Stock Photo)

Rubio's hawkishness was matched by hard-liners on the Cuban side. Some
key US officials who visited Cuba with Obama sensed a backlash by elements
within the government. Less than a month after Obama's visit, the blowback
became clear when a top Cuban foreign ministry official characterized the
Obama thaw as "an attack on our history, culture, and symbols." The US journalists Adam Entous and Jon Lee Anderson note that during military proces-
sions Cuban troops threatened not only to wage war if US imperialism came to
the island but also to make Obama "a hat out of bullets to the head." This rigid
antinormalization cohort may have included Fidel Castro himself. In a letter to
"Brother Obama" published in the Communist Party outlet *Granma* just days
after Obama's visit, the aged Fidel affirmed that "nobody should be under the
illusion that the people of this noble and selfless country will renounce
the glory, the rights, or the spiritual wealth they have gained." He waved away
the carrot of US-driven economic development too: "We do not need the empire
to give us anything." Faced with such opposition, bilateral relations remained
decidedly chilly, with the trade embargo remaining in place and the expected

flood of tourists failing to materialize. It goes without saying that Cuban Americans by no means represented the only obstacle to the proceedings.

Havana Syndrome

Starting in late 2016 and lasting through August 2017 roughly two dozen US diplomats working in Havana started reporting a range of symptoms including hearing loss, double vision, headaches, and even acute cognitive impairment. A University of Pennsylvania neurosurgeon studied the patients, including eight Canadian diplomats who claimed similar symptoms, and reported that they appeared "exactly like the patients we would see in a concussion clinic." Yet none of them reported suffering any type of head collisions. Some suspected a kind of sonic attack successfully carried out by either the Cuban government, rogue Cuban agents, or a third party like Russia in cahoots (or not) with hard-liners in Havana.

Benjamin Rhodes was an Obama White House aide who participated in the nine rounds of secret negotiations to broker the bilateral deal of 2014. In his calculus, "The Russians would have every interest in fucking with us in Cuba." Moscow must be reckoning, Rhodes surmised, that "you're in our neighborhood [referring to Eastern Europe, especially Ukraine], and we're going to mess around in yours." Assuming it was indeed an attack, the motive was presumably the same: to torpedo the thaw, to use a mixed metaphor. But another interpretation might be that an otherwise routine Cuban intelligence mission was utilizing a surveillance technology that went haywire, causing inadvertent health damages.

In late September 2017 Secretary of State Rex Tillerson ordered all nonessential personnel evacuated from the embassy. The Cuban government vehemently denied any involvement, attributing the episode to a case of mass hysteria, a clinical condition in which collective stress and anxiety manifest in shared physical symptoms among a group. Soon after Tillerson's decree, Havana issued a statement: "Cuba has never allowed, or will it allow, the Cuban territory to be used for any action against accredited diplomatic officials or their families, without exception." It also called the embassy drawdown and expulsions "hasty, inappropriate and unthinking."

Certainly Marco Rubio knew the answer during the hearings he convened in early 2018: "Two things we know for sure: people were hurt and the Cuban government knows it." Conservative foreign policy circles in Washington were also not convinced of the Cuban government's innocence. José Cárdenas, for one, alleged that Havana's "historical record" of harassment was overwhelming, making the sonic attack something the Cuban regime would be "perfectly willing to do."

Accusations of Cuban abuse of American personnel had circulated for decades. For example, in 2003 reports surfaced that the Cuban intelligence service had deposited excrement in US diplomats' houses. A top US envoy stationed in Havana, James Cason, explained other tactics: "They would come into your house and erase the pictures of your kids off your computer, or turn all the books around on your bookshelf, just to show you that you had no privacy." But there were limits. "They never did anything physical to anybody," Cason said.

In contrast to Rubio, Rhodes was skeptical that the Cubans who had just brokered the rapprochement would now go Cold War on the US: "It just doesn't strike me as something the Cuban government would do. They've been pragmatic about Trump." The mention of the freshly inaugurated President Trump is telling here, given that he had denounced the Cuban thaw as a "terrible and misguided deal" and announced the reimposition of travel and trade curbs in June 2017. This raises questions about the extent to which Tillerson's embassy evacuation order (save twenty-seven essential personnel) was in fact a political move. The timeline is important. The personnel move was presumably about the health and safety of US diplomats, but Foggy Bottom also issued a travel warning to Americans considering a trip. Within a week Trump expelled fifteen Cuban diplomats working in the United States. Tillerson's reasoning was that it was necessary to keep Havana's embassy personnel in a similarly reduced capacity as the US embassy in Havana.

The Cuban regime blamed all of these moves on cynical domestic politics designed to thwart the thaw, and it may have had a point: Trump was explicitly against closer relations. But just because Havana is a David to Washington's Goliath does not mean that the Cubans couldn't have been up to something with the embassy—sonic or otherwise. Ultimately, as Peter Kornbluh says: "This is likely another installment in the long saga of spy-vs.-spy in U.S.–Cuba relations." In late 2020, the National Academies of Sciences, Engineering, and Medicine reported that "directed, pulsed radiofrequency energy" was the "most plausible mechanism" to cause what the world had come to call the Havana syndrome.

Back to the Cold

Trump's antipathy toward the détente would soon have teeth. In the middle of 2019 American newspaper readers were being told that, due to Trump's new tightening of sanctions on Cuba, "just like that, the cruise ships are gone, along with thousands of cash-toting Americans who oohed and aahed—and shopped—amid the crumbling grandeur of Old Havana." As the *Washington Post* correspondent Anthony Faiola put, it, this had to seem to Cubans like a "bitter reversal of fortune" given Obama's restoration of relations and the history-making visit in 2016. Chefs, artists, and high-tech entrepreneurs were supposedly going to thrive in the "seemingly lucrative détente." Instead, increasingly desperate Cubans were lining up for scarce goods in what had become the island's most searing crisis since the economic and social catastrophes during the so-called special period in the early 1990s when Havana lost its key sponsor, the Soviet Union.

Most Cuba watchers attributed the most recent severe economic contraction to the implosion of Cuba's key patron, oil-swollen Venezuela as well as Havana's incompetence in managing the day-to-day-economy. But the Trump sanctions, doled out to punish Cuba for its continued ties to Venezuela, appeared to have caused some of the most recent and immediate pain. Justifying the new restrictions on US citizens' travel to the island and oil deliveries from Venezuela, a senior Trump official explained the policy logic: "We are talking about funding and financing that goes to a regime that is repressing 11 million people and is supporting a regime that is repressing 31 million people in Venezuela. We are serious. These are times for maximum pressure, and that is what has informed our thinking."

Cuban authorities countered that US actions were not weakening the communist regime but hurting ordinary Cubans. Local Cubans agreed that Trump was the problem. "This situation we are living in can only be attributed to one single problem, the U.S. blockade from this disgraceful Trump," one elderly resident told Faiola. "The man is crazy, a paranoid. . . . The situation has become worse for us since he's been there." Others, however, were inclined to blame their own government. "This will never be fixed," lamented an anonymous citizen. "The problem is political. Leaders who only think they know what they are doing."

Coda: *Our Woman in Havana*

Vicki Huddleston first started working in and on Cuba as a US Foreign Service officer in the late 1990s, before going on to work at the Pentagon. This period was an especially precarious time for Castro's regime, what with the American embargo tightening and Soviet subsidies worth around $5 billion annually coming to an end. In her gripping memoir *Our Woman in Havana*,

Huddleston recounts her experiences as chief of the US Interests Section (effectively the ambassador) in Havana during the Bill Clinton and George W. Bush presidencies.

In Huddleston's analysis Washington's "Cuba policy is actually domestic policy, not foreign policy," driven by the Cuban–American lobby's desire for harsh, punitive measures against the Cuban regime. She herself expressed no patience for the "myths and contradictions" behind the rhetoric outlining how Cuban Americans must "fight to regain the country they lost." In her words the Cuban American voting bloc has "seduced Democrats and Republicans alike": hardcore conservatives like Ronald Reagan and George W. Bush played to the Cuban American electorate, but so did John F. Kennedy and Bill Clinton. During the 2000 presidential election the so-called *voto castigo* (punishment vote) went against Al Gore as payback for Clinton's (mis)handling of the tortured repatriation case involving Cuban boy Elián González, giving the election to Bush. To Huddleston the punitive US approach to Cuba, driven by these interests, is insupportable: "It is well past time that we stop making Cuba a glaring exception to the way we engage with countries around the world whose political systems we oppose. Cuba is the only country against which we maintain a comprehensive unilateral economic embargo and the only country in which we occupy part of its territory [Guantánamo Bay] against its wishes."

Huddleston argued further against punitive measures: "Economic embargoes hurt people more than they hurt governments," she wrote, critiquing one of the foundational elements of US policy toward Cuba going back fifty years. In the absence of political and economic engagement, Huddleston expressed certainty that Washington would needlessly alienate a "potential strategic ally" while fomenting unnecessary division among its existing allies.

The former diplomat was elated when Barack Obama created a diplomatic opening with Cuba in late 2014. She believed that the conditions became even better for a thaw in relations after Fidel Castro's brother Raúl stepped down in April 2018, as for the first time in almost sixty years "a Castro will no longer rule Cuba."

The problem was Donald Trump's efforts to undo Obama's historic bilateral agreements with a regime in Havana that demonstrated a remarkably deft ability to maintain a hermetic grip on political life in Cuba. The fact that the communist regime survived the end of the Castros should give one pause for thought in predicting any swift change in Cuba's political direction, whatever the US might or might not do. Taking the temperature of the Cuban thaw remains an uncertain business.

41 • Poor Mexico
So Far from God, So Close to Trump

I don't care about Mexico, honestly. I really don't care about Mexico.
—Donald Trump, November 2015

As just about everyone on both sides of the Rio Grande knows, ties between the United States and Mexico run deep and wide. Given the more than thirty-five million Mexicans and Mexican Americans living in the United States; a two-thousand-mile border that is crossed, legally or otherwise, more than a million times each year; and hundreds of billions of dollars of annual trade, it is hard to overstate the interconnectedness between the two countries.

In some ways the relationship is equal. For example, to policy makers in both countries the neighboring country is simultaneously a domestic and a foreign policy portfolio. But in most ways the relationship is not symmetrical. Given its wealth, power, and global footprint, the United States is Mexico's preeminent global partner, so Mexicans tend to pay close attention to and know a fair bit about the goings-on in its northern neighbor. But most Americans, elite and otherwise, tend not to return the favor. They don't follow this country of 130 million closely nor do they concern themselves with the domestic affairs south of the border unless they directly affect them. It's a slanted form of apathy that is roused only when the attention-grabbing issues of narco violence and immigration are bandied about by politicians and the media.

El Donald Lashes Out

This asymmetry of attention was revealed during the 2016 US presidential campaign. Despite the fact that Donald Trump made Mexico a major theme, it rarely dawned on most Americans, convulsed inward by their own political drama, to ask how the whole tawdry psychodrama appeared to Mexicans. Given how sensitive the Mexican national psyche is to slights from the Colossus to the North, Trump's June 2015 fulminations about Mexican rapists and murderers marauding north of the border did not go unnoticed nor did his threats to tear down NAFTA and build a wall along the border. Fher Olvera, the lead singer of Maná, Mexico's closest equivalent to U2, told a Los Angeles concert audience, "We feel sorry for that Miser. He is incompetent. I haven't heard a speech so violent and so filled with hate since Hitler." Using his trademark deflection technique, Trump soon tweeted, "I like Mexico and love the spirit of the Mexican people." This did not placate critics like the former Mexican president Felipe Calderón, who responded, "Hypocrite." President Peña Nieto, by contrast, was excoriated for not demanding an apology from Trump, who was at the time still a dark-horse Republican primary candidate.

Peña Nieto's fortunes took a further nosedive in August 2016 after Trump, now the Republican presidential nominee, accepted Peña Nieto's invitation to visit Mexico City, where the two held a press conference on trade and crime and conducted a restrained discussion of Trump's proposal to build a wall between the two countries. However, any progress from this sit-down was soon undone at a rally in Phoenix hours later, where Trump told ebullient supporters, "While there are many illegal immigrants in our country who are good people, this doesn't change the fact that most illegal immigrants are lower-skilled workers with less education who compete directly against vulnerable American workers, and that these illegal workers draw much more out from the system than they will ever pay in."

The candidate also had sharp words for those he deemed too indulgent of low-skilled immigration, saying they were out of touch with the core concerns of the American people and spent "too much time in Washington." Trump's solution? Hard-line rhetoric to deter the masses from coming: "Our message to the world will be this: You cannot obtain legal status or become a citizen of the United States by illegally entering our country. Can't do it. This declaration alone will stop the crisis of illegal crossing. You can't just smuggle in, hunker down, and wait to be legalized. Those days are over." Trump's message of fear in Phoenix was corroborated by the parents of American citizens who said that undocumented immigrants had murdered their children. One mother told the rally, "If you don't vote for Trump, we won't have a country."

Trump's visit to Mexico City and the Phoenix speech, taken together, amounted to a kind of political bait-and-switch gambit, and President Peña Nieto paid the price. His popularity among Mexicans, already weakened by

President Donald Trump discusses proposed border wall prototypes alongside
Border Patrol Sector Chief Rodney Scott, San Diego, California. March 13, 2018.
(CBP Photo / Alamy Stock Photo)

domestic scandals and yet another spike in narco violence, took a huge hit owing to the perception that he had been played by Trump. His popularity continued to sink after Trump was elected. The Mexican paper *El Financiero*
reported that an astoundingly low proportion of Mexicans, a mere 2 percent,
held a favorable opinion of Trump, and Peña Nieto's meek showing in the face
of Trump's attacks pulled him down to about the same level.

Mexico's economy paid a similar price from the "Trump Effect." The
strength of the peso vacillated according to the perceived likelihood of a Trump
victory, but on November 9, when his victory was confirmed, the volatility
ended: the peso sank to an all-time low, crossing a new threshold of twenty
pesos per dollar. Following the election, Minister of Finance José Antonio
Meade declared that the Mexican government had a contingency plan for this
doomsday scenario, but these assurances did little to assuage concerns. President-elect Trump's early January 2017 tweets claiming that he would punish
US companies that moved their production to Mexico added another layer of
anger and anxiety.

But Trump succeeded in doing something almost unheard of in Mexico's
motley politics: create unity. Citizens crafted piñatas in El Donald's likeness,

while in June 2015 Univisión, the exclusively Spanish-language network in the United States, summarily dropped its link to the Trump co-owned *Miss USA* pageant, set to take place in only a few weeks. When as president Trump announced plans to build the wall along the southern border "Mexicans of all political stripes," as described by the *Wall Street Journal* editorial page, considered it an insult. Trump then tweeted that President Peña Nieto should cancel the upcoming bilateral meeting between the two heads of state if Mexico wasn't prepared to cough up the cash for building said wall. Backed by the entire, normally fractious spectrum of Mexican politics, Peña Nieto promptly canceled the meeting. Attempting to quell this international incident, Trump soon spoke directly with Peña Nieto, and both described the call as productive.

A Man in History

History plays a part in Mexican perceptions of Donald Trump. Seen from Mexican eyes, Trump is the embodiment of the rich, smug gringo boss who unsettles Mexico's deeply nationalist and *machista* self-identity. Mexicans do not like being dictated to, especially by *gabachos* (slang for the slang, gringo). The ire that Trump evokes in Mexicans is real and founded in key events over the course of the countries' two-century history.

The Mexican–American War of 1846 was a calamity for Mexicans. Generations of Mexicans have learned in school, not inaccurately, that Texas and California were "territories usurped by the United States" in the 1830s and 1840s. The official US Marine Corps hymn starts with "From the Halls of Montezuma," referencing the vaunted Battle of Chapultepec in September 1847, when marines overran Mexico City's main citadel. US citizens might not remember these names and places; most Mexicans do.

The important element of the Mexican psyche was that the jaded view of the United States was not just due to actual Punitive Expedition–style invasions or pejorative rhetoric but to how the Mexican state in the postrevolutionary decades constructed a sweeping *mexicanidad* (Mexicanness) identity that made anti-Americanism as reflexively Mexican as, say, apple pie is American. Now it would be the Mexican state and, even better, the ruling party, or PRI, that would protect Mexico's oft-violated sovereignty. Vote for the PRI, the architects of the "perfect dictatorship," to use the novelist Mario Vargas Llosa's inimitable phrasing, and you're voting for Mexico.

The PRI's dirty secret—and what made the dictatorship all the more perfect—was that despite its incessant nationalist and antiyanqui rhetoric, its ideology and policies were remarkably adaptive and flexible. It sought and maintained better relationships in and with Washington than any radical Mexico City newspaper editorial or presidential address delivered from Los Pinos palace would have the Mexican public believe. A fine example of this contrast between appearances and reality occurred around the massive earthquake that demolished Mexico City in 1985. At first the PRI ceremoniously refused assistance from the United States but then quietly changed its mind soon after. In the end Mexican authorities were widely deemed negligent in their emergency response efforts, and public opinion toward the ruling party soured. Some observers feel that this development was the first nail in the perfect dictatorship's coffin en route to its death via democratic elections in 2000 after seventy-one years in power.

Bilateral Blues or Bliss?

With the PRI gone, the last of Mexico's all-but-official anti-Americanism ended. Indeed, since NAFTA began in 1994, and especially after the PRI's peaceful transition out of power, the bilateral relationship improved in myriad ways. Mexican enmity toward the United States became a fraction of what it once was, replaced by an almost "special relationship" of bilateral consultation and respect on issues ranging from drugs and thugs to trade. Exhibit No. 1 was the capture of El Chapo Guzmán in January 2016, when US counternarcotics agents disguised themselves as Mexican marines to aid in the hunt for the Mexican drug kingpin.

One of the ironies of Trump's hostile rhetoric toward Mexico and Latin American immigrants more broadly was that in so many respects the two nations were more culturally and economically intertwined than ever before. As the researcher Andrew Selee noted, constant bidirectional flows of people and capital were producing "vanishing frontiers." And these borders, it seemed, were vanishing in expected places like the San Diego–Tijuana region, where a joint international airport operates on the Mexican side of the border and US Republican politicians extol their unified economic zone. But they were disappearing also in places located far from Mexico, such as Hazleton, Pennsylvania, and Knoxville, Tennessee. In Rust Belt cities across the Northeast, borders faded away, as was apparent in the Mexican bakery giant Bimbo that employed US workers and the *taquerías* that were adored by gringos.

When US media did pay attention to Mexico, it tended to fixate on the undeniable and incessant gangland horrors there. Less covered, however, was the economic and social revolution that took place in Mexico starting in the early 1990s. In a single generation Mexicans' life expectancy jumped four years, bringing it within two years of that of Americans. Median income rose by one-third since the early 1990s, and education levels over the same period increased by over half. By the 2010s a quarter of Mexican children were attending institutions of higher learning, triple the rate of previous decades. Indeed, Mexico had become a middle-class country: 40 percent of the population is defined as such. These changes partly explain why Mexicans were no longer entering the United States illegally as they once did. Between 2010 and 2020 more Mexicans returned to their home country than migrated to the United States, contrary to Trump's conservative, base-rousing rants.

Enter AMLO

In July 2018 Mexico experienced its most stunning electoral moment since its transition to democracy in 2000, when, in his third attempt to secure the Mexican presidency, Andrés Manuel López Obrador won in a landslide victory. Surprisingly, given his strident left-wing ideologies and prior rebukes of Trump, AMLO's initial approach to his US counterpart was circumspect, in no small part due to his sense that Mexico had much to lose—above all, economically—in a deteriorated bilateral climate. Trump, by contrast, pushed hard on immigration, issuing multiple threats about closing the US–Mexico border and levying tariffs of roughly $346 billion if Mexico did not do more to stop Central American immigrants from transiting through its territory. Critics, including free-market Republicans, slammed Trump for using trade policy and NAFTA—at this point the three governments had signed but not all had ratified NAFTA 2.0 with a few updates—to leverage the separate issue of unauthorized immigration.

AMLO eventually agreed to boost security at the border, but in so doing he took many resources away from the fight against the cartels in the Mexican heartland. And then came the 2020 outbreak of the coronavirus and its associated restrictions on the international movement of people—the perfect fuel for Trump's anti-immigrant agenda. Now, using a public-health angle, Trump could drastically and justifiably restrict cross-border movement from Mexico. But in one of the more bizarre twists of the US–Mexico relationship, the pandemic ended up bringing the two heads of state closer together. AMLO described the relationship as a friendship, while Trump promised Mexico one thousand ventilators and praised López Obrador in return. Some critics asserted that AMLO had no choice but to please Trump. Whatever the case, his accommodation of a president with such a notorious record of denigrating Mexico and Mexicans threatened to pose a crucial challenge to AMLO's domestic credibility.

Ultimately, it seemed that in the time of Trump, Mexico had to dance to its powerful neighbor's increasingly divisive tune. The lesson from history—that which affects Mexico also affects the United States—appeared lost on Trump, even if the consequences were real. Time showed that the border between the two countries was never fixed or impermeable, and Trump's short-term vote-winning rhetoric and strong-armed policies eroded the fragile trust between the two governments.

Coda: Borderlands

Francisco Cantú studied international relations as an undergraduate at Georgetown University in Washington, DC, and expected to pursue a career in public policy. But, infused with wanderlust, Cantú also wanted to work in the outdoors and experience real life outside the Washington Beltway. A bilingual, third-generation Mexican American reared near the border, Cantú felt drawn to the US Border Patrol because his mother was a National Park ranger. In his memoir, *The Line Becomes a River*, Cantú recalls explaining to his dubious mother that he was "tired of reading about the border in books" and added that "stepping into a system doesn't mean that the system becomes you." He joined the Border Patrol in 2008 at the age of twenty-three. During his first year or so he was stationed at the border itself, after which he carried out relatively staid, desk-bound intelligence work in Arizona, New Mexico, and Texas—the vast, arid, and often inhospitable borderlands of which straddle the three-thousand-kilometer-long US–Mexican frontier.

Cantú's exquisitely crafted, distressing memoir brings readers face to face with the reality of the border, a place most Washington pundits forever launch comments at without seeing firsthand. Cantú documents his time working for *la migra*, the term Latino migrants use to refer to the Border Patrol, as well as his experiences after he left the agency in 2012. He expresses ambivalence about the agency's professionalism and humanity, writing of agents slicing the water containers that desperately parched migrants depend on for their lives and of a higher-up's assigning migrants to one of two categories, "scum-bags" or "P.O.W.s," that is, plain ol' wetbacks. In an especially harrowing and heartrending scene that occurred after Cantú's departure from the agency, an unauthorized Mexican migrant with whom Cantú had developed a friendship is deported. Virtually powerless to do anything other than help his friend pursue a conventional legal response, Cantú's despair is on full display. "It's like I never quit," he tells his mother. "It's like I'm still part of this thing that crushes."

42 • Exodus from the Northern Triangle

They haven't done a thing for us.
—President Donald Trump, referring to the Salvadoran, Honduran,
and Guatemalan governments on immigration to the United
States, March 29, 2019

Sometime in 2018 a Honduran citizen named Manuela Hernández, who lived in a town called San Pedro Sula, decided she could no longer pay a local gang's fifty-dollar-a-month war tax. Her alternative to paying was to take a step that countless other Hondurans have made: to migrate with her young daughter to the United States. "I have to go," she told the *Wall Street Journal* correspondent Ryan Dube. "You can't have a life with the gangs," she said, miming having her throat cut. A fellow San Pedro Sula resident named Erasmus Salinas, a sixty-four-year-old street vendor, told Dube a similar story. Gangs had killed his brother-in-law a few years earlier, but he had little hope the authorities would apprehend the perpetrators. "There is no justice," he said. Legions more desperate people from El Salvador and Guatemala, which, together with Honduras, make up the so-called Northern Triangle of Central America, faced a similar choice: endure life-threatening conditions at home or seek a better life elsewhere.

There was little reason to doubt these grim accounts of life in the Northern Triangle. A May 2017 report by Médecins Sans Frontières described the region as suffering "unprecedented levels of violence outside a war zone," adding that "citizens are murdered with impunity" and "kidnappings and extortion are daily occurrences. Non-state actors perpetuate insecurity and forcibly recruit individuals into their ranks, and use sexual violence as a tool of intimidation and control." Girls as young as eleven were taken as *jainas*, or sex slaves, and boys were forcibly recruited into the gangs.

To some extent the myriad ills afflicting the Northern Triangle were nothing new: the region had been victimized by corruption, domestic violence, extortion, male underemployment, and adolescent recruitment into gangs, among other problems, ever since its constituent countries came into being in the first half of the nineteenth century. In the twentieth century, seeking to emulate Fidel Castro's spectacular revolutionary triumph in Cuba in 1959, Marxist guerrillas in all three countries (though far less so in Honduras) picked up arms to topple military juntas or civilian governments. The Guatemalan revolution lasted from 1960 to 1996, while the Salvadoran revolution raged from 1980 to 1992.

Although the end of the Cold War bolstered the role of the ballot box in these previously war-torn nations, it was not enough to yield adequate state institutions or to confer sufficient legitimacy on democratic governments. Making matters worse, drug traffickers began shifting their transit routes for cocaine through Central America as their once-preferred maritime routes came under pressure during the US-led war on drugs. The festering wounds of the Cold War era and the weaknesses of the quasi-democratic era that followed were exploited by gangs and other malignant actors to further destabilize the Northern Triangle. A vicious downward cycle resulted: civilian insecurity delegitimized vulnerable public institutions, while ineffective public institutions produced civilian insecurity.

In addition, the US government's strategy on immigration changed drastically between the end of the Cold War and the migrant crises of the 2000s and 2010s. During the Cold War the US prided itself on an immigration policy that welcomed political refugees from communist countries as a means of cultural one-upmanship against the Reds, but when the Cold War ended, that need disappeared. Immigration remained relatively under the radar as a domestic issue until the 9/11 attacks changed everything. The first foreign-launched attack on US soil catalyzed anti-immigration sentiment among conservatives, initially directed at the global Muslim community, and then, starting in 2015, Donald Trump's campaign for president ratcheted up the rhetoric against immigrants from Latin America as well.

Reasons to Leave: Life under El Salvador's MS-13

The emergence of the MS-13, El Salvador's dominant gang, is a salient tale of the lasting impact of the political instability experienced by Central American countries during the Cold War and another instance of US policy blowback under the Clinton administration. In the 1970s and 1980s hundreds of thousands of Central Americans, a majority of them Salvadorans, fled dictatorial repression and ideological violence in their home countries and landed in the United States. In Los Angeles Salvadoran youth at the mercy of predatory gangs from other Latin American countries organized the first iteration of MS-13, which expanded across the United States and then inevitably sent feelers back to El Salvador. US policies of deporting gang-related criminals further expedited the exportation of *mara* (gang) behavior and structures back to Central America. There, in the absence of an effective state, the organization sprouted like a weed and spread into Honduras.

In 2018 El Salvador's defense ministry estimated that more than 500,000 Salvadorans, in a country with a total population of less than 7,000,000 were involved with gangs, taking into account the gang members' relatives and children who had been forced to commit crimes. MS-13 was present in 248 of El Salvador's 262 municipalities and raked in $600,000 a month in extortion revenues from bus operators and other small and medium-sized retail businesses. Indeed, MS-13 and Barrio 18, a rival gang, might have been El Salvador's largest employers, besting multinational textile outfits such as Hanesbrands Inc. and Fruit of the Loom. Carlos Arguetta, a former gang member who once brought in $1,000 per month extorting his neighbors, explained to Dube that "one of the main reasons the gangs are so strong [is that] if someone offers you $25 to sell drugs or do an errand, a lot of times that's the only door [opportunity] you'll find."

El Salvador's gangster woes had their surreal aspects as well. One was the booming business in coffin making and funeral services. In San Pedro Perulapán, a nondescript town not far from El Salvador's capital, reporters investigated the town's funeral home bonanza. A funeral home employee going by the pseudonym Rogelio told a reporter, "We are selling coffins like hot bread!" Funeral home workers had even coined a verb, *muertear,* meaning to search the streets for dead bodies. Given the surging demand, Rogelio had grown accustomed to the particular challenge of preparing bullet-riddled cadavers. One gang member's body arrived at the funeral home with twenty-three gunshots in his chest, five in one hand, and several more in the face. Rogelio attributed the spike in business to the violence that had riven his town and the surrounding countryside, where locals lived at the whim of Barrio 18.

Murder became an everyday occurrence, with 1,616 people violently killed in El Salvador in 2017 compared with a total of 953 across Spain, Switzerland, Portugal, and the Netherlands. Few homicides, however, resulted in judicial punishments for the perpetrators, highlighting the pervasive climate of impunity in El Salvador. In 2018 El Salvador's minister of justice and security, Mauricio Ramírez Landaverde, acknowledged that gangs' control was so pervasive that "you don't know where the state ends and the criminal organizations begin." As Dagoberto Gutiérrez, a former commander of the Marxist FMLN insurgency, lamented in a recent interview, "We are living in the worst war of our history, but no one wants to acknowledge it as a war."

A logical response to these kinds of conditions was to flee, and many Central Americans did just that, mostly to Mexico and the United States. Violence and criminality were not the only reasons people left Central America. Economic underperformance was chronic. Dube spoke to a teenager named Iván Buezo in Honduras after he had been returned from the US in 2018. He was already planning to make his way back to *el norte,* explaining that "you can't make any money here." His daily wage as a farmworker was a paltry five dollars. In 2018 a surge in Guatemalan migration was driven by economic hardships and food shortages in the country's majority-ethnic-Mayan highland communities. The pull of familial ties was yet another driver: in a single Catholic parish in El Salvador, for example, more than one in two children had a parent living outside the country as of 2016. Young people often arrived at the border by themselves, a trend that vastly increased in 2014.

The Summer of Living Dangerously

In the spring and summer of 2014 tens of thousands of children from the Northern Triangle streamed across the US–Mexico border. In total, almost seventy thousand were recorded between October 2013 to September 2014. This was the peak of a migration boom that had taken off in the early 2000s, with huge demographic effects. Between 2007 and 2015 the total number of Northern Triangle nationals living and working inside US borders swelled by a whopping 25 percent, while Mexican residents slid by 6 percent.

The overwhelming number of desperate migrants created an array of moral and logistical challenges in the United States. Most of those who came through official asylum-seeking channels at the border were first processed by US Customs and Border Protection officers, whose task it was to triage migrants as asylum seekers, those seeking alternative forms of legal protection, and all other categories. The vast majority were turned away. For the most part the American media and public paid scant attention to the structural issues driving the migrant crisis, preferring instead to worry about the security of the border and focus on horror stories. Fewer than ten miles from Capitol Hill, the Maryland suburb of Langley Park was, according to the *Post*, being "plagued by MS-13 drug dealing, prostitution, robbery, extortion and murder." Around forty-five hundred unaccompanied Central American minors landed in Prince George's County, where Langley Park is located, during 2014's "summer of living dangerously." A proportion of them were recruited directly into the gang.

The Obama administration responded to the crisis with the proposed Alliance for Prosperity announced in 2014, a five-year regional plan involving hundreds of millions of dollars of emergency aid to help Northern Triangle governments with anticorruption and economic initiatives. The recipient governments also pledged $8.6 billion of their own to confront the crisis, but people continued to attempt the journey to the US. Capitol Hill was supportive of the administration's budget request, appropriating $750 million to fund the plan, a figure representing nearly double the aid to the Northern Triangle. In January 2016 Vice President Joe Biden appealed for public support for the nascent program, publishing an op-ed in the *New York Times* entitled "A Plan for Central America" in which he stated that the "security and prosperity of Central America are inextricably linked to our own." What the White House's statements and Biden's op-ed did not mention was that between 2008 and 2015 the United States had given just over $1 billion through the Central America Regional Security Initiative, an extension of the George W. Bush administration's Mérida Initiative to support Mexico's war against drug gangs. As far as any objective observer could tell, the differences between the Bush and Obama administrations' aid-based approaches to the problem were nonexistent.

In some instances joint initiatives yielded results. The Obama administration enlisted the UN to open screening centers for migrants in Northern Triangle nations hoping to reach the United States, thus offering an alternative to the arduous journey out of their native lands through cartel-infested Mexico. In 2016 Honduras ranked third among Northern Triangle countries sending unaccompanied children to the US, down from first place in 2014. Its murder rate dropped precipitously in the same period. Part of this improvement, as the journalist Sonia Nazario reported, was the result of a joint effort between the US and Honduran governments to mobilize local communities in violence-prevention efforts. In 2014 USAID and the Bureau of International Narcotics and Law Enforcement Affairs set up neighborhood outreach centers, which, among other activities, provided vocational training and mentors for unemployed residents.

 While there was little indication that the Northern Triangle's endemic ills had been permanently ameliorated, there was plenty of evidence that well-

Two migrants from Guatemala sleep on train tracks in Arriaga, Mexico.
August 8, 2014. (Jorge Lopez / Reuters Pictures)

considered social, public security, and military programs could have some
effect. Some of the innovative and necessary reforms that were already underway, such as the modernization of El Salvador's sole forensics lab and the
building of new prosecutors' quarters, were also funded by Washington.

However, the Obama administration also controversially doubled down on
a long-standing policy of deporting MS-13 and Barrio 18 criminals from US
prisons back to the Northern Triangle. The plan was essentially the reverse of
the kingpin extradition strategy deployed in Colombia and Mexico and thus
repeated the policy that had led to the rise of the gangs in Central America in
the first place. While US authorities deported around twenty thousand criminals to all of Central America between 2000 and 2004, in fiscal year 2015 they
deported over twenty-six criminals to the Northern Triangle alone.

In addition to shipping off immigrants and criminals caught in the US to
what amounted to failed states, the US enlisted the Mexican government to do
the same. Urged on by Washington, Mexico apprehended 70 percent more
Northern Triangle migrants in 2015 than in the previous year and returned
nearly two hundred thousand of them to their home countries, thereby preventing them from potentially reaching the US. Mexico's more muscular

stance likely accounted for a precipitous drop in Northern Triangle apprehensions along the US border. However, the push–pull dynamic set in motion by the deportation of criminals caused a rebound. A new wave of seventeen thousand Northern Triangle minors fleeing violence hit the border in the summer and fall of 2015, and in 2016 just under half of the individuals arrested near the border were from the Northern Triangle, a jump from 13 percent in 2010.

All told, between 2010 and 2016 the United States and Mexico apprehended more than one million Northern Triangle immigrants, deporting eight hundred thousand of them, including forty thousand children. In that same period asylum pleas from Northern Triangle citizens swelled by 800 percent, and between October 2017 and June 2018 76 percent of the seventy-three thousand asylum claimants interviewed by US officials demonstrated a "credible fear" of returning home.

Enter the Caravans

Seeking protection from gangs and other predators and encouraged by indications that migrating with their families would bolster their case for asylum, migrants from Central America changed their approach in 2018, traveling in family units and occasionally as part of large so-called caravans. In September 2018 the Border Patrol reportedly arrested 16,658 family members journeying together, and the total for fiscal year 2018 broke 100,000 for the first time. According to the *Washington Post*'s Nick Miroff, "Families are coming in caravans and on their own because it works. Only 1.4 percent of migrant family members from Guatemala, Honduras and El Salvador who crossed the border illegally in 2017 have been deported to their home countries."

In April 2018 President Trump expressed outrage at reports that a twelve-hundred-strong caravan from the Northern Triangle had set out for Mexico, apparently en route to the United States. In the end, however, only a few hundred managed to make it to the US border. In an Oval Office meeting Trump is said to have demanded that US border officials "close the whole thing!" Apparently Trump's aides had to tell him that such a move would cost billions in lost bilateral trade for the president to back down. Trump had a similar reaction upon hearing that a caravan originating in Honduras was on the move in October 2018. Over several days he told his supporters both in person at campaign-style rallies and via Twitter that he would close the US–Mexico border and consider military action to defend it. Tweeting on October 22, Trump wrote, "Sadly, it looks like Mexico's Police and Military are unable to stop the

Caravan heading to the Southern Border of the United States. Criminals and unknown Middle Easterners are mixed in. I have alerted Border Patrol and Military that this is a National Emerg[enc]y. . . . Every time you see a Caravan . . . blame the Democrats for not giving us the votes to change our pathetic Immigration Laws!"

In what was dismissed as both a cynical electoral ploy and an inappropriate, even illegal, use of armed forces in a domestic context, Trump ordered fifty-nine hundred active-duty personnel to the borderlands of Texas, California, and Arizona just days before the midterm elections on November 6. The caravan was more than a thousand kilometers from the border. A few weeks later the Pentagon acknowledged that the deployment had cost $72 million. Leading up to the midterm elections, the president described the vote as a referendum on his immigration policies: "an election of the caravan." Although Trump's border campaign might have made sense from a political perspective, given that 90 percent of Republicans approved of his hard-line stance, the Republican Party still lost forty seats in the House of Representatives in the midterms. Many of these losses were in moderate suburban and exurban districts. Beyond electoral numbers, Trump's approach also gave rise to scenes that sparked widespread outrage among Americans.

On November 25 what had been a slow-moving saga erupted into bedlam and violence when a subgroup of the caravan attempted to walk across the border at San Ysidro, a high-traffic land crossing between San Diego and Tijuana. A few individuals threw rocks at US agents, who responded with tear gas. The San Ysidro port of entry was then closed for several hours. In the midst of the chaos a Reuters photographer, Kim Kyung-Hoon, captured a soon-to-go-viral image of a Honduran girl retching from the gas. Attempting to deflect the impression that his policy had led to the traumatization of defenseless children, Trump insisted that agents had acted in self-defense. He then threatened to "close the border permanently." High-ranking Democrats like California governor-elect Gavin Newsom condemned the situation, tweeting, "These children are bare-foot. In diapers. Choking on tear gas. Women and children who left their lives behind—seeking peace and asylum—were met with violence and fear. That's not my America. We're a land of refuge. Of hope. Of freedom. And we will not stand for this."

The incident cast many to recall the most controversial of Trump's policies, the so-called zero-tolerance anti-immigration policy initiated in April 2018. Migrant children were separated at the US border from their parents, who were criminally charged with entering the country illegally and jailed. The policy sparked such outrage and protests that the president rescinded the order in June 2018. Yet reports of children continuing to be held in detainment centers away from their parents persisted for months, and as of 2021 over a hundred children had still not been reunited with their parents.

Deterrence

While cracking down on the migrants, Trump also castigated Latin American countries for not doing enough to stem the northward flow. In 2018 Trump threatened to cut off aid to the Northern Triangle governments if they "allow their citizens, or others, to journey through their borders and up to the United States, with the intention of entering our country illegally." But the migrants continued to come. In a single day, May 24, 2019, fifty-eight hundred migrants crossed the border; soon after, more than one thousand, overwhelmingly from the Northern Triangle, crossed en masse at night to request asylum.

Trump made good on his threats in late May 2019, announcing that the US would stop all direct development assistance to the Northern Triangle countries, approximately $550 million. Furthermore, he said he would slap an escalating scale of tariffs on Mexican imports if the country did not "[take] action to dramatically reduce or eliminate the number of illegal aliens crossing its territory into the United States." A former senior Mexican official described the tariff conditions as the "biggest challenge for Mexican diplomacy" since Lázaro Cárdenas's 1938 expropriation of foreign petroleum holdings.

A little over a week after he issued the tariff ultimatum and after taking withering criticism from Democrats as well as probusiness Republicans, Trump quietly backed down. He acceded to assurances by the incoming president, AMLO, that he would impose greater border enforcement. AMLO delivered by deploying six thousand Mexican troops from the newly formed National Guard to the Mexico–Guatemala border, the principal pathway for most Northern Triangle migrants. Trump touted AMLO's willingness to vastly expand what became a bilateral agreement that forced asylum seekers to wait in Mexico while their judicial reviews were underway. Trump officials added that this so-called Remain in Mexico plan would alleviate overcrowded detention facilities along the southwest border. AMLO's bet was that these sorts of deals with the devil (Trump), including the indirectly related renegotiation of NAFTA, would ultimately bolster Mexico's bilateral interests.

The "Invisible Wall"

Three years into his presidency, Trump often heralded his "big, beautiful wall," but it was conspicuous only by its absence, despite the president's frequent boasts that it was underway and even almost done. Perhaps due to its difficulties in putting up a physical barrier, the Trump administration was soon described as erecting "an invisible wall" to deal with the migrant crisis: a collection of legal rulings and redefinitions had made it increasingly difficult for migrants to claim asylum in the US. In June 2018 Attorney General Jeff Sessions announced that fleeing gang or domestic violence would no longer be adequate grounds for seeking asylum, though this ruling was later overturned by a federal court. In July 2019 the Trump administration introduced new immigration rules that required migrants to apply for asylum in countries they transited before reaching the US. For example, a Guatemalan migrant who arrived at the US–Mexican border without having first attempted to claim asylum in Mexico would have his US asylum request refused. And through it all Trump continued to speak through and leverage via aid: when the Central American countries agreed to the rules he had set, in October 2019 Trump reinstated some of the financial assistance cut in July.

Conclusion

Two centuries of US–Latin American history have seen many changes that have shaped the world as we know it today. At the beginning of this history the US had just won its independence from its former colonial ruler, the United Kingdom, and Latin America was still predominantly under the rule of the Old World powers Spain, France, and Portugal. Slave plantations abounded in the Caribbean and the United States, but huge swathes of territory, such as California, Texas, and parts of Mexico, remained in the hands of the First Nation inhabitants. This land was, however, considered fair game for annexation by the rising nation-states of the region. Borders were provisional, a fact demonstrated by the rampant expansion of the United States in the age of Manifest Destiny. Yet this was also a time of growing regional solidarity as the independence movements began to spread across Latin America, occasionally inspirited and supported by the US. The Monroe Doctrine formally put a seal on the self-identity of a region that would not answer to its former imperial overlords, though European interference and influence continued.

Fast forward to 2021, and the world looks very unsettled and fractured. The United States has maintained its position as a global superpower, outlasting the United Kingdom and the Soviet Union and coming through two world wars. But it now looks anxiously across the Pacific to China, which, despite being communist, does all the capitalist things America used to do so well: make, buy, and sell, everything except invent.

Latin America, in turn, has become, if anything, more complex and convoluted. At times it appears as though each county is entirely its own ecosystem, from Nicolás Maduro's iron rule over an imploding "Bolivarian socialist" Venezuela to AMLO's attempts to tackle organized crime in Mexico with hugs. But at the same time, they are tied together by inextricable historical, cultural, economic, and political bonds. Perhaps nothing illustrates this interconnectedness better than the Brazilian anticorruption investigation Operation Carwash, which traced a cobweb of corruption that reached from Brazil all the way to Argentina, El Salvador, Guatemala, Panama, Colombia, Ecuador, and Peru, resulting in the fall of several prominent politicians and the implication of over a dozen corporations.

As the vignettes that constitute this book show, the trajectory of US–Latin American relations has been turbulent, contentious, and complex. The Cold War left a deep scar in relations between the two, with the undeniable hegemony of the US in that period giving rise to accusations of manipulating Latin American domestic affairs and jettisoning democratic ideals in pursuit of geopolitical exigencies, all in the name of tackling the perceived communist threat. As Henry Kissinger once quipped, "America has no permanent friends or enemies, only interests." Fragile democratic systems in places crumbled, and states were usurped by strongmen, often wearing shiny epaulets; corruption and coercion were rife (see also the US in the time of Watergate and the Iran–Contra scandals). We have seen how, toward the end of the Cold War, organized crime began to exploit both the tenuous grip of state power in the region (and the booming US drug market) to rake in vast profits, using extreme violence to cement their control over huge areas.

The fall of the Berlin Wall and the collapse of communism seemed to offer a moment of panhemispheric hope. Latin American countries rushed to adopt free-market practices and the so-called Washington Consensus, and NAFTA came into being. But fragile economies sank into the fiscal mire, and dreams of a hemispheric trade compact foundered on the rocks of hemispheric rivalry. Today, with migration dominating the headlines, it can seem as though the dividing line between the US and Latin America is firmer and more unyielding than ever, the relationship fraught with antagonism and heavy-handedness.

But to paint the picture in such a bleak way is misleading. Although the US–Latin America train has at times derailed, the general commitment to the republican, democratic principles that first fired the wave of independence movements in the hemisphere has persisted through times of abeyance. Yes, there have been juntas, dictators, strongmen, and, recently, a resurgence in populists. We are also more than cognizant of the US interventions that drastically backfired. But there have been bilateral success stories, and billions of dollars in aid ranging from JFK's New Frontier Alliance for Progress to Plan Colombia and the 2010 rebuilding in Haiti after the earthquake. And we cannot forget that bilateral relations are not made from government policy alone.

Rather, it is often anonymous, often ordinary citizens who try to hold those in power to account, who bravely protest against injustice, and who forge a better path for their societies. Among the (in)famous names of leaders, generals, and officials, we hope we have given some sense of the currents generated by a nation's people that also shape its history.

Ultimately, though the relationship between the United States and Latin America has had its moments of crisis, it is simply too important to ignore: what the US does affects Latin America, and vice versa. Implicit in John Bolton's assertion that Latin America is "our hemisphere" is a recognition that the US has a crucial (albeit in Bolton's analysis proprietorial) stake in the hemisphere, even if, as in all relationships, there are moments of disagreement and distance.

An Impartial Eye

Scholars have attempted to synthesize the motivations behind US actions over the arc of its two-century history, the veritable gamut from tyrannical bully to idealistic saint. The United States has usually been on the powerful side of the equation, and this, as students of International Relations 101 dutifully learn, is what allows the powerful to determine outcomes: as Thucydides quoted the ancient Athenians, "The strong do what they can and the weak suffer what they must." But just because the US has been the predominant power in the region's history does not mean we must always interpret its actions through the lens of realpolitik. Likewise, it may be tempting to reduce US motivations to, say, racism, which we can see in our survey is undoubtedly the case in numerous instances. But we must bear in mind that while US policy makers could be (and were) undoubtedly racist, racism, as opposed to economic interest or ideological bent, may not have always been the key driver of policy.

We must also be aware that we are living in a very different time from that when most of the events in this history took place, and it is incumbent on us to attempt to understand these various historical eras as they were, not as what they appear as in hindsight. As scholars of history we must not let our understandable desire to hold the United States to account for its mistakes or machinations in Latin America result in the neglecting of any attempt to tease out a more exacting picture of what transpired and, hopefully, what will transpire. Perhaps now more than ever, it matters tremendously whether or not we have our facts right and have examined all of the available evidence. Given the stakes in play, ideological blinders—right or left wing—are no substitute for clear-eyed analysis and reasoned debate.

ACKNOWLEDGMENTS

Two colleagues contributed enormously to greatly enhancing the coherence of our initially bloated draft. Bowdoin College emeritus historian Allen Wells read the entire manuscript at least twice and came back with especially keen and voluminous suggestions that we eagerly and gratefully integrated into the final version. Formerly at the International Institute for Strategic Studies in London, editor Alex Goodwin wielded his equally deft brain and pen on every page, even if his name is not in the title.

The four keen blind reviewers via Yale were patient and supportive, especially in the case study selection as well as in our final rounds of revisions. Yale's august team of Jaya Chatterjee, Eva Skewes, and Joyce Ippolito aided the manuscript in one way or another. Lawrence Kenney's exquisite copyediting of the final draft of the manuscript was a gift from heaven.

Russell Crandall would like to thank his three professors—Michael Mandelbaum, Piero Gleijeses, and the deceased Fred Holborn—at the Johns Hopkins School of Advanced International Studies, who introduced this wet-behind-the-ears graduate student to the wonder of diplomatic history.

A veritable army of full-time or part-time, current or past Davidson College (and in one case, Bowdoin College) students served as research assistants. In some cases this was research conducted for our prior books and articles that we then adapted in the chapters and stories seen here: Jack Richardson, Mattie Engleby, Michael Hall, Peter Roady, Caroline McDermott, Marshall Worsham, Katie Hunter, Maria Antonia Bravo, Savannah Haeger, Haley Rhodes, Becky Contreras, Sarah Sears, Eliza Patterson, Lauren Martinez, Gustavo Orozco, Eduardo Estrada, Laura Dunnagan, Akilah J. Kinnison.

The following people, in what is certainly an incomplete list, contributed in ways big and small to our shared undertaking: Greg Weeks, Joe Gutekanst, Daniel Lynds, Lisa Forrest, James Sponsel, Jason Radcliffe, Trish Johnson, Shannon O'Neil, Tom Shannon, Brian Winter, Benjamin Russell, Michael Shifter, Andy Rhodes, Richard Feinberg, Denis McDonough, Kari McDonough, Guadalupe Paz, Anne McKenzie, Francisco González, Jonathan Stevenson, Hal Brands, Chris Sabatini, Carolyn West, Lucy Cáceres, Dane Erickson, Eduardo Estrada, Rebecca Bill-Chavez, Ralph Levering, Clayton Rose, Carol Quillen, Phil King, Philip Jefferson, Chris Chivvis, Pam Dykstra, Ramiro Orias.

Davidson College provided a subvention to cover publishing-related expenses.

BIBLIOGRAPHY

Listed chapter-by-chapter for ease, the following sources contain sufficient material to construct our stories for this volume. To save paper and keep under a very strict word count that forced us to shave the first (and admittedly bloated) manuscript by fifty thousand words, we excluded listing sources not directly linked to our text. All quotations appear in at least one of the sources listed here. Additional source material along with other pedagogical, scholarly, and policy materials related to this book is at: russellcrandall.com

Introduction

Baker, James. *The Politics of Diplomacy.* New York: Putnam, 1995.

Crandall, Russell. "Dueling Doctrines: Biden vs. Miller." *Americas Quarterly,* May 2020.

———. "The Post-American Hemisphere." *Foreign Affairs* (May/June 2011).

———. *The United States and Latin America after the Cold War.* New York: Cambridge University Press, 2008.

Dirzauskaite, Goda, and Nicolae Cristinel Ilinca. "Understanding 'Hegemony' in International Relations Theories." Aalborg Universitet, 2017.

Drezner, Daniel W. "A Post-Hegemonic Paradise in Latin America?" *Americas Quarterly,* Winter 2015.

Filkins, Dexter. "John Bolton on the Warpath." *New Yorker,* April 29, 2019.

"HBO History Makers with James Baker." *Council on Foreign Relations,* June 15, 2006, available at: https://www.cfr.org/event/hbo-history-makers-series-james-baker-iii-0.

Londoño, Ernesto, and Nicholas Casey. "Trump Administration Discussed Coup Plans with Rebel Venezuelan Officers." *New York Times,* August 8, 2018.

Prengaman, Peter. "Brazil's Bolsonaro Considers US Base to Counter Russia." *Sydney Morning Herald,* January 5, 2019.

Winter, Brian. "The Tropical Trump? If He's Lucky." *Americas Quarterly,* March 20, 2019.

Chapter 1. The Black Spartacus Who Balanced Washington

Baptist, Edward E. "The Bittersweet Victory at Saint-Domingue." *Slate,* August 6, 2015.

Bell, David A. "The Contagious Revolution." *New York Review of Books,* December 19, 2019.

Crandall, Russell. "The Black Bonaparte." *Survival* 59, no. 4 (September 2018): 183–90.

Forsdick, Charles, and Christian Høgsbjerg. "Black Jacobin Ascending: 1793–98." In *Toussaint Louverture: A Black Jacobin in the Age of Revolutions,* 54–80. London: Pluto Press, 2017.

Furstenberg, François. *In the Name of the Father: Washington's Legacy, Slavery, and the Making of a Nation.* New York: Penguin Books, 2007.

Geggus, David. "The Changing Faces of Toussaint Louverture: Literary and Pictorial Depictions." The John Carter Brown Library, 2013.

———. "The French Slave Trade: An Overview." *William and Mary Quarterly* 58, no. 1 (2001): 119–38.

Girard, Philippe. "Black Talleyrand: Toussaint Louverture's Diplomacy, 1798–1802." *William and Mary Quarterly,* Third Series, 66, no. 1 (2009): 87–124.

———. *Toussaint Louverture: A Revolutionary Life.* New York: Basic Books, 2016.

Gonzalez, Johnhenry. *Maroon Nation: A History of Revolutionary Haiti.* New Haven: Yale University Press, 2019.

Hazareesingh, Sudhir. *Black Spartacus: The Epic Life of Toussaint Louverture.* New York: Farrar, Straus and Giroux, 2020.

"Hispaniola Smallpox Epidemic of 1507." *Encyclopedia of Plague and Pestilence: From Ancient Times to the Present.* New York: Facts on File, 2008, 139.

Lepore, Jill. *These Truths: A History of the United States.* New York: Norton, 2019.

Perl-Rosenthal, Nathan. "An Opening for Haiti." *Wall Street Journal,* August 27, 2020.

Peterson, Robert K. D. "Insects, Disease, and Military History: The Napoleonic Campaigns and Historical Perception." *American Entomologist* 41 (1995): 147–60.

Schuller, Mark. "Haiti's 200-Year Ménage-à-Trois: Globalization, the State, and Civil Society." *Caribbean Studies* 35, no. 1 (2007): 141–79.

Scott, Julius S. *The Common Wind: Afro-American Currents in the Age of the Haitian Revolution.* New York: Verso, 2019.

Chapter 2. When Americans Loved Simón Bolívar

This chapter is adapted from: Crandall, Russell. "When Americans Loved Simón Bolívar." *Survival* 50, no. 6 (2017): 157–64, copyright © The International Institute for Strategic Studies, reprinted by permission of Informa UK Limited, trading as Taylor & Francis Group, www.tandfonline.com on behalf of The International Institute for Strategic Studies.

Arana, Marie. *Bolívar: American Liberator.* New York: Simon and Schuster, 2013.

Beschloss, Michael. *Presidents of War: The Epic Story, from 1807 to Modern Times.* New York: Crown, 2018.

Bullen, Roger. "France and the Problem of Intervention in Spain, 1834–1836." *Historical Journal* 20, no. 2 (1977): 363–93.

Crandall, Russell. "Review of Gaddis Smith, The Last Years of the Monroe Doctrine." *SAIS Review* 16, no. 1 (1996): 254–56.

Fitz, Caitlin. *Our Sister Republics: The United States in an Age of American Revolutions.* New York: W. W. Norton, 2016.

LaFeber, Walter. *Inevitable Revolutions: The United States in Central America.* New York: Norton, 1993.

Lynch, John. *Simón Bolívar: A Life.* New Haven: Yale University Press, 2006.

McDougall, Walter A. *Promised Land, Crusader State: The American Encounter with the World since 1776.* Boston: Houghton Mifflin, 1997.

———. *The Tragedy of American Foreign Policy: How America's Civil Religion Betrayed the National Interest.* New Haven: Yale University Press, 2017.

Robertson, William Spence. "South America and the Monroe Doctrine, 1824–1828." *Political Science Quarterly* 30, no. 1 (1915): 82–105.

Sedgewick, Augustine. *Coffeeland: One Man's Dark Empire and the Making of Our Favorite Drug.* New York: Penguin, 2020.

Zimmermann, Warren. *First Great Triumph: How Five Americans Made Their Country a World Power.* New York: Farrar, Straus and Giroux, 2004.

Chapter 3. La Doctrina Monroe

Arana, Marie. *Bolívar.* New York: Simon and Schuster, 2014.

Beschloss, Michael. *Presidents of War: The Epic Story, from 1807 to Modern Times.* New York: Crown, 2018.

Crandall, Russell. "Review of Gaddis Smith, The Last Years of the Monroe Doctrine." *SAIS Review* 16: 254–56.

LaFeber, Walter. *Inevitable Revolutions: The United States in Central America.* New York: Norton, 1993.

Lepore, Jill. *These Truths: A History of the United States.* New York: W. W. Norton, 2019.

McDougall, Walter A. *Promised Land, Crusader State: The American Encounter with the World since 1776.* Boston: Houghton Mifflin, 1997.

———. *The Tragedy of American Foreign Policy: How America's Civil Religion Betrayed the National Interest.* New Haven: Yale University Press, 2017.

Robertson, William Spence. "South America and the Monroe Doctrine, 1824–1828." *Political Science Quarterly* 30, no. 1 (1915): 82–105.

Zimmermann, Warren. *First Great Triumph: How Five Americans Made Their Country a World Power.* New York: Farrar, Straus and Giroux, 2004.

Chapter 4. Destiny Manifested

Bulmer-Thomas, Victor. *Empire in Retreat: The Past, Present, and Future of the United States*. New Haven: Yale University Press, 2018.

Calhoun, John C. "Calhoun, Speech on Mexico 1848." Indiana University, January 4, 1848.

Henderson, Timothy J. *A Glorious Defeat: Mexico and Its War with the United States*. New York: Hill and Wang, 2008.

McDougall, Walter A. *Promised Land, Crusader State: The American Encounter with the World since 1776*. Boston: Houghton Mifflin, 1997.

Merk, Frederick, Lois Bannister Merk, and John Mack Faragher. "Manifest Destiny." In *Manifest Destiny and Mission in American History: A Reinterpretation*, 46–47. Cambridge: Harvard University Press, 1995.

O'Sullivan, John. "Annexation." *United States Democratic Review*, August 1845.

———. "The Great Nation of Futurity." *United States Democratic Review*, 1839.

Wood, Gordon S. *The Radicalism of the American Revolution*. 1st Vintage Books ed. New York: Vintage Books, 1993.

Chapter 5. A Lone Star Is Born

"Acquisition of Florida: Treaty of Adams-Onís (1819) and Transcontinental Treaty (1821)." Department of State Office of the Historian.

Adams, John, and Charles Francis Adams. *The Works of John Adams, Second President of the United States: With a Life of the Author, Notes and Illustrations*. Boston: Little, Brown, 1856.

"Annexation Process: 1836–1845, A Summary Timeline." Texas State Library and Archives Commission, April 3, 2012.

Beschloss, Michael. *Presidents of War*. New York: Crown, 2018.

Blight, David W. *Frederick Douglass: Prophet of Freedom*. New York: Simon and Schuster, 2018.

Bulmer-Thomas, Victor. *Empire in Retreat: The Past, Present, and Future of the United States*. New Haven: Yale University Press, 2018.

Calvert, Robert A., Arnoldo De León, and Gregg Cantrell. "Mexican Texas, 1821–1836." In *The History of Texas*, 57–58. UK: Wiley-Blackwell, 2014.

Fitz, Caitlin. *Our Sister Republics: The United States in an Age of American Revolutions*. New York: Liveright Publishing, 2016.

Gates, E. Nathaniel, ed. "Manifest Destiny." In *Race and U.S. Foreign Policy in the Ages of Territorial and Market Expansion, 1840–1900*, 3. London: Routledge, 2014.

Greenberg, Amy S. *A Wicked War: Polk, Clay, Lincoln, and the 1846 U.S. Invasion of Mexico*. New York: Vintage Books, 2013.

Henderson, Timothy J. *A Glorious Defeat: Mexico and Its War with the United States*. New York: Hill and Wang, 2008.

"Inaugural Address of James Knox Polk." The Avalon Project (Yale Law School), March 4, 1845.

McPherson, James M. "America's 'Wicked War.' " *New York Review of Books*, February 7, 2013.

Merry, Robert W. *A Country of Vast Designs: James K. Polk, the Mexican War, and the Conquest of the American Continent*. New York: Simon and Schuster, 2011.

Polk, James. "President Polk Calls on Congress to Declare War on Mexico." Digital History, May 11, 1846.

Reséndez, Andrés. *Changing National Identities at the Frontier: Texas and New Mexico, 1800–1850*. New York: Cambridge University Press, 2004.

Rodriguez, Sarah K. M. " 'The Greatest Nation on Earth': The Politics and Patriotism of the First Anglo American Immigrants to Mexican Texas, 1820–1824." *Pacific Historical Review* 86, no. 1 (2017): 50–83.

Schoultz, Lars. *Beneath the United States: A History of U.S. Policy toward Latin America*. Cambridge: Harvard University Press, 1998.

Smith, Gaddis. *The Last Years of the Monroe Doctrine, 1945–1993*. New York: Hill and Wang, 1994.

"The Treaty of Annexation—Texas." The Avalon Project (Yale Law School), April 12, 1844.

Yardley, Jonathan. " ' "A Wicked War": Polk, Clay, Lincoln, and the 1846 U.S. Invasion of Mexico' by Amy S. Greenberg." *Washington Post*, November 12, 2012.

Zimmermann, Warren. *First Great Triumph: How Five Americans Made Their Country a World Power*. New York: Farrar, Straus and Giroux, 2004.

Chapter 6. A Wicked War

Beschloss, Michael. *Presidents of War*. New York: Crown, 2018.

Bulmer-Thomas, Victor. *Empire in Retreat: The Past, Present, and Future of the United States*. New Haven: Yale University Press, 2018.

Chernow, Ron. *Grant*. New York: Penguin Press, 2017.

Greenberg, Amy S. *A Wicked War: Polk, Clay, Lincoln, and the 1846 U.S. Invasion of Mexico*. New York: Vintage Books, 2013.

Guardino, Peter. *The Dead March: A History of the Mexican–American War*. Cambridge: Harvard University Press, 2017.

Henderson, Timothy J. *A Glorious Defeat: Mexico and Its War with the United States*. New York: Hill and Wang, 2008.

Holden, Robert H., and Eric Zolov, eds. *Latin America and the United States: A Documentary History*. 2nd ed. New York: Oxford University Press, 2011.

Kimmage, Michael. *The Abandonment of the West: The History of an Idea in American Foreign Policy*. New York: Basic Books, 2020.

"Lincoln's Spot Resolutions." National Archives, August 15, 2016.

Loveman, Brian. *No Higher Law: American Foreign Policy and the Western Hemisphere since 1776.* Chapel Hill: University of North Carolina Press, 2010.

McDougall, Walter A. *Promised Land, Crusader State: The American Encounter with the World since 1776.* Boston: Houghton Mifflin, 1997.

McPherson, James M. "America's 'Wicked War.' " *New York Review of Books,* February 7, 2013.

Merry, Robert W. *A Country of Vast Designs: James K. Polk, the Mexican War, and the Conquest of the American Continent.* New York: Simon and Schuster, 2011.

Oakes, James. "Our 'Wicked War.' " *New York Review of Books,* November 23, 2017.

Schoultz, Lars. *Beneath the United States: A History of U.S. Policy toward Latin America.* Cambridge: Harvard University Press, 1998.

Yardley, Jonathan. " ' "A Wicked War": Polk, Clay, Lincoln, and the 1846 U.S. Invasion of Mexico' by Amy S. Greenberg." *Washington Post,* November 12, 2012.

Zimmermann, Warren. *First Great Triumph: How Five Americans Made Their Country a World Power.* New York: Farrar, Straus and Giroux, 2004.

Chapter 7. California Conquest

Arax, Mark. *The Dreamt Land: Chasing Water and Dust across California.* New York: Alfred A. Knopf, 2019.

Bancroft, Hubert Howe. *History of the Pacific States of North America.* San Francisco: A. L. Bancroft, 1882.

Barrows, H. D. "Mexican Governors of California." *Annual Publication of the Historical Society of Southern California and Pioneer Register, Los Angeles* 5, no. 1 (1900): 25–30.

Brands, H. W. *Andrew Jackson: His Life and Times.* New York: Doubleday, 2006.

Denton, Sally. "Frémont Steals California," *American Heritage* 60, no. 4 (Winter 2011).

DeVoto, Bernard. *The Year of Decision, 1846.* New York: St. Martin's Press, 2000.

Dillon, Richard. *Fool's Gold. A Biography of John Sutter.* New York: Coward McCann, 1967.

Frémont, John Charles. *Memoirs of My Life.* Lanham, MD: Cooper Square Press, 2001.

Hackel, Steven W. *Junípero Serra: California's Founding Father.* New York: Farrar, Straus and Giroux, 2013.

Hurtado, Albert L. "Empires, Frontiers, Filibusters, and Pioneers: The Transnational World of John Sutter." *Pacific Historical Review* 77, no. 1 (2008): 19–47.

Madley, Benjamin. *An American Genocide: The United States and the California Indian Catastrophe, 1846–1873.* New Haven: Yale University Press: 2017.

Nunis, Doyce B. "Alta California's Trojan Horse: Foreign Immigration." *California History* 76, no. 2/3 (1997): 299–330.

Polley, Frank J. "Americans at the Battle of Cahuenga." *Annual Publication of the Historical Society of Southern California, Los Angeles* 3, no. 2 (January 1894): 47–54.

Rolle, Andrew F. *John Charles Fremont: Character as Destiny*. Norman: University of Oklahoma Press, 1999.

Tenney, William Jewett. *The Military and Naval History of the Rebellion in the United States*. Arkose Press, 2015.

United States v. Sutter 62 U.S. 170 (1858).

Walker, Dale L. *Bear Flag Rising: The Conquest of California, 1846*. New York: Forge, 1999.

White, Ronald C. *American Ulysses: A Life of Ulysses S. Grant*. New York: Random House, 2017.

Chapter 8. ¡Viva Grant!

Blight, David W. *Frederick Douglass: Prophet of Freedom*. New York: Simon and Schuster, 2018.

Boyle, T. "The Venezuela Crisis and the Liberal Opposition, 1895–96." *Journal of Modern History* 50, no. 3 (September 1978): D1185–D1212.

Chernow, Ron. *Grant*. New York: Penguin Press, 2017.

"French Intervention in Mexico and the American Civil War, 1862–1867." Department of State Office of the Historian, 2016.

Guyatt, Nicholas. "America's Conservatory: Race, Reconstruction, and the Santo Domingo Debate." *Journal of American History* 97, no. 4 (March 2011): 974–1000.

Hamnett, Brian R. "Liberalism Divided: Regional Politics and the National Project during the Mexican Restored Republic, 1867–1876." *Hispanic American Historical Review* 76, no. 4 (1996): 659–89.

Kimmage, Michael. *The Abandonment of the West: The History of an Idea in American Foreign Policy*. New York: Basic Books, 2020.

Kirk, John. "José Martí and the United States: A Further Interpretation." *Journal of Latin American Studies* 9, no. 20 (November 1977): 275–90.

Pinkett, Harold T. "Efforts to Annex Santo Domingo to the United States." *Journal of Negro History* 26, no. 1 (January 1941): 12–45.

Pitre, Merline. "Frederick Douglass and the Annexation of Santo Domingo." *Journal of Negro History* 62, no. 4 (October 1977): 390–400.

Sexton, Jay. *The Monroe Doctrine: Empire and Nation in Nineteenth-Century America*. New York: Hill and Wang, 2011.

Thomson, P. C. "Popular Aspects of Liberalism in Mexico, 1848–1888." *Bulletin of Latin American Research* 10, no. 3 (1991): 265–92.

"Venezuela Boundary Dispute, 1895–1899." U.S. Department of State, Office of the Historian, https://history.state.gov/milestones/1866–1898/venezuela.

White, Ronald C. *American Ulysses: A Life of Ulysses S. Grant*. New York: Random House, 2017.

Chapter 9. Yellow Fever

This chapter is adapted from: Crandall, Russell. "Staining the Flag." *Survival* 60, no. 6 (2018): 189–98, copyright © The International Institute for Strategic Studies, reprinted by permission of Informa UK Limited, trading as Taylor & Francis Group, www.tandfonline.com on behalf of The International Institute for Strategic Studies.

Baker, Russell. "The Performer." *New York Review of Books*, April 11, 2002.

Chace, James. "Tomorrow the World." *New York Review of Books*, November 21, 2002.

Crandall, Russell. *America's Dirty Wars: Irregular Warfare from 1776 to the War on Terror.* New York: Cambridge University Press, 2014.

Drabelle, Dennis. "Tough Questions the Nation Faced after the Spanish–American War." *Washington Post*, January 27, 2017.

Immerwahr, Daniel. *How to Hide an Empire: A History of the Greater United States.* New York: Farrar, Straus and Giroux, 2019.

Kinzer, Stephen. *The True Flag: Theodore Roosevelt, Mark Twain, and the Birth of the American Empire.* New York: Henry Holt, 2017.

Lind, Michael. "Teddy Roosevelt, Mark Twain, and the Fight over American Imperialism." *New York Times*, January 10, 2018.

McKinley, William. "Message to Congress Requesting a Declaration of War with Spain," April 11, 1898. Online by Gerhard Peters and John T. Woolley, *American Presidency Project.*

Merry, Robert W. *President McKinley: Architect of the American Century.* New York: Simon and Schuster, 2017.

Milne, David. *Worldmaking: The Art and Science of American Diplomacy.* New York: Farrar, Straus and Giroux, 2017.

Pérez, Louis A. *Cuba between Empires, 1878–1902.* Pittsburgh: University of Pittsburgh Press, 1998.

———. *The War of 1898: The United States and Cuba in History and Historiography.* Chapel Hill: University of North Carolina Press, 1998.

Risen, Clay. *The Crowded Hour: Theodore Roosevelt, the Rough Riders, and the Dawn of the American Century.* New York: Scribner, 2019.

———. "The Rough Riders' Guide to World Domination." *New York Times*, May 31, 2019.

Smith, Mark. "The Political Economy of Sugar Production and the Environment of Eastern Cuba, 1898–1923." *Environmental History Review* 19, no. 4 (Winter 1995): 31–48.

Thomas, Evan. *The War Lovers: Roosevelt, Lodge, Hearst, and the Rush to Empire, 1898.* New York: Little, Brown, 2010.

Trask, David. "The Spanish–American War—The World of 1898: The Spanish–American War." Library of Congress, June 22, 2011.

Zwonitzer, Mark. *The Statesman and the Storyteller: John Hay, Mark Twain, and the Rise of American Imperialism.* Chapel Hill, NC: Algonquin Books, 2016.

Chapter 10. TR's Soft Talk and Big Stick

Bishop, Joseph Bucklin. *Theodore Roosevelt and His Time Shown in His Own Letters.* New York: C. Scribner's Sons, 1920.

Collin, Richard H. "The 1904 Detroit Compact: U.S. Naval Diplomacy and Dominican Revolutions." *The Historian* 52, no. 3 (1990): 432–52.

Ellsworth, Harry Allanson. *One Hundred Eighty Landings of the United States Marines, 1800–1934.* Washington DC: History and Museums Division, Headquarters, U.S. Marine Corps and U.S. Government Printing Office, 1974.

Hill, Howard C. *Roosevelt and the Caribbean.* Chicago: University of Chicago Press, 1927.

Maass, Matthias. "Catalyst for the Roosevelt Corollary: Arbitrating the 1902–1903 Venezuela Crisis and Its Impact on the Development of the Roosevelt Corollary to the Monroe Doctrine." *Diplomacy & Statecraft* 20, no. 3 (November 2009): 383–402.

Marks, Frederick W. *Velvet on Iron: The Diplomacy of Theodore Roosevelt.* Lincoln: University of Nebraska Press, 1982.

Maurer, Noel. *Setting the Trap: The Rise and Fall of U.S. Intervention to Protect American Property Overseas, 1893–2013.* Princeton: Princeton University Press, 2013.

Mitchell, Nancy. *The Danger of Dreams: German and American Imperialism in Latin America.* Chapel Hill: University of North Carolina Press, 1999.

———. "The Height of the German Challenge: The Venezuela Blockade, 1902–3." *Diplomatic History* 20, no. 2 (1996): 185–209.

Mitchener, Kris James, and Marc Weidenmier. "Empire, Public Goods, and the Roosevelt Corollary." *Journal of Economic History* 65, no. 3 (September 2005): 658–92.

Morris, Edmund. " 'A Matter of Extreme Urgency': Theodore Roosevelt, Wilhelm II, and the Venezuela Crisis of 1902." *Naval War College Review* 55, no. 2 (Spring 2002).

Munro, Dana G. "The Genesis of the Roosevelt Corollary." In *Intervention and Dollar Diplomacy in the Caribbean, 1900–1921,* 65–111. Princeton: Princeton University Press, 1964.

Nester, William R. *Theodore Roosevelt and the Art of American Power: An American for All Time.* Lanham, MD: Lexington Books, 2019.

Parsons, Edward B. "The German-American Crisis of 1902–1903." *The Historian* 33, no. 3 (1971): 436–52.

Reter, Ronald Francis. "The Roosevelt Corollary to the Monroe Doctrine and the Santo Domingo Receivership of 1905: Big Stick or Big Brother?" Master's Thesis, Loyola University Chicago (1969), accessed at: https://ecommons.luc.edu/luc_theses/2377

Ricard, Serge. "The Roosevelt Corollary." *Presidential Studies Quarterly* 36, no. 1 (2006): 17–26.

Veggeberg, Vernon T. "A Comprehensive Approach to Counterinsurgency: The U.S. Military Occupation of the Dominican Republic, 1916–1924." Marine Corps University, 2008.

Chapter 11. Mr. Roosevelt's Canal

Ameringer, Charles D. "The Panama Canal Lobby of Philippe Bunau-Varilla and William Nelson Cromwell." *American Historical Review* 68, no. 2 (1963): 346–63.

Bishop, Joseph Bucklin. *Theodore Roosevelt and His Time Shown in His Own Letters.* New York: C. Scribner's Sons, 1920.

"Building the Panama Canal, 1903–1914." *Office of the Historian, U.S. Department of State Foreign Service Institute.* Access at: https://history.state.gov/milestones/1899-1913 /panama-canal.

"Cape Horn: A Mariner's Nightmare." *NASA Observatory,* July 12, 2014, accessed at: https://earthobservatory.nasa.gov/images/91472/cape-horn-a-mariners-nightmare.

Crandall, Russell. *America's Dirty Wars: Irregular Warfare from 1776 to the War on Terror.* New York: Cambridge University Press, 2014.

———. "Staining the Flag." *Survival* 60, no. 6 (2018): 189–98.

Immerwahr, Daniel. *How to Hide an Empire: A History of the Greater United States.* New York: Farrar, Straus and Giroux, 2019.

"May 4, 1904: U.S. Dives into Panama Canal." *Wired,* May 4, 2011, accessed at: https:// www.wired.com/2011/05/0504us-panama-canal-construction/.

Milne, David. *Worldmaking: The Art and Science of American Diplomacy.* New York: Farrar, Straus and Giroux, 2017.

"On This Day: Panama Regains the Panama Canal." National Constitution Center. Accessed July 18, 2018.

Roosevelt, Theodore: "Annual Message to Congress," December 6, 1904, accessed at: https://millercenter.org/the-presidency/presidential-speeches/december-6-1904-fourth-annual-message.

———. "Special Message," November 16, 1903. Online by Gerhard Peters and John T. Woolley, The American Presidency Project.

Snapp, Jeremy S. *Destiny by Design: The Construction of the Panama Canal.* British Columbia, Canada: Heritage House, 2000.

Wills, Matthew. "How a Postage Stamp May Have Helped Create the Panama Canal." *JSTOR Daily,* December 14, 2017.

Zimmermann, Warren. *First Great Triumph: How Five Americans Made Their Country a World Power.* New York: Farrar, Straus and Giroux, 2004.

Zwonitzer, Mark. *The Statesman and the Storyteller.* Chapel Hill, NC: Algonquin Books, 2016.

Chapter 12. Imperial Idealism

Blaisdell, Lowell L. "Henry Lane Wilson and the Overthrow of Madero." *Southwestern Social Science Quarterly* 43, no. 2 (1962): 126–35.

Brown, L. Ames. "A New Era of Good Feeling." *Atlantic Monthly,* January 1915.

Christie, Thomas Walter. "Diplomacy of Intervention: The ABC Conference Niagara Falls 1914." Graduate Student Theses, Dissertations, and Professional Papers, 1986, 5152.

Coerver, Don M., and Linda B. Hall. *Tangled Destinies: Latin America and the United States*. Diálogos. Albuquerque: University of New Mexico Press, 1999.

Crandall, Russell. *America's Dirty Wars: Irregular Warfare from 1776 to the War on Terror*. New York: Cambridge University Press, 2014.

Eisenhower, John S. D. *Intervention!: The United States and the Mexican Revolution, 1913–1917*. New York: W. W. Norton, 1993.

Hall, Linda B., and Don M. Coerver. *Revolution on the Border: The United States and Mexico, 1910–1920*. Albuquerque: University of New Mexico Press, 1990.

Hart, John Mason. *Empire and Revolution: The Americans in Mexico since the Civil War*. Berkeley: University of California Press, 2002.

Katz, Friedrich. *The Life and Times of Pancho Villa*. Stanford: Stanford University Press, 1998.

Link, Arthur S. "Mexico: The Background of Wilsonian Interference." In *Wilson, Volume 2: The New Freedom*, 347–78. Princeton: Princeton University Press, 1956.

McPherson, Alan. *A Short History of U.S. Interventions in Latin America and the Caribbean*. UK: Wiley-Blackwell, 2016.

Milne, David. *Worldmaking: The Art and Science of American Diplomacy*. New York: Farrar, Straus and Giroux, 2017.

"President Wilson and Latin America." *American Journal of International Law* 7, no. 2 (1913): 329–33.

Rausch, George J. "Poison-Pen Diplomacy: Mexico, 1913." *The Americas* 24, no. 3 (1968): 272–80.

Sweetman, Jack. *The Landing at Veracruz: 1914: The First Complete Chronicle of a Strange Encounter in April, 1914, When the United States Navy Captured and Occupied the City of Veracruz, Mexico*. Annapolis: U.S. Naval Institute, 1987.

Ulloa, Bertha. "La Discordia Huertista." In *La Lucha Revolucionaria*, 123–66. Mexico, D.F.: Colegio de México, 2010.

Welsome, Eileen. *The General and the Jaguar: Pershing's Hunt for Pancho Villa, A True Story of Revolution and Revenge*. New York: Little, Brown, 2006.

Chapter 13. Hunting Sandino

This chapter is adapted from: Crandall, Russell. *America's Dirty Wars: Irregular Warfare from 1776 to the War on Terror*. New York: Cambridge University Press, 2014. © Russell Crandall 2014, published by Cambridge University Press. Reproduced with permission of the Licensor through PLSclear.

McPherson, Alan L. *The Invaded: How Latin Americans and Their Allies Fought and Ended U.S. Occupations*. Oxford: Oxford University Press, 2014.

Chapter 14. Sumner Welles Goes to Havana

Aguilar, Luis E. *Cuba 1933: Prologue to Revolution*. Norton Library N712. New York: Norton, 1974.

Dur, Philip, and Christopher Gilcrease. "U.S. Diplomacy and the Downfall of a Cuban Dictator: Machado in 1933." *Journal of Latin American Studies* 34, no. 2 (2002): 255–82.

Franklin D. Roosevelt Presidential Library & Museum. "Sumner Welles Papers," n.d. Accessed August 16, 2019.

Gellman, Irwin F. *Good Neighbor Diplomacy: United States Policies in Latin America, 1933–1945.* Baltimore: Johns Hopkins University Press, 1979.

———. *Roosevelt and Batista: Good Neighbor Diplomacy in Cuba, 1933–1945.* Albuquerque: University of New Mexico Press, 1973.

Green, David. *The Containment of Latin America: A History of the Myths and Realities of the Good Neighbor Policy.* Chicago: Quadrangle Books, 1971.

Haines, Gerald K. "Has Anything Changed? The United States and Its Relations with Latin America," edited by Joseph Smith. *Diplomatic History* 17, no. 4 (1993): 627–31.

———. "Under the Eagle's Wing: The Franklin Roosevelt Administration Forges an American Hemisphere." *Diplomatic History* 1, no. 4 (1977): 373–88.

Langley, Lester D. *The United States and the Caribbean in the Twentieth Century.* 4th ed. Athens: University of Georgia Press, 1989.

O'Sullivan, Christopher D. *Sumner Welles: Postwar Planning and the Quest for a New World Order, 1937–1943.* New York: Columbia University Press, 2014.

Pérez, Louis A. *Cuba under the Platt Amendment, 1902–1934.* Pittsburgh: University of Pittsburgh Press, 1986.

Schmitz, David F. *Thank God They're on Our Side: The United States and Right-Wing Dictatorships, 1921–1965.* Chapel Hill: University of North Carolina Press, 1999.

Varg, Paul A. "The Economic Side of the Good Neighbor Policy: The Reciprocal Trade Program and South America." *Pacific Historical Review* 45, no. 1 (1976): 47–71.

Wood, Bryce. *The Making of the Good Neighbor Policy.* New York: Columbia University Press, 1961.

Chapter 15. Nuestro Petróleo

Balderrama, Francisco E., and Raymond Rodriguez. *Decade of Betrayal: Mexican Repatriation in the 1930s.* Albuquerque: University of New Mexico Press, 1995.

Becker, Marjorie. *Setting the Virgin on Fire: Lázaro Cárdenas, Michoacán Peasants, and the Redemption of the Mexican Revolution.* Berkeley: University of California Press, 1995.

Cárdenas, Lázaro. "Document #7: 'Speech to the Nation.'" Brown University Library Center for Digital Scholarship, 1938.

Dickter, Arturo Grunstein. "In the Shadow of Oil." *Mexican Studies/Estudios Mexicanos* 21, no. 1 (2005): 1–32.

Mateos, Abdón. *De la Guerra Civil al exilio.* Madrid: Biblioteca Nueva, 2005.

Maurer, Noel. "The Empire Struck Back: Sanctions and Compensation in the Mexican Oil Expropriation of 1938." *Journal of Economic History* 71, no. 3 (September 2011): 590–615.

McConahay, Mary Jo. *The Tango War*. New York: St. Martin's Press, 2018.

Meyer, Lorenzo. *The Mexican Revolution and the Anglo-American Powers: The End of Confrontation and the Beginning of Negotiation*. Translated by Sandra del Castillo. La Jolla: University of California, San Diego, 1985.

Montes, Juan. "A New Oil Boom in Mexico's Aging 'Golden Belt.'" *Wall Street Journal*, November 4, 2014.

Chapter 16. The Shadow War

Becker, Marc. *The FBI in Latin America: The Ecuador Files*. Durham: Duke University Press, 2017.

Bratzel, John T., and Leslie B. Rout. "FDR and the 'Secret Map.'" *Wilson Quarterly* 9, no. 1 (1985): 167–73.

McConahay, Mary Jo. *The Tango War*. New York: St. Martin's Press, 2018.

Mitchell, Nancy. "Protective Imperialism versus 'Weltpolitik' in Brazil: Part One: Pan-German Vision and Mahanian Response." *International History Review* 18, no. 2 (May 1996): 253–78.

Prengaman, Peter. "Brazil's Bolsonaro Considers US Base to Counter Russia." *Sydney Morning Herald*, January 5, 2019.

"RG 84: Argentina." U.S. Department of State, 1940, available at: https://www.archives.gov/research/holocaust/finding-aid/civilian/rg-84-argentina.html.

Rhodes, Andrew. "The Geographic President: How Franklin D. Roosevelt Used Maps to Make and Communicate Strategy." *The Portolan* 107 (Spring 2020).

Sedgewick, Augustine. *Coffeeland: One Man's Dark Empire and the Making of Our Favorite Drug*. New York: Penguin, 2020.

Slany, William. "U.S. and Allied Wartime and Postwar Relations and Negotiations with Argentina, Portugal, Spain, Sweden, and Turkey on Looted Gold and German External Assets and U.S. Concerns about the Fate of the Wartime Ustasha Treasury; Supplement to Preliminary Study on U.S. and Allied Efforts to Recover and Restore Gold and Other Assets Stolen or Hidden by Germany during World War II." U.S. Department of State, 1998.

Vertuno, Jim. "Long before World Cup, Natal a Key Spot for U.S. in World War II." *Washington Times*, June 15, 2014.

"World War II: Mexican Air Force Helped Liberate the Philippines." *HistoryNet*, June 12, 2006.

Part III. Hot Cold War, 1950–1991

Brands, Hal. *Latin America's Cold War*. Cambridge: Harvard University Press, 2010.

Crandall, Russell. "Hot Cold War." *Survival* 54, no. 1 (2012): 183–90.

Rabe, Stephen. *The Killing Zone*. 2nd ed. Oxford: Oxford University Press, 2015.

Chapter 17. Mr. Kennan Goes to Latin America

Gaddis, John Lewis. *George F. Kennan: An American Life*. New York: Penguin Press, 2011.

Immerman, Richard H. *John Foster Dulles and the Diplomacy of the Cold War*. Princeton: Princeton University Press, 1992.

Kennan, George F. *Memoirs*. 2 vols. Boston: Little, Brown, 1967.

———. "Memorandum by the Counselor of the Department (Kennan) to the Secretary of State." U.S. Department of State Office of the Historian. Washington, DC, March 29, 1950.

Koppes, Clayton R. "The Charge in the Soviet Union (Kennan) to the Secretary of State," February 22, 1946. National Security Archive, accessed at: https://nsarchive2.gwu.edu/coldwar/documents/episode-1/kennan.htm.

———. "Solving for X: Kennan, Containment, and the Color Line." *Pacific Historical Review* 82, no. 1 (2013): 95–118.

LaFeber, Walter. *Inevitable Revolutions*. New York: Norton, 1983.

Steil, Benn. *The Marshall Plan*. New York: Simon and Schuster, 2019.

Trask, Roger R. "George F. Kennan's Report on Latin America (1950)." *Diplomatic History* 2, no. 3 (1978): 307–11.

Chapter 18. Getting Jacobo

Anderson, Jon Lee. *Che Guevara: A Revolutionary Life*. New York: Grove Press, 1997.

"Cleaning up America's Backyard." *Association for Diplomatic Studies and Training: Moments in U.S. Diplomatic History* (blog), June 7, 2016.

Coy Moulton, Aaron. "Amplia ayuda externa contra 'la gangrena comunista': las fuerzas regionales anticomunistas y la finalización de la operación PBFortune, Octubre de 1952." *Revista de historia de América*, no. 149 (2013): 45–58.

Crandall, Russell. *America's Dirty Wars*. New York: Cambridge University Press, 2014.

Cullather, Nicholas. "Operation PBSUCCESS: The United States and Guatemala 1952–1954." CIA Historical Review Program, Washington, DC, 1997, https://www.cia.gov/library/readingroom/docs/DOC_0000134974.pdf

———. *Secret History: The CIA's Classified Account of Its Operations in Guatemala, 1952–1954*. 2nd ed. Stanford: Stanford University Press, 2006.

Dorn, Glenn J. "Pushing Tin: U.S.–Bolivian Relations and the Coming of the National Revolution." *Diplomatic History* 35, no. 2 (2011): 203–28.

Eisenhower, Dwight D. "Eisenhower on Guatemala, 1954." In *Mandate for Change: The White House Years, 1953–1956*, 421–26. New York: Doubleday, 1963.

"Foreign Relations of the United States, 1950, The United Nations; The Western Hemisphere; Volume II." U.S. Department of State, Office of the Historian.

Gaddis, John Lewis. *George F. Kennan*. New York: Penguin Press, 2011.

Gleijeses, Piero. "The Agrarian Reform of Jacobo Arbenz." *Journal of Latin American Studies* 21, no. 3 (October 1989): 453–80.

———. *Shattered Hope.* Princeton: Princeton University Press, 1991.

Grandin, Greg. *The Last Colonial Massacre.* Chicago: University of Chicago Press, 2011.

Immerman, Richard H. *The CIA in Guatemala.* Texas Pan-American Series. Austin: University of Texas Press, 1982.

Kinzer, Stephen. *The Brothers: John Foster Dulles, Allen Dulles, and Their Secret World War.* Reprint edition. St. Martin's Griffin, 2014.

———. *Overthrow: America's Century of Regime Change from Hawaii to Iraq.* New York: Times Books, 2007.

Lehman, Kenneth. "Revolutions and Attributions: Making Sense of Eisenhower Administration Policies in Bolivia and Guatemala." *Diplomatic History* 21, no. 7 (Spring 1997): 185–213.

McCann, Thomas. *An American Company: The Tragedy of United Fruit.* New York: Crown, 1976.

Schlesinger, Stephen C., and Stephen Kinzer. *Bitter Fruit: The Story of the American Coup in Guatemala.* Cambridge: Harvard University Press, 2005.

Streeter, Steven M. "Overthrow of Jacobo Arbenz (1954)." In *Encyclopedia of U.S. Military Interventions in Latin America,* edited by Alan McPherson. Santa Barbara, CA: ABC-CLIO, 2013.

Young, Kevin. "Purging the Forces of Darkness: The United States, Monetary Stabilization, and the Containment of the Bolivian Revolution." *Diplomatic History* 37, no. 3 (2013): 509–37.

Chapter 19. Containing Cuba

Anderson, Jon L. *Che Guevara: A Revolutionary Life.* New York: Grove Press, 1997.

Crandall, Russell. *America's Dirty Wars.* New York: Cambridge University Press, 2014.

———. "Fidel's Secret." *American Interest,* February 3, 2015.

———. "Irreconcilable Differences." *Survival* 54, no. 3 (2012): 179–88.

Crandall, Russell, and Frederick Richardson. "Castro's Revolutionary Coming of Age." *Survival* 62, no. 2 (2020): 153–64.

Fursenko, Aleksandr, and Timothy Naftali. *One Hell of a Gamble: Khrushchev, Castro, and Kennedy, 1958–1964.* New York: Norton, 1998.

Guerra, Lilian. *Visions of Power in Cuba: Revolution, Redemption, and Resistance, 1959–1971.* Chapel Hill: University of North Carolina Press, 2012.

LeoGrande, William, and Peter Kornbluh. *Back Channel to Cuba: The Hidden History of Negotiations between Washington and Havana.* Chapel Hill: University of North Carolina Press, 2015.

Rasenberger, Jim. *The Brilliant Disaster: JFK, Castro, and America's Doomed Invasion of Cuba's Bay of Pigs.* New York: Scribner, 2011.

Voss, Michael. "Bay of Pigs: The 'Perfect Failure' of Cuba Invasion." *BBC*, April 14, 2011.

Welch, Richard E. "Herbert L. Matthews and the Cuban Revolution." *The Historian* 47, no. 1 (November 1984): 1–18.

Chapter 20. Washington and the Dominican Republic

Bishop, Marlon. "80 Years On, Dominicans and Haitians Revisit Painful Memories of Parsley Massacre." *NPR.Org*, October 7, 2017.

Carrozza, Anthony R. *William D. Pawley: The Extraordinary Life of the Adventurer, Entrepreneur, and Diplomat Who Cofounded the Flying Tigers*. Washington, DC: Potomac Books, 2012.

Committee on Intelligence Activities. *Alleged Assassination Plots Involving Foreign Leaders: Interim Report of the Select Committee to Study Governmental Operations with Respect to Intelligence Activities*. The Mary Ferrell Foundation, 2007.

Crandall, Russell. *Gunboat Democracy: U.S. Interventions in the Dominican Republic, Grenada, and Panama*. Lanham, MD: Rowman and Littlefield, 2006.

Crassweller, Robert D. *Trujillo: The Life and Times of a Caribbean Dictator*. New York: Macmillan, 1966.

Diederich, Bernard. *Trujillo: The Death of the Goat*. London: Bodley Head, 1978.

Drum, Kevin. " 'But He's Our Son of a Bitch,' " *Washington Monthly—Politics*, May 16, 2006.

Gleijeses, Piero. *The Dominican Crisis: The 1965 Constitutionalist Revolt and American Intervention*. Baltimore: Johns Hopkins University Press, 1978.

Horrock, Nicholas M. "C.I.A. Is Reported to Have Helped in Trujillo Death." *New York Times*, June 13, 1975.

Montgomery, Paul L. "Plotters Against Trujillo Doubt Any C.I.A. Involvement in Assassination of Dictator." *New York Times*, June 23, 1975.

Pulley, Raymond H. "The United States and the Trujillo Dictatorship, 1933–1940: The High Price of Caribbean Stability." *Caribbean Studies* 5, no. 3 (1965): 22–31.

Rabe, Stephen G. "Betancourt, Castro, and Trujillo, 1958–1963." In Peter L. Hahn and Mary A. Heiss, eds., *The United States and the Third World since 1945* Columbus: Ohio State University, 2001.

———. *Eisenhower and Latin America: The Foreign Policy of Anticommunism*. Chapel Hill: University of North Carolina Press, 1988.

———. "Eisenhower and the Overthrow of Rafael Trujillo." *Journal of Conflict Studies* 6, no. 1 (January 1986).

———. *The Killing Zone: The United States Wages Cold War in Latin America*. New York: Oxford University Press, 2016.

Young, Thomas. "40 Years Ago, Church Committee Investigated Americans Spying on Americans." *Brookings*, May 6, 2015.

Chapter 21. Washington and the Dominican Republic

Crandall, Russell. *Gunboat Democracy: U.S. Interventions in the Dominican Republic, Grenada, and Panama*. Lanham, MD: Rowman and Littlefield, 2006.

Felten, Peter G. "The Path to Dissent: Johnson, Fulbright, and the 1965 Intervention in the Dominican Republic." *Presidential Studies Quarterly* 26, no. 4 (Fall 1996): 1009–18.

Gleijeses, Piero. *The Dominican Crisis: The 1965 Constitutionalist Revolt and American Intervention*. Baltimore: Johns Hopkins University Press, 1978.

McPherson, Alan. "Misled by Himself: What the Johnson Tapes Reveal about the Dominican Intervention of 1965." *Latin American Research Review* 38, no. 2 (2003): 127–46.

Chapter 22. A Very Brazilian Coup

Aragon, Daniel P. "Chancellery Sepulchers: Jânio Quadros, João Goulart, and the Forging of Brazilian Foreign Policy in Angola, Mozambique, and South Africa, 1961–1964." *Luso-Brazilian Review* 47, no. 1 (2010): 121–49.

Binder, David. "U.S. Assembled a Force in 1964 for Possible Use in Brazil Coup." *New York Times*, December 30, 1976.

"Brazil Coup Affects Whole Continent: Overthrow of Goulart Is Expected to Bolster the Moderates and Set Back the Communists." *New York Times*, April 5, 1964.

Crandall, Britta. *Hemispheric Giants: The Misunderstood History of U.S.–Brazilian Relations*. Lanham, MD: Rowman and Littlefield, 2011.

Leacock, Ruth. *Requiem for Revolution: The United States and Brazil, 1961–1969*. Kent, OH: Kent State University Press, 1990.

Loureiro, Felipe Pereira. "The Alliance for Progress and President João Goulart's Three-Year Plan: The Deterioration of U.S.–Brazilian Relations in Cold War Brazil (1962)." *Cold War History* 17, no. 1 (January 2017): 61–79.

———. "The Alliance For or Against Progress? US–Brazilian Financial Relations in the Early 1960s." *Journal of Latin American Studies* 46, no. 2 (April 2014).

Morel, Edmar. *O Golpe Começou em Washington*. Jundiaí, SP: Paco Editorial, 2014.

Pereira, Anthony W. "The US Role in the 1964 Coup in Brazil: A Reassessment." *Bulletin of Latin American Research* 37, no. 1 (June 2016).

Quadros, Jânio. "Brazil's New Foreign Policy," *Foreign Affairs* 40, no. 1 (October 1961): 19–27.

Skidmore, Thomas E. *Brazil: Five Centuries of Change*. Second ed. Oxford: Oxford University Press, 2010.

———. *The Politics of Military Rule in Brazil, 1964–1985*. New York: Oxford University Press, 1990.

Stepan, Alfred C. *The Military in Politics: Changing Patterns in Brazil*. Princeton: Princeton University Press, 1971.

Walters, Vernon A. *Silent Missions*. New York: Doubleday, 1978.

Chapter 23. Killing Che

"Alliance for Progress (Alianza Para El Progreso)." *John F. Kennedy Presidential Library and Museum,* n.d.

Brands, Hal. *Latin America's Cold War.* Cambridge: Harvard University Press, 2012.

Casey, Michael. *Che's Afterlife: The Legacy of an Image.* New York: Vintage, 2009.

Crandall, Russell. *America's Dirty Wars.* New York: Cambridge University Press, 2014.

———. "A Hot Cold War." *Survival* 54, no. 6 (December 2012): 183–90.

Grimmett, Richard F., and Mark P. Sullivan. "United States Army School of the Americas: Background and Congressional Concerns." Congressional Research Service, April 16, 2001.

Harmer, Tanya. *Allende's Chile and the Inter-American Cold War.* Chapel Hill: University of North Carolina Press, 2014.

Kennedy, John F. "Address at a White House Reception for Members of Congress and for the Diplomatic Corps of the Latin American Republics." John F. Kennedy Presidential Library and Museum, March 13, 1961.

Ryan, Henry Butterfield. *The Fall of Che Guevara: A Story of Soldiers, Spies, and Diplomats.* New York: Oxford University Press, 1999.

Selvage, Donald R. "Che Guevara in Bolivia." Marine Corps Command and Staff College, April 1, 1985.

Chapter 24. What Really Happened in Chile?

"Allende, a Man of the Privileged Class Turned Radical Politician." *New York Times,* September 12, 1973.

Devine, Jack. "What Really Happened in Chile." *Foreign Affairs* 93, no. 5 (September/October 2014): 168–74.

Devine, Jack, and Peter Kornbluh. "Showdown in Santiago." *Foreign Affairs* 93, no. 5 (2014): 168–74.

Falcoff, Mark. "Kissinger and Chile: The Myth That Will Not Die." *Commentary.* November 2003.

Gustafson, Kristian C. "CIA Machinations in Chile in 1970: Reexamining the Record." *Studies in Intelligence* 47, no. 3 (2003): 35–49.

Harmer, Tanya. *Allende's Chile and the Inter-American Cold War.* Chapel Hill: University of North Carolina Press, 2014.

Haslam, Jonathan. *The Nixon Administration and the Death of Allende's Chile: A Case of Assisted Suicide.* New York: Verso, 2005.

Hersh, Seymour M. "The C.I.A. Is Linked to Strikes in Chile that Beset Allende." *New York Times,* September 20, 1974.

———. "The Price of Power." *The Atlantic,* December 1, 1982.

Hitchens, Christopher. *The Trial of Henry Kissinger.* London: Verso, 2001.

Howe, Marvine. "Chile Calls Truck Strike 'Catastrophic.' " *New York Times,* August 18, 1973.

Kornbluh, Peter. "Chile and the United States: Declassified Documents Relating to the Military Coup, September 11, 1973." National Security Archive.

———. *The Pinochet File: A Declassified Dossier on Atrocity and Accountability.* New York: New Press, 2004.

Maxwell, Kenneth. "The Other 9/11: The United States and Chile, 1973." *Foreign Affairs,* December 2003.

"Papers Show I.T.T. Urged U.S. to Help Oust Allende." *New York Times,* July 3, 1972.

Rogers, William. "Crisis Prevention." *Foreign Affairs.* March 2004.

Rogers, William D., and Kenneth Maxwell. "Fleeing the Chilean Coup: The Debate Over U.S. Complicity." *Foreign Affairs,* January 2004.

Sigmund, Paul E. "The 'Invisible Blockade' and the Overthrow of Allende." *Foreign Affairs,* January 1974.

Treverton, Gregory. "Covert Intervention in Chile, 1970–73." Carnegie Council on Ethics and International Affairs Case No. 503, 1990, distributed by the Institute for the Study of Diplomacy, Georgetown University, Washington, DC.

Chapter 25. Guatemala's "Scorched Communists"

Alterman, Eric. "The Upside of Genocide." *The Nation.* June 19, 2013.

Bonner, Raymond. "Behind the Guatemala Coup: A General Takes Over and Changes Its Course." *New York Times,* March 29, 1982.

———. "Guatemala Enlists Religion in Battle." *New York Times,* July 18, 1982.

Broder, Tanya, and Bernard Lambek. "Military Aid to Guatemala." *Yale Journal of International Law* 13, no. 1 (1988): 111–45.

Carothers, Thomas. *In the Name of Democracy: U.S. Policy toward Latin America in the Reagan Years.* Berkeley: University of California Press, 1991.

Clinton, William J. "Remarks in a Roundtable Discussion on Peace Efforts in Guatemala City, March 10, 1999," American Presidency Project, accessed at: https://www.presidency.ucsb.edu/documents/remarks-roundtable-discussion-peace-efforts-guatemala-city.

Crandall, Russell. *America's Dirty Wars: Irregular Warfare from 1776 to the War on Terror.* New York: Cambridge University Press, 2014.

Culpepper, Miles. "Ronald Reagan's Genocidal Secret: A True Story of Right-Wing Impunity in Guatemala." *Salon,* March 24, 2015.

Doyle, Kate. "The Final Battle: Ríos Montt's Counterinsurgency Campaign." *National Security Archive.* March 19, 2013.

———. "Guatemala's Genocide on Trial," *The Nation,* May 22, 2013.

———. "Indicted for Genocide: Guatemala's Efraín Ríos Montt." *National Security Archive.* March 19, 2013.

———. "The Pursuit of Justice in Guatemala." *National Security Archive*, March 23, 2012.

Gall, Norman. "Slaughter in Guatemala." *New York Review of Books*, May 20, 1971.

Garrard-Burnett, Virginia. *Terror in the Land of the Holy Spirit: Guatemala under General Efraín Ríos Montt, 1982–1983*. Oxford: Oxford University Press, 2011.

Grandin, Greg. *Denegado en su totalidad: documentos estadounidenses liberados*. Guatemala City: AVANCSO, 2001.

Malkin, Elisabeth. "Former Leader of Guatemala Is Guilty of Genocide Against Mayan Group." *New York Times*, May 10, 2013.

———. "Trial on Guatemalan Civil War Carnage Leaves Out U.S. Role." *New York Times*, May 16, 2013.

Meislin, Richard J. "Guatemalan Chief Says War Is Over." *New York Times*, December 11, 1982.

"Obituary: Efraín Ríos Montt." *BBC News*, April 2, 2018.

Reagan, Ronald. *Public Papers of the Presidents of the United States*. Book 2 (July 3 to December 31, 1982). U.S. Government Printing Office, 1983.

———. "Question-and-Answer Session with Reporters on the President's Trip to Latin America." December 4, 1982, American Presidency Project, accessed at: https://www.presidency.ucsb.edu/documents/question-and-answer-session-with-reporters-the-senate-override-fiscal-year-1982.

Schirmer, Jennifer G. *The Guatemalan Military Project: A Violence Called Democracy*. Philadelphia: University of Pennsylvania Press, 1998.

Sikkink, Kathryn. *Mixed Messages: U.S. Human Rights Policy and Latin America*. Ithaca: Cornell University Press, 2007.

United States, General Accounting Office. "Military Sales." Report to the Chairman, Subcommittee on Western Hemisphere Affairs, Committee on Foreign Affairs, House of Representatives. National Security and International Affairs Division, January 20, 1986.

"U.S. Ambassador Frederic Chapin Says the Government of Guatemala . . ." *UPI*, April 16, 1982.

"Who Is Elliott Abrams, US Special Envoy for Venezuela?" *Al Jazeera*, February 12, 2019.

Wilkinson, Daniel. *Silence on the Mountain: Stories of Terror, Betrayal, and Forgetting in Guatemala*. Durham: Duke University Press, 2004.

Wills, Santiago. "Did U.S. Back Genocide in Guatemala?" *ABC News*, May 14, 2013.

Chapter 26. Nicaragua under the Sandinistas

This chapter is adapted from: Crandall, Russell. *America's Dirty Wars*. New York: Cambridge University Press, 2014, 280–303. © Russell Crandall 2014, published by Cambridge University Press. Reproduced with permission of the Licensor through PLSclear.

Crandall, Russell. *The Salvador Option: The United States in El Salvador, 1977–1992.* New York: Cambridge University Press, 2016.

Gould, Jeffrey L. "Toward Revolution in the Countryside, 1974–1979." In *To Lead as Equals: Rural Protest and Political Consciousness in Chinandega, Nicaragua, 1912–1979,* 270–91. Chapel Hill: University of North Carolina Press, 1990.

Kagan, Robert. *A Twilight Struggle: American Power and Nicaragua, 1977–1990.* New York: Free Press, 1996.

Lake, Anthony. *Somoza Falling.* Amherst: University of Massachusetts Press, 1990.

LeoGrande, William M. *Our Own Backyard: The United States in Central America, 1977–1992.* Chapel Hill: University of North Carolina Press, 2007.

Sobel, Richard. "Contra Aid Fundamentals: Exploring the Intricacies and the Issues." *Political Science Quarterly* 110, no. 2 (1995): 287–306.

Timbers, Edwin. "Legal and Institutional Aspects of the Iran–Contra Affair." *Presidential Studies Quarterly* 20, no. 1 (1990): 31–41.

Chapter 27. Why Invade Grenada?

Binder, David. "Soviet Brigade: How the U.S. Traced It." *New York Times,* September 13, 1979.

Crandall, Russell. *Gunboat Democracy: U.S. Interventions in the Dominican Republic, Grenada, and Panama.* Lanham, MD: Rowman and Littlefield, 2008.

Duffy, Gloria. "Crisis Mangling and the Cuban Brigade." *International Security* 8, no. 1 (Summer 1983): 67–87.

Klein, Ezra. "Jimmy Carter's 'Malaise' Speech Was Popular!" *Washington Post,* August 9, 2013.

"The U.S. Invades 'A Little Island Called Grenada.'" *Association for Diplomatic Studies and Training,* October 10, 2014.

Chapter 28. The Salvador Option

This chapter is adapted from: Crandall, Russell. *The Salvador Option: The United States in El Salvador, 1977–1992.* New York: Cambridge University Press, 2016. © Russell Crandall 2016, published by Cambridge University Press. Reproduced with permission of the Licensor through PLSclear.

Chapter 29. Getting Rid of Pinochet

Bawden, John R. "Cutting Off the Dictator: The United States Arms Embargo of the Pinochet Regime, 1974–1988." *Journal of Latin American Studies* 45, no. 3 (August 2013): 513–43.

Branch, Taylor. "The Letelier Investigation." *New York Times,* July 16, 1978.

"Chile: 40 Years on from Pinochet's Coup, Impunity Must End." *Amnesty International,* September 10, 2013.

Christian, Shirley. "Chile Arms Caches Are Laid to Cuba." *New York Times,* October 19, 1986.

"CIA: 'Pinochet Personally Ordered' Letelier Bombing." *National Security Archive,* n.d.

"CPD: October 6, 1976 Debate Transcript." *Commission on Presidential Debates.* Available at: https://www.debates.org/voter-education/debate-transcripts/october-6-1976-debate-transcript/

DeYoung, Karen, David Montgomery, Missy Ryan, Ishan Tharoor, and Jia Lynn Yang. " 'This Was Not an Accident. This Was a Bomb.' " *Washington Post,* September 20, 2016.

Falcoff, Mark. "Chile: The Dilemma for U.S. Policy." *Foreign Affairs* 64, no. 4 (1986): 833–48.

Fermandois H., Joaquín. *Mundo y Fin de Mundo: Chile en la Política Mundial, 1900–2004.* Santiago: Ediciones Universidad Católica de Chile, 2005.

" 'The First Terrorist Attack in the U.S.'—The Letelier–Moffitt Assassinations." *Association for Diplomatic Studies and Training,* February 4, 2014.

Franklin, Jonathan. "US Considered Offering Asylum to Chilean Dictator Augusto Pinochet." *Guardian,* September 11, 2014.

Goshko, John M., and Timothy S. Robinson. "U.S. Eying Cutback in Aid to Chile." *Washington Post,* October 18, 1979.

Kirkpatrick, Jeane J. "Dictatorships & Double Standards." *Commentary* 68 (November 1979): 34–45.

Kornbluh, Peter. "Declassifying U.S. Intervention in Chile." *NACLA,* September 25, 2007.

———. "The Pinochet File." *National Security Archive,* n.d.

———. *The Pinochet File: A Declassified Dossier on Atrocity and Accountability.* New York: New Press, 2013.

———. "Why the Obama Administration Is Giving Old State Secrets to Latin American Allies." *Washington Post,* September 16, 2016.

———. "Why the State Department Finally Confirmed Augusto Pinochet's Role in International Terrorism." *The Nation,* October 13, 2015.

Kornbluh, Peter, and Yvette White. "Pinochet: A Declassified Documentary Obit." *National Security Archive.*

Lee, Diz. "Chile's 1988 Plebiscite and the End of Pinochet's Dictatorship." *Association for Diplomatic Studies and Training,* November 18, 2014, https://adst.org/2014/11/chiles-1988-plebiscite-and-the-end-of-pinochets-dictatorship/.

Lyons, Richard D. "Senate Votes Overhaul of Military Aid." *New York Times,* February 19, 1976.

Meneses, Emilio C. "Heraldo Muñoz y Carlos Portales." *Revista de Ciencia Política* 9–10, no. 1–2 (1987).

Montes, Rocío. "New US Documents Show Pinochet Ordered Ex-Minister's Murder in 1976." *El País*, October 12, 2015.

Morley, Morris. *Reagan and Pinochet: The Struggle Over U.S. Policy toward Chile*. New York: Cambridge University Press, 2015.

Onis, Juan de. "U.S. Lifts Carter's Ban on Trade Assistance for Chile." *New York Times*, February 21, 1981.

Pastor, Robert A. *The Carter Administration and Latin America: A Test of Principle*. Atlanta, GA: Carter Center, 1992.

"Pursuing the Past: U.S. Policy Toward Chile's Augusto Pinochet." *PBS NewsHour*, February 20, 2001.

Rickard, Stephen A., Cynthia G. Brown, and Alfred C. Stepan. *Chile: Human Rights and the Plebiscite*. Americas Watch Report. New York: Americas Watch Committee, 1988.

Santibañez, Abraham. *El Plebiscito de Pinochet: Cazado en Su Propia Trampa*. Santiago, Chile: Editorial Atena, 1988.

Sater, William F. *Chile and the United States: Empires in Conflict*. The United States and the Americas. Athens: University of Georgia Press, 1990.

Schoultz, Lars. *Human Rights and United States Policy Toward Latin America*. Princeton: Princeton University Press, 1981.

"Siege Imposed in Chile after Military Escorts Are Slain in Ambush; Leftists Blamed." *Los Angeles Times*, September 6, 1986.

Sigmund, Paul E. *The United States and Democracy in Chile*. Baltimore: Johns Hopkins University Press, 1993.

Slattery, Gram. "Kerry to Deliver Declassified Papers on Argentina's 'Dirty War.' " *Reuters*, August 4, 2016.

Part IV. Post–Cold War, 1989–

Cárdenas, José R. "RIP, Inter-American Democratic Charter." *Foreign Policy*, January 24, 2014.

Costa, Eduardo Ferrero. "Peru's Presidential Coup." *Journal of Democracy* 4, no. 1 (1993): 28–40.

Crandall, Russell. "The Post-American Hemisphere." *Foreign Affairs* (May/June 2011).

———. *The United States and Latin America after the Cold War*. New York: Cambridge University Press, 2008.

Human Rights Watch. "Venezuela: OAS Should Invoke Democratic Charter." *Human Rights Watch*, May 16, 2016.

Nowrasteh, Alex. "Proposition 187 Turned California Blue." *Cato Institute*, July 20, 2016.

Organization of American States. "Inter-American Democratic Charter." Organization of American States Department of Public Information, July 9, 2001.

Ward, Alex. "Pompeo Says 'Military Action Is Possible' in Venezuela If Maduro Doesn't Step Down." *Vox*, May 1, 2019.

Chapter 30. Invading Panama

Crandall, Russell. *Drugs and Thugs: The History and Future of America's War on Drugs.* New Haven: Yale University Press, 2020.

———. *Gunboat Democracy: U.S. Interventions in the Dominican Republic, Grenada, and Panama.* Lanham, Md.: Rowman and Littlefield, 2006.

Gugliotta, Guy, and Jeff Leen. *Kings of Cocaine: Inside the Medellín Cartel, an Astonishing True Story of Murder, Money, and International Corruption.* New York: Simon and Schuster, 1989.

Jonnes, Jill. *Hep-Cats, Narcs, and Pipe Dreams: A History of America's Romance with Illegal Drugs.* Baltimore: Johns Hopkins University Press, 1999.

Kempe, Frederick. *Divorcing the Dictator: America's Bungled Affair with Noriega.* New York: G. P. Putnam's Sons, 1990.

Shultz, George P. *Turmoil and Triumph: Diplomacy, Power, and the Victory of the American Deal.* New York: Scribner, 2010.

Chapter 31. The Washington Consensus Goes South

This chapter is adapted from: Crandall, Russell. *The United States and Latin America after the Cold War.* New York: Cambridge University Press, 2008. © Russell Crandall 2008, published by Cambridge University Press. Reproduced with permission of the Licensor through PLSclear.

Agarwal, Prateek. "Washington Consensus." *Intelligent Economist,* available at: https://www.intelligenteconomist.com/washington-consensus/.

Chapter 32. Haitian Tragedy

This chapter is adapted from: Crandall, Russell. *The United States and Latin America after the Cold War.* New York: Cambridge University Press, 2008. © Russell Crandall 2008, published by Cambridge University Press. Reproduced with permission of the Licensor through PLSclear.

Girard, Philippe R. "Operation Restore Democracy?" *Journal of Haitian Studies* 8, no. 2 (2002): 70–85.

———. "Peacekeeping, Politics, and the 1994 US Intervention in Haiti." *Journal of Conflict Studies* 24, no. 1 (June 1, 2004): 20–41.

Idelson, Molly. "Supreme Court: Administration Holds to Policy of Haitian Repatriation." *CQ Weekly,* February 27, 1993, 462.

U.S. Government Accountability Office (U.S. GAO). "Peacekeeping: Cost Comparison of Actual UN and Hypothetical U.S. Operations in Haiti," no. GAO-06-331 (February 21, 2006).

Warren, Christopher. "Shaping a New World: U.S. and Brazilian Leadership in a Democratic, Prosperous Hemisphere." *US Department of State Dispatch* 7 (1996): 77.

Chapter 33. Haitian Tragedy

This chapter is adapted from: Crandall, Russell. *The United States and Latin America after the Cold War*. New York: Cambridge University Press, 2008. © Russell Crandall 2018, published by Cambridge University Press. Reproduced with permission of the Licensor through PLSclear.

Christopher, Warren. "Shaping a New World: U.S. and Brazilian Leadership in a Democratic, Prosperous Hemisphere." *US Department of State Dispatch* 7 (1996): 77.

Girard, Philippe R. "Operation Restore Democracy?" *Journal of Haitian Studies* 8, no. 2 (2002): 70–85.

———. "Peacekeeping, Politics, and the 1994 US Intervention in Haiti." *Journal of Conflict Studies* 24, no. 1 (June 1, 2004): 20–41.

Gros, Jean-Germain. "Haiti's Flagging Transition." *Journal of Democracy* 8, no. 4 (October 1, 1997): 94–109.

"Replacement of U.S.–Led Force in Haiti with UN Peacekeeping Mission." *American Journal of International Law* 98, no. 3 (2004): 586–88.

Sciolino, Elaine. "Clinton Says U.S. Will Continue Ban on Haitian Exodus." *New York Times,* January 15, 1993.

Shacochis, Bob. "Bill Clinton's Shameful Haiti Legacy." *Daily Beast,* January 19, 2010.

Chapter 34. Haitian Tragedy

This chapter is adapted from: Crandall, Russell. *The United States and Latin America after the Cold War*. New York: Cambridge University Press, 2008. © Russell Crandall 2008, published by Cambridge University Press. Reproduced with permission of the Licensor through PLSclear.

Falcoff, Mark. "Where Does Haiti Go from Here?" *American Enterprise Institute for Public Policy Research,* April 2004.

Grossman, Marc. "U.S. Policy toward Haiti." Testimony before the Senate Foreign Relations Committee, 108th Cong., 2nd sess., July 15, 2003.

"Haiti: Human Rights Developments." *HRW World Report, 2000.* New York: Human Rights Watch, 2001.

Taft-Morales, Maureen. "Haiti: Developments and U.S. Policy since 1994 and Current Congressional Concerns." *Congressional Research Service.* Washington, DC: Library of Congress, January 19, 2005.

United States Government Accountability Office (U.S. GAO). "PEACEKEEPING: Cost Comparison of Actual UN and Hypothetical U.S. Operations in Haiti." GAO-06-331, February 2006.

Wilentz, Amy. "René Préval: The Unassuming President Who Wanted to Save Haiti." *Politico,* December 28, 2017.

Zacharia, Janine. "Washington v. Aristide: Oppo Research." *New Republic,* March 3, 2004.

Chapter 35. Supply Side

Cawley, Marguerite. "Montesinos Is Gone, But Peru's Narco-Political Brokers Continue Tradition." *InSight Crime*, October 20, 2014.

Crandall, Russell. *Drugs and Thugs: The History and Future of America's War on Drugs.* New Haven: Yale University Press, 2020.

DeYoung, Karen. " 'The Doctor' Divided U.S. Officials." *Washington Post*, September 22, 2000.

"El Coronel Absuelto." *Caretas*, June 23, 2005.

"La Intervención de Alberto Fujimori." Corte Suprema de Justicia de la República (2001), available at www.gacetajuridica.com.pe/noticias/sente-fujimori/P2C15_Intervencion.pdf.

Lama, Abraham. "Drogas y Narcotráfico—Perú: Edecán y ex avión presidencial involucrados en narcotráfico." *Inter Press*, May 19, 1996.

"Montesinos: The End of the Road." *BBC*, June 24, 2001.

Quiroz, Alfonso. *Corrupt Circles: A History of Unbound Graft in Peru.* Baltimore: Johns Hopkins University Press, 2008.

Rempel, William, and Sebastian Rotella. "Arms Dealer Implicates Peru Spy Chief in Smuggling Ring." *Los Angeles Times*, November 1, 2000.

Youngers, Coletta, and Eileen Rosin, eds. *Drugs and Democracy in Latin America: The Impact of U.S. Policy.* Boulder, CO: Lynne Rienner, 2004.

Chapter 36. Supply Side

Anderson, Jon Lee. "The Fall of Evo Morales." *New Yorker*, March 16, 2020.

Crandall, Russell. "Blow Hard." *American Interest*, January 1, 2008.

———. *Drugs and Thugs: The History and Future of America's War on Drugs.* New Haven: Yale University Press, 2020.

———. "Reports from the Revolution." *Survival: Global Politics and Strategy* 50, no. 6 (2008): 193–98.

Curiel, John, and Jack Williams. "Did Evo Morales Win?" *Wall Street Journal*, February 27, 2020.

Doward, Jamie. "Leaked Paper Reveals UN Split over War on Drugs." *Guardian*, November 30, 2013.

Friedman-Rudovsky, Jean. "Bolivia's Surprising Anti-Drug Success." *Time*, August 5, 2008.

Guillermoprieto, Alma. "Bolivia's Parched Future." *New York Review of Books*, December 18, 2009;

"How Bolivia Fights the Drug Scourge." Editorial Board, *New York Times*, September 14, 2016.

Hudak, John, et al. "Uruguay's Cannabis Law: Pioneering a New Paradigm." Brookings Institute Center for Effective Public Management and the Washington Office on Latin America, March 2018.

"International Cocaine Industry." Interagency Intelligence Memorandum, November 1987, accessed at: https://www.cia.gov/library/readingroom/docs/CIA-RDP89 M00699R002201800002-5.pdf.

Montes, Juan, and José de Córdoba. "Evo Morales Offers to Sit Out Bolivia's Next Election If He Can Finish Term." *Wall Street Journal,* November 20, 2019.

Radwin, Max. "Is Bolivia's Coca Policy a Solution to Drug Trafficking—or Part of the Problem?" *World Politics Review,* June 5, 2018.

Chapter 37. Supply Side

"A New Plan for Colombia." *The Economist.* January 23, 2016.

Crandall, Russell. *Driven by Drugs: U.S. Policy toward Colombia.* Boulder, CO: Lynne Rienner, 2002.

———. *Drugs and Thugs: The History and Future of America's War on Drugs.* New Haven: Yale University Press, 2020.

———. "Drug War Divide." *American Interest,* October 3, 2014.

———. "Drug Wars." *Survival* 55, no. 4 (August–September 2013): 229–40.

———. *The United States and Latin America after the Cold War.* New York: Cambridge University Press, 2008.

Dudley, Steven, et al. "Colombia Elites and Organized Crime." *InSight Crime,* August 9, 2016.

McDermott, Jeremy. "Criminal Activities of the FARC and Rebel Earnings." *InSight Crime,* May 21, 2013.

White House, Office of the Press Secretary. "Fact Sheet: Peace Colombia—A New Era of Partnership between the United States and Colombia," February 4, 2016.

Yagoub, Mimi. "Are New Groups Already Moving in on FARC Drug Empire?" *InSight Crime,* August 19, 2016.

Chapter 38. The (Almost) Coup in Caracas

Anderson, Jon Lee. "The Revolutionary." *New Yorker,* September 3, 2001.

Bachelet, Pablo. "State Department Documents Reveal U.S. Dealings with Venezuela's Chavez." *McClatchy Washington Bureau,* December 9, 2007.

Corrales, Javier. "The Logic of Extremism: How Chavez Gains by Giving So Much to Cuba." Inter-American Dialogue Working Paper. Washington, DC, December 2005.

"Coup and Counter-Coup." *The Economist,* April 15, 2002.

Crandall, Russell. *The United States and Latin America after the Cold War.* New York: Cambridge University Press, 2008.

Crane, Mary. "U.S.–Venezuela Relations." CFR Backgrounder. Washington, DC: Council on Foreign Relations, May 18, 2005.

Forero, Juan. "A Chávez Comeback More Astounding Than His Fall." *New York Times,* April 14, 2002.

————. "Documents Show C.I.A. Knew of a Coup Plot in Venezuela." *New York Times,* December 3, 2004.

Gott, Richard, and Georges Bartoli. *Hugo Chávez and the Bolivarian Revolution.* New York: Verso, 2011.

Lapper, Richard. "Living with Hugo: U.S. Policy toward Hugo Chávez's Venezuela." Council Special Report 20, November 2006. Washington, DC: Council on Foreign Relations.

"A Review of U.S. Policy Toward Venezuela, November 2001–April 2002." United States Department of State and the Broadcasting Board of Governors Office of Inspector General, 2002.

"Venezuela: Hugo Chávez's Revolution." Latin America Report No. 19, February 22, 2007. Washington, DC: International Crisis Group.

Chapter 39. El Narco Mexicano

Crandall, Russell. "Democracy and the Mexican Cartels." *Survival: Global Politics and Strategy* 56, no. 3 (2014): 233–44.

————. *Drugs and Thugs: The History and Future of America's War on Drugs.* New Haven: Yale University Press, 2020.

Crandall, Russell, and Savannah Haeger. "Latin America's Invisible War." *Survival: Global Politics and Strategy* 58, no. 5 (2016): 159–66.

————."Mexico's Cartels and the Rule of Law." *IISS Strategic Comments,* January 2020.

de Córdoba, José, and Jessica Donati. "Mexico's Failure to Stem Violence Strains Relationship with U.S." *Wall Street Journal,* October 25, 2019.

Ellis, Evan. "Strategic Insights: Mexico—New Directions, Continuity, and Obstacles in the Fight Against Transnational Organized Crime." *U.S. Army War College,* March 31, 2016.

Gibler, John. *To Die in Mexico: Dispatches from Inside the Drug War.* San Francisco: City Lights Books, 2011.

Graff, Garrett M. "The Green Monster." *Politico Magazine,* November/December 2014.

Grillo, Ioan. *El Narco: Inside Mexico's Criminal Insurgency.* New York: Bloomsbury Press, 2012.

Hernández, Anabel. *Narcoland: The Mexican Drug Lords and Their Godfathers.* London: Verso, 2013.

Looft, Christopher, and Steven Dudley. "Most Guns in Mexico Traced to US Dealers: Govt Data." *Insight Crime,* May 1, 2012.

"Mérida Initiative." *Insight Crime,* November 1, 2010.

Okeowo, Alexis. "A Mexican Town Wages Its Own War on Drugs." *New Yorker*, November 27, 2017.

Radden Keefe, Patrick. "Cocaine Incorporated." *New York Times*, June 15, 2012.

Chapter 40. Washington–Havana Whiplash

Aho, Matthew D. "U.S.–Cuba Policy Whiplash." *America's Quarterly*, December 9, 2019.

Anderson, Jon Lee. "The Diplomat Who Quit the Trump Administration." *New Yorker*, May 28, 2018.

Anderson, Jon Lee, and Adam Entous. "The Mystery of the Havana Syndrome." *New Yorker*, November 19, 2018.

Buncombe, Andrew. "Where Is Rolando Sarraff Trujillo?" *The Independent*, January 1, 2015.

Cárdenas, José R. "Targeting American Diplomats, Cuba Is Up to Its Dirty Old Tricks." *Foreign Policy* (blog), August 16, 2017.

Crandall, Russell. "Mr. Obama goes to Cuba." *Survival Editors' Blog*, March 23, 2016.

Crandall, Russell, and Sarah Sears. "Review of *Our Woman in Havana: A Diplomat's Chronicle of America's Long Struggle with Castro's Cuba* by Vicki Huddleston." *Survival* 61, no. 3 (May 2019).

"Cuba Has Never Perpetrated, nor Will It Ever Perpetrate Attacks of Any Sort Against Diplomatic Officials or Their Relatives, without Any Exception." *Granma*, October 3, 2017.

Cullen, Catherine. "Canada Sending Home Families of Diplomats in Cuba after Cases of 'New Type' of Brain Injury." *CBC Radio-Canada*, April 16, 2018.

"Declarations of Cuban Minister of Foreign Affairs: Cuba Has Never and Will Never Commit Attacks Against Diplomats." *Representaciones Diplomáticas de Cuba en el Exterior* (blog), October 4, 2017.

DeYoung, Karen. "Obama Moves to Normalize Relations with Cuba as American Is Released by Authorities in Havana." *Washington Post*, December 17, 2014.

———. "Trump Administration Ends Group Travel to Cuba by Americans." *Washington Post*, June 4, 2019.

Erickson, Amanda. "Scientists Can't Explain Why Diplomats in Cuba Are Suffering from 'Traumatic Brain Injury.' " *Washington Post*, April 17, 2018.

Erikson, Daniel P. "Cuba Wars Redux." *Global Americans*, May 22, 2018.

Faiola, Anthony. "As Sanctions Bite in Cuba, the U.S.—Once a Driver of Hope—Is Now a Source of Pain." *Washington Post*, June 23, 2019.

Harris, Gardiner. "16 Americans Sickened after Attack on Embassy Staff in Havana." *New York Times*, August 24, 2017.

Harris, Gardiner, Julie Hirschfeld Davis, and Ernesto Londoño. "U.S. Expels 15 Cuban Diplomats, in Latest Sign Détente May Be Ending." *New York Times*, January 20, 2018.

Huddleston, Vicki. *Our Woman in Havana: A Diplomat's Chronicle of America's Long Struggle with Castro's Cuba.* New York: Overlook Press, 2018.

Jordan, Mary. "Marco Rubio's Hard Line on Cuba Says Much about How He Views the U.S. Role in the World." *Washington Post,* January 24, 2016.

Kessel, Jonah M., Melissa Chan, and John Woo. "How an Alleged Sonic Attack Shaped U.S. Policy on Cuba." *New York Times* video, 2018.

National Academies of Sciences, Engineering, and Medicine. 2020. *An Assessment of Illness in U.S. Government Employees and Their Families at Overseas Embassies.* Washington, DC: The National Academies Press. https://doi.org/10.17226/25889.

Obama, Barack. "Statement by the President on Cuba Policy Changes." The White House Office of the Press Secretary, December 17, 2014.

Palus, Shannon. "A Comprehensive List of All the Potential Causes of the Cuban 'Sonic' Attacks." *Slate Magazine,* July 26, 2019.

Robles, Frances, and Kirk Semple. " 'Health Attacks' on U.S. Diplomats in Cuba Baffle both Countries." *New York Times,* August 12, 2017.

Rubio, Marco. *An American Son: A Memoir.* New York: Sentinel, 2012.

"Rubio Presses State Department on Response to Attacks on U.S. Diplomats in Cuba." U.S. Senator for Florida Marco Rubio, January 9, 2018, https://www.rubio.senate.gov/public/index.cfm/2018/1/rubio-presses-state-department-on-response-to-attacks-on-u-s-diplomats-in-cuba.

Small, Gary. "Mass Hysteria Can Strike Anywhere, Anytime." *Psychology Today* blog, September 28, 2010.

Swanson, Ana, and Edward Wong. "Report Points to Microwave 'Attack' as Likely Source of Mystery Illness That Hit Diplomats and Spies." *New York Times,* December 5, 2020.

Tumulty, Karen, and Anne Gearan. "Cuba Decision Marks a Bet by Obama that Cold War Politics Have Turned a Corner." *Washington Post,* December 17, 2014.

Weeks, Greg. "Bolton's Bay of Pigs Anniversary Speech: Tough Talk, Election Politics and Failed Policies." *Global Americans,* April 18, 2019.

Whitefield, Mimi. "Cuba on U.S. Diplomats' Health Attacks: No Way It's Sonic Weapons. Maybe It's Stress." *Miami Herald,* February 8, 2018.

Zimmer, Carl. "A 'Sonic Attack' on Diplomats in Cuba? These Scientists Doubt It." *New York Times,* October 5, 2017.

Chapter 41. Poor Mexico

Barbaro, Michael, Alex Burns, Maggie Haberman, and Kirk Semple. "Highlights of Donald Trump's Immigration Speech and Mexico Trip." *New York Times,* August 31, 2016.

Cantú, Francisco. *The Line Becomes a River: Dispatches from the Border.* New York: River-head Books, 2018.

Cheng, Evelyn. "Mexican Peso Plunges More than 12% to Record Low vs. Dollar on Trump Election Upset." CNBC, November 9, 2016.

"The Diplomatic Meaning of El Chapo's Extradition." *Economist,* January 28, 2017.

Dodds, Eric. "Univision Drops Miss USA Pageant after Trump's Mexico Remarks." *Time,* June 25, 2015.

Goldberg, Michelle. "Congratulations on Fixing the Border, Mr. President!" *New York Times,* June 10, 2019.

Grillo, Ioan. "Trump's Bullying Won't Fix the Migrant Crisis." *New York Times,* June 10, 2019.

Karni, Annie, Ana Swanson, and Michael D. Shear. "Trump Says U.S. Will Hit Mexico With 5% Tariffs on All Goods." *New York Times,* May 30, 2019.

"Mexico under AMLO." *International Institute for Strategic Studies Strategic Comments,* August 2018.

Miroff, Nick, Kanye Sieff, and John Wagner. "How Mexico Talked Trump Out of Tariff Threat with Immigration Crackdown Pact." *Washington Post,* June 11, 2019.

Oppenheimer, Andres. "Fallout from Trump's Visit to Mexico: A Rise of Anti-Americanism?" *Miami Herald,* September 9, 2016.

Saldana, Janel. "Maná's Fher Compares Donald Trump to Hitler after Racist Comments Against Mexicans." *Latin Times,* June 19, 2015.

Shear, Michael D., Zolan Kanno-Youngs, and Ana Swanson. "Trump Says No Deal with Mexico Is Reached as Border Arrests Surge." *New York Times,* June 5, 2019.

Sherman, Christopher. "Mexico's Leader Bonding with Trump." *Associated Press,* April 23, 2020.

Snider, Annie. "Trump Win Churns U.S.–Mexico Water Talks." *Politico,* November 26, 2016.

Winter, Brian. "Old School: What a Hostile Mexico–Trump Relationship Might Look Like." *Americas Quarterly,* January 9, 2017.

Woolf, Nicky, Scott Bixby, and Ben Jacobs. "Trump Announces Trip to Mexico for Talks with President Peña Nieto." *Guardian,* August 31, 2016.

Chapter 42. Exodus from the Northern Triangle

This chapter is adapted from: Crandall, Russell, "Exodus from the Northern Triangle," *Survival* 61, no. 1 (2019): 91–104, copyright © The International Institute for Strategic Studies, reprinted by permission of Informa UK Limited, trading as Taylor & Francis Group, www.tandfonline.com on behalf of The International Institute for Strategic Studies.

"Yearbook of Immigration Statistics 2015." U.S. Department of Homeland Security, available at https://www.dhs.gov/immigration-statistics/yearbook.

Conclusion

Misculin, Nicolás. "Argentina, Brazil Reach Deal to Share Evidence in Corruption Cases." *Reuters*, August 3, 2018.

Shiel, Fergus, and Sasha Chavkin. "Bribery Division: What Is Odebrecht? Who Is Involved?" *International Consortium of Investigative Journalists*, June 25, 2019.

INDEX

Note: Page numbers in italics refer to maps or photographs.

Republic, 190; and Latin America, 216; Moncada Attack, 169; Operación Verano (Summer Operation), 172; Playa Girón invasion, 178–79; refugees from, 332; relationship with Venezuela, 376; revolt against Batista, 170–72, 174; Revolt of the Sergeants, 133; revolutionary training in, 216–17, 245; sovereignty for, 89; Soviet troops in, 260; support for Nicaragua from, 252; support from Soviet Union, 179, 182; supporting guerrillas in Chile, 293; trade embargo, 398; US intervention in, 107, 130–35; US relationship with, 83–84, 96, 156, 398–405; US sanctions against, 403–5; and Venezuela, 404. *See also* Batista, Fulgencio; Castro, Fidel; *Maine*, USS

Cuban Commission of Human Rights and National Reconciliation, 398
Cuban Expeditionary Force, 177–78
Cuban Missile Crisis, 181–83
Curran, Brian Dean, 342–43
Customs and Border Protection (CBP), 389–90, 417
Czechoslovakia, 276

Dam, Kenneth, 267–68
Dana, Charles, 65
Daniel, Jean, 183
Darién Gap, 97
Darío, Rubén, 76
D'Aubuisson, Roberto, 282–83
Davis, Arthur, 306
Davis, Nathaniel, 230
Davis, Richard Harding, 84
DEA (Drug Enforcement Administration), 302, 346, 347, 361, 385, 391
Dearborn, Henry, 191–92
Decena Trágica (Ten Tragic Days), 107

Declaration of the Rights of Man and of the Citizen, 13
declassification diplomacy, 296
de la Maza, Antonio, 192
De la Rúa, Fernando, 323
de Lesseps, Ferdinand, 98–99
del Valle, Reginald Francisco, 110
democracy: in Brazil, 291, 298; in Mexico, 389; in Uruguay, 291; in Venezuela, 380–81
Department of Homeland Security, 389
Dessalines, Jean-Jacques, 15
Devine, Jack, 229, 231–32
Dewey, George T., 91
DeYoung, Karen, 351–52, 354
Díaz, Adolfo, 120, 121–22, 126
Díaz, Porfirio, 47, 137
Dillon, C. Douglas, 191
Dobbins, James, 341
Dodd, Christopher, 366
Doheny, Edward L., 137
Dole, Robert, 305, 320
Dollar Diplomacy, 108, 120
Dolphin, USS, 111
Dominica, 266
Dominican Customs Receivership, 94
Dominican National Guard, 185
Dominican Republic, 93–94, 184; after the civil war, 200–204, *203*; Batista's exile in, 172, 190; civil war in, 198–200; communism in, 190, 196, 199, 202; Cuban invasion of, 190; insurrection in, 216; relationship with US, 94; US assistance for, 195; US intervention in, 107, 117–19, 120, 127–28, 198–201; US involvement in, 185; US occupation of, 185, 187. *See also* Santo Domingo
Dominican Revolutionary Party (PRD), 195
Donaldson, Kevin, 349

Maitland, Thomas, 12

Malary, Guy, 335

Malley, Robert, 55

Manifest Destiny, 7, 32–38, 47, 48, 61, 425

Manila Bay, Battle of, 91

Mann, Thomas, 198, 200, 210, 211

Maoism, 351

Mao Zedong, 169

Marcos, Ferdinand, 378

Martí, José, 71, 84

Martin, John Bartlow, 196–97

Martínez, Gerson, 286

Martner, Gonzalo, 230

Marulanda, Manuel "Sureshot," 370

Marxism, 169, 235; in Central America, 415; in Chile, 227; in Colombia, 350, 367; in El Salvador, 239, 247; in Grenada, 259; in Nicaragua, 239, 244, 247. *See also* Farabundo Martí National Liberation Front (FMLN)

Massing, Michael, 310

Matthei, Fernando, 295

Matthews, Herbert, 171–72

Maxwell, Kenneth, 233

Mazzilli, Pascoal, 213

McConahay, Mary Jo, 142

McCoy, Frank, 125

McCurdy, Clarke, 214

McDougall, Walter, 30, 36, 63–64, 82–83

McKinley, William, 76, 80, 85–86, 99

McNamara, Robert, 197, 217

McPherson, Alan, 128

Meade, José Antonio, 408

Médecins Sans Frontières, 414

Medeiros, Rostand, 145

Medellín Cartel, 303, 304, 348, 385, 386–87, 391

Meese, Edwin, 255

Mena, Luis, 120

Menem, Carlos, 315, 321, 323

Mengele, Joseph, 143

Mérida Initiative (Plan Mexico), 388–89, 391, 418

Merritta, Ezekiel, 59

Merry, Robert, 79

Mesa, Carlos, 363

Mexican Air Force (FAM), 145

Mexican-American War, 7–8, 35, 37–38, 46–47, 49, 55, 409; in California, 60–61; map, 50; opposition to, 51, 52–54; Treaty of Guadalupe Hidalgo, 54–55, 56

Mexican Eagle Oil Company, 137–38

Mexico, 29, 35; anti-drug efforts in, 386–87, 391, 392–94; anti-yanqui protests in, 111; border enforcement by, 420–22; Clinton's bailout, 319–20, 324; Colonization Law (1824), 41; Constitutionalist movement, 110, 113; Constitution of 1917, 137; corruption in, 391; debt default, 316; democracy in, 389; drug trafficking, 385; drug-related violence in, 387–88, 391–94; drugs in, 297, 373; immigrants from, 412–13; improvements in, 410–11; independence of, 40; Kennan's assessment of, 154; map of war with US, 50; and NAFTA, 319; nationalization of petroleum assets, 136, 138–41, 139; response to Central American refugees, 419–20; as source of drugs in US, 346, 347, 386, 391–92; territories seized from, 46; troubled economy, 318–19; and the Trump presidency, 406–13; US antidrug efforts, 388–96, 418; US intervention in, 107–16; war with US, 7–8, 35, 37–38, 46–47, 49, 55; and the Washington Consensus, 315; during WWII, 145–46; Zapatista insurrection, 318

Sutter, Johann August (John A.), 56–58, 59, 61–62
syndicalism, 122
Szulc, Tad, 198

Taft, William Howard, 108, 120
Task Force on Latin America, 207
Taylor, John, 322
Taylor, Zachary, 49, 51
Teller Amendment, 88
Tello, Jorge, 391
tercermundismo (third worldism), 216
terrorism: in Lebanon, 263–64; Sept. 11, 2001, attacks, 298, 367–68
Texas, 7, 33, 37, 39, 44; annexation of, 47–48, 51, 55, 58; independence of, 44–45; map, 43; settlement of, 40–41
Thatcher, Margaret, 264
Thomas, Evan, 83, 84
Thoreau, Henry David, 51
Thurman, Max, 308
Tillerson, Rex, 402–3
Tocqueville, Alexis de, 36–37
Todd, William, 60
Tomic, Radomiro, 226
Tonton Macoutes, 327, 329, 334
Torres, Manuel, 22
Torrijos, Omar, 303
Torrijos-Carter Treaties, 313
Toussaint Clause, 12
TransAfrica, 336
Treaty of Annexation, 47
Treaty of Cahuenga, 60
Treaty of Guadalupe Hidalgo, 55, 56
Treviño Morales, Miguel Ángel (Z-40), 394
Trist, Nicholas, 54, 55
Trujillo, Héctor, 194
Trujillo, José Arismendy, 194
Trujillo, Ramfis, 190, 194
Trujillo, Rolando Sarraf, 399

Trujillo Molina, Rafael Leonidas, 94, 172, 184, 185–93, 188; assassination of, 192–93, 194; and the Cold War, 189
Truman, Harry S., 106
Trump, Donald, 299, 324, 364, 408; on Central American immigration, 420–22; and Cuba, 403–5; on Mexican immigration, 407–12, 415, 423; and Mexico, 393–94
Tupamaro guerrillas, 218
Tuskegee Institute, 118
Tuthill, John, 214
Tyler, John, 47–48
Tyson, Brady, 289

Ubico, Jorge, 159, 160
Ungo, Guillermo, 283
unilaterally controlled Latino assets (UCLAs), 253
United Fruit Company (UFCO), 160–62, 163, 165, 166
United Nations, 147, 164, 257; Commission for Human Rights, 289; Commission of Inquiry on the Coca Leaf, 359; and the Governors Island Accords, 334; and Haiti, 335, 340, 343; Mission in Haiti (UNMIH), 336; peacekeeping force in Haiti (MINUSTAH), 343–44, 345; Resolution 940, 336; Single Convention on Narcotic Drugs, 359, 361–62
United Province of Rio de la Plata, 29
United States: abolitionist movements in, 14, 24, 44; aid to El Salvador from, 276–78; aid to Mexico, 410; annexation of Texas, 47–48, 51, 55, 58; anti-drug efforts in Mexico, 388–92; concerns about communism, 2, 150–51, 153, 155–56, 157, 158, 162, 163, 165, 194, 206–7, 211, 237, 241, 291;